AF522626

CASE FOR RAM

A foreign invader brutally attacks a sacred temple of an indigenous community, destroys it and builds a mosque on top of it. This has happened often. The response was rare. For the indigenous Hindu community agitated for five hundred years, refusing to forget their God, their Ram Lalla. The temple was finally restored the way Maryada Purushottam Ram would have liked it—through the process of law. Understanding the legal court cases is critical to understanding how the temple was built; because the case for Lord Ram was not built through the force of arms, but the power of arguments and proof. The Archaeological Survey of India proved that it was a structure of the indigenous community since 1st century bce and the Ram devotees proved their continued worship. This book by Anirudh Sharma and Sridhar Potaraju recounts in detail, but also in an easily readable manner, what legal evidence was presented and how the case for the Ram Janmabhoomi temple was proved in the Supreme Court. Read this book to understand one of the most important cases in Indian history. Even more, to understand how an indigenous community can restore its rights, while still following the process of law. A must-read.

Amish Tripathi,
bestselling author

An unbiased account of devotion and courtroom drama, as I witnessed it unfold in the Supreme Court. Read it slowly and discover the life story of the Bhishma Pitamaha of Indian law—who, at 92, fought a gladiatorial battle for Lord Ram's case. A media-shy, living legend and one of India's greatest lawyers, about whom little is known publicly. A compelling recommendation for both believers and non-believers. This is the first non-fiction legal thriller of its kind.

Arunachalam Vaidyanathan,
former Senior Resident Editor (Legal), NDTV

Beyond the TV debates, the noise, and the din, the real battle was fought in the courtroom. Through a Ram Bhakt, Shri Ram Lalla had to prove—via the secular code of law—the exact place of his birth, the spot where he was *Virajmaan*. Bhagwan Ram was the epitome of one who remained steadfast through pain and suffering to uphold *Dharma*—the rule of law. His *Bhakta*s too had to walk the same path to seek justice. *Case for Ram* merits a thorough reading. Riveting!

Anand Narasimhan,
Senior TV Media Journalist

CASE FOR RAM

The Untold Insiders' Story

ANIRUDH SHARMA
SRIDHAR POTARAJU

RUPA

First published by
Rupa Publications India Pvt. Ltd 2025
161-B/4, Gulmohar House,
Yusuf Sarai Community Centre,
New Delhi 110049

Sales centres:
Bengaluru Chennai
Hyderabad Kolkata Mumbai

Photos courtesy: Sridhar Potaraju, Sunil Kumar Tiwari, and court records

P-ISBN: 978-93-7003-241-5
E-ISBN: 978-93-7003-543-0

First impression 2025

10 9 8 7 6 5 4 3 2 1

Printed in India

Contents

Foreword *vii*
Prologue: Traversing Centuries *ix*

SECTION I
GOD'S OWN LAWYER

1. The Imminent Clash 3
2. Lord Ram's Lawyer 13
3. The Legal Team 23
4. The Suits 31
5. A Case of Great Significance 41
6. A Beautiful Mind and the Factual Matrix 48
7. God Arrives in Court 60

SECTION II
THE CASE BEGINS

8. Of Twists and Turns 75
9. Raining Surprises 83
10. Court, Janmabhoomi and the Bhakt 91
11. The Janmabhoomi Conundrum 100
12. Of Prayer and a Barrage of Questions 114
13. Archaeology and the Temple: Evidence from 1 BCE to 1528 CE 126
14. History, Evidence and Parikrama 139
15. Nirmohi Akhara's Challenge 147

SECTION III
THE OPPOSING SIDE

16. The Opposing Side 161
17. Of 'Rights', 'Wrongs', 'Belongs To', and 'Threats' 173
18. A Tectonic Shift 183
19. On Whose Side Was History? 195
20. A Stumbling Block or an Ashwamedha? 207

SECTION IV

1885

21. The Focal Point 221
22. The Riddle of 1885 233
23. Who Won in 1885? 246
24. The Worth or Worthlessness of Archaeology: Reply to ASI Report 258
25. What Do Experts Want? What Do Courts Want? 267

SECTION V

THE CASE OF THE TEMPLE

26. The Last Wish 281
27. The Test of Indianness 290
28. The Form of God: Importance of the Worshipper 301
29. The World of Temples and Statues 311
30. Judges—Idgah and Archaeology 326
31. Juristic Person: Final Round 342

SECTION VI

THE SPIRIT OF THE LAW

32. Witnesses and Their Evidence 355
33. Hair-Splitting Law 366
34. Evidence of the Sunni Central Waqf Board 376
35. Possession, Ownership and Questions 387
36. The Last Act 399
37. Prayers and Oral Evidence 411
38. The Judgement 424

Afterword/Client's Corner 436
Annexures 442
List of Lawyers who Participated in the Case on behalf of Lord Ram Lalla 444
Acknowledgements 447
Glossary 451
Index 456

Foreword

When the authors approached me with a request to pen a foreword for this book, I could hardly turn down fellow members of the Bar whom I have known for many years now.

The Ram Janmabhoomi case, one can safely say, was among the significant and contentious legal battles that we have seen. More than a mere legal dispute, it was an amalgam of religion, faith, history and legal principles. The Supreme Court's verdict in 2019, which provided a resolution to the conflict surrounding the disputed land in Ayodhya, marked the culmination of a long and complex journey.

As the final verdict settled the legal dispute over the ownership of the land, it also marked the beginning of a new chapter for India's religious and social fabric. The decision, though a historic one, was met with disappointment by some.

This book provides an exhaustive account of the courtroom journey. It not only explores the legal intricacies of the case, but also provides a first-hand account of the courtroom drama that unfolded in the Supreme Court. The painstaking preparation for the case and the role played by the lawyers for the contesting parties is explained in some detail, with an emphasis on the seminal contribution of two of India's leading Senior Advocates, Shri. K Parasaran and Shri C.S. Vaidyanathan. Since the authors were themselves involved in the conduct of the case before the Supreme Court, the book presents an authentic and well-informed perspective.

A treasure trove of information which the reader is unlikely to find anywhere else, this book is a treat for history buffs, lawyers and anyone interested in the subject. Through its pages, the reader will feel transported inside the courtroom, hearing the arguments and counterarguments, understanding the evidence and legal precedents that shaped the case, and witnessing how the final judgement came to be.

K.K. Venugopal
Senior Advocate

Prologue
Traversing Centuries

When divinity appears in court, millions follow the proceedings in rapt attention. Revered and admired by many across the world, Lord Ram's name transcends borders and languages. The legend of Lord Ram—the Ramayana—has been retold innumerable times in different parts of the world, including Cambodia, Nepal, Sri Lanka, Indonesia, Java, Myanmar, Malaysia, Laos, Thailand, the Philippines, Japan, Mongolia, Vietnam, China and Iran.

In Cambodia, the Ramayana is retold as *Reamker* (Ramakerti: Ram + *kirti* or glory); in Nepal as *Siddhi Ramayan*; in Sri Lanka as *Janakiharan*; in Indonesia as *Ramakavaca*; and as *Ramavijaya* in the Javanese version. In Myanmar, it is *Yama Zatdaw*; in Malaysia, it is known as *Hikayat Seri Rama*; the Laos national epic is *Phra Lak Phra Ram*; and in Thailand, it is *Ramakien*. Found even in Iran, the Ramayana is known there as *Dastan-e-Ram*.

Most versions can be traced back to Maharishi Valmiki, whose hero transcends the mortal plane, exemplifies virtue, and triumphs over evil. In India, it is not uncommon to find the Ramayana being recited every day in many households, including by a ninety-two-year-old top lawyer who was the lead counsel of team Ram Lalla.

A Courtroom for the Divine

Therefore, it is no small matter when the deity Lord Ram becomes a litigant in a long-running legal dispute over a plot of land in the North Indian town of Ayodhya. When a court of mere mortals is tasked with determining his birthplace, the case is fraught with legal complexities, emotional resonance, and a tryst with the unknown.

The quest for Ram Janmabhoomi has spanned nearly 500 years. In recent history, India witnessed massive social and political movements to reclaim this land considered most sacred. Across the centuries, these movements were never led by lawyers, nor did lawyers initiate the political struggle. The earliest legal cases, beginning in 1949, were filed by others like Gopal Singh Visharad and Rajender Singh. The role of lawyers, therefore, was limited. They were neither responsible for maintaining law and order in the country nor for eventually having the temple constructed. The credit for that lay elsewhere.

As the lead counsel for Ram Lalla—infant Ram—clearly stated, credit belongs to social organizations, political leaders, religious figures, and of course to the executive, which ensured peace and executed the judgement. But inside the court, it was only lawyers who could present Lord Ram's case.

Inside the Lead Counsel's War Room

Case for Ram: The Untold Insiders' Story attempts to capture key moments of the Ayodhya case as seen from within the chambers of the lead counsel for Lord Ram. It draws on the perspective of the legal team that assisted in building the argument for a temple at the disputed site. Based on true events, it represents how the case was seen unfolding by team Ram Lalla in the Supreme Court of India, highlighting dramatic legal twists and unexpected turns, a few of which some believe could have entirely derailed the case.

In lead counsel K. Parasaran's opinion, this was a case where one had to be careful. There was a total of five suits. Suits 3 and 5 were to be taken up first by the court. Senior Advocate Sushil Kumar Jain was to start Suit 3. Jain was the counsel for the suit filed by Nirmohi Akhara. Senior Parasaran had asked his team to remember that, in a way, it was a case where everyone on the

Hindu side was a claimant for the land. There were two main Hindu sides: Ram Lalla Virajman, the deity himself, and Nirmohi Akhara, which claimed historical possession, management and control of the disputed site. In 2010, the Allahabad High Court awarded one-third of the disputed land to Nirmohi Akhara. But the status of Nirmohi Akhara as a manager was itself disputed. A manager of a property can never claim ownership over the property, so Lord Ram had to enter the dispute himself. The Allahabad High Court had accepted that Ram Lalla was a Juristic Person (explained later in detail in Chapter 7), represented by his 'next friend', or in this case, friend of God. But the catch was that the argument for Bhagwan Shri Ram Lalla could destroy the suit of Nirmohi Akhara, and vice versa. But more on that later.

There was also some urgency—our lead counsel was a nonagenarian, painfully aware of life's uncertainties. Would he live to see the case through? That doubt was one he voiced himself. Then there was the matter of evidence—evidence to identify the precise location of Lord Ram's birth. What happened in 1885 that became critical in this regard? Can a birthplace be disputed, or even relocated?

The *janmabhoomi*, or birthplace, is central to Lord Ram's story, affirmed across the various versions of the Ramayana. The evidence explored in this book includes archaeological findings, travelogues of Christian missionaries, and British colonial gazetteers. The first case in independent India was filed in 1949, but the narratives go farther back—perhaps as far as 1000 BCE. Few, if any, legal cases in the world have dealt with a timeline so vast.

When Faith Meets the Constitution

The right to faith, belief, worship and religious freedom is protected by the Constitution of India. Religion is intrinsic to Indian life—even today, children are named after gods: Durga,

Shiv, Krishna, etc. So, it is not surprising that in India, deities enjoy legal rights akin to human beings. For centuries, a deity or idol has been treated as a 'Juristic Person' in Indian law. A devotee or temple trustee typically acts on its behalf. In light-hearted legal terms, this representative is often described as a 'friend' of God.

To believers, Lord Ram is revered as an avatar of Lord Vishnu. His name is invoked at birth and in death. *'Hey Ram'* is even inscribed at Raj Ghat, the memorial to Mahatma Gandhi, regarded as Father of the Nation. *'Ram Naam Satya Hai'*—meaning 'the name of Ram is the ultimate truth'—is chanted during Hindu funeral rites in many parts of India. But what holds meaning for the soul does not always suffice in court.

India's courts have witnessed religious disputes both between different faiths and within different sects of the same religion. A monumental legal challenge arises when two religious communities claim the same land. While interfaith land disputes are not new, the Ayodhya case stands apart. Arguably the first of its kind in the world, it captured both the legal imagination and public emotion.

Reconstructing the Untold Narrative

As time passed, memories faded. To reconstruct an accurate account, we referred to public records, news reports and legal web portals such as *Live Law*, *Supreme Court Observer*, *Bar & Bench*, and *LatestLaws.com*. We also revisited our own scattered notes, and conversations in Mr K. Parasaran's chambers. We have viewed the story from the chambers of Mr K. Parasaran and we do therefore have a slant. We took this approach because of a question we were often asked: 'How did a ninety-two-year-old man manage such an enormous task?' And just as often: 'What was going through the minds of the lawyers during this case?'

Of course, in narrating such an epic case, a few creative

liberties have been taken. In hindsight, some moments seemed dramatic, while others were tinged with humour. But above all, this book is a record of events as we witnessed them. It is a work from our perspective of issues deemed most relevant by us.

Some people raised doubts regarding the final judgement of the Supreme Court, declaring that it was not based on evidence, and as a result communal harmony was threatened. The present work seeks to present the life story of the lawyers as well as the story of the evidence relied upon and the courtroom drama from public records, in an age where the Hon'ble Supreme Court of India has allowed livestreaming of its proceedings and word-by-word reporting from Supreme Court is a norm.

In true Indian tradition, every reader has the freedom to reach their own conclusion.

SECTION I

GOD'S OWN LAWYER

1

The Imminent Clash

The library and the canteens of the Supreme Court are regular haunts of the country's top lawyers. New entrants, struggling lawyers, and students also crowd these spaces to be in the pulse of things. The Ram Janmabhoomi case naturally accrued a lot of attention and curiosity. After the 2010 Allahabad High Court judgement, whenever there was a development in the case, lawyers or journalists interested in the case would often spend a few minutes to discuss the ruling, which ran into around 8,000 printed pages. Its very length reflects the intricacies involved and the immense pressure riding on the judges during the period. Justice S.U. Khan of the Allahabad High Court had summed up the lives of the anxious judges who wrote the judgement. In the Ayodhya title dispute judgement, he wrote:

> *Here is a small piece of land (1500 square yards) where angels fear to tread. It is full of innumerable land mines. We are required to clear it. Some very sane elements advised us not to attempt that. We do not propose to rush in like fools lest we are blown. However, we have to take a risk. It is said that the greatest risk in life is not daring to take the risk when the occasion for the same arises. Herein follows the judgement the entire country is waiting for with bated breath.*[1]

'Several prime ministers of India had attempted but failed to resolve this issue of the land conflict between those who claimed it to be the Babri Masjid and those who called it

---

[1]Prelude to Allahabad Judgment by Justice S.U. Khan, *Vada Prativada*, https://tinyurl.com/3ke6bkyf. Accessed on 21 September 2025.

Ram Janambhoomi.'[2] Prime ministers came and went, but the dispute outlived them, often snowballing into a political, social or communal issue at various points in times. However, within the framework of a modern democracy, it was eventually the court which had to decide the issue as the final arbitrator.

The Allahabad High Court, after detailed final hearings going into 91 days, finally delivered its judgement on 30 September 2010, after the case had begun in 1949–50. The land was partitioned into three parts: two parts were awarded to two Hindu sides who advanced arguments fit enough to destroy each other's case, and one part was awarded to the Uttar Pradesh Sunni Central Waqf Board (*hereinafter referred to as Sunni Board)* representing the Muslim population. The partition did not end the conflict. Appeals were filed by all three sides, and the highest court of the land, the Supreme Court of India, was brought in to resolve this issue.

Property Dispute: Lord Ram and the Court

It may be useful to quickly sum up the issue at hand—about 1,500 sq. yd of land. While one community claimed ownership of the land, which was Lord Ram's birthplace comprising the shrine at which they had been worshipping for centuries, the other claimed rights over the same plot of land, asserting that it had been an active mosque for hundreds of years. But the contest was not merely about the right to property of two religious groups: Hindus and Muslims. It was also, very clearly, about the right to property of Hindu groups versus other Hindu groups and Muslim groups versus other Muslim groups. However, it wouldn't be inaccurate to say that this fact wasn't known to the public and this lack of awareness largely led to the misunderstanding that

[2]Khan, M. Tariq, 'How former Prime Ministers, spiritual gurus have failed to resolve Ayodhya dispute', *Hindustan Times*, 9 March 2019, https://tinyurl.com/mu7b4vfp. Accessed on 2 September 2025.

it was a Hindu-Muslim dispute, thus wrongly giving it religious connotations. It was quite rightly pointed out by a segment of the press: 'In the media, these parties have been broadly categorized as the Hindu side and the Muslim side. But there are significant differences in what these parties seek.'[3] Nirmohi Akhara refused to recognize Ram Lalla or Ram Janmasthan as valid parties before the law, while the latter opposed the Akhara's claim as the manager of the disputed site. Similarly, on the other side, while 'the Sunni Central Waqf Board wanted control of the land to build a mosque, the Shia Waqf Board was ready to part with the land to facilitate the construction of a Ram Temple.'[4] Before the actual case began, specific administrative creases had to be ironed out.

Many Documents, Many Languages

English is the official language of the Supreme Court of India; many important documents that were required by parties to prove one point or the other were not in English. Even the evidence/deposition of witnesses were not in English. There were suggestions at various points in time that proceedings could not commence as numerous documents were in Arabic, Sanskrit, Persian and Hindi; many documents, relied upon by the Allahabad High Court for its judgement, had yet not been translated into English. Finally, on 11 August 2017, the Supreme Court ordered:

> *Mr. Tushar Mehta, learned Senior Counsel and Mr. Raghawendra Singh, learned Advocate General for the State of UP, shall file the English translation of the entire oral evidence within ten weeks. Needless to say, copies of the*

---

[3]Yamunan, Sruthisagar, 'Not just Hindu versus Muslim: Ayodhya dispute has several parties battling each other in Court', *Scroll.in*, 16 October 2019, https://tinyurl.com/535wueu8. Accessed on 18 January 2025.

[4]Ibid.

translation shall be in bound volumes and shall be handed over to all the learned counsels appearing for the parties.

The case saw lawyers and judges look for precedents of similar conflicts in Jerusalem or elsewhere (there is no case instituted in Jerusalem). Some lawyers looked for relevant materials from judgements of the International Court of Justice. The case also led to a frantic search for the surviving members of Lord Ram's clan after the Supreme Court of India queried the possibility of descendants of Lord Ram being around.[5] The country of one billion nearly came to a standstill on discovering this new angle. *The New Indian Express* brought out a story titled 'Meet the eight individuals who claim to be Lord Ram's descendants.'[6] *Hindustan Times* reported, '"We are Lord Ram's Descendants," say Mewar royals, [the] third claim in a week.'[7] What happened to such claims finally remains unknown.

There was a way of looking at the dispute solely from a religious perspective and not as a pure and simple property dispute. Mr Subramanian Swamy wanted to intervene and raise Constitutional Law issues.[8] He wished to prioritize the question of the Fundamental Right to Worship on the disputed site in his pending application for intervention. Contrary to the views of Mr Tushar Mehta (currently Solicitor General of India), appearing for the State of Uttar Pradesh (UP), and Senior Advocate C.S. Vaidyanathan appearing for Ram Lalla, Mr Swamy argued that Hindus' right to worship at the birthplace

---

[5]PTI, 'Are descendants of Lord Ram still there at Ayodhya, asks SC', *The Economic Times*, 9 August 2019, https://tinyurl.com/swuaxskc. Accessed on 18 January 2025.

[6]Sarda, Kanu, and Rajesh Asnani, 'Meet the eight individuals who claim to be Lord Ram's descendant', *The New Indian Express*, 26 August 2019, https://tinyurl.com/2buxr8mn. Accessed on 18 January 2025.

[7]Rawal, Urvashi Dev, '"We are Lord Ram's descendants", say Mewar Royals, third claim in a week', *Hindustan Times*, 12 August 2019, https://tinyurl.com/2xy58ez9. Accessed on 18 January 2025.

[8]'Day 1 Arguments, Ayodhya Title Dispute', *Supreme Court Observer*, 11 August 2017, https://tinyurl.com/4t2ryszv. Accessed on 18 January 2025.

of Lord Ram needed to be heard first. This was because, as per Mr Swamy, if the court concluded this was a religious issue, the fundamental right would take precedence over the land ownership issue. This contention was vehemently opposed by Mr Tushar Mehta, as well as Dr Rajeev Dhavan, who was representing the Sunni Central Waqf Board, on the grounds that a five-judge Bench had separated matters such as religious rights issues from the ownership of the disputed land[9] issue. If Mr Swamy's plea was accepted, it would mean that the case would be decided primarily on religious aspects, and evidence of parties dealing with other aspects would be relegated to the background.

The question was, when should the matter be heard? Mr Tushar Mehta, the then Additional Solicitor General[10], appearing for the state of Uttar Pradesh, pointed out the need to simplify the procedural and factual backgrounds of the case in the haze of appeals; he emphasized in his submission that the matter was already getting delayed and that the time was ripe for the case to be finally adjudicated as a property dispute.[11]

A total of 14 appeals were filed in the Supreme Court against the 2010 Allahabad High Court judgement. It seemed that every side was aggrieved by the ruling of the Allahabad High Court on some point or the other. There was also the issue of the national parliamentary elections coming up in 2019. No one could dispute that Ayodhya was also a political issue and could be raised in the election campaigns. The final hearing in the case could be before the election campaigns started, during the campaign, or after the elections were over.

When the matter was to finally be heard in 2018, it was debated whether the case should be referred to a larger Bench

---

[9]Ibid.

[10]Mr Tushar Mehta rose to the office of Solicitor General of India and is currently holding the position.

[11]'Day 1 Arguments, Ayodhya Title Dispute', *Supreme Court Observer*, 11 August 2017, https://tinyurl.com/4t2ryszv. Accessed on 18 January 2025.

comprising five judges rather than three. It was decided that three judges would hear the matter. Just as things seemed to reach a quietus, came a five-judge Bench, with Justice Ranjan Gogoi taking over as Chief Justice of India. The Bench constituted then comprised judges who were tipped to become future Chief Justices of India, along with Chief Justice Gogoi. The Bench further changed with the recusal of Justice U.U. Lalit.[12] The final Bench was constituted of the then Chief Justice of India Ranjan Gogoi, Justice S.A. Bobde, Justice D.Y. Chandrachud, Justice Ashok Bhushan and Justice S. Abdul Nazeer.

This further piqued the media's interest, leading to a flurry of discussions around the case. They anticipated that as the case progressed, and as jurists with contrasting styles prepared to debate with each other, it would give rise to a great legal tussle. This would, in turn, present young lawyers with a marvellous opportunity to hear the doyens of the bar on issues of civil law and the evaluation of evidence.

The Final Hearing

As the 2019 general elections approached, the clamour for an early hearing of the dispute grew louder, mainly outside the court and, to a certain extent, among a few lawyers. The court dashed the hopes of an early hearing as further time was given to the officials in the Supreme Court to prepare the records.[13] Earlier, mediation had failed time and again. The court made a final attempt for an out-of-court settlement, even though some parties were not keen on mediation. An eminent mediation panel was constituted under the chairmanship of Justice Fakkir Mohamed Ibrahim Kalifulla, former judge of the Supreme

---

[12] 'Ayodhya case: Five-judge constitution Bench reconstituted', *The Hindu*, 3 December 2021, https://tinyurl.com/23kffywy. Accessed on 18 January 2025.

[13] *M. Siddiq (D) Thr. Lrs v. Mahant Suresh Das & Ors*, Civil Appeal No. 10866-10867 of 2010 – Record of Proceedings of Supreme Court dated 26.02.2019.

Court of India, also comprising renowned spiritual guru Sri Sri Ravi Shankar and Shri Sriram Panchu, Senior Advocate. There were some objections reported in the press[14] against the inclusion of Sri Sri Ravi Shankar, as well as the fact that he had been trying for a peaceful settlement for long with formulas[15] and was part of some dialogues from the time of Prime Minister Atal Bihari Vajpayee.[16] The mediation process now was to be kept confidential, and the media was restrained from reporting about the mediation proceedings to prevent many sensitive issues from cropping up.

On 10 May 2019, when the campaign for the general elections was at its peak in India, the mediation committee was given a further extension, and the possibility of an early hearing was completely ruled out.

In early August 2019, the Supreme Court of India ruled that the court-mandated mediation in the Ayodhya title dispute was not progressing as desired. For the many mediation processes over decades, it had been claimed that they had reached very close to a settlement. Later, it was said that even this mediation panel came very close to arriving at a settlement.[17] But the law did not accept any agreement unless each and every party consented. The mediation process did restart again later by a court order, only to never close. However, a two-judge Bench, led by Chief Justice of India Ranjan Gogoi, announced a day-to-day hearing of all appeals and cross-appeals by a Constitution Bench from 6 August 2019.

---

[14]'Ayodhya case: Muslims raise objections over Sri Sri Ravi Shankar in SC mediation panel', *The Indian Aawaaz*, 8 March 2019, https://tinyurl.com/ya874r22. Accessed on 18 January 2025.

[15]'Walk the Talk: Sri Sri Ravi Shankar', *NDTV* on *YouTube*, 22 August 2013, https://tinyurl.com/88ftwv6f. Accessed on 18 January 2025.

[16]Ray, Shantanu Guha, 'The Sri Sri hand in Ayodhya settlement', *The Times of India*, 24 November 2019, https://tinyurl.com/37munc4c. Accessed on 18 January 2025.

[17]Rajagopal, Krishnadas, 'Ayodhya mediation was close to a settlement', *The Hindu*, 1 December 2021, https://tinyurl.com/mt64pp6c. Accessed on 18 January 2025.

The legal dispute originating in 1950 was finally reaching its culmination.

The courts had the arduous task of adjudicating the rights of communities within and between religions. It was a puzzle they had to solve by decoding the riddles of lawyers and the mysteries of expert witnesses. Beyond this was the enigma of archaeology and the ghost of history. The first to confront this problem was the Allahabad High Court. Doubts were raised: 'Will Allahabad High Court succeed in settling the Ayodhya dispute?'[18]

The Allahabad High Court ended up partitioning the land three ways. The same doubts returned when the Supreme Court took up the case. There were questions within questions: Where exactly was Lord Ram born? Was there any structure? Which was the exact spot?

Such questions revealed the enormity of the situation. The key to solving one of the greatest legal puzzles of the birthplace of Lord Ram was in decoding terms such as 'Juridical or Juristic Person'[19] and 'Preponderance of Probability'[20], terms that would be repeated quite often.

You Don't Represent God in Court Every Day

When the Supreme Court suddenly announced it would begin hearing the case, it took most lawyers by surprise. Team Ram Lalla hadn't expected the final hearing to start so soon. But since the mediation had not given the desired result, and the case had been pending in the Supreme Court for nine years, the court decided it was time to move forward. However well one is prepared, whether you are Sachin Tendulkar or Don Bradman, you can lose your wicket. Lionel Messi can miss a penalty. So,

---

[18]PTI, 'Will Allahabad HC succeed in settling Ayodhya dispute?', *The Economic Times*, 30 September 2010, https://tinyurl.com/55jk9kws. Accessed on 18 January 2025.
[19]*See* Glossary.
[20]*See* Glossary.

lawyers are doubly careful. It is not about being nervous or unsure, but one must be careful in all situations, especially with the Ram Janmabhoomi case because you don't represent God in court every day.

Four Senior Counsels were engaged on behalf of Ram Lalla. For such a case involving intricate questions of facts and law besides being steeped in antiquity, emotions and religion, a lawyer of eminence, age, stature and learning was required. Mr K. Parasaran, then aged ninety-two, former Attorney General for India and one of India's top lawyers, was chosen as child Ram's lead lawyer. Mr Parasaran—also addressed as Senior Parasaran to differentiate him from his son Mohan Parasaran, also a lawyer of repute, and former Solicitor General of India—was the lead counsel. The nature of the Ayodhya conflict required the dexterity of an experienced legal eagle, and Senior Parasaran had an exceptional career in law spanning seventy years of impeccable integrity and outstanding scholarship[21].

Mr C.S. Vaidyanathan, formerly Additional Solicitor General of India, had a crucial role to play along with Senior Parasaran. Mr Vaidyanathan knew the intricacies of the case thoroughly and was to deal with issues arising from evidence of the case, and then also became a backup for Mr Parasaran because he took great care to cover the same ground that Mr Parasaran was covering. The third and fourth pillars of Ram Lalla's counsel were Mr Ranjeet Kumar, former Solicitor General of India, and Mr P.S. Narsimha, former Additional Solicitor General who was always ready with all aspects related to the case. God had chosen four pairs of capable hands.

Whether it was a god's case or a human being's, the die was cast. Subsequently, the lawyers would be the actual players. Since the lead lawyer for God was a nonagenarian, the case proceeded at an uneven pace—sometimes fast and sometimes slow.

---

[21]*See* Letters from Nani A. Palkhivala and Justice V.R. Krishna Iyer in Annexures.

Consistency, quality and depth of preparation were the keywords. For an outsider, it would be a roller-coaster ride, some of which would be easy to understand and some difficult. In all this, it wasn't that members of God's team didn't have differences among themselves or that God's own lawyer did not have humongous personal difficulties to overcome. The old man depended on infant Ram to support him just as infant Ram needed the old man's counsel; Ram wanted to come back to his place of birth, was what the nonagenarian believed—whether he could serve his lord well was for time to decide. The nonagenarian believed he was facing a young man—a septuagenarian who had the relative advantage of youth—on the opposing side.

God's team was ready to lay claim to Lord Ram's birthplace. The opposing side was equally hardworking. Though much younger than Senior Parasaran, the opposition lawyers were equally respected and eminent. For law students, it was a masterclass from the masters themselves. It was a unique case—after all, for the nonagenarian, this property dispute was God's case fought out by humans where even a parallel theory of a place as Ram's birthplace was suggested.

2

Lord Ram's Lawyer

The Ayodhya Ram Mandir case generated large-scale interest not only across India but also around the world, particularly among the Indian diaspora that was keenly following its progress. The question that perplexed those not closely familiar with the distinguished assemblage of Indian lawyers was why they hadn't heard of this lawyer who was being referred to in the legal circles and the media as the *pitamah* (patriarch in this context) of the Indian Bar[22]. You couldn't blame them. To date, Senior Parasaran remains notoriously media-shy. He won't write articles; he won't give interviews; he doesn't come on television and never speaks on legal issues outside the court. A veritable hermit within the Indian legal pantheon! Ask him to write his views, and his answer would be, 'Half the people will not agree with my views, some may be offended. I don't want to offend anyone at the tail end of my life.' Or he will say, 'There are many things which are best left unsaid. That's what my experience of ninety years in the world has taught me.'

Unostentatious, Senior Parasaran was a man who wore a *veshti* (traditional Indian lower garment for men popular in South India, particularly Tamil Nadu), and in a world full of BMWs, Mercedes Benz, Jaguars, Rolls Royce, Audis and Lexus, he stuck to the humble Ambassador till the car manufacturers themselves had enough and discontinued it. However, even though Mr Parasaran habitually kept a low profile, there were

---

[22]Roy, Debayan, 'Parasaran, the "Pitamah" of Indian lawyers got his wish when Ayodhya hearings ended', *The Print*, 18 October 2019, https://tinyurl.com/bdf3mkez. Accessed on 18 January 2025.

many who had heard of him because of the numerous high-profile cases he had undertaken, though only a few would be able to recognize him. Now he was lead counsel in the Ayodhya case. For a man not giving interviews and making it a point to stay away from the media glare, he was surprised to find an article in *The Indian Express* featuring his life as a lawyer: '*At 92, Key Face in Ayodhya case K. Parasaran Is a Trusted Voice of Many Governments*.'[23] Suddenly, newspapers were carrying columns on the nonagenarian and his face was splashed across print media and TV screens. Now the name and face could be tallied. Young lawyers, common men and women, and law students wished to have their pictures clicked with Mr Parasaran. For an old gentleman, whose pictures were seldom seen and whose video clips were not available in abundance on *YouTube* in the internet age, the man was taken aback as people lined up to get themselves clicked with him.

The Ayodhya case was garnering more and more interest. Curiosity about Lord Ram's counsel also kept growing. As public interest grew, so did requests from journalists for interviews. But all such interview requests were turned down, no matter where they came from. Senior Parasaran refused to talk about himself to journalists, so they rushed in droves to Mohan Parasaran for information. He would melt at seeing a young, disappointed journalist's face earnestly trying to convince him how people in this age of right to information wanted to know more and more about every issue, including the life of Lord Ram's lawyer. Mohan Parasaran would then kindly give out some information about his father. 'After completing his graduation, Senior Parasaran had taken up a job at Madras University. But he soon quit and joined Law College. He then tried unsuccessfully to be a part-time law lecturer. So, in a way, the senior had an occupation before he

[23]Vishwanath, Apurva, 'At 92, key face in Ayodhya case K Parasaran is a trusted voice of many governments', *The Indian Express*, 12 August 2019, https://tinyurl.com/y45jf8w8. Accessed on 18 January 2025.

joined the [legal] profession.'

A sketch here of Senior Parasaran would inform the curious that he was born in Srirangam, the holy town in Tamil Nadu, to Shri R. Kesava Iyengar and Shrimati Ranganayaki. Unfortunately, he lost his mother at a very young age, and though his father remarried, Parasaran missed his mother intensely. Kesava Iyengar was a legend, a top lawyer of his time, and a doyen of Hindu Law. He also practised well into his nineties. He was respected not only as a lawyer but also as a Vedic scholar.

Senior Parasaran's career started under his father. He was still a law student when he began working in his father's office; he would take dictations, and do the clerical work, such as making bundles of files and arranging the office and the books. His father was a perfectionist. In Senior Parasaran's opinion, today's young boys and girls rely too much on computers and phones. When Parasaran was young, if they made mistakes, or didn't remember the exact citations or principles in their training, it would fetch them a rap on their knuckles. In those days, everyone had very good memory. What distinguished Kesava Iyengar from others was the tremendous range of his knowledge, even by the standards of those days.

'My father was a noble soul, a great scholar, and then a brilliant lawyer. He knew Sanskrit, Tamil, Telugu, English, Latin and Greek. Even British judges were very fond of him. I was lucky enough to have seen a lawyer like him and to have trained under him. It is rare to get a guru like him,' was Senior Parasaran's honest admission.

As years went by, in the legal profession Senior Parasaran became a living legend himself, with undisputed stature and respect accorded to few. However, if anyone extolled his legal abilities, they were sure to get an earful. In his opinion, he was not even a 'patch on the learning and advocacy of his father or lawyers like Lal Narayan Sinha or C.K. Daphtary.'

Unfortunately, differences on certain issues led to the father and son living separately for a while. So, despite being the son of such an eminent lawyer, Senior Parasaran faced innumerable struggles in his youth due to financial problems. He had to walk from home to the courts because he didn't have money to travel by bus, and lived in a shed/garage with his family during his initial years of struggle. He shared this shed/garage with two other families. Getting cases and work was difficult. Money was a distant dream and buying anything for his newborn child was a challenge. Life looked bleak; and then Lord Ram entered his life. On one occasion, he went to a religious gathering where the priest said, 'If you read the Ramayana, the fate lines in your hands change.' So he started reading the Ramayana, and things changed for him. He often says, 'If Ram comes into your life, your life starts changing for the better.'

Senior Parasaran began his practice before the Supreme Court in 1958. From the 1970s, he has been sought after by almost every administration.[24] This luminary became Advocate General of Tamil Nadu in 1976 and then was appointed Solicitor General of India in 1980. From 1983 to 1989, he served as Attorney General for India. Despite this, he did not shy away from disagreeing with the political leadership.

> *In 1985, as Solicitor General of India, he advised the government to not act on the show-cause notice issued to demolish the Indian Express building as it was legally untenable. However, when the Indira Gandhi government ignored his opinion, he refused to defend the government in court and offered to resign if he was forced to appear. The government, despite his public statement, not only kept him in office but promoted him to Attorney General of India in two months.*[25]

---

[24]Express Web Desk, 'Who is K Parasaran?' *The Indian Express*, 6 February 2020, https://tinyurl.com/yesnx5t3. Accessed on 18 January 2025.
[25]Ibid.

Some journalists highlighted the fact that Senior Parasaran was one of the rare awardees of top civilian honours from opposing ends of the political spectrum. During the NDA tenure of 1999–2004, former Prime Minister Atal Bihari Vajpayee appointed him as a member of the drafting and editorial committee tasked with reviewing the working of the Constitution. The Vajpayee government also awarded this former Attorney General of India the Padma Bhushan. The successive Manmohan Singh-led UPA-1 government awarded him the Padma Vibhushan and nominated him to the Rajya Sabha.

Does Age Matter?

Those who knew him, also knew that he had a phenomenal memory that served him well whenever he demanded. He was a scholar, sharp as a knife and had seventy years of experience at the Bar. He was what one calls a real heavyweight fighting in the client's corner. That Senior Parasaran was in the top layer of the legal pack was now clear, but then it dawned on the public that he was a nonagenarian! How was he going to manage it all? Would he be able to successfully argue for possession of the entire disputed land in the Supreme Court, in favour of the deity Ram Lalla Virajman? Members of Mr Parasaran's team also recall many people asking them if a ninety-two-year-old could prepare and argue such a historic case. These were not questions asked by onlookers alone. Mr Parasaran would objectively express similar concerns himself. He calmly accepted that advanced age had given him a frail body with multiple health issues. He objectively wondered whether he would be alive to see the case through. So many things could go wrong. For example, the case could get adjourned till the next session, the Chief Justice could retire and the matter would have to be reheard from the beginning. Add to this, another concern—old age, a ruthless master, had left Mr Parasaran without teeth, hearing impaired, and with glaucoma. Due to insufficient rest, glaucoma would often tire out his eyes. They would be red, unable to take further stress. He walked slowly. Climbing stairs was painful and his strained eyes streamed incessantly. Most of this was not visible to the onlookers.

To us, the members of his team and other associates, it was heart-wrenching to see him struggle. It was even more painful to watch him wave away concerned requests to rest when he was tired or ailing. Senior Parasaran had fought many landmark cases, but none was more important to him than Ram Lalla's case. He would reiterate that it was his good fortune that at the end of his life, he was able to serve his Lord. 'Ram has defined and changed my life. My last wish is to see a temple come up at his birthplace. Whatever must be done, only Ram will do; any other lawyer or I will just be a medium of his wishes, a *nimittamatra* (mere instrument) of Lord Ram's plans,' he would say.

On his team members coaxing him to rest, more often than not, he chose to not heed their advice. Then he had to be reminded that he had undergone a difficult and risky heart valve replacement surgery a few years back. Besides leaving him physically frailer, the surgery also meant that he could not take too much stress at work. On Senior Parasaran's recovery, his doctor marvelled, 'Maybe God has kept you back for a very special purpose.' After all, he was to fight Lord Ram's case.

Naturally, this frailty was of immense concern for his family. Mohan Parasaran and his wife, Nandini Parasaran, always urged Senior Parasaran to be mindful of his age and health. 'On the personal front, take breaks, relax, and then keep working as much as you want,' they insisted. Ever the disciplined person, Mr Parasaran would always agree, saying only in exceptional circumstances would he stray.

All his life, Senior Parasaran had been disciplined about work, food as well as medicines, if any. Nandini Parasaran was responsible for ensuring her father-in-law did not deviate much from maintaining a disciplined lifestyle, and took to surprise checking. 'Medicines have to be taken on time,' his team hurriedly reminded him if Nandini was spotted anywhere close to him. Mr Parasaran didn't like that one bit. Any interruption was a distraction. His discipline and dedication to his work for Lord Ram were non-negotiable. Hence, when it came to medicines versus law for his god, medicines were an option, though seldom a priority. That took a toll. Mr Parasaran was a study in contrast. As a lawyer, he was devoted to the case and a disciplined worker, but as a patient, he often behaved like a truant child.

The patient had to be quiet and keep his eyes closed for at least five minutes after being administered a drop in each eye, especially during work. Senior Parasaran would invariably jump out of his enforced rest and silence a bare 1–2 minutes later. As the discomfort grew and family members protested, the disciplined gentleman and the difficult patient had no choice but to agree to adhere to the medicine schedule, though with great reluctance. Such diversions from the work for Lord Ram came with its discomforts for the nonagenarian. He would ask impatiently if the five minutes were up. He was in love with his work, his cases, and his religious texts. Nothing else mattered to him.

Senior Parasaran hated these breaks but knew he had to rest to be able to continue working. Moreover, Nandini Parasaran was invariably around with polite reminders that real health challenges could arise if he did not follow the doctor's advice at this age. The legal battle on behalf of Lord Ram would go on for months. He had to listen to the doctors to be able to deliver his best. It was only after continuous persuasion by his elder son that Senior Parasaran agreed to take intermittent breaks. He was wary that the other side would raise some challenging points. He wanted to concentrate on these time frames but not by ignoring his health.

During the last few years, Parasaran had been working intensively on this case. The past eight months were especially hectic. Long discussions and conferences had become the norm. The nonagenarian never complained. These conferences would often be joined by Bhupendra Yadav, who by that time was a prominent Member of Parliament of the Rajya Sabha, and a top leader of the Bharatiya Janata Party (BJP). In fact, Yadav, along with Vikramjit Banerjee (who rose to the position of Additional Solicitor General of India), Madan Mohan Pandey, Bhakti Vardhan Singh, and Saurabh Shyam Shamsheryhad formed the Ram Lalla team for the Allahabad High Court. For the final hearing, Ravi Shankar Prasad had come down to Allahabad in addition to the other team members.

The Ram Setu Case

Senior Parasaran had been fighting for a long time to preserve religious institutions and temples. He was deeply concerned about the weakening Indian culture and values. When asked about politics, he was unequivocal: 'I am not in any party, but yes, I am in the party of the believers and in the party of those who believe in divine powers and the existence of gods.' He would discuss how he appeared in cases of gods. As legend would have it, when he appeared in the Ram Setu case, one of the judges reminded him that he was generally seen supporting the government's policy decision in such cases.[26] So, why was he appealing against the government's decision to dredge through the Ram Setu? Both sides—one in favour of preserving the Ram Setu and the other in favour of dredging through it—had approached Mr Parasaran to appear for them. He could not decide whether to stay neutral or appear for any contesting sides. He would say that he was in a *dharma sankat* (moral dilemma).

---

[26]Sinha, Ashish, 'Legal Luminary K. Parasaran, Fought for Ramlalla in Supreme Court at the age of 92', *The Daily Guardian*, 13 January 2024, https://tinyurl.com/2nnf76df. Accessed on 18 January 2025.
Also *see*: Venkatesan, V., 'Sethusamudram case: K. Parasaran's Submissions', *law and other things*, 6 May 2008, https://tinyurl.com/3mvzhxyv. Accessed on 18 January 2025.

One evening, on a weekend, he went for a walk at a beach in Chennai but kept pondering over the issue. That night, he could not sleep and remained awake till 2 a.m. His mind debated on whether to accept the case from either side or not. According to Senior Parasaran, his mind finally veered to the point where he began reading the Ramayana daily. He also recalled a special mention of Ram Setu in the *Skanda Purana*. As a follower and reciter of the Ramayana daily, he concluded that Ram Setu was special and should not be destroyed. He questioned himself on whether deciding not to argue the case wasn't a mistake. 'This is the least I could always do for Ram,' he thought. Armed with this belief, Senior Parasaran appeared in the Ram Setu case. He intended to protect it and suggest possible alternatives that the court could investigate. He had suggested that there were three routes, and while one route required damage and dredging through the Ram Setu, the other two routes could yet result in the completion of the project, and the Ram Setu could be saved as well.[27]

For quite some time now, the man was not taking other cases and restraining himself to only giving opinion in some matters. Even opinions were now postponed till end of the case. He was engrossed in Ayodhya and Sabarimala. He would often say, 'In my nineties, I have a right to think only of God, talk only of God, and do my prayers. These cases sync with that. I want to finish these two cases and go back to Chennai. I am an old man now; people must understand when pressuring me to take cases. These days, in my nineties, I don't want to stray from temples and my gods. How can I take up cases?' He would repeat that he had 'no interest in anything other than his religious and spiritual pursuits and things connected with them'.

One could not help but agree that it was a reasonable point of view for a man in his nineties who had a right to pursue his

[27]The case is still pending.

religious and spiritual callings. However, it was not a formal retirement. His team members knew Senior Parasaran's first love.

Over the years, one after another, gods and religious communities were reaching the courts. There were cases from the church, dargahs, gurudwaras as well as temples.

Finally, Lord Ram was in court. This worried the nonagenarian.

3

The Legal Team

In Senior Parasaran's team were six lawyers. Of them, P.V. Yogeswaran and Bhakti Vardhan Singh had the longest association with the Ram Janmabhoomi case. Bhakti Vardhan Singh's association goes back even earlier—to the time when he was still a student of law in Allahabad. Bhakti was in his mid-thirties with a receding hairline. Amiable, medium-built, and about 5'7", Bhakti's calm demeanour perfectly complemented Yogeswaran's exuberance, the latter having been associated with the case since 2010. Their chalk-and-cheese personalities made them a good team. Bhakti Vardhan Singh and Bhupendra Yadav were the only ones from the Allahabad High Court days who were still active in the team. However, if anyone wished to ascertain the main issues of this property dispute from the perspective of the case of Ram Lalla, then the man to be contacted was Yogeswaran, for Yogi, as he was called, was the Advocate-on-Record for Ram from 2010. An advocate-on-record is a lawyer who is authorized to file a case in the Supreme Court of India. He is the main man for the client, or the main strategist of the case. An advocate-on-record can argue the case himself or he may hire a senior counsel; senior counsels cannot appear on their own. Yogi was the man chosen to be Advocate- on-Record for Lord Ram. He was often spotted at the South Delhi residence-cum-office of the Parasarans.

Yogi is a live wire. He has a way of talking that immediately draws your interest. There is never a dull moment with him around—just that his bespectacled face lends a deceptive aura of innocence and gentleness. Full of energy and enthusiasm, he rarely allowed Bhakti to speak. Yogi was a selfless warrior who would often get involved neck-deep in the case. The risk was that sometimes he would let the warrior in him overtake the lawyer. Those moments were challenging. Thankfully, he usually reserved the warrior in him for his close circle of friends and his teammates.

Before you could enter the Parasarans' office, Rama Mutthuswamy (Mutthu), a long-time court clerk of Senior Parasaran, generally recorded your attendance and identification from behind a desk. Such was the overwhelming presence of Mutthu that one could gauge how a day in office would unfold from his greetings, which depended on the mood he was in. He was usually in a state of savageness and foul mood—a minefield or a booby trap ready to blow you apart before you entered; this side though was reserved for chamber juniors. On the rare lucky day, a good mood ensured safe passage to the associates' work area.

The office had a small cubicle with photographs of Senior Parasaran with former presidents and prime ministers adorning the walls. Rows of well-stacked bookshelves neatly lined the walls. The workstations were arranged across four rows with two columns, and somewhere within those columns would be seated a lost and scholarly Aditi Dani and Ashwin Kumar D.S. Aditi and Ashwin were two juniors of Mohan Parasaran. Senior Parasaran used to say in jest, 'I have misappropriated them from my son.' The victims of this misappropriation, though, were not complaining. Mohan Parasaran was not complaining either. He had problems only with his father not being mindful of his age.

Steel Wrapped in Smiles

Yogi's lean, thinly framed stature belied his aggressiveness. But he was not the only one-of-his-kind, innocuous-looking young lawyer in the team; Aditi was the other one. Neither was harmless to their opposing counsels' clients. Their looks were deceptive, and so were their smiles if you were not hiring them. If one were to ask who among the two looked more deceptively young, the answer would be Aditi. She could easily pass off for a fresh graduate or law school intern.

Aditi is an effective young lawyer. She is full of energy with very strong ideas that can at times go against building consensus in the team on some points. Many times, her thoughts conflicted with those of her team members and she had the full licence to use her right to freedom of expression.

However, there was a challenge looming that had to be dealt with. Like all other team members, Aditi had marked out her caveats from 8,000 printed pages of the Allahabad High Court judgement. If Yogi and Bhakti had worked day and night to master the facts, then Aditi was the court-master[28]-cum-probable-judge. She was in absolute command. Playing the devil's advocate, she left the colleague beside her, Ashwin, smiling and cringing in equal measure. A quiet and helpful friend, Ashwin was left to Aditi's mercy when she would fire salvos at him in the quizzing round, and he would respond with a few hits and many misses, oscillating between 'happy' and 'hapless' with equal ease. Ashwin had varied experience, but within the band of boys, only the lady was privileged to play the lead 'caveator', someone who was given the right to object.

In one way, the difference of opinion within the team helps as it leads to a thorough vetting of ideas. But sometimes, differences can also be worrisome. Expectedly, during the case, there were many such moments of worry.

The team members would become engrossed in serious case-related conversations, with serious moments interspersed with humour to lighten the intensity of the discussions. Yogeswaran always sought his colleagues' opinions. He once asked Bhakti if

[28]Someone who assists judges in court.

his knowledge of the matter was enough to get a certificate from him. 'Sir, you are the only team member who participated in the hearings before the Allahabad High Court. You saw all the evidence as well as heard all the arguments. You are the person who can give me a certificate stating if I am clear or not with the facts,' said Yogi. Bhakti, however, could gauge the reason behind such a frivolous question. 'Yogeswaran, your nervousness is increasing with the approach of the final hearing. You are repeating the same things,' he pointed out.

By now, Yogeswaran was sleeping and dreaming about this case. He had almost lost his objectivity and had converted from a lawyer to a client by then. A lawyer should never get emotionally involved with the outcome of the case. But in the Ram Janmabhoomi case, the lawyers were getting as personally concerned and emotionally involved as a client.

Mutthu often felt tempted to join in their discussions but usually refrained. He jumped in only when anyone erred, often citing the first lapse of the day. If nothing else, Mutthu would point out that someone was late: 'Where are the latest entrants to the team? Where are Sridhar Potaraju and Anirudh Sharma? The boss had called everyone upstairs. It seems the duo are late!'

We had both been closely associated with Senior Parasaran. Sridhar had earlier worked with Mr P.S. Narasimha, senior advocate and former Additional Solicitor General of India, and handled several temple-related matters, including the Tirumala Tirupati Devasthanam Board case from 2004. Anirudh was a student of Mr Parasaran and had trained under him since 2005, and witnessed a wide range of constitutional, commercial and civil cases. But like Ashwin and Bhakti, even we couldn't match the sheer energy of Yogi and Aditi—the firebrands of the team, and a clear threat for both the opposition and their own team members.

Benchmarks of Brilliance

Senior Parasaran's advancing age had made it difficult to use the flight of stairs, so his workplace was moved up from the basement to the ground floor, which still required climbing a few steps. But he was always ahead of his team in terms of readiness. They always walked into office to find fresh handwritten notes with dates lying on the table—a testimony to his meticulous approach and evidence that Mr Parasaran was an early riser. 'He wakes up at 4 a.m.,' his domestic help, who was privy to his daily routine, would inform us. Coffee was the fuel that kept him going. The handwritten notes often held our attention, particularly Sridhar's, who was not only a lawyer in the Ayodhya case, but his office also handled all the legal logistics of this case.

Senior Parasaran's living room was partitioned to accommodate his worktable. Spread out on it were law cases dating back to the 1920s and 1930s, judgements of the Privy Council, Indian appeals, books, digests and journals. There were also Supreme Court cases and those aforementioned handwritten notes on green paper. Those handwritten notes always stood out.

Every case had not only handwritten notes by Senior Parasaran but, in fact, many versions of the same notes. There was version one of a note, followed by version two, version three, the note made just before going to bed or the note made in the morning of the day of the hearing, and lastly, the final version; sometimes, even these came with a semi-final version. Just as the team would be admiring the as-yet new and fresh version of the handwritten notes, the nonagenarian—taking slow, small, measured steps with a stick in his hand to keep his balance—would appear on the scene. Undoubtedly, Yogeswaran was the master of facts in this case. But then, facing a person with the reputation of being a master craftsman was a tough call. Yogi's, Aditi's, Bhakti's, and Ashwin's ingenuity was to face the ultimate test at Mr Parasaran's desk. And we could only anticipate the challenge that would come from the nonagenarian.

Senior Parasaran, if in his element, would start addressing his team as soon as he saw them from a distance, and the initiation for the final preparation started in the same manner: 'Every structure has an unseen foundation, and archaeologists often deal with such hidden foundations. This Ram Temple/Ayodhya case, too, had many silent strategists. My predecessor in the office of the Attorney General, Lal Narayan Sinha, is the architect of the present case.'

Dressed in a veshti and a white shirt, he held a walking stick in one hand and a small box containing his hearing aids and a set of dentures in the other. That was Senior Parasaran at first glance, ready for the legal tug of war without effectively working ears, eyes, or any natural teeth, struggling to balance himself as he walked.

He read the *sarga*s (chapter or section within a *kanda* or canto) of the Ramayana, chanted prayers, remembered the Lord, and smeared *thirunamam* (sacred mark) on his forehead before shifting his attention to his other important morning ritual. It was his staple—a cup of steaming hot filter coffee that got him in work mode, and once done with it, he was ready for the day. He would sit at his work table, fold his hands with his neck jutting out a bit, and look at a simple Parthasarathi calendar that hung right opposite his seat. Behind his seat lay books of law. The hearing aids were duly placed where they belonged. When assisting counsels greeted him on the morning of 3 August 2019, he quickly showered his blessings on them. Apart from the six, others in the queue to seek his blessing were Mukul Singh, Praneet Pranav and Amit Sharma. The trio were working behind the scenes and had spent hours working with the evidence and sorting out papers. They were as much part of the group, well versed with the case, and often entrusted with managing the humongous load of documents and tracing relevant evidence from those documents for senior counsels.

By then, Senior Parasaran would be comfortably seated in his chair, interlocking his fingers as his elbows rested on the table. He would remain silent for a few moments and then slowly start bringing his fingers to life, twiddling them into motion. That meant deep contemplation. Mr Parasaran warned the team members that a humongous challenge awaited them. 'The inner conflict between the Hindu sides could destroy the case of temple. The catch is that the suit filed on behalf of Bhagwan Shri Ram Lalla could destroy the suit of Nirmohi Akhara and the suit filed by Nirmohi Akhara could destroy the suit filed by Bhagwan Sri Ramallah.' No one from the team differed.

Cross-Talk and Cross-Exams

Senior Parasaran had been working on this matter for a long time. In fact, for the last two years, this case had been completely occupying his mind. He alleged that Yogeswaran had been after his life for eight long months since October 2018. To get his revenge against Yogi, Mr Parasaran would plant him in the place of a judge: 'Yogeswaran will tell me whether I have got the factual matrix of the case right or not!'

An embarrassed Yogi's response would usually be of complete surrender: 'Sir, you know everything; you have read everything.'

'No one knows everything, Yogeswaran. I don't have ten heads to know everything. I am on Ram's side, don't make me Ravan,' Parasaran would respond.

Sticking to the facts, Senior Parasaran would lament that the factual matrix was not what newspapers and casual readers had been reporting to date. It was much more. Mr Parasaran had finished a detailed list of the events for his team to check later and give suggestions. But he would check all the factual matrices himself, with special instructions to Yogeswaran to pay attention so that he could correct any inaccuracies.

Incorrigible, Yogi would fire a smiling reply, 'What will I correct, sir? You know it all!'

Senior Parasaran had a standard retort. When calm, he would lean back in his seat, but when aggressive, he would move forward and lean on the table. 'At ninety-two, my faculties—memory, hearing, eyesight—are functioning at fifty per cent, while my strength and efficiency are less than fifty per cent. I have no natural teeth left. You are a terrible fellow, Yogeswaran. I have told you before that I don't have ten heads, and you say I know it all! Is this how you treat a person surviving on dentures?' he would say with mock sternness. A comparison with Ravan while representing Ram seemed quite misplaced. Mr Parasaran had a great sense of humour, this being only a figurative reflection of his wit and wisdom.

Factual matrix was just the beginning—he could pull out the whole development of various branches of law from memory. He may have been right about the unmatchable standards of top lawyers, admitting that he was at half his abilities. Yet, we mere mortals would acknowledge that at ninety-two, and with fifty per cent of his efficiency, he was still a class apart and in a league of his own, something only a gifted few could ever achieve. The rest of the team was no match for his memory, knowledge, efficiency and sheer excellence at his craft.

All these compliments generally infuriated Senior Parasaran. However, retorts that were not known were brought into vogue to explain the phenomenon called age. For the nonagenarian, age itself was a challenge. 'You young people must understand. I am serious. Age is an ailment, which only the elderly understand,' was his staple statement.

4

The Suits

The case of Lord Ram arose through a civil suit. Simply stated, a civil suit is a legal proceeding brought to enforce a civil right or to obtain redress for a wrong. The game of civil suits tests a lawyer's competence in its entirety. A civil suit states the facts against another party. The other party has the right to accept or deny these allegations. On the basis of that, the issues in dispute are framed and thereafter, the parties are allowed to lead and provide evidence backing their claims. The evidence presented can be documentary, expert or oral in nature. The next step is the examination and cross-examination of witnesses which takes place through the procedure established by law. Then come the final arguments which are followed by a judgement. Therefore, a civil suit creates the base of the case being argued and is played out on a fresh slate in the courts. Contrary to this, an appeal is based on the records generated through the civil suit itself.

The initial point of action for the first suit filed was the events of the night between 22 and 23 December 1949, when 'the idol of Bhagwan Shri Ram was installed with due ceremony_under the central dome of the building.'[29] This would, of course, have made national news, but also laid the foundation for what some would say was a 'unique civil case'.

[29]Visharad, Gopal Singh, O.S. NO. 1 of 1989, Reg. Suit 2 of 1950, *Vada Prativada*, https://tinyurl.com/y7t7xwpm. Accessed on 18 January 2025.

From Here Started the Saga of the Suits

The first suit (Suit 1)[30] was filed on 16 January 1950. It is with this suit that the courts took over the land of Ram Janmabhoomi. The order of attachment of the land was passed and the receiver was appointed. So, both the Hindu as well as the Muslim parties to this legal case lost possession, and the receiver arrived on the scene to take possession. The date 22/23 December 1949 was marked as 'very important'.

Everyone went out; the receiver came in. This meant that the government was now in control and the possession of the property was not with any individual or religious group. So, did prayers continue at the disputed site and Ram Janmabhoomi from the Ram *bhakt*'s (devotee's/worshipper's) perspective?

A civil suit (Suit 1 of 1950) for an injunction order (preventing the other side from doing certain acts listed in a petition) was filed by Gopal Singh Visharad on 16 January 1950. On the same day, the case was taken up and orders were passed, resulting in the idols of Ram Lalla continuing to occupy the space below the central dome of the structure. This order was slightly modified on 19 January 1950. The modified and final order of injunction reads as follows:

> *Opposite parties are hereby restrained by means of temporary injunction to refrain from removing the idols in question from the site in dispute and from interfering with pooja etc. as at present carried on.'*[31]

Now the aforementioned order dated 19 January 1950 was confirmed in the plaintiff's favour (effectively Ram bhakts' favour), granting facilities to pray after considering all objections.

---

[30]Khan, Justice S.U., *Vada Prativada*, https://tinyurl.com/4ba5ukfs. Accessed on 18 January 2025

[31]Pleadings in all suit, Volume-A, Bhagwan Sri Rama Virajman& Ors. v. Sri Rajendra Singh & Ors., Civil Appeal No. 4768-4771 of 2011, *Vada Prativada*, https://tinyurl.com/m5jv6j6y. Accessed on 18 January 2025.

For Senior Parasaran, this order was very important: 'We said, and we say again, that we have only one Ram Janmabhoomi. We could not have and we cannot change it. How can we change anyone's birthplace?' But the order recorded a fact which was crucial.

It was also observed in the order dated 3 March 1951 that there were several other mosques in the vicinity of the disputed site. The order of 3 March 1951 recorded what would later be picked up by the media as a statement from Senior Parasaran during the final days of the hearing:

> *[...] As to the balance of convenience, it is obvious that the effect of vacating the interim injunction at this stage is likely to deprive the plaintiff of the right claimed by him in this suit. Moreover, it is a matter of admission between the parties that there are several other mosques in the mohalla in question. The local Muslims will not, therefore, be put to much inconvenience, if the interim injunction remains in force during the pendency of the case.*[32]

Senior Parasaran's instruction was to make a note and highlight it for later reference. This finding of fact was not challenged by anyone and had, therefore, stood the test of legal scrutiny over time. He wanted to use this statement in court someday, because it was not his deduction or opinion, but a recording of the court. This observation was made in 1951 and was still holding forth from 1951 to 2019.

The second suit, Suit 25 of 1950 (later numbered as OOS 2 of 1989), was filed by Paramhans Ram Chandra Das. It sought an injunction order restraining the defendants from interfering with the worship of Lord Ram at the janmabhoomi, and further to not disturb or remove the idols. Overall, this suit was not of much

[32]Order passed by the Trial Court on 03.03.1951 which was extracted by Justice Sudhir Agarwal in his judgment in Para 128 of the Allahabad High Court Judgment, *elegalix.allahabadhighcourt.in*, https://tinyurl.com/hazp52zs. Accessed on 18 January 2025.

importance to the fate of the dispute.

Then came the third suit. This suit was very interesting. Nirmohi Akhara filed the original Suit 26 of 1959 (renumbered as OOS 3 of 1989).[33] Nirmohi Akhara, in common parlance, could be described as a group of Hindu ascetics. They were an ancient group having organized themselves as a math and could be termed as the Ramanandi sect of Bairagis. Nirmohi Akhara still owns and manages several temples. They claimed the disputed land, identified by Hindus to be Ram Janmabhoomi, as belonging to them. The prayer in the suit was to the effect that the receiver, who had got charge of the temple due to the order passed by the court, should be removed from the management, and charge of the temple and its management (of the Janmabhoomi) should be delivered to Nirmohi Akhara.

Nirmohi Akhara also stated that the land, which is the Janmasthan, belongs to them and has always belonged to them. Therefore, they too identified the spot of Ram's birth—the same as in Ram Lalla's case. However, they differed on other points raised in Suit 5 of Ram Lalla. Ultimately, with the turn of events, Nirmohi Akhara ended up challenging Lord Ram Lalla—God's suit itself.[34]

Suit 4: The dispute carried on, and on 18 December 1961, the Sunni Central Waqf Board filed a suit.[35]

The suit number was R.S. No. 12 of 1961, which was renumbered as Suit 4 of 1989. This was filed with an application to represent the entire Muslim community and was one of the most important suits. The relief sought in the case was: (*See maps in photo inserts*)

---

[33]Nirmohi Akhara, O.S. No. 26 of 1959 (renumbered as OOS 3 of 1989), *Vada Prativada,* https://tinyurl.com/yc6zc3vj. Accessed on 18 January 2025.

[34]Nirmohi Akhara unnecessarily opposing deity's plea, both stand or fall together in Ayodhya case: SC', *The New Indian Express*, 27 August 2019, https://tinyurl.com/2t2mbfek. Accessed on 18 January 2025.

[35]Sunni Central Waqf O.S. No. 4 of 1989, Reg. Suit No. 12 of 1961, *Vada Prativada*, https://tinyurl.com/mrxxz5jt. Accessed on 18 January 2025.

> *A declaration to the effect that the property indicated by letters A B C D in the sketch map attached to the plaint is a public mosque commonly known as 'Babari Masjid' and that the land adjoining the mosque shown in the sketch map by letters E F G H is a public Muslim grave yard as specified in para 2 of the plaint and it may be decreed.*

Though the process of reading, re-reading, marking and re-marking had been done many times, Senior Parasaran would still make a point loud and clear. The Sunni Board stated that the entire area, ABCD, is a mosque. Ram Lalla's suit also stated that the entire area, ABCD, is a *temple*. So, none of the parties pleaded for the land as divided into the inner and outer courtyards. 'So, how can divisions of the land be affected? Both sides identify the land as one indivisible composite unit.' The prayer clause of the Sunni Central Waqf Board Suit, among other things, read:

> *(b) That in the case in the opinion of the court, delivery of possession is deemed to be the proper remedy, a decree for delivery of possession of the mosque and graveyard in a suit by removal of the idols and other articles which the Hindus may have placed in the mosque as objects of their worship be passed in plaintiff's favour, against the defendants.*
>
> *(bb) That the statutory Receiver is commanded to hand over the property in dispute described in the Schedule 'A' of the Plaint by removing the unauthorized structures erected thereon.*[36]

Then came the Suit of God—Suit 5.

On 1 July 1989, a fifth suit was filed by former Allahabad High Court Judge Deoki Nandan Agarwal as a 'next friend' of Ram Lala Virajman[37] (the deity, deemed a minor legal person)

[36]Sunni Central Waqf O.S. No. 4 of 1989, Reg. Suit No. 12 of 1961, Para 24 of the plaint, https://tinyurl.com/mrxxz5jt. Accessed on 18 January 2025.

[37]*M. Siddiq (D) Thr. Lrs v. Mahant Suresh Das & Ors*, Civil Appeal No. 10866-10867

before the civil judge in Faizabad. It prayed that the whole disputed site be handed over to Ram Lalla for the construction of a new temple. The suit of Lord Ram was important as none of the earlier suits had claimed ownership of the land. It was a suit, a well-thought-about legal document and finalized after intense research, and referred to the aspirations of Mahatma Gandhi. A few salient features of Suit 5 of Ram Lalla are worth noting:

> *19. That it is manifestly established by public records of unimpeachable authority that the premises in dispute is the place where maryadaPurushottam Shree Ramchandra Ji Maharaj was born as the son of Maharaja Dashrath of the solar dynasty, which according to the tradition and the faith of the devotees of Bhagavan Shriram is the place where he manifestly himself in human form as an incarnation of bhagwanvishnu. The place has since ever been called Shriram Janmabhoomi by all end sundry through the ages.*
>
> *20. That the place itself or the ASTHAN SHREE RAM JANMABHOOMI, as it has come to be known, has been an object of worship as a deity by the devotees of bhagwan Shri ram, as it personifies the spirit of the divine worshipped in the form of Shri ram lala or Lord ram the child. The asthan was thus deified and has had a juridical personality of its own even before the construction of a temple building or the installation of the idol of bhagwan Shri ram thereat.*
>
> *[...]*
>
> *22. That according to the faith of the devotees of bhagwan Shri ram lala, or Lord ram the child, it is the spirit of bhagwan Shri ram as the divine child which resides at aasthanshriramjanmabhoomi and can be experienced by those who pray, there and invoke the spirit for their spiritual*

---

of 2010 [Part N, Para 354 (p. 402)] *Supreme Court Judgment*, https://tinyurl.com/3bwykemu. Accessed on 18 January 2025.

uplift. The spirit is the deity. An idol is not necessary for invoking the divine spirit. Another example of such a deity is that of kedarnath. The temple of kedarnath has no ideal in it. It is the undulating surface of stone which is worshipped there as the deity. Still another example of such a deity is the Vishnu pad temple at Gaya, that too has no idol in it. The place which is believed to have born the footprints of bhagwanvishnu is worshipped as deity. Similarly, at Ayodhya, the very asthan shri ram janmabhoomi is worshipped as a deity through such symbols of the divine spirit as the charan and the sitarasoi. The place is a deity. It has existed in this immovable form through the ages, and has ever been a juridical person. The actual and continuous performance of pooja of such an immovable deity by its devotees is not essential for its existence as a deity. The deity continues to exist so long as the place exists, and being land, it is indestructible. Thus, Asthana shriramjanmabhoomi is an indestructible and immovable deity who has continued to exist throughout the ages.

[...]

30. That the Hindu public and the devotees of the plaintiff deities, who had dreamed of establishing ram Raja in free India, that is, the rule of dharma and righteousness, of which maryadapurushottam Shri ramachandrajimaharaj was the epitome have been keenly desirous of restoring his janmasthan to its pristine glory, as a first step towards that national aspiration given to us by mahatma gandhi. For achieving this, they are publicly agitating for the construction of a grand temple in the nagar style.

"Plans and a model of the proposed temple have already been prepared by the same family of architects who build the somnath temple. the active movement is planned to commence from September 30, 1989 and foundation stone of

> *the new temple building, it has been declared, shall be laid on November 9, 1989.*[38]

The Sunni Central Waqf Board's Suit (4 of 1989) also had some interesting averments from the viewpoint of Senior Parasaran's team. Their plea was twofold. The first being that the mosque was built on totally unused and vacant land, and alternatively, even if the mosque was built on an erstwhile temple land through the fiction of/by virtue of the law of 'adverse possession' (ownership through hostile, uncontested possession of property belonging to someone else), the board would still be the owner.

> *2. That in the sketch map attached herewith, the main construction of the said mosque is shown by letters A B C D and the land adjoining the mosque on the east, west, north and south, shown in the sketch map attached herewith, is the ancient graveyard of the Muslims, covered by the graves of the Muslims, who lost their lives in the battle between emperor Babar and the previous ruler of Ajodhiya, which are shown in the sketch map attached herewith. The mosque and the graveyard is vested in the almighty. The said mosque has since the time of its construction been used by the Muslims for offering prayers and the graveyard has been used as graveyard. The mosque and the graveyard are in mohallakot Rama Chander also known as Rama kot Town, Ayodhya, The khasra number of the mosque and the graveyard in suit are shown in the schedule attached which is part of the plant.*
>
> *[…]*
>
> *11. That the Muslims have been in peaceful possession of the aforesaid mosque and used to recite prayer in it, till 23.12.1949 when a large crowd of Hindus, with the mischievous intention of destroying, damaging or defiling the*

[38]Sri Ram Lalla Virajman & Ors., O.S. No. 5 of 1989 Reg. Suit 236 of 1989, Para 30, https://tinyurl.com/5c5nw827. Accessed on 18 January 2025.

said mosque and thereby insulting the Muslim religion and the religious feelings of the Muslims, entered the mosque and desecrated the mosque by placing idols inside the mosque. The conduct of Hindus amounted to an offence punishable under sections 147, 295 and 448 of the Indian Penal code.

11(a). That assuming, though not admitting. That at one time there existed a Hindu temple as alleged by the defendants representatives of the Hindus on the site of which emperor Babur built the most, some 433 years ago, the Muslims, by virtue of their long exclusive and continuous possession beginning from the time the mosque was built and continuing right up to the time some mosque, some mischievous persons entered the mosque and desecrated the mosque as alleged in the preceding paragraphs of the plaint, the Muslims perfected their title by adverse possessions and the right title or interest of the temple and of the Hindu public if any, extinguished.[39]

In 1989, the Uttar Pradesh Shia Waqf Board had also moved in and became a party in the case. Finally, in the Supreme Court, the case not only became a symbol of a Hindu-Muslim divide but also of an inter se divide between the Muslim and the Hindu parties on certain points, and unanimity on certain points.

The order dated 3 March 1951 hinting at the conflict between one Janmabhoomi and multiple mosques was holding the field till now but as history would have it, Lord Ram's suit had succeeded on most counts before the Allahabad High Court. Hence, the focus was maximized on Suit 5. The plaintiffs in the original Suit No. 5 (filed 01.07.1989) claimed exclusive ownership of the disputed site. They were Bhagwan Sri Ram Virajman (idol), Sri Ram Janmabhoomi (birthplace).

The discussions concerning Suit 5 in Senior Parasaran's chambers were time-consuming. A particular point in Suit 5 on

---

[39]Sunni Central Waqf O.S. No. 4 of 1989, Reg. Suit No. 12 of 1961, Para 11(a), https://tinyurl.com/2s2mfb4m. Accessed on 18 January 2025.

whether the Ram Janmabhoomi can itself be a Juristic Entity, became a bone of contention and even created a deep divide in Mr Parasaran's team. This worried Mr Parasaran.

But all said and done, God did arrive in court and the team began pulling their oars together to attend to God's case led by 'God's Own Lawyer'.

5

A Case of Great Significance

The top court of any country always decides cases that hold much significance for the future. The Supreme Court of India has also undertaken many such cases in the past. The Ayodhya case was certainly among them. It was acknowledged that the case of Lord Ram dealt with many sensitive issues. Therefore, to err on the side of caution, journalists would often speak to lawyers to discuss the case or to confirm their viewpoints, and sometimes, to gain information or clear their doubts. Ordinary citizens too may have wanted to follow the everyday proceedings of the Ayodhya case.

A judgement in the first instance is not the end. Like all institutions, a court can err. In that case, one can appeal to a higher court. There are lesser chances of a mistake and greater chances of a mistake being corrected if multiple trained eyes scrutinize a case. A total of 14 appeals were filed in the Supreme Court against the 2010 Allahabad High Court judgement. It seemed that every side was aggrieved by the Allahabad High Court's ruling on some point or the other.

In an appeal that challenges a judgement given in a civil suit by the first court, the case can be completely analysed, supported by robust evidence by a higher court. That implies that the case can be reopened in absolute terms for discussion (this kind of appeal is called first appeal). Before the Supreme Court of India, such cases are rare where a High Court has decided a civil suit, and an appeal knocks directly on its door. Generally, a round of appeal lies before the higher courts, where the second round of in-depth scrutiny of evidence is allowed.

The Supreme Court was to hear the Ayodhya case as a first appeal where the conclusions derived from evidence could also be challenged. Evidence in detail could be delved into and examined. The Supreme Court rarely undertook such tasks where in-depth oral evidence and cross-examinations of witnesses in a suit were witnessed. Any other kind of petition filed in the Supreme Court is decided based only on affidavits and documents. Rarely is there cross-examination in the Supreme Court.

The emotions the Ayodhya case could arouse had even compelled a veteran like Senior Parasaran to tread with caution. He would take care of the minutest details while addressing his briefing counsel in this case. He would insist on reading every page of the case brief (case file) from cover to cover, himself. Top senior counsels would often be fast, quick and to the point, having narrowed down controversies with their long experience of conducting thousands of cases at the Bar. But not in this case, not by this counsel. Mr Parasaran's conferences and discussions with his team delved deep into the case, and his factual recaps were detailed.

Senior Parasaran repeated, 'The most important points are the facts and the history which this case has seen.' As was his habit, he would lean back in his chair when contemplating his next moves. He had already dictated a list of events as all lawyers do. Being cautious, he wanted to test himself and continued, 'It is the Ayodhya case, so we all must be careful,' he would politely remind us all. Detailed meetings and conferences became the norm. The final rounds of discussions were precise and to the point. Senior Parasaran was unequivocal in his statements: 'We must start from the fact that the land in the dispute/suit land is the entire premises of Shri Ram Janambhumi, which is situated in village Kot Rama Chandra (Ram Kot at Ayodhya) Pargana Haveli Avadh, Tehsil Sadar, District Faizabad, UP. The area of the suit land in dispute is limited to about 130 x 80 sq. ft only as of now. Less than 1,500 sq. yd. It is not in dispute by any party that Sita

Rasoi and Ram Chabutra are within the disputed area.'

To make it simpler for the judges to understand the area's topography, a map had to be used.

Senior counsels are generally systematic in their ways of working, and with around seventy years of experience as a lawyer, Senior Parasaran had the points crystallized. From the long conferences on the issue, the following points had come to the fore for the team:

1. Since time immemorial, Hindus have believed and had faith in the fact that Ayodhya is the birthplace of Shri Ram. This faith and belief have been put into practice till now. No one can dispute it, and no one has disputed it. Even the opposing parties accept that Lord Ram was born in Ayodhya.
2. The time frame of the case could be divided roughly into four periods. The first period lasted from 1 BC till 1528. What were the faiths, practices and worships prevalent till 1528 before the disputed structure was constructed at the disputed site? These were the questions to be answered by the team. Modern archaeological evidence was now available to provide the land's ancient history.
3. The second period was from 1528, when the disputed structure was constructed, till 1857, when the British took over, and an iron railing/grill was erected on the land. The issue of faith and worship arose again from 1528 to 1857–58. Who worshipped on the disputed land? Who did not worship? What did the independent observers see? Who says we have evidence? Who says we don't have any proof? All these questions were to be answered with the help of evidence substantiated by history.
4. The third phase fell between 1857 and 1949. In furtherance of their divide-and-rule policy, the British constructed an iron railing/grill affecting an artificial division and identification of the land around 1857 So, the land dispute, as it went to court, had the land marked as the inner courtyard and the

outer courtyard separated by the iron railing/grill. The factual position arising from this artificial division could be gauged through a map submitted on 6 December 1885 in the Court of the Sub-Judge, Faizabad; the map showed the position of the disputed place as it stood at that time. Ram Chabutra, Sita Rasoi and Bhandara (community kitchen) were in the outer courtyard, while the disputed structure was in the inner courtyard.

The third phase was the legally intriguing period from 1857 to 1949. What was the status of faith and worship until the idols were placed inside the Garbha Griha (sanctum sanctorum) as referred by one party and the central dome by another? Who worshipped there? Who did not worship there? What did people see and write about? What could the people not see or write about? These questions resurfaced.

5. The last phase started from 1950 when the first civil suit was filed, till the culmination of all the cases before the Allahabad High Court.

At each stage, concurrence was taken from the team members, particularly, from Yogeswaran and Bhakti. Senior Parasaran was clear: 'We must put the case in a manner where we show the least number of disputes. The best evidence is the admission from opposite parties.[40] So, we must carefully work on their admissions on evidence and practice of faith by Ram bhakts at the disputed site.' Yogi always had multiple points to discuss. The nonagenarian would often calm him down with a reminder, 'If required, in certain cases, one should argue less and let your opposing side argue to their heart's content.' This was contrary to Yogi's idea of existence. Yogi believed that he or we must have the maximum say. In fact, Yogi always believed that he must have the maximum say.

With disappointment in his voice, Senior Parasaran would remind his team, 'Because of my age, I will not be taking the

---

[40]When claimant A makes a statement and B cannot deny it, or accepts it.

court through pieces of evidence. Till a few years back, I could have managed the strength to cover all aspects myself, but that is not possible anymore.' In his opinion, Mr C.S. Vaidyanathan was an outstanding choice for dealing with facts in addition to his command over the law. He was informed that Mr Vaidyanathan was getting himself ready on all issues of fact and law.

The nonagenarian had covered all evidence from what he admitted was his fading memory. He would quietly let slip some samples of efficiency. 'Evidence has been advanced as noted by the High Court that Guru Nanak Devji visited Ayodhya in 1510–11 AD and that too, to have *darshan* (auspicious sighting) of the janmabhoomi of Shri Ram.' This, in his opinion, did support the faith and belief of his clients, but no evaluation of this evidence came up in the High Court's judgement. There was evidence of Hindus worshipping on the site before and even after 1528 when Babur it is claimed, came near Ayodhya.

As pointed out, the important aspect was that even the Sunni Board had said that the disputed structure was constructed in 1528 at the behest of Babur.[41] Ram Lalla's case also said it was constructed at the behest of Babur in 1528. Ram Lalla's side, however, contended that the building does not meet the pre-requisites of being a mosque under Islam, that it never religiously and validly turned into a mosque. Since the Sunni Board claimed that Babur had dedicated the building as a mosque, to Senior Parasaran's mind, the burden was on the Sunni Board to prove that Babur had dedicated the building as a mosque. When was it dedicated? How was it dedicated? These were issues that had to be proved by the Sunni Board.

In his warrior-like manner, Yogeswaran would emphasize, 'Sir, we have historical evidence to prove all our points.' In many discussions, even lawyers would ponder over how the courts would analyse history, but that stood as a legal proposition.

---

[41]Sunni Central Waqf O.S. NO. 4 of 1989, Reg. Suit no. 12 of 1961(Para 18), https://tinyurl.com/2s2mfb4m. Accessed on 18 January 2025.

Aditi would caution Yogi in the team, 'All that we say has to sail through as evidence.'

The senior counsel considered Bhakti's repeated request for time on the issues of evidence mired in history. Despite Yogi and Bhakti's assertion, Senior Parasaran would remind everyone, 'No, Vaidyanathan will deal with evidence. I am here to help with the law. I am an old man.'

Senior Parasaran would get worked up when a law point decided way back in time had to be discussed. He would immediately point out that there were cases where the Privy Council and the Supreme Court had already decided how hearsay evidence and historical documents like travelogues, etc., throw light on the history and can be used as evidence. Generally, a person can be a witness of what she/he directly sees or witnesses and not on the basis of what one hears about an incident from a third person. What one hears from a third person is hearsay evidence. Aditi would ring in a caveat on such issues to remind her colleagues that both sides could present historical evidence in their favour. Mr Parasaran was always happy to hear such doubts. He would smile when young lawyers were eager to test themselves.

In 2005, while assisting Senior Parasaran as his chamber junior in some important cases, Anirudh too had his queries, like Aditi had hers in 2019. Nevertheless, a lawyer playing the devil's advocate is an asset to the team though she/he may sometimes seem challenging. The questions she/he raises help fine-tune arguments and give a clearer perspective while the lawyer just does her/his duty. Hence, Aditi's point of not throwing caution to the winds was valid. But aren't younger people excited about probing, testing, and discovering? There is no substitute for experience; no one gains experience without raising doubts and questions.

The case was gaining interest. It was, therefore, natural that certain questions from the relatives and friends of team members would reach the nonagenarian: 'Sir, in your nearly seventy years of experience, did you see a case of this nature where varied types of evidence coexist?' The answer was obvious: 'No!'

Senior Parasaran had seen all types of cases. He had seen the Supreme Court since the 1950s. Times had changed, and he often said, 'These days, the court is overworked.' For him, what hadn't changed in the last many years was that ninety per cent of the cases filed as Special Leave Petitions questioning the judgement of any inferior court or forum got dismissed in the Supreme Court. 'The problem is not that lawyers don't work hard. Sometimes the judges work harder.' Such answers were preceded by a wink from behind the wrinkles and a hearty laugh.

But the Ayodhya dispute was the only case where archaeological evidence took us back to 1 BCE. The seasoned lawyer was ready to delve into history and accurately evaluate the case from his work done in the past two years. In lawyers' terms, a list of dates was ready which could summarize the whole timeline of the case. That's from where the lawyers start.

6

A Beautiful Mind and the Factual Matrix

Every case in court starts with a 'List of Dates and Events' that simplifies the case and arranges it in chronological order. This is prepared for every case in all law offices; if required, it could be handed over to the court. A look at the detailed list of dates prepared by Senior Parasaran left not an iota of doubt, even in the minds of Yogeswaran and Bhakti, that he had been working on his own too, apart from the long hours spent with them. In fact, till a few years ago, Mr Parasaran, with his photographic memory and insatiable appetite for reading at breakneck speed, would not require such detailed interactions with his team.

Senior Parasaran was clear: 'The whole case had at its base not only a positive affirmation of existence of faith but also evidence of the practice of faith.' Mr Parasaran, however, had given it his all and now wanted to run his thoughts and preparations by his team. Maybe for this case, he wanted a dry run. For the uninitiated, Mr Parasaran's construction of the facts of the case would be sufficient to understand and follow the case. He would keep the papers down and, from his memory, dish out facts, even if those facts were derived from different sets of case files.

'The place (disputed site) itself is divine and is of religious importance as it is the birthplace of Lord Ram. The place or the Asthan Shri Ram Janambhumi, as it has come to be known, has been an object of worship as a "deity" by the devotees of Bhagwan Shri Ram, as it personifies or reflects the spirit of the "divine" worshipped in the form of Shri Ram Lalla, the child, since time immemorial. The asthan was thus deified and, therefore, has a characteristic/personality of its own even before the construction of any temple building or the installation of the idol of Bhagwan Shri Ram there. It is believed that the mere darshan of the land grants salvation. So, the place of birth is important. The emphasis was on the "place of birth", which cannot be changed,' was assertion of the senior counsel.

With no contention challenging the faith of Hindu devotees and Ram bhakts regarding the birth of Lord Ram at Ayodhya as described in the Valmiki Ramayana, or, as existing today, the dispute was narrowed down. 'Ram was born in Ayodhya' was a statement of fact in the case. It was, however, disputed and denied by the opposing side that the site of the disputed structure/Babri Masjid was Lord Ram's birthplace. Mr Parasaran's case, in short, was that there existed a temple at the site since the era of Vikramaditya, and that the mosque stands on the same demolished temple structure. So, it was said that the disputed structure/mosque was not constructed on vacant land, while the Sunni Board and others say that the disputed structure/mosque was constructed on vacant land and no structure existed below it. That was the core dispute. The attempt was to prove Ram Lalla's case through religious documents, historical travelogues and gazettes, and establish that the same site has been worshipped as Ram Janmabhoomi.

Top lawyers are good storytellers. After a thorough discussion, the factual matrix of the case could be told as a story, based on Senior Parasaran's dictated list of dates. Aditi would invariably scrutinize the typed 'List of Dates and Events', while Yogeswaran easily recorded all of it in his head. The rest were just required to assist either of the two, Aditi or Yogi. The practice was simple. As a rule, all dates were on the left and the events associated on the right. However, there was a method.

When a team is ready, well prepared and committed, a couple of people do organically emerge as facilitation points;

and as rules of banter would have it, they can be called some tag names. Senior Parasaran would go over all the points in detail while keeping his team in the loop. In essence, he enumerated the following salient points—the factual matrix, culled from his reading of the history of the site which we present in Tables 1.1 and 1.2.

Table 1.1: Factual Matrix

1528	As per Ram Lalla's case, the disputed structure/mosque building was constructed at the site of the destroyed temple. The material used included that taken from the temple, including its pillars, which were made of Kasauti or touchstone, with figures of Hindu gods and goddesses carved on them. So, the presence of figurines of Hindu beliefs never ceased to be present in the building. Irrespective of that, Ram bhakts' faith in the land remained intact; they kept worshipping the land despite a new building at the janmabhoomi site.
Between 1528 and 1858	Various records about the nature of worship performed at the Janam Asthan/Babri Masjid disputed complex by independent sources exist. Important aspects of history are present there. Most importantly, independent sources identify the spot of Ram's birthplace. These sources include European travellers, Christian missionaries, and British officers. The first among the many documents was the travelogue of William Finch, who visited India between 1608 and 1611, and which was published in *Early Travels in India (1583–1619)*. The second was *Description Historique et Géographique de l'Inde* (1786) by Father Joseph Tieffenthaler, who visited Oudh between 1766 and 1771. He refers to worship by Hindus

	at the disputed site, the practice of *parikrama* or circumambulation of a scared spot, and of prostrating in front of the revered site. The third was Walter Hamilton's *East India Gazetteer* of 1828. The fourth was Robert Montgomery Martin's *The History, Antiquities, Topography and Statistics of Eastern India* (1838), while the fifth was Edward Thornton's *A Gazetteer of the Territories Under the Government of East-India Company* (1858), which were all published close to 1855.

All these and many other sources had already been presented to the Allahabad High Court. These documents identified the disputed site as one of religious practice, faith, belief, and worship for Ram bhakts. Senior Parasaran emphasized every time these documents were discussed: 'All these are independent sources to which no mala fide can be attached; these are old, reliable and credible accounts.'

Bhakti and Yogeswaran filled in the details of such evidence, as instructed and each document would later be studied minutely. When Yogi would point out that all these are ancient facts, Senior Parasaran's answer would be terse: 'Ancient facts cannot be proved by direct evidence. You cannot summon witnesses from ancient periods. Summoning witnesses from ancient times would be scary. Only Yogeswaran and Aditi can, to some extent, handle such witnesses. I would run away!'

Such punches kept the team on their toes and the nonagenarian agile. The butt of these jokes also enjoyed such light moments. Senior Parasaran would quickly move on to more serious stuff of the law. Hearsay evidence would come into play. For historical facts, hearsay evidence, could be brought in a court of law. On such points of law, Mr Parasaran would quickly move to the past in his own fixed pattern: 'Digressing from facts, let me tell you about a very old judgement. All of you must note it down.

It's a 1925 Privy Council case,[42] p. 113. The judgement says that in certain cases and stages, direct evidence may not be available. So, to prove historical facts, customary facts, hearsay evidence is admissible. It means that evidence about faith, belief, practice, and customs which may have travelled down from generation to generation through stories, word-of-mouth or customs would be admissible. The case to my now-fragile memory was called *Raja Rajendra Narain v. Kumar Gangananda & Ors*. It was held that after the existence of a custom for some years, proved by direct evidence, it can, as a rule, be shown to be immemorial by hearsay evidence[43], and it is for this reason that such hearsay evidence is allowed as an exception to the general rule, deviating from the rule of non-admissibility of hearsay evidence. So, the law is that all hearsay evidence will be admitted in such matters.'

Senior Parasaran, as he often did, was again recalling judgements that had been passed ninety-four years ago. He was habitually doing so even with such an old memory card. Ashwin and Anirudh were two of his fanboys in the room. Every top lawyer has a fan club, and so does Mr Parasaran. To his fans, he was a man with a beautiful mind!

When the book titled *All India Reporter 1925*, or *AIR 1925*, arrived, the contemplative mood would return. Senior Parasaran would be at work, digging deep into his memory. After a pause and flipping through the pages, he would come to the golden law point: 'I think the Supreme Court has relied upon this 1925 Privy Council ruling in the 1989 case of Shakuntalabai or Shardabai or something like that. Justice Saikia's judgement, you can look that up on the internet.' (Computers were certainly not the nonagenarian's first love.) 'You young boys and girls only play

---

[42]Important past and present judgements are reported in journals. One such journal is the *All India Reporter*, or AIR.

[43]Evidence is normally given only of which one has been an eye witness. What someone hears from others is hearsay evidence and not admissible in a court of law. Hearsay evidence is accepted by the court only as an exception to the rule.

with computers. That's what you all youngsters do. Even senior counsels whom I have seen as young boys use computers now. Human memory is fading.'

His eyes would grapple with the pages of the book. Senior Parasaran was a study in himself when he was with law books. In fact all top lawyers are, but with distinct habits and styles. He would flip through a few pages with an expression of dismay. It was evident that his eyes were straining with the small fonts. He would widen his eyes to read, then shut one eye and read with the other. The physical challenges while dealing with this case were humongous. It was, therefore, natural to expect the nonagenarian to experience eye problem and physical discomfort.

Senior Parasaran would often ask for the right book but with age, sometimes would cite the wrong page number. 'My memory is failing me these days. I can't depend on it,' he would say with a wry smile. But once the correct page was found—213 instead of the 113 he had mentioned—he would quickly get to the heart of the matter. 'So, customs and traditions of religion need to be proved by practice, for which there can be hearsay evidence,' he explained, before directing that targeted searches be run through computer databases. Everyone's views on the detailed list of dates and events[44] were taken. The most contentious timeline was from 1528 to 1885. In a short, simplified format, the notes reflected some salient points for the team's understanding, concerning the Hindu parties' continued claim over the disputed structure and continued attempts to assert their faith in an era of British divide and rule.

[44]Note for discussion in the office of Mr K. Parasaran.

Table 1.2: Factual Matrix (contd)

1856–57	The disputed premise was divided into two parts by constructing an iron-grilled wall. It was an artificial partition between the Hindu and Muslim areas. This partition was to maintain law and order and had no connection with the issue of who owned the land.
28 November 1858	Nihang Singh Fakir Khalsa entered the disputed structure. A complaint was lodged, and a report was prepared by Sheetal Dubey, *Thanedar* (Station Officer), against the prayer offered by Nihang Singh Fakir in the middle of the Masjid Janam Asthan, and for erecting the Nishan Sahib (Sikh religious flag) there. Twenty-five Sikhs were also present for the hoisting of the religious flag at the Masjid Janam Asthan. Certain events finally led to an order stating that the place was to be vacated. However, as per the case of Ram Lalla, no evidence exists of offering any prayers/namaz at that site before 1855.
1860–61	Applications were filed by mosque supporters who wanted Hindus out of the premises, with prayers to get Ram Chabutra removed. The proceedings failed, and Ram Chabutra continued to exist within the disputed structure. These applications are proof of the continued worship at the Ram Janam Asthan by Ram bhakts, thus establishing their claim.

August 1863–September 1865	The opposite side (Sunni Board) had communications with the British government about certain grants, etc., for the disputed land. But no document establishes their ownership/title, and no exclusive possession of the disputed site was made. This was the case on Ram Lalla's side. Our case was that even in their documents, on which the opposite side/Sunni Board relies, the place is called Masjid Janam Asthan. This also comprises the first set of evidence of the period after 1857, brought by the opposite side to challenge the case of the Ram bhakts.
1865–73	Similar communication between the other side/Muslim side and the British existed till 1873. Certain claims were also filed for the title of the *kabaristan* (graveyard), etc. But none could succeed, and none of the documents of the opposite side says a word about the offering of namaz within the premises till 1873.
14 May 1877	Due to the heavy rush on days when a fair was held at the Janam Asthan, it was felt that an extra door had to be opened for Hindus within the disputed structure. This was in pursuance of the continued faith and worship that attracted a considerable number of people—so much so that the rush endangered the life of Ram bhakts. The opening of the door was sought to be stopped through legal proceedings. However, the proceedings failed, and a new door was opened.

18 June 1883	Another case was filed. The Ram bhakts regularly worshipped within the disputed site and Ram Chabutra. Suit No. 374/943 was filed by Mohd. Asghar against Raghubar Das in 1882; he claimed rent for the use of the Chabutra and Takht for organizing the Kartik Mela on the occasion of Ram Navami. The Sunni Board side failed again, and the suit was dismissed.[45]
12 January 1884	By this time, the British government displayed a growing tendency to instigate and sustain the tension between the Hindu and Muslim communities. Continued tension suited their divide-and-rule game. But these past orders of 1877 and 1883 substantiate Ram bhakts' continued claim on the land where they performed prayers on the disputed structure.

Hence, the issues were answered with the conclusion that tensions existed between the communities. But why was this so? This was because Ram bhakts were present on the disputed site. Senior Parasaran reiterated, 'In my opinion, we prove our presence before 1528 and after 1528 till date. We will go into the pre-1528 era with religious and other historical evidence later. Of course, archaeological evidence is also there for Vaidyanathan to deal with. We establish continued practice, presence, faith, and devotion. Even those documents primarily starting after the 1860s, which record the other side's presence, also record not merely our presence, but the devotion, perseverance, worship, and faith of Ram bhakts, who were retaining their presence against all odds and trying to regain administrative control of the remaining part which went out of their control due to the artificial partition.'

[45]*M. Siddiq (D)* Thr. *Lrs v. Mahant Suresh Das & Ors*, Civil Appeal No. 10866-10867 of 2010 [Part D.1, Para 46 (x) (p. 68)] *Supreme Court judgment* https://tinyurl.com/mr2arh5b. Accessed on 18 January 2025.

If Senior Parasaran looked for a response from his team members, Sridhar always liked to sum up on behalf of everyone else: 'So, Sir, even our worst case is that we were always present on the land and worshipping.' But Mr Parasaran would not move on without Yogeswaran's approval.

Certain secrets about the case would also be revealed when Yogeswaran talked. Senior Parasaran's rule was clear: 'If Yogeswaran says yes, it's final. He has been working on the case from even before 2010.' If someone commented that Mr Parasaran was privy to many secrets as an advisor to prime ministers, the nonagenarian replied, 'Well, I myself don't know about the secrets Yogeswaran knows. I don't know of any secret lying with me.'

The team was told that the senior counsel would not give any exclusive information that he may have of events buried deep in the past, even at the tail end of his career. Senior Parasaran would cut short these chats by getting the team back to work with a warning not to intrude into his personal history as a Ram bhakt but to stick to the history of the case. The case itself had revealed many mysteries which none had anticipated. Further twists and turns in the case could take team Ram Lalla by surprise.

Authentic South Indian filter coffee and some snacks were always served at Senior Parasaran's chamber; the team lapped these up with delight but could never beat Mr Parasaran at the game of drinking coffee—no one could have coffee as fast as he did. After a mini break that included an exchange on Sanskrit poetry between Mr Parasaran and Sridhar Potaraju, the juggernaut would roll again. Sridhar had a deep interest in Indian knowledge systems in spite of not being trained in Sanskrit language. He was also exploring writing on the timeless wisdom of the Mahabharata and Ramayana. Sometimes, anecdotes from the Ramayana and Mahabharata were exchanged between Mr Parasaran and Sridhar. Mr Parasaran then would end it with a quick, short statement, 'Whatever is there in the world, good or bad, you will find its reflection in the Mahabharata, and there is no text like the Bhagavad Gita. All problems, solutions to existing problems and the highest knowledge are found in the Mahabharata.'

As soon as a break ended, Senior Parasaran would be back to dictating the factual matrix from 1885 onwards—all facts arranged chronologically. Yogeswaran, the master of facts, was to correct him if he went wrong. That seldom happened. 'Others must also pay attention and point out any errors they discover. There can be mistakes because of my age,' Mr Parasaran had warned them.

But a few questions did require last rounds of discussions which sometimes stretched into the night:

1. What cases were filed earlier concerning Ram Janam Asthan preceding Ram Lalla's suit?
2. If cases were filed earlier, say in the 1880s, for Ram Janam Asthan, what was decided in those cases?
3. Was anything decided against Hindus or was anything decided against the other side?
4. Was anything decided in cases filed around 1880–90, or was the decision not to arrive at any judgement pronounced in these cases?

These questions significantly affected the case. If some issue was already decided in favour of one party and against the other, it was the end of the matter. But was it already the end of the road for Ram bhakts?

Could what happened in 1885 throw light on such issues? For this reason, Senior Parasaran went through each fact and event that occurred between 1858 and 1949 multiple times in detail. After a factual matrix was finalized, he was back to modifying his notes again, creating a flow chart of facts, and trying to simplify each proceeding as much as possible in his handwriting. Though he would be called to answer these issues much later, he wanted to be ready in all matters, barring one, and for good reason. This issue would haunt Mr Parasaran much later and even divide the team.

As he went over timelines and evidence, Senior Parasaran's primary focus was on whether the parties got delayed in filing these cases. Non-filing the case within the time limit prescribed by law could kill a case. Mr Parasaran was, therefore, concentrating equally on that aspect, but what had caught his team's and people's attention in general was the evidence of the case, the religious connotations involved in it, the nature of the land at the Janam Asthan and the lawyer arguing the case. Mr Parasaran never imagined that for a media-shy individual, media persons had begun to research the man representing Ram in this historical legal tussle.

However, a new development disturbed Senior Parasaran's family.

7

God Arrives in Court

In the Supreme Court, on most occasions advocates-on-record speak in the first person for their clients. A young AOR of, say, thirty-five years might be heard making a statement in court in the following terms: 'My lords, I am seeking custody of my grandchildren from my third child.' The AOR wears the identity of his clients while making such statements. All this is done to serve and get justice for the client. Yogeswaran was the AOR for Ram Lalla. And in this manner, God arrived in court.

Often, questions about their outstanding accomplishments are posed to successful professionals. In the context of the Ram Janmabhoomi case, the question that arose was, whether Suit 5, the suit of Ram Lalla, stood as one of the most important cases in Senior Parasaran's approximately seven decade-long legal career? Mr Parasaran's reply was unequivocal: 'When God arrives in court, it becomes the most important case.' For him, representing Ram Lalla was not only a professional task but a work for his soul as well: 'The most interesting arguments in this case would be in Suit 5 of Ram Lalla with respect to the identity and nature of the land Janmabhoomi, and the evidence that has come around it.'

At this point, it behoves the authors to share that a case can completely take over a lawyer's life if he/she doesn't ensure separation of the professional from the personal. Such was the nature of this case that the separation was waning for Senior Parasaran while it had already dissipated for Yogeswaran.

For the first time, in this case, God became a party in Suit 5.

The plaintiffs in Suit 5 were God—Ram Lalla Virajman—

and the land, Ram Janmabhoomi, the birthplace of God! The proposition that the Ram Janmabhoomi land must be looked at as a Juristic Person was first canvassed in Suit 5. This novel proposition of land as a Juristic Person would present various dimensions of the Hindu faith and practices under which the belief in the land, the practice of worshipping it and the evidence around it would come up for evaluation. It could bring to the fore many unchartered dimensions and propositions of property law, faith, and worship.

The five different suits had five different tangents and different prayers. While the Shia-Sunni cases could destroy each other, so could the suits of Ram Lalla and Nirmohi Akhara.

Henceforth, the team discussions would focus on the details of these five cases—some in favour and some against Ram Lalla's case. Senior Parasaran had already done his part of the hard work by crystallizing the points, putting the factual matrix in a chronological flow. The complication primarily was that the points and facts in nearly all cases were scattered. Therefore, the next task for the team was to correlate all the documents with the points dictated and emphasized. Indeed, this stood as a milestone because correlating everything from a heap of pages typed on both sides was easier said than done.

The team was now discussing the next set of dates from the list. They were all post-Independence.

The most important suit among all was Suit 5 of Ram Lalla from the temple or the Hindu side's perspective, while Suit 4 of the Sunni Central Waqf Board along with all those defendants named in the earlier suits remained the most important from the mosque or the Muslim side. Senior Parasaran would repeatedly remind his team: 'Suit 5 is a brilliant piece of work from one of the best all-time lawyers that this country has produced. It was all done in Patna by Lal Babu.' Lal Narayan Sinha was a stalwart, so much so that he was hero-worshipped even by top lawyers such as Harish Salve in his younger days.[46]

Even after several rounds of readings and scrutiny, the protocol for Senior Parasaran remained the same: conferences/discussions would start with him reminding us that Suit 5 was drawn by his predecessor on the post of Attorney General of India. A few important pleadings of the suits were again jotted down as fresh handmade notes. Notes, which were dictated earlier were not considered notes; notes that others made and presented were not considered notes. Only handmade notes were elevated to the status of notes. So, the notes for Suit 5 started again. In common language, the suit raised, among others, the following important points, which constituted the basic premise of the case on which Lord Ram's case was based in court.[47]

1. What is being worshipped in Ayodhya by Hindus in the disputed area? The land Janmabhoomi, the place, the asthan itself is being worshipped. The prayers of devotees are not dependent on the construction of a temple building or the installation of the idol of Bhagwan Shri Ram there.
2. What was sacred in Ayodhya? In the case of Ayodhya, not only was the land sacred, but the idol of the deity was also present there. However, an idol is not necessary for invoking the divine spirit. Another example of such a deity is that of Kedarnath. The Kedarnath Temple does not have an idol in it. It is the undulating surface of a stone which is worshipped there as the deity. Yet another example of such a deity is the Vishnupad Temple at Gaya. That, too, has no idol in it.
3. The worship of Shri Ram Janmabhoomi had continued since time immemorial at the same place. The place itself is a deity and belongs to God.

---

[46]Bhan, Indu, *Legal Eagles: Stories of the Top Seven Indian Lawyers*, Penguin Random House India, New Delhi, 2015. Also referred to Chandrachud, Chintan, *The Cases that India Forgot*, Juggernaut Books, New Delhi, 2019.

[47]Sri Ram Lalla Virajman & Ors, O.S. No. 5 of 1989, Reg. Suit No. 236 of 1989, https://tinyurl.com/5c5nw827. Accessed on 18 January 2025.

4. No valid waqf or valid mosque was ever created or could have been created at the place or any part of it, given the title and possession of the Hindu deities on the land.
5. Kasauti pillars with figures of Hindu gods carved still existed inside the building. The case of Suit 5 was that Ram Bhakts had been worshipping on Shri Ram Janmabhoomi despite the presence of the building/mosque.
6. Was there a huge delay in deciding the case? Suit 5 filed in 1989 also raised the issue of delay in deciding the case. The first case was filed in 1950. The issues were also framed in all four suits more than 25 years ago, but the hearing had not yet commenced. This delay had led to continued mismanagement of the place.
7. Why was Suit 5 required to be filed in 1989? Devotees, despite the building of the mosque, which had kasauti pillars, worshipped the place as Shri Ram Janmabhoomi and were desirous of having a new temple, befitting its pristine glory, constructed at Shri Ram Janmabhoomi, Ayodhya.
8. Was the disputed land a composite whole? The whole area cannot be looked at in a fragmented manner as the entire premises at Shri Ram Janmabhoomi, along with the courtyards, enclosures and buildings constitute one integral complex. The complex comprising the inner and outer courtyards had a single identity.

Therefore, the suit of God, apart from presenting a history of the place, indicated that the Janam Asthan was in an area known as Ram Kot; it marked the birthplace of Ram, where in 1528 an ancient temple was destroyed and on its site was built Babur's Mosque. Suit 5 raised interesting points about both law and spirituality. The aforementioned point in legalese read as follows in Suit 5 or the Suit of God:

> *1. That the plaintiff Nos 1 and 2, namely, Bhagwan Shri Rama Virajman at Shri Rama Janambhumi, Ayodhaya, also*

called Shri Rama Lal Virajman and the Asthan Shri Rama Janambhumi, Ayodhya with the other idols and places of worship situate there at, are juridical persons with Bhagwan Shri Rama as the presiding deity of the place [...]

14. That the plaintiff Deities and their devotees are extremely unhappy with the prolonged delay in the hearing and disposal of the said suits, and the deteriorating management of the affairs of the Temple, particularly the way in which the receiver has been acting. It is believed that a large portion of the money offered by the worshippers, who come in great numbers, is being misappropriated by the Pujaris and other Temple staff, and the receiver has not controlled this evil. Further, the devotees of the plaintiff deities are desirous of having a new temple constructed, befitting their Pristine glory, after removing the old structure at Shri Rama Janambhumi, Ayodhya.

20. That the place itself, or the ASTHAN SHRI RAM JANAMBHUMI, as it has come to be known, has been an object of worship as a deity by the devotees of SHRI RAM as it personifies the spirit of the divine worshipped in the form of SHRI RAM LALLA or LORD RAM the child. The Asthan was thus deified and has had a juridical personality of its own even before the construction of a Temple building or the installation of the idol of Bhagwan Shri Ram there. [...]

24. That such a structure raised by the force of arms on land belonging to the plaintiff Deities after destroying the ancient temple situated thereat, with its materials including the kasauti pillars with figures of Hindu gods carved thereon, would not be a mosque and did not become one despite the attempts to be treated as a mosque during the British rule after the annexation of Avadh.

25. That the worship of the plaintiff Deities has continued since ever throughout the ages at Shri Rama Janambhumi. The place belongs to the Deities. No valid waqf was ever created or could have been created of the place or any part of it, in view of the title and possession of the Plaintiff Deities thereon.

[…]

33. That the entire premises at Shri Rama Janambhumi, Ayodhya, which contain, besides the presiding deity of the plaintiff no. 1, other idols and the Ram Chabutra and the Charan and the Sita Rasoi, etc., along with the yards, enclosures and buildings, including the Sita Koop, and all that, constitute one integral complex. They had a single identity.

Senior Parasaran would then ask for the plaint to be read in its entirety. The plaint accepted all are children of God; Muslims are as much children of God as Hindus, but in essence, the plaint stated that no one can change the birthplace. This birthplace itself is divinity personified. The devotees had worshipped at the place from time immemorial, and hence, were claiming this as the only birthplace of Lord Ram, hence this was Lord Ram's property. 'Ram bhakts have no other option.' It was clear to the nonagenarian that this was not a matter of My God v Your God but a matter of exercise and practice of faith by Hindus at the only place of Lord Ram's birth.

But then why did it necessitate the filing of Suit 5 nearly 40 years after Suit 1 by Gopal Singh Visharad of the Hindu Mahasabha was filed? In Senior Parasaran's knowledge, all the clients and organizations espousing the Hindu cause in the case went to Lal Babu to seek his opinion on the matter. When he read all the plaints, he was shocked. In none of the suits for the Hindu party, an express title claim had been made. The situation was grave. Even if a new suit were to be filed, it would be futile as having been barred in law due to delay and therefore barred by limitation. But this brought forth the work of geniuses. Mr Parasaran would point out, 'Lal Babu drew a suit based only on the future cause of actions. The future is never time-barred. Though the suit talked about all the past suits, it looked only at the situation prevailing as on date and plans of the future.' It was on these premises of what Ram bhakts wanted in the future and the problems prevailing in 1988–89 that the suit was drawn. It was this Suit 5 which had succeeded before the Allahabad High Court.

At times such as these, Aditi would be ready with a caveat, 'But Sir! Land on its own having a Juristic Personality like a company—is that not a difficult or a far-fetched proposition?' In her opinion, Senior Parasaran could allocate some additional time to other issues. For Anirudh, however, this was the point, and Mr Parasaran had to argue this point. Many a time, opinions would differ. Now, Yogeswaran, Aditi and Ashwin on one side, and Anirudh, Bhakti and Sridhar were taking contrarian viewpoints. Yogi strongly felt that land as a Juristic Person was a proposition that should not be argued. Aditi's and Ashwin's feelings were even stronger on the issue. There was an intense debate on this point. As the debate escalated, Senior Parasaran became grim. The nonagenarian gave full latitude to his team and evaluated all points. However, he didn't expect a heated discussion.

Senior Parasaran had accepted that when he first saw the proposition of a Juristic Person, it had made him contemplate, and prima facie, he had agreed with Aditi, Ashwin and Yogi's views. However, there were many facets to this point that required further contemplation, so it became the only point on which work was postponed for later and for good reason, including the fact that his team was getting divided. The High Court had held that the land Janam Asthan/Janmabhoomi was a Juristic Person. With this point in his favour and his team divided, Mr Parasaran contemplated answering only after the

Sunni Central Waqf Board had argued out its attack on the High Court holding in favour of Janam Asthan being a Juristic Person.

Those in the legal profession by virtue of their experience know how top legal eagles can develop a point systematically and logically and present a multitude of perspectives on issues that seemed like an open-and-shut case. It was no surprise, therefore, that Senior Parasaran was of the view that the issue of a Juristic Person would have wide ramifications. Years earlier, Mr Parasaran had told Anirudh that though one may lose arguments made on a point, the lost point would have positive ramifications on other points. Differences in the team were escalating. Sridhar would insist that 'the point of Ram Janmabhoomi being divine has been taken to be proven by a top experienced lawyer.' Bhakti would point out that the belief which was practised was that God himself chose the land where he could descend in human form. Janmabhoomi was God's chosen land.

Senior Parasaran had reflected for a while on Aditi's question. For land to be a Juristic Personality, it would require a completely disjoint and distinct identity of its own like a company, trust, or government department. He had conducted some preliminary discussions with Anirudh which had led to some interesting points. Land, purely as a piece of land, could not be a Juristic Person, but could it be also said that for having a place of worship, a temple must necessarily be there?

Can there be a Hindu place of worship without a temple? Bhakti had examples. Suit 5 itself had given examples of the Vishnupad Temple of Gaya where not idols but footprints are worshipped. Examples of *swayambhu* (self-manifested) deities are commonly found in India. The place or the site is important. Here, too, a place is important. Idols of gods are sometimes replaceable, but, as Senior Parasaran emphasized, 'the place, the piece of land is of primary importance.'

'But what if a place is of reverence to Hindus and there is no temple over it? Or there is a temple and no idol in it? What if there is a temple, which for some reason is abandoned? What happens to its status as a temple after it is abandoned? What if idols are stolen from the temple? Can the temple get those idols back? Should not idols stolen from the temples of India and smuggled out of India be returned to India? Can someone discover an abandoned temple and start worshipping there again? Can anyone tell a devotee that she/he is worshipping in a dead temple? Can a temple die? Lots of questions arise.'

A decision was made to work on the issue of a Juristic Person, and the entitlement of Ram Janam Asthan suing in its own name later, and then decide the course of action to be taken.

Aditi's and Ashwin's queries continued: 'Should we go deep into Hindu practices for land to be proven as a Juristic Person or just concentrate on legal premises?'

During these discussions, the shelved term 'Juristic Person' crept back many a time. One junior associate Shiwani Tushir, working with Sridhar, questioned, 'Can land also be a Juristic Person?' To this, the reply was another question, 'If you have to explain what a Juristic Person is to a layman, how would you explain that?'

Human beings pay tax, companies pay tax. Human beings earn money, companies earn money. So sometimes companies act like humans while earning money and paying taxes. Similarly, a trust or a registered society can also hire people, fire people, buy land, sell land like a company, and so, a company, trust or anything of the same kind can be assumed to be a person for the sake of law and are treated as if they are 'living persons' or 'Juristic Persons'. One can file cases against governments and banks, though they are not human beings but Juristic Persons—persons in the eyes of law though not a human being. Banks give loans and if a person does not repay the loans and stands in default, the banks move the courts and take over the defaulter's property. This question was one of the points on which the whole case of Ram Lalla hinged. *Can land have a Juristic*

Personality? Later, many people were going to ask this. However, as mentioned, there was no unanimity among the team members.

Such points were unique, and the answer to such questions could shape laws in different branches for decades to come. In fact, it would be pertinent to state that lawyers and their Bars waited to hear masters of the Law or legends like Mr K. Parasaran, Mr Ram Jethmalani, Mr Fali S. Nariman, Mr Harish Salve, Dr Rajeev Dhavan and others, who by their decades of hard work and brilliance, had achieved legendary status on questions or legal matters like these. Some patience, some suspense, some mystery or maybe even some drama may arise during such hearings. One must wait for one of the most senior lawyers in their eighties or nineties to come up with their propositions on such issues. In this case, another top lawyer, Dr Rajeev Dhavan was on the other side. Those who followed the law would also wait to hear Dr Dhavan on such points. For students of law, whichever side one supported, these were occasions to look forward to.

Is It Five Minutes?

While there were differences between the team members on the point of land being a Juristic Person, Aditi and Ashwin were worried that the nonagenarian with his health in shambles was taking on too much workload, and that he had to be dissuaded from bearing the burden of arguing points related to Juristic Person. A lot of questions and suggestions from juniors younger than him by sixty years or more were coming in. Senior Parasaran appreciated varied thinking and listened patiently to the young and eager ones.

For Ashwin and Aditi, the youngest in the team, the toil was double. They had to complete their work with Mr Mohan Parasaran and then assist Senior Parasaran. They would then get Senior Parasaran's submissions, as dictated, typed and ready only to find that the submissions changed the next day. Senior Parasaran's misappropriation of his son's juniors was going ahead full steam and as mentioned earlier, the 'victims' were not complaining. Then D-Day arrived, and the case was about to get into action mode. With intermittently watering eyes, Senior Parasaran continued his long hours of work. Looking at the nonagenarian, Sridhar had to break the workflow many a time.

A tab on medicine time was kept. The challenge was to convey to one of the seniormost lawyers in the country that he had already prepared all these points and all the work had been done. At best, very politely, the team members could remind him of his frail health and suggest appropriate scheduling of work. Senior Parasaran's usual reply to such a suggestion was always: 'Yes, I have covered those issues earlier, but in this case, I need to be doubly sure. I want to do that again. This is arising from a civil suit. This is the first appeal. For me, it's a mental mortgage.'

There was no arguing with 'I want to do that again.' If Senior Parasaran was in the flow, he would keep speaking even as eye drops were being administered. Announcements like 'I will continue reading Suit 3 and Suit 4 again' and 'I am into a mental mortgage to do that' would be repeated to the team, raising concerns.

Those five-minute rituals of keeping the eyes closed were repeated time and again. The medicine would finally be given only partial respect, and the rest period was not a peaceful one. Living legends are difficult to comprehend, not because they inherently come across as difficult, but probably because their difficulty arises from their love for their craft. So, as soon as medicine time was over, the master got busy with the documents and suit pleadings. Work would go on into the early hours of the morning.

As health played seesaw with the nonagenarian, he sometimes called in sick, which meant he would start work as late as 8 a.m. Of course, the day would not end earlier than 11 p.m.

Senior Parasaran would retire for the day with a parting shot in a serious and sombre tone, 'Listen, you people, we have to read all the evidence as well, though Vaidyanathan will argue on that. But the important thing to share is this, I am an old man; and one has to be practical. Vaidyanathan must be ready. Brief him assuming I am not there. God has spared me till now, but the call can come any day, any time. I don't know with failing health in this manner, what all can I cover. I have been speaking to Vaidyanathan as well. Ensure he is ready on all points, even those which I am covering.'

The problem for the briefing team was that there also were instructions from other senior advocates of the team, Mr Vaidyanathan, Mr Ranjit Kumar and Mr Narasimha, that Senior Parasaran must cover as much of the case as possible, though they would also be ready on every point and for every eventuality. So, the team had to convince Mr Parasaran to cover more points and the task was handed over to Anirudh, his own student. Mr Parasaran still had that passion for his trade and craft and this was not a client's case. This was 'cause-lawyering'.

But like any ninety-two-year-old man, Senior Parasaran had difficulty getting up after sitting for long hours as his knees would get locked. The hearing of the case was about to begin and his practical, recurrent talks about the fragility of life unnerved the whole team every time it started.

SECTION II

THE CASE BEGINS

8

Of Twists and Turns

To cope with their nerve-racking schedule, lawyers often work even on weekends. It is only during court vacations that busy lawyers get time to rest and recharge. This wasn't true for Lord Ram's legal team. Every year, during the annual summer vacation of the court, Yogeswaran and Bhakti would arrive wherever Mr Vaidyanathan would be vacationing. Even when Mr Vaidyanathan spent his summer vacations in Arya Vaidya Pharmacy, Coimbatore, to get some Ayurvedic rejuvenation therapy, Yogi and Bhakti would diligently follow him there for detailed conferences.

The Supreme Court declared that the court hearing was to begin on 6 August 2019. Senior Parasaran and Mr Vaidyanathan had prepared and discussed the case from the perspective of Suit 5. As the court had directed that appeals arising from Suit 3 and 5 would be taken up first, it was decided that Suit 3 would be argued by Mr Vaidyanathan. The evidence, including archaeological evidence, would be carefully gone through.

Mr Vaidyanathan had a somewhat different working style from Senior Parasaran; it reminded people of Mr Parasaran's work style of younger days. He would read on his own, and not with the briefing counsels, after which, he would have pointed discussions on his queries, and on those topics which the briefing counsels would want to discuss or clarify with him. Over a period of five years, complete facts and evidence, including archaeological, were discussed. As the case reached its crescendo, the whole exercise was undertaken again.

Hourly discussions would stretch into the entire day, even on

Saturdays and Sundays. Many a time, lunch, for Sridhar, Bhakti, and Yogeswaran, was at Mr Vaidyanathan's house and dinner at Mr Parasaran's house.

In Senior Parasaran's office, both in Delhi and Chennai, multiple people were applying their minds and trying to locate any additional points. Mr Mohan Parasaran would often complete his work and take an update of the case from Aditi and Ashwin and then join in on the conference. Mohan Parasaran had his own share of cases where both Lord Ram and Ramayana were involved. As a believer in Ram, he had recused himself from taking a stand that endangered the existence of the Ram Setu. The Ram Setu case in the Supreme Court had created a lot of controversies. Mr Mohan Parasaran had been serving as the Solicitor General of India on that day and was briefed to appear for the government.[48]

Even when in Chennai, Senior Parasaran often had enough support and lawyers with whom he could discuss his thoughts. His Chennai office also had to handle the regular flow of suggestions and additional legal and religious points from people from all walks of life, for the case.

Twist in the Tale

The court had directed that Suit 3 of Nirmohi Akhara would be taken up first. Senior Parasaran and Mr Vaidyanathan had prepared and discussed the case from the perspective of Suit 5 of Ram Lalla, and the last couple of days before the start of the case were devoted to Suit 3. Even as one of the most contested cases of independent India was about to reach its denouement, in a way, the media still had not gotten hold of the fact that the dispute in court was now reduced to less than 1,500 sq. yd of land.

Suit 3 was filed by Nirmohi Akhara whose *sanyasis*/priests

[48]'I have faith that Lord Rama exists: Solicitor General Mohan Parasaran', *Rediff.com*, 21 September 2013, https://tinyurl.com/5b827ds9. Accessed on 18 January 2025.

claimed to serve Ram Lalla, and it was on this basis that Nirmohi Akhara claimed to have *shebaiti* rights (right of performing service to Lord Ram and all incidental work attached to it). (*See* Chapter 15 for more details.)

Now here comes the twist, marking the beginning of several blind turns that came our way. The Supreme Court Bench had directed that arguments on Suit 3 of Nirmohi Akhara would herald the start of the proceedings of this historical case. The counsel for Nirmohi Akhara was Mr Sushil Kumar Jain who was to start Suit 3, but he had other plans. In deference to Senior Parasaran's stature and seniority, Mr Jain called up Mr Parasaran and requested him to open the case. Many others too felt that it would be in the fitness of things that such a once-in-a-lifetime case be opened by a lawyer who had attained such stature and eminence. The issue at hand was that this meant beginning with Suit 5 of Ram Lalla. At that time, Mr Parasaran was neck-deep into Suit 3 and it was reasonably calculated that Suit 3 of Nirmohi Akhara would lay claim to the court's attention for at least a week. According to his habit, and not too difficult for us to guess, a fresh note was being prepared till a day back to effectively reply to Mr Jain's arguments as well as whatever arguments may be raised by the Sunni Board. Now Mr Parasaran had to do a 180-degree turn and mentally step out of Suit 3 and into the intricacies of Suit 5 of Ram Lalla Virajman.

For a Senior Counsel, there was no way of turning down such a request. To reiterate, this was a sudden turn of events because it meant that the case would not start with Suit 3 of Nirmohi Akhara but with Suit 5 of Ram Lalla Virajman. It also meant, to our secret dismay, that the fresh notes for Suit 3 would be discarded, and yet another round of fresh notes would be prepared for Suit 5. Aditi would again burn the midnight oil to give Senior Parasaran's dictated notes a final colour.

The sheer magnitude of records of the Ayodhya case was overwhelming. People often asked how the records became so humongous. In one of the orders dated 26 February 2019,[49] the Supreme Court had recorded the answers to such questions:

> *[...]*
>
> *: [...] The Bench has been informed that the original records are lying in 15 sealed trunks in a room which has also been sealed. Whether the depositions and documents which are in Persian, Sanskrit, Arabic, Gurumukhi, Urdu and Hindi, etc. have been translated is not clear...*
>
> *[...] The members of the Second Committee with the assistance of officials of the Registry, opened all the trunks one after the other. The record was physically inspected. It will be appropriate to mention here that the original record from the High Court of Judicature at Allahabad, Lucknow Bench was received in two consignments, consisting of 8 trunks (numbered 1 to 8) and 7 trunks (numbered 1 to 7) respectively. The first consignment was received on 24.3.2014 and the second on 17.8.2017.*
>
> *It is revealed that the record consists of 38,147 pages of which 12,814 pages are in Hindi, 18,607 pages are in English, 501 pages are in Urdu, 97 pages are in Gurumukhi, 21 pages are in Sanskrit, 86 pages are in other language scripts, 14 pages contain images and 1,729 pages are in combination of more than one language script, viz. Hindi, English, Urdu, Sanskrit and Gurumukhi. The record also includes 4,278 blank pages, though numbered yet not relevant for the purpose of translation [...]*
>
> *The Judgment runs into 8,170 pages. The deposition is in 14,385 pages: out of these 2,548 pages are in English and 10,907 pages are in Hindi. The deposition also includes various documents of which 97 are in Punjabi (Gurumukhi),*

---

[49]Supra 13.

824 are in multiple languages, 5 are in Sanskrit, 2 are in Urdu and 2 are in other language scripts.

There are 453 documents which have been marked with exhibits. The said exhibits consist of 3,609 pages which include 2,188 pages in English, 572 in Hindi, 395 in Urdu, 402 in multiple language scripts and 52 in other language scripts. It has further been noticed that, barring a few, the record received from the High Court does not include translation of vernacular documents in English. Thus, the documents/exhibits which are not in English will have to be translated […]

In the last two years, each party might have condensed the records into 3,000/4,000 pages as it sought to rely on selected documents and not focus on the rest. Team Ram Lalla was not an exception. Senior Parasaran discussed every point, starting from the history of the filing of the suit and then went on to reiterate the point that Suit 5 was all about the cause of action arising in the 1980s, which troubled the Ram bhakts in offering their prayers to the Lord, their wish for the construction of a Ram Temple at the sacred birthplace of Lord Ram. It did not delve into the past.

And then Senior Parasaran made his notes. As usual, he investigated his previous notes to prepare fresh ones, but as habit would have it, he had to read the suit afresh and note the issues framed by the Allahabad High Court with respect to Suit 5 and the findings given on those issues. The issues overlapped on many points and were also common to issues in the other suits.

One of the most important issues in Suit 5 was whether Asthan Ram Janmabhoomi, which was only a piece of land, was a Juristic Person capable of filing a case in its name (i.e. the case being filed in the name of the land) and defending its interest or not. Senior Parasaran, while covering all issues, decided that due to paucity of time, and a last-minute change of focus from Suit 3 to Suit 5, the issue of a 'Juristic Person' would be discussed later. There were many reasons for this decision:

1. That on this point—as to whether the land, Ram Janam Asthan, in its name, could file a suit/institute a claim/defend a claim—the ruling was in favour of Ram Lalla Virajman's, side in the High Court.
2. Since the ruling of the Allahabad High Court on this point was in favour of Ram bhakts and Ram Lalla Virajman, it was imperative for the other side to attack this finding/judgement of the Allahabad High Court on the point of the piece of land, Asthan Ram Janambhoomi, being a Juristic Person, and then a reply would be given by team Ram Lalla.
3. That the point, though initially thought by Senior Parasaran to be difficult to prove, was a very interesting one and could open the whole legal game and change perspectives. There were two views. While Aditi, Yogeswaran and Ashwin argued against this point of view of the land being a Juristic Person, Anirudh, Bhakti and Sridhar supported the proposition. Even if it did not prove the land to be a Juristic Person, it would achieve many a collateral purpose.

Anirudh and Aditi had a similar trait of inquisitiveness and Anirudh instinctively knew when Aditi had a query. 'Should we go deep into Hindu practices or just concentrate on legal premises?' she asked. As he heard her, Senior Parasaran would catch Anirudh's eye and smile benignly as he recalled that Anirudh too would have a question every 10 minutes, back in 2005. The reply to her question nonetheless was, 'We will see. Whatever this bhakt of Ram has to do for the case, he will do, but only from the records of the case, from the observation of the courts below, and only from the perspective of justice for the Ram bhakts and not to run down anyone or any community.' In such circumstances, Ashwin, as Aditi's friend and philosopher, would smile politely. He would discuss all his points with Aditi and then let the lady in the team lead him. He made the general believe she was commanding.

The immediate problem on hand, however, was that with a change in the series of the case, frantic searches were launched to trace the notes of Suit 5. Sometimes, hours went into finding the relevant notes and getting the relevant documents rearranged as per Suit 5 of Ram Lalla, which had earlier been arranged as Suit 3 of Nirmohi Akhara. All notes looked similar, hence only the author of the notes would know what to look for. With the notes all mixed up, the team dreaded the worst.

Though Mr Jain offered a gesture of respect by requesting Senior Parasaran to open the case, it resulted in its own problems. Unfortunately, this was not the time when the nonagenarian could burn the midnight oil at his own sweet will. Mr Parasaran, as usual, disposed of his old notes and started making fresh ones to open Suit 5. His eyes, under heavy medication, were posing their own challenges. As concerns began growing in the team, he would say: 'I am only a nimitta matra, an instrument of the gods. God will do the work; he may be having other plans. I am not the doer. We do not do any work worth taking credit for. We just have to work hard. I can't leave this work midway. Whatever God wants, only that will happen. No need for being too analytical. God will take care of me. He has already given me a full and good life.'

A huge number of documents were gathered, academicians in India and abroad were consulted. From 1949, people were involved; there were social and political movements which everyone knew about. Even if the case was won, he believed it would not be the lawyers who would be taking up the onerous responsibility of getting the temple constructed. The credit belonged somewhere else. As multiple notes of Suit 3 kept popping up from the mix, Senior Parasaran decided to write down a new set of notes.

Since the case was to start in a couple of days, Sridhar, Bhakti and Yogi had to divide their time between the office of Senior Parasaran and Mr Vaidyanathan. They could also return to Mr Parasaran's place when required without missing a step, thanks to the strong backroom support given by Praneet Pranav, Mukul Singh, and Amit Sharma, while Anirudh, Ashwin and Aditi managed the task with Mr Parasaran. The problem was that many a time, some clerical work still needed to be executed, such as the preparation of documents to be depended upon or the compilation of case laws that was to be relied upon by the senior counsels, Mr Parasaran and Mr Vaidyanathan. The burden fell on Mr Sridhar Potaraju's office, his juniors, and his paralegal team. As lawyers and their clerks negotiated their way between the seniors, assuming things had finally settled to a manageable rhythm, fate continued to roll the dice.

9

Raining Surprises

If Senior Parasaran thought that his seventy years of courtroom experience sans or with all its drama couldn't hold any more surprises for him, he had another think coming. Multitasking as a bhakt, a lawyer and a client was a different ball game than being a lawyer. Perhaps this role of multitasking was the only novel thing left for him to experience as a lawyer. So, here it was.

Finally, the notes of Suit 5 (Ram Lalla's suit) were concretized on the morning of 6 August 2019. As usual, the points to be argued were arranged in green paper notes. Suit 5 was ready to be heard. The court started at 10.30 a.m. As per discipline, Senior Parasaran had to be in court by 9.30 a.m. if he had to open a case or whenever there was a hearing. Since it was raining heavily that morning, Mr Parasaran ensured that he left home well before 9 a.m. after hurriedly wolfing down breakfast under the benign eyes of Nandini Parasaran. The drive from home to the Supreme Court normally took 20–25 minutes. In any case, a little before 9 a.m. was not the time when one typically encountered Delhi traffic from GK-I to the Supreme Court. It was, therefore, not presumptuous on the part of the driver to suggest that even if there was waterlogging, a 20-minute drive would, at most, take 40 minutes. But it seems the heavens heard and decided on having their own way.

It was 10 a.m., and there was still no sign of the ever-punctual Senior Parasaran. Hearts beat faster, and though the rains had ensured that the weather was pleasant, palms turned sweaty for those waiting for Mr Parasaran to arrive. Yogeswaran's phone rang, and Mr Parasaran informed him about the unprecedented level of traffic jams on the streets. The instructions to Yogi were clear: 'Inform Mr Sunil Kumar Jain that he has to start in case I am not able to make it on time.'

Mr Jain waited as long as possible while a very concerned Senior Parasaran tried his best to reach the court on time. It was past 10.30 a.m. now, and there was still no sign of Mr Parasaran. The judges arrived and Mr Jain informed them about the decision taken by the lawyers that Mr Parasaran would start with Suit 5. The judges were also informed that he had started from his residence early but was still stuck in a dreadful traffic jam. However, the judges were very clear in their minds that the case had to start with Suit 3; it was something they had already communicated to the counsels. *Man proposes, God disposes.* Mr Sunil Kumar Jain opened the case on behalf of Nirmohi Akhara. The case of Ram Lalla was to follow only after Suit 3 was completed

With this twist in the tale, the case filed in 1949 finally started its denouement on 6 August 2019.

Senior Parasaran was still in his car, the lawyer in him calm and the bhakt concerned; the traffic wasn't helping matters either. But someone did step out of the Chief Justice's court—Courtroom No.1 of the Supreme Court of India—to keep him informed of the proceedings. The old gentleman heaved a sigh of relief when he was told of the initiation of the proceedings along with the fact that Mr Jain had started with Suit 3 of Nirmohi Akhara.

Even at ninety-two, Senior Parasaran could walk on his own if there was no commotion or rush around. The Supreme Court and its now narrow corridors presented a different picture altogether. The court building was constructed in 1950 when the population of India was 359 million. The population of the country in 2019 had reached around 1,360 million. The number of judges in the Supreme Court had increased from 8 to 34. The number of cases being filed had also increased manifold. In 1950, only 1,215 cases were filed in the Supreme Court, while between 2010 and 2019, it would have been anywhere between 55,000 and 60,000 per year.[50] On many days, lawyers jostled for space. Many courtrooms had to be redesigned to increase capacity and space, and yet the space always seemed inadequate. In such a scenario, the hustle and bustle of the Supreme Court warranted a couple of people walking with Mr Parasaran. Finally, Mr Parasaran arrived at Courtroom No.1, flanked by two of his team members. This would become a familiar sight in the days to come.

Courtroom No.1 of the Supreme Court of India looks slightly different from other courts. Spacious, it has an elegant finish, with a huge chandelier hanging just below the dome. The walls are adorned with portraits of former Chief Justices of India, lending quiet dignity to the courtroom as well as serving as a reminder of its hallowed history. A witness to many a doyen both from the Bar and the Bench, this courtroom was perhaps witnessing for the first time a battle of history meeting its fate, with the embellishment of archaeology, scriptures, evidence and law. Of course, history would be played out by the lawyers, and finally judged by unemotional judges for whom what mattered was evidence, law and precedents, and in a civil trial, preponderance of probabilities.

Lawyers and students of law had many questions, the first being: 'Can the issue of worship by competing communities be decided by secular courts of law?'

There was an unequivocal answer. The issue of competing claims of communities and between sub-sects of the same communities, such as the Digambars or Shwetambars, or a mosque and a gurudwara, or Shias and Sunnis, or between two sub-communities of Hindu society has resulted in many landmark judgements and memorable headlines. Such cases, if

---

[50]PTI, 'Over 88% rise in pending cases in Supreme Court since inception in 1950', *The Economic Times*, 18 January 2017, https://tinyurl.com/5b784zcv. Accessed on 18 January 2025.

not resolved judicially, would usually meet their judgements on the streets in the most unfortunate and violent ways imaginable. All through the legal history of India, such cases have reached the courts for final adjudication. The right to worship is a civil right, and when such rights clash and the title of land is in question, then civil suits are the only remedy and the only choice possible.

The suit of Nirmohi Akhara was now in focus. Nirmohi Akhara as a group of ascetics had a well-known history. It is said that Rani Lakshmibai of Jhansi breathed her last in Gwalior, in one of the temples of Nirmohi Akhara after her battle with the English and the East India Company forces during the First War of Independence in 1857. The saints of Nirmohi Akhara had the last rites of the Rani performed as per her wish—that she may not be captured dead or alive by the soldiers of the East India Company. The civil suit pleadings of Nirmohi Akhara in Suit 3, inter alia, read as follows:

> *Para 4A: That Nirmohi Akhara, plaintiff, is the Panchyati Math of 'Ram Nandi' sect of Vairagies, and as such, is a religious denomination following its own religious faith and pursuit according to its own custom prevalent in Vairagies sect of Sadhus. The customs of Akhara, Nirmohi have reduced in writing on 19 March 1949 by registered deed.*
>
> *Para 4B: That plaintiff Nirmohi Akhara owns several temples in […] and manages all of such temples through Panches and Mahants of Akhara. The whole temples and properties vest in Akhara i.e., plaintiff. The plaintiff, being a Panchyati Math, acts on democratic pattern. The management and right to management of all temples of Akhara vest absolutely with Panches of Akhara, and Mahant being the formal head of the institution, is to act on majority opinion of the Panches.*

Nirmohi Akhara's entire case rested on the fact of whether it was the *shebait* of Ram Lalla Virajman. Shebait is the institution, minded by human beings who have managerial rights or charge of the property of the deity/divinity, including the idol or any other form of divinity present at the site. Therefore, a shebait is a person who, in law, is a manager with all the powers of an overall caretaker. This would also include financial powers. A shebait can thus be equated with the manager of a property that belongs to a minor, but in the absence of any parent or guardian, the manager looks after the property of the minor. The manager does not become the owner of the property of the minor while taking care of the said property.

Nirmohi Akhara opened the arguments with the title of possession. The possession in a civil suit is of vital importance. The current suit filed by the parties also had a claim of dispossession, which meant that a party was complaining that they were forcefully thrown out, and therefore, dispossessed from the land. Nirmohi Akhara claimed that they were in possession of Ram Janam Asthan for the past over 100 years, till the time the court intervened and appointed a receiver who took charge and possession of the property.

The importance of this submission/claim of being in possession for over 100 years was that if Nirmohi Akhara succeeded in proving their possession or worship of Ram Lalla, there was a good chance that the worship of Ram Lalla would continue within the disputed premises as had happened in the past. Even if Nirmohi Akhara did only prove the point that it continued its worship of Ram Lalla for over 100 years, in deciding the dispute, interesting results could crop up.

Nirmohi Akhara's presence at the site could have also proved another cardinal point in the case—within the composite land complex, the worship of Ram Lalla Virajman had continued, even if there was a structure of the mosque present within that composite land complex. It would also prove the presence of the worshippers of Ram, and of course, the worshippers would be there only if Ram Lalla Virajman was present within the disputed site. It would also lead to substantiating the fact that

Ram Lalla Virajman was being worshipped on that piece of land only because it was Ram Janmabhoomi. No one had made any written claim in the suits that the land was not one composite complex. On the contrary, the marking of the disputed site by the main contesting parties was similar and one composite whole (including both the inner and outer courtyards).

The history of worship even during the last 100 years was crucial as it would substantiate the practice of faith and would be a concrete set of evidence. In epics, there are always twists, and sometimes, turns. Life is also not simple in epic legal battles. There was a challenge to surpass for Senior Parasaran, Mr Vaidyanathan, and their team. This Himalayan challenge came from Nirmohi Akhara itself. Nirmohi Akhara had opposed the presence of Ram Lalla Virajman (the idol of God himself) as well as Ram Janmabhoomi, the piece of land, as parties to the suit in their written statement. The opposition continued even in the Supreme Court.[51]

Nirmohi Akhara started its case and went into the theory of management of property by the shebait. Nirmohi Akhara took all of 6 August 2019 and indicated that it would take at least a day or two more for its arguments. That gave Senior Parasaran some time to rest his overworked eyes, we thought. For a change, he could now turn up for work after appropriate rest and sleep. And as there was every reason to believe that Nirmohi Akhara would take the entire day of 7 August for its arguments as well, Mr Parasaran could get up early in the morning and work extra hours. That's what the team thought, but not Mr Parasaran. He worked late into the night and woke up early in the morning. As he was not supposed to argue for a couple of days, the nonagenarian could conserve energy while arguments went on.

Nirmohi Akhara advanced the theory of its shebait rights a

[51]'Nirmohi Akhara unnecessarily opposing deity's plea, both stand or fall together in Ayodhya case: SC', *The New Indian Express*, 27 August 2019, https://tinyurl.com/3r9tkajs. Accessed on 18 January 2025.

bit further the next day. It presented its arguments that it was the manager of God's property (at the place) in its entirety. The court asked Nirmohi Akhara to provide evidence to prove its claim of title based on revenue records or any other piece of document that they might have. But Nirmohi Akhara was not prepared with the evidence that it wanted to rely on, and therefore, asked for some reprieve and sought more time from the court. Suit 3 was cut short for the time being.

All this while, Mr Parasaran had been taking notes on the arguments of Nirmohi Akhara. The Bench, while offering time to Nirmohi Akhara to get its evidence in order, had another surprise in store. Suddenly, Mr Parasaran was asked to start with his arguments in Suit 5. Nirmohi Akhara would argue its suit later. It was raining surprises in this case; no one knew what turn the case would take next. Now even the lawyers did not know when their turn to present their case would come.

There was also the issue of time. *The Hindu*[52] reported the proceedings of the day:

> *[...] The court had asked Mr. Parasaran to commence his arguments after Nirmohi Akhara sought more time to produce oral, historical and documentary evidence to establish their claim over the entire area of the disputed Ram Janmabhoomi.*
>
> *The court was on a tight schedule as the CJI had about 50 working days left before retirement in November, decided to hear the deity and gave the Akhara time to prepare the evidence.*
>
> *When a lawyer protested the move from the back row of the courtroom, Chief Justice Gogoi gave him a dressing down,*

---

[52]Rajagopal, Krishnadas, 'Ayodhya hearing: "Unshakeable faith is proof of Rama's birthplace"', *The Hindu*, 28 November 2021, https://tinyurl.com/2ew4zdyu. Accessed on 18 January 2025.

> *saying: 'the First Court of this country should remain the First Court of this country. Don't try to make it anything else.'*
>
> *Earlier, the court did not agree when senior advocate Sushil Kumar Jain, for Nirmohi Akhara, suggested reading the documentary evidence from the judgments of the lower courts in the case.*
>
> *'These would be just excerpts. We want the original documents,' Justice D.Y. Chandrachud, on the Bench, reacted.*
>
> *Mr. Jain said documentary evidence like revenue records, etc., to establish the Akhara's claim of having managed and controlled the 'temple' in the Ram Janmabhoomi went missing in a 'dacoity' in 1982."*
>
> *Cutting Mr. Jain short in his arguments of Suit 3 meant that Mr. Parasaran had to start Suit 5 of Ram Lalla when his thoughts were mired in Suit 3 of Nirmohi Akhara.*

Senior Parasaran had to immediately gather his thoughts regarding Suit 5, but now his notes of Suit 5 were not at hand! Were the notes missing or were the notes left behind at his residence? Frantic efforts to trace the notes were initiated as Mr Parasaran moved to the first chair to address the court.

No one, not even the nonagenarian was expecting the Supreme Court Bench to make an offer that it had never made before, not as far as any lawyer or journalist who regularly covered the court could remember.

10

Court, Janmabhoomi and the Bhakt

The story of how the day unfolded, leading up to the gracious yet surprising offer and the court action that followed, shall forever remain etched in our memory. As usual, the day for Senior Parasaran started at 4.30 a.m.; he was busy grappling with his old notes, very old notes, yet older notes and fresh notes along with new ideas. Many a time, the arguments would be extempore without any reference to the notes prepared in advance for the case. It required only an idea on the spot to change the arguments. In fact, this happened quite often.

Senior Parasaran had been quite relieved that not only were his notes for Suit 3 of Nirmohi Akhara ready but also that Mr Sushil Kumar Jain had informed him that he would argue for at least one more full day for Nirmohi Akhara and might even stretch it to two full days. This meant that the nonagenarian would just have to take notes only, and this would help him regain his energy. Since he was not to argue that day, he could get up early and work on finalizing his submissions/arguments for Suit 3. Working late at night and getting up early in the morning to work, of course, posed challenges. A slight fever was only making matters worse.

An under-slept and overworked Senior Parasaran was not in an ideal physical condition to argue. Mentally, though, the nonagenarian remained sharp and ready. However, his notes prepared to argue Suit 5 were missing. Just as the adrenaline was beginning to surge and he stepped forward to take the first chair, the then Chief Justice of India Ranjan Gogoi—presiding over the five-judge Bench—departed from convention and suggested that Mr Parasaran may remain seated while presenting his arguments. Despite his age, physical challenges and CJI Ranjan Gogoi's invitation to sit and argue the case, Mr Parasaran politely declined. He had perhaps not expected this kind gesture from the Chief Justice. Though he was grateful to the judges who were all not less than twenty-seven years younger than him, this gesture perhaps unsettled an already surprised senior counsel and mellowed him down: 'It's okay. Your Lordships are too kind. The tradition of the bar has been to stand and argue, and I am concerned about the tradition,' the lawyer said.[53]

Kindness aside, nothing else went smoothly. In addition to the issue of the missing notes on the suit, the nonagenarian running a temperature was faced with the challenge of microphones not being placed correctly, as a result of which people sitting at the back of the courtroom found it difficult to hear him. Ram Lalla's case did not take off as planned.

Retaining his composure despite the unexpected turn of events around him, Senior Parasaran informed the Bench that unlike other cases and the Ram Setu case, he was appearing in this case not only as a lawyer but also as a believer and client. 'Ram has shaped my life,' he went on to declare as the reason for his commitment to the case. The litigation was in the form of a representative suit and a title dispute/property dispute between two communities. As a Ram bhakt, he owed everything he had achieved in life to Ram. In fact, he made it later known publicly, 'It is my last wish to see a Ram Temple come up at the site of Ram's birth.'[54]

But law courts are law courts and not wish-granting institutions. The hearing of the day was marked by some religious

---

[53]'Verdict on a Saturday, addendum judges' dinner—How SC's Ayodhya judgment saw many firsts', *The Print*, 5 August 2020, https://tinyurl.com/586jadzb. Accessed on 18 January 2025.

[54]Roy, Debayan, 'Parasaran, the "Pitamah" of Indian lawyers got his wish when Ayodhya hearings ended', *The Print*, 18 October 2019, https://tinyurl.com/3y3ky6db. Accessed on 18 January 2025.

points submitted by Senior Parasaran. Ram's birthplace was special because one's motherland stands as totally different from all other places. A version of the Ramayana describes the glory of the motherland thus: *Janani janmbhoomishcha swargadapi gariyasi* (One's motherland is higher than heaven).

Just as Senior Parasaran was trying to build the case of the absolute importance of Ram Janmabhoomi from the scriptures, there was another bolt from the blue. The issue of the land being a Juristic Person was raised, which no one expected. The land, janmabhoomi, in Suit 5 was made a plaintiff on the premise of the land itself being divine in the eyes of worshippers.

The Supreme Court, hearing the Ayodhya land dispute case, asked Senior Parasaran how the birthplace of Lord Ram, or Janamasthan, could be recognized as a Juristic Person with legal rights in the matter. Though the Bench, led by Chief Justice Ranjan Gogoi, acknowledged that Hindu deities had been treated in law as Juristic Entities and could own property and pursue litigation, the catch was whether the birthplace itself could hold the same legal status. They indicated that this would be a cardinal issue and a challenge.

Senior Parasaran, representing Ram Lalla Virajman, submitted that in Hinduism idols are not mandatory for a site to be sacred. He highlighted that rivers and the Sun are worshipped, suggesting that a birthplace too could be viewed as a Juristic Person.

Certain observations were made by the Bench with reference to the Uttarakhand High Court decision that declared the holy river Ganga as a Juristic Person with a view to protect it. Senior Parasaran then continued with other submissions, highlighting that Ram Lalla Virajman was not made a party when the disputed site was originally attached by a magistrate and placed under a court-appointed receiver.[55]

---

[55]'Ayodhya case: SC asks how birth place can be made party to land dispute', *The Pioneer*, 8 August 2019, https://tinyurl.com/5x5h7bjd. Accessed on 18 January 2025. Also *see*: Dixit, Mala, *Ayodhya se Adalat Tak Bhagwan Shri Ram*, Namyapress.com.

Joining in, Senior Advocate Rajeev Dhavan, appearing for the Muslim side, stressed on the point that the claims filed by Ram Lalla Virajman and Nirmohi Akhara were contradictory. He said that if one succeeded, the other would automatically fail. Dr Dhavan suggested that the mosque side should be required to respond collectively in one go.

Leave of the court was granted to answer the question about land being a Juristic Person on the next day of the hearing in detail, though a preliminary answer was given immediately. There was a threat to the case of Ram Lalla too. A few glances were exchanged recalling the fact that Mr Dhavan had reminded the Bench that Nirmohi Akhara and Ram Lalla's suits were at loggerheads. This issue was of deep concern, as was the nonagenarian's physical fitness.

On some points, Suit 3 of Nirmohi Akhara and Suit 5 of Ram Lalla Virajman were at loggerheads, and on some points, they were not. It had to be seen whether the points on which the two suits agreed would come to haunt Dr Dhavan's clients or not. Maybe, Nirmohi Akhara's Suit 3 might come as a clincher! But a clincher for which side? That was the point yet to unfold.

In the courtroom, Senior Parasaran continued with his arguments in a low voice, giving instances from the Ramayana and reciting shlokas to build up the base of faith of Ram bhakts for worshipping in Ayodhya. It would be pertinent to mention here that the Ramayana in its entirety was exhibited as evidence before the Allahabad High Court during the proceedings of the case. Mr Parasaran was clear that unshakable faith and the practice of that faith could be the only self-sufficient proof of such issues as identifying the birthplace of Ram. If that was proved, even archaeological evidence might not be required.

The arguments in Suit 5 started, and interesting questions came to the fore. Every day, a recap of the arguments would take place back in the office. The team did not know that they would be researching into the night, seeking answers to questions that were seldom asked. Before coming to the use of hearsay evidence in his submissions, Mr Parasaran laid out the base for his arguments that Lord's Ram birthplace could not be pinpointed with a needle, but pointed out in an area.

In light of the submission that it was the existence of the unshakable faith of believers that was evidence that the disputed site in Ayodhya was the birthplace of Lord Ram, Senior Parasaran made his submission by posing this question:[56] *How will we prove after so many centuries that Lord Ram was born there?*

The court then asked Parasaran if questions of this nature—about the birth of a religious figure—had ever arisen in any court. The Bench asked Parasaran 'whether issues like [the] birth of Jesus Christ at Bethlehem have been questioned and dealt with by any court in the world,' to which Mr Parasaran said that he would check and inform the court.

Questions such as the birth of Jesus had never crossed anyone's mind; the team was completely at sea. The journey from Ayodhya to Jerusalem was far from comfortable. Ram Lalla's case was unlike any other. For queries to which he lacked immediate answers, Mr Parasaran respectfully requested the judges for time to respond after verifying the facts.

Perhaps the judges also wanted counsels to proceed in their own manner. Earlier, during various rounds of preparations, Senior Parasaran was clear that he would make the points listed below while arguing Suit 5. These points were used and repeatedly emphasized during the arguments and were used to start the arguments even while the notes were being traced:

1. The unshakable faith of devotees is proof of Ram's birthplace. This place has withstood the test of time, tragedies, and innumerable and insufferable challenges.

---

[56]PTI, 'Unshakeable faith of Hindus enough to prove Lord Ram born at Ayodhya's disputed site: Supreme Court told', *The Economic Times*, 7 August 2019, https://tinyurl.com/vrvnxkhk. Accessed on 10 September 2025.

Also *see*: Dixit, Mala, *Ayodhya se Adalat Tak Bhagwan Shri Ram*, Namyapress.com.

2. 'How can I, after so many years, prove the exact spot of [the] birth of Ram with a needle? I can only prove the area of birth of Ram as existing in [the] belief of devotees.' The only evidence in such cases was to be the practice of faith, and from that faith, the land had to be identified. The concept of the practice of faith at the site since time immemorial, and the fact that travelogues and gazetteers noted the presence of Ram bhakts pointed to only one conclusion, and that was in favour of the Ram bhakts.
3. The birthplace is not any other place. The whole world has been created by the Lord himself. God chose to take birth in human form and descend on earth to alleviate the sins of humankind. He chose a place that could hold divinity in itself. That place is divine and Ram Janmabhoomi. The question for Senior Parasaran was: 'Why and why was only this place chosen by God?' In this context, the Valmiki Ramayana was relied upon to show that,
   i. Dashratha was chosen by God as his father.
   ii. Janmasthan was chosen to be Ayodhya.
   iii. The Valmiki Ramayana mentions in three places that Lord Ram was born in Ayodhya.

The work of a lawyer is less in the courtroom and more in his reading room. Burning the midnight oil and the toil that a lawyer undertakes are understood only by those in the legal profession. Lawyers slog, irrespective of age, seniority, and stature. A rest of not more than half an hour or so would see the nonagenarian back at work after completing the day's proceedings. Fatigue would of course be visible. Senior Parasaran was not satisfied with the day's hearing because his notes of Suit 5 were not available at the beginning of his submissions, he was running a temperature, the kind gesture shown by the judges had caught him off guard and due to his emotional attachment to the case, he felt that he had not met his own standards.

Yogeswaran insisted that everyone, including all the team

members, persuade Senior Parasaran to sit and argue. Sensing reluctance, Yogi insisted that Mr Parasaran must accept the offer of the Chief Justice of India to sit and argue, more so because Mr Parasaran was already under medication. The answer from Mr Parasaran was a firm 'No'. Yogi, the warrior, was not going to give up without a fight. He persisted with the old gentleman. However, he did not expect such a spirited fightback from Mr Parasaran.

The floodgates opened. An emotional Senior Parasaran had tears rolling down his cheeks: *'It is my Lord's case. It's Ram's case. I argued all kinds of cases for all kinds of people throughout my life standing in the court. Now, I cannot be asked to argue my own Lord's case, who has rescued me when my life was in (the) doldrums, without due respect. I cannot be sitting and arguing. You all are worried about my age. I don't mind even if I die arguing this case. I will stand and argue.'*

Yogi was speechless. His demand had triggered the unimaginable. Vanquished, he dropped his request. Warrior Yogeswaran had just lost a battle.

Now that Suit 5 had abruptly started, Mr C.S. Vaidyanathan, Mr Ranjit Kumar and Mr P.S. Narasimha were to visit Senior Parasaran to discuss the case strategy. It was rare to see such eminent counsels with such seniority and vast experience, coming across for discussions and briefings, and that too in a case of cause lawyering. But this was not just any case, and the person whom they were visiting was not just any counsel. One could sense that this was more than a professional engagement. It was clear in the meeting that the team felt that the change of precedence—starting with Suit 4, then as per the court's order changing it to starting with Suit 5, and then again changing it to starting with Suit 3, and yet again abruptly changing from Suit 3 to Suit 5 was a bit too much of a flip-flop for a senior citizen on medication. Overall, the situation resulted in deep concern within the team. Would Senior Parasaran's physical and emotional health allow him to see the case through?

After the conclusion of a short meeting, Senior Parasaran started preparing all points with effective support from his old notes, and another new note needed to be prepared. Fortunately, the new note was to Mr Parasaran's satisfaction, and things went smoothly till he realized that he could not locate his earlier notes on the point of how land could be a 'Juristic Person', and maintain Suit 5 in its name. A frantic search did not yield any result. Mr Parasaran checked and rechecked. There were reams of notes on facts, lists of dates, law points and history, but none on 'Juristic Person'. This was a topic that Mr Parasaran had prepared all by himself, much earlier. He was still labouring, and the stress of tracing out his notes, or the notes getting misplaced was adding up. Standing for hours and arguing in court are both taxing physically, as well challenging mentally. At such an age, running a temperature and subjecting the body to such a gruesome work schedule resulted in unforeseen effects. Finally, the body gave distress signals. Glaucoma took over and due to consistent water welling up in the eyes, it became nearly impossible for Mr Parasaran to read. There was no other option but to rest the eyes and hope that things would be better by morning. God's lawyer required some divine help.

The first sign of age affecting Senior Parasaran's memory was now visible. He was not able to recall his points of law and the judgements that he wanted to rely on for the point of 'Juristic Person'. This was a job that this lawyer could do at a snap of a finger. Maybe Mr Parasaran was not an efficient client, and a client in him was blocking his lawyer's mind.

Mr Mohan Parasaran was informed, and he had to intervene and convince his father: 'Take some rest, respect your age. You have to last the whole case,' Mohan Parasaran had to plead. With his memory failing him for the first time, Senior Parasaran closed the day on a tense note. His condition was such that Mrs Nandini Parasaran and Mr Mohan Parasaran ordinarily would have passed a decree forcing him to rest the next day and not go to court. But it was Lord Ram's case. They held themselves back. While Yogeswaran, Sridhar and Bhakti were busy with archaeological, oral and documentary evidence, Mr Parasaran's in-house team of Anirudh, Ashwin, and Aditi were tasked with getting the relevant case laws on the identity of the land ready overnight. For old-time followers of Mr Parasaran, for the first time, age had finally breached the wall. With his health in a precarious balance, the question was, what would happen next?

11

The Janmabhoomi Conundrum

The night was tense. Anirudh, Ashwin and Aditi kept researching previously decided law that justified at least from some angle the possibility of the piece of land, Ram Janam Asthan, as a Juristic Person. It was very important to the case. Hours went by, and all the hard work was beginning to feel futile when, finally, in the morning around 4 a.m., something significant was found. The findings were communicated to all. In all this pressure and shock of having to navigate through the whirlpools and eddies at court that resulted in fresh research and preparation, and with original notes being lost, everyone had forgotten that the Allahabad High Court judgement had also deliberated on the point concerning the Juristic Person and had given its findings. So, an English appeal case was discovered. Indeed, even in the 1980s and 1990s, English jurists were engaged in deliberations over whether Hindu temples could be recognized as 'Juristic Persons'. This line of thought was later advanced through a series of Supreme Court judgements, which provided a foundation for further legal arguments. Long nights such as these—nights that could make or break a case—are all too familiar to lawyers. The interest of the case and that of the client stand paramount. This takes a toll on the personal life and health of many lawyers. Cancelled events, absence from family and social get-togethers, and so on become sort of routine.

Fortunately, because of medicines, Mr Parasaran, the bhakt, finally slept well—at least for one night. He finally accepted that overwork was taking a heavy toll on his body. Senior Parasaran started working a little late, and that meant he was in his reading room anywhere between 6 and 6.15 in the morning. His associates, despite the advantage of their age and comparative youth, could only reach between 7 and 7.15 a.m. The situation at the office was grim. Within half an hour or so, Senior Parasaran's eyes started watering again. The effect of over-exertion, against which his family had warned him, resurfaced. There was no one to give him a printout of the email Anirudh had sent at 4 a.m. Even if someone had been there, Senior Parasaran would not have been able to read. So, when associates reached the office, they found Mr Parasaran visibly disturbed, dejected and upset. 'For the first time, my memory is failing me,' were the words they were greeted with. He asked if they had been able to get any points. An affirmative answer offered some relief and he immediately asked for any judgement or case law to be read aloud where they may have found evidence of property in any circumstances being elevated to the status of a Juristic Person.

It took only the first two lines of the judgements to be read, for Senior Parasaran to immediately recall the names of the judges who had written the judgements. He then gave the rest of the details of the case himself, all from memory—without reading those judgements. In his usual style, he gave all the para numbers and page numbers of the judgements. The brilliant mind was back after just a little bit of sleep, rest and one trigger. There was relief on everyone's face as Mr Parasaran started adding more to the list, eyes closed, water flowing from his eyes as it does in elderly persons suffering from glaucoma. Simultaneously, all the points he was raising from his memory were being jotted down. Mr Parasaran's memory was now working; the ageing engine indeed had warmed up, as he would say in jest.

Since many judgements had to be read in court and the day was long, it was decided that Senior Parasaran would rest and then come to court. Persistent hard work was Mr Parasaran's work ethics and discipline. He had to remember that he was appearing in Lord Ram's case as his lawyer and not as a bhakt. If emotions could be held in check, then the entire case could be argued by the professional without opening the brief or the notes. But that was easier said than done. Adhering to Nandini and Mohan Parasaran's request to look after himself, the morning was spent with Mr Parasaran listening with eyes closed as the team read out the judgements to him.

For a change, the morning session of Mr Parasaran's work was not as long as it usually was.

Senior Parasaran made it clear to the team that since their side had already succeeded on the point of the land being a Juristic Person before the High Court, he would cite only one or two judgements—out of deference to the court's query—and place the onus on the opposing side to challenge Suit 5 and demonstrate that Ram Janmabhoomi was not significant enough to possess a distinct legal personality. 'Let them argue,' he said, 'what practices we follow, what we do not; what we worship, what we do not; what holds importance for us and what does not.' Only after the other side had made their case would he respond in full measure on the question of Ram Janmasthan being a Juristic Person.

For the assisting team, mornings comprised reading and discussing reports of the previous day's arguments in the newspapers. These newspapers were also read by their relations and friends, some of whom would unfailingly call them either to offer advice or out of devotion or inquisitiveness. One common query was whether lawyers were getting angry as the media reports suggested.

Do judges and lawyers get angry? Well, lawyers are as human as anyone else. Lawyers, like all human beings, work hard, laugh, are happy, get angry, are irritated, and have to wear black coats in the sultry Indian weather. Moreover, like every human being is different, lawyers, including top lawyers, are unique and different. Yet, at times they do get irked. *The Hindu* ran a report titled

'Ayodhya case: advocate objects to five days a week hearing.'[57]

Senior advocate Rajeev Dhavan, appearing for a Muslim party, on Friday objected to the Supreme Court about the five-days-a-week hearing of the politically sensitive Ram Janmabhoomi–Babri Masjid land dispute case in Ayodhya, saying he would 'not be able to assist' the court if the hearing was 'rushed through'.

The submission was made by him when the Supreme Court commenced hearing on the fourth day of the case.

Breaking tradition, the apex court decided to hear the sensitive case on Monday and Friday, also days reserved only for fresh cases.

As the counsel for deity Ram Lalla Virajman started advancing their submissions before a five-judge Constitution Bench headed by Chief Justice Ranjan Gogoi, Mr. Dhavan got up and interjected the proceedings.

'It is not possible to assist the court if it is heard on all days of the week. This is the first appeal and the hearing cannot be rushed in this manner and I am put to the torture,' he told the Bench. He said the apex court was hearing first appeals after the Allahabad High Court had delivered the verdict in the case and the hearing as such could not be rushed through.

Being the first appeal, documentary evidence had to be studied. Many documents were in Urdu and Sanskrit, which had to be translated, Mr. Dhavan said. He said that if the court decided to hear the case on all five days of the week, then he might have to leave the case.

'We have taken note of your submissions. We will revert to

[57]'Ayodhya case: advocate objects to five days a week hearing', *The Hindu*, 9 August 2019, https://tinyurl.com/4cmjms93. Accessed on 18 January 2025.

you soon,' CJI Gogoi said and proceeded with the hearing.

The Bench began hearing the submissions of senior advocate K. Parasaran on behalf of deity Ram Lalla Virajmaan.

The apex court had asked how the Janmasthanam (birthplace of the deity) could be regarded as a Juristic Person having stakes as a litigant in the case.

The discussion of Senior Parasaran with his team members, apart from the issue of Juristic Person, was around those points that had been argued and those points that were still left to be argued. The team often went into recap mode. The challenge was to first establish the true nature of the deity, Ram Janam Asthan as well as Ram Lalla Virajman. This, along with the relevant gist of events, would establish the continued practice of faith at the birthplace of Ram. This continued practice of faith would be evidence. The distinction was between only arguing about belief and faith in divinity, and demonstrating that the belief and faith were put into action. Faith in the belief that Ram was born in Ayodhya in the Ram Kot area itself, had already been established from various sources. Senior Parasaran was to address the court on these lines. The *Supreme Court Observer* reported a part of the argument of Mr Parasaran in its day proceedings as follows:

2.1 Ram was born in Ayodhya

First, he stated that he must establish the nature of the deity, Lord Ram, and the relevant history of events. Parasaran submitted that the spirit of Lord Ram is present at Janmabhoomi and can be experienced by those who pray there, reasoning that the presence of [an] idol is not necessary for the presence of [a] deity.

On the issue of whether Ram was born at Ayodhya, he submitted that Valmiki's Ramayana states that Lord Ram's place of birth is Ayodhya. He further submitted that what has to be proven is that the custom of worshipping at the site (on the belief that Ram was born there) has existed for a significant number of years. He added that the unshakeable faith of millions of believers is itself evidence.[58]

The nonagenarian, who was already under the weather, was put on a regular dose of Oral Rehydration Solution to boost his flagging energy because he wasn't going to rest voluntarily. The basis on which the suit of Ram Lalla Virajman was filed was set out at Para 20 of Suit 5:[59]

20. That the place itself, or the ASTHAN SHRI RAMA JANMA BHUMI, as it has come to be known, has been an object of worship as a deity by the devotees of a BHAGWAN SHRI RAMA, as it personifies the spirit of the Divine worshipped in the form of SRI RAMA LALA or Lord RAMA the child. The Asthan was thus Deified and has had a Juridical personality of its own even before the construction of a Temple building or the installation of the Idol of Bhagwan Sri Rama thereat.

So, what was the area that constituted Ram Janmasthan/Janmabhoomi? Was it merely a spot/exact spot where Ram was believed to be born, or was it a wider area? If it is the exact spot, then what should be its dimension? Is scientific precision required to prove issues of faith or a place of birth? The line of arguments as discussed by Senior Parasaran with the team was that the place has been worshipped as the birthplace of Lord Ram—Ram Janmabhoomi. The place is impressed with a divine and sacred character. The place has been worshipped as personifying divinity; this is applicable even without there being any worshipping of an idol within the disputed structure.

The argument shaped sought to simplify things. Ram

---

[58]'Day 23 Arguments: Ayodhya Title Dispute', *Supreme Court Observer*, 7 August 2019, https://tinyurl.com/yrpnbyhw. Accessed on 18 January 2025.

[59]Sri Ram Lalla Virajman & Ors, O.S. NO. 5 of 1989, Reg. Suit 236 of 1989, Para 20, https://tinyurl.com/5c5nw827. Accessed on 18 January 2025.

Janmabhoomi did not only mean the exact spot where Ram was born but the wider area. Various sources had mentioned that Lord Ram was born in the palace of Dashratha in Ayodhya, and the place was in the Ram Kot area where the presently disputed land existed. It is unnecessary to identify the spot or room as the place of birth. The disputed area constructed was now approximately 1,500 sq. yd (1,460 sq. yd to be precise), and the palace would have certainly occupied a larger area. The practice of devotees was to worship the larger area as Ram Janmabhoomi/ Janmasthan. That is where faith was being crystallized and practised. That was where the right to worship, which is a civil right, had to be granted. The area was the identified area of the practice of faith.

The idea was to have a solid ground for proving the land as Ram Janmabhoomi as per law, even without relying on archaeological evidence. But then, how did these preparations ultimately fructify? The arguments as reported by *Supreme Court Observer*[60] were:

> *2.4 Ram Janmasthan (birthplace of Lord Ram) is not merely the ground of the main dome of the mosque, but the surrounding area as well.*
>
> *[...] K. Parasaran then submitted that the Ram Janmasthan (birthplace of Lord Ram) is not merely the ground of the main dome of the mosque, but the surrounding area as well. He argued that although sthan means a specific place, it is not restricted to a specific dimension in size and that the Janmasthan is considered to be a very sacred site in Hinduism on account of its nature and the fact that holy yatras are conducted through it. He explained that in legal understanding, a building is not merely the constructed building alone but also the incidents to the building.*

[60]'Day 24 Arguments, Ayodhya Title Dispute', *Supreme Court Observer*, 8 August 2019, https://tinyurl.com/32u9dbd9. Accessed on 18 January 2025.

Drawing on this example, he claimed that the Janmasthan is therefore not merely the ground below the main dome of the mosque but the surrounding land which is considered by Hindus to be the birthplace of Lord Ram. He explained that the unshakeable faith of the people over the area of land considered as the Janmasthan should be included in the ground below the dome when deciding on the title of the disputed Ayodhya land title. He further argued that due to its nature and significance, the Janmasthan was at the core of Hinduism and could not be broken up into three parts.

2.5 A Temple Existed before the Mosque Was Built

K Parasaran then made submissions relating to the existence of a temple before the mosque was built. He primarily relied on the existence of the faith and belief of Hindu people and contended that it is undisputed that Lord Ram existed before Emperor Babar, who built Babri Masjid.

The answer to the issue of land as a Juristic Person had to be given and Senior Parasaran shortlisted two cases. With basic legal premises laid out, it was time to move to evidence. The issue of the parikrama of Ram bhakts of the disputed site was going to be a bone of contention between the parties.

The first round from Mr Parasaran had seen, inter alia, the following:

1. *Attempt to give the history and importance of the piece of land*
2. *Explain the belief and the practice of belief with respect to the land (Ram Janmabhoomi)*
3. *Explain that the identity of the land gave the land a distinct identity and qualified the land as a Juristic Person in itself.*

C.S. Vaidyanathan

It was time now for evidence. The role of Mr C.S. Vaidyanathan was crucial. Bhakti, Sridhar and Yogeswaran now had additional responsibilities—to ensure ready access to the evidence. The issues to be covered by Mr Vaidyanathan were factual, requiring in-depth understanding of the evidence, deposition of witnesses, cross-examination of witnesses, as well as the archaeological evidence. Mr Vaidyanathan also had the responsibility of being prepared for all issues that Senior Parasaran was covering. Mr Parasaran, much to the discomfort of the team assisting him, would continue to remind the team that 'I am living on borrowed time. God has been kind to spare me for this long.' Therefore, Mr C.S. Vaidhyanathan was vital to the case.

There was now growing inquisitiveness about Mr Vaidyanathan as well.

If Mr Parasaran had his struggles with adversity, Mr Vaidyanathan too had a life story straight out of some drama series.

He had lived mostly in villages, though he was born in Coimbatore. His father, the late Mr Shankar Narayan, was associated with the revenue department of the state government, a job that placed the family in villages and provided enough for a respectable living but not affluence. These villages had little to no access to either electricity or piped water supplies. He studied mostly in government schools in the villages. If asked, he would recall that he went to school without wearing the humblest of slippers. Most of his education was in Tamil medium. He had the benefit of a close-knit extended family, and within his house, he credited his mother for efficiently running the household with nine children. He had one brother and seven sisters. That is where his appreciation for all-time family bonds and joint and extended families came from.

Interestingly, Mr Vaidyanathan completed his schooling

at the age of thirteen and a half, while the minimum age for admission to Madras for further studies at that time was fourteen and a half years. Hence, his family had to send him to Mysore to study till graduation.

Later, Mr Vaidyanathan's father became a lawyer, too. Having contracted typhoid while working with the government, Mr Vaidyanathan's father was advised medical rest. Subsequently, he had to quit his job. This brought Mr C.V. Shankar Narayanan to Bangalore University where he stood first in his class and topped in law. He took up law practice in revenue laws and land reforms, among others, while his son completed law even before he had turned twenty, which was below the minimum age required to enrol in the Bar Council in 1969. You could say in jest that Mr Vaidyanathan derived pleasure in not following the laws of age.

As fate would have it, Mr Vaidyanathan, therefore, had to enrol in LL.M. (Master's in Law) which he coupled with a Master's in Social Work. With exposure to different fields to his credit, an advertisement from DCM caught his attention, and that started his tryst with Delhi. Between 1970 and 1974, he worked as a senior management trainee for DCM in Delhi. During this time, he also got married and started a family. The question of taking up law as a profession still existed at the back of his mind. However, the struggle between career choices reached its denouement in 1974, when there was a strike in DCM. It presented him with an opportunity to contemplate his past, present and future. He had to take a call on whether law would be a suitable career option.

As the tug of war continued in Mr Vaidyanathan's mind, further opportunity for contemplation presented itself on a train journey of two full days. The train journey fulfilled its purpose; the decision was made to take up the legal profession for the rest of his professional life. He accepted the fact that since his father had started practising, there was enough encouragement to take up law as a profession. When he finally arrived on the scene to take up law practice, in June 1974, his father introduced him to Mr K.K. Venugopal, another lawyer who has a legendary status in the legal profession.

Indira Gandhi infamously levied a state of Emergency which gripped India from 1974 to 1977. One of the star juniors of Mr Venugopal's team then was Mr P. Chidambaram, who, even in those days, was a Congress leader. Hence, Mr Chidambaram could not appear in matters where steps taken concerning the Emergency were under challenge. For Mr Vaidyanathan, this presented opportunities to appear independently and to assist Mr Venugopal in such cases. Encouragement from his senior was never lacking for Mr Vaidyanathan, and that was the key to his success. When the Emergency finally ended, Mr Vaidyanathan's second tryst with Delhi was about to start.

Mr K.K. Venugopal was appointed Additional Solicitor General of India in 1979. As he shifted to Delhi, he invited all his juniors to join him in Delhi. The one to volunteer among the whole lot had already been in Delhi, and that is how Mr Vaidyanathan returned to Delhi again. As his juniorship continued, the recognition and basis for independent practice came from pro bono cases.

Through all this, his long experience of life, navigating from villages with no electricity to the politically charged city of Delhi, and then to being a top law officer of Government of India as well as being a very successful senior counsel, Ram Lalla's case was perhaps the most important case for Mr Vaidyanathan. He was a bhakt, too, On the flip side there was always this lurking threat of objectivity getting lost if the bhakt took over from the lawyer.

When it was his turn to make submissions in court, he quickly removed his shoes—he was appearing for the god that he believed in. For him, this case was devotion. Back home, it was his wife who was making sure that Ram Lalla's case was well taken care of. Like Mr Parasaran, she, too, was waiting to see Lord Ram's birthplace get a temple befitting the religious belief prevalent in the country. It was no surprise that Mr Vaidyanathan's son, Harish, himself a lawyer, was taking care of the comfort of team Ram Lalla, especially when they were spending long hours in conferences at his place. As far as food goes, there was no dearth of it.

Temples had held great significance in the lives of both Senior Counsels in the Ram Lalla case. Just as temples had shaped Senior Parasaran's worldview, Mr Vaidyanathan too had grown up in their midst. In fact, his early exposure to music came from festivals and temple rituals where music was inseparable from daily life. Each year, during the music season, he would return to Chennai to attend the festival. He often remarked that he had absorbed music through 'osmosis', never having undergone any formal training. Both Mr K. Parasaran and Mr C.S. Vaidyanathan, accomplished professionals as they were, came together as a well-oiled team for this case. They may have different working methods—Mr Vaidyanathan preferring to do his thinking by himself, while Senior Parasaran often spoke his thoughts out aloud—but both were believers in Ram and fought this case pro bono. The next counsel for Lord Ram Lalla was Mr Ranjit Kumar.

> *Mr. Ranjit Kumar was a reputed Senior Counsel and former Solicitor General of India. He journeyed from Patna to Delhi. From being a struggling first-generation lawyer to being an Advocate-on-Record and now a top Senior Counsel, he had for long appeared as an amicus (friend of the court) in environmental cases as well. When the court asked for rupees fifty lakh to be paid to him by Delhi government, having considered his services as Amicus Curiae for over two decades, he politely and with humility refused to accept such payment. He had in cases like Challenge to then President Shankar Dayal Sharma's election, Prosecution of former Prime Minister Shri P.V. Narasimha Rao and had been Amicus Curiae in a number of cases before the Supreme*

> *Court. His life had moved along the flow of River Ganga. He was born in Varanasi and was married also in Varanasi while his paternal side was in Bhagalpur in Bihar. His father was a government servant in a transferable job and he changed many schools. Religion, culture and his grandmothers were all part of same set for Mr. Kumar. As a child, he was diligent in providing help to his paternal and maternal grandmothers in gathering flowers and making garlands and that is where his tryst with temples started and ultimately took him on a journey to temples of South India with Senior Parasaran and Mohan Parasaran. Since the guest had to be given first priority, Senior Parasaran would command Mohan Parasaran to come in some other car so that he could inform Ranjit Kumar of the history of the place, the nature of worship and the reason for that particular kind of temple and worship. The condition of some temples taken over by the government was an issue of concern for Mr Kumar. Now here he was trying his bit so that Lord Ram's idol comes back to his birthplace permanently and people may worship the idol with an appropriate structure befitting the grandeur of faith and belief that people lived with every day.*[61]

Sri P.S. Narasimha was the youngest of the four senior advocates who led the case on behalf of Sri Ram Lalla, as he was then a prominent senior advocate and a former Additional Solicitor General. His in-depth study of Indian history and the *shastra*s (scriptures and treatises) remains a lesser-known facet of his personality. While leading a hectic professional life, he took out time to learn Sanskrit to relish Indic knowledge in ancient shastras. In fact, he used to take time out from his worldly affairs to engage with Vedic scholars and participate in discourses

[61]Chaudhary, Nilasish, '"Really Moved": SC says After Sr Adv Ranjit Kumar Refuses to Accept Rs 50 Lakhs for Service as Amicus', *Live Law*, 25 August 2020, https://tinyurl.com/ttd232x8. Accessed on 18 January 2025.

on the Dharma Shastras. His father, Late Justice P. Kodanda Ramaiah, after retiring as a judge of the Andhra Pradesh High Court, dedicated his life as a philanthropist to researching and publishing books on the essence of *itihasa*s (histories) such as the Ramayana and the Mahabharata. His association with the case went back to the time when the Allahabad High Court pronounced its judgement, and the same had to be challenged in appeals before the Supreme Court. In fact, he was one of the most tech-savvy senior advocates. He started using an iPad since 2010 to read the Allahabad High Court judgement in the course of settling the appeals filed before Supreme Court. He pursued his work and life seamlessly, with science and spirituality as his guiding principles even while appearing in the case of God! But what about evidence?

Now evidence spanning hundreds of years was to be rolled out.

12

Of Prayer and a Barrage of Questions

The appeals challenging the High Court judgement on the Ayodhya case had been closely scrutinized by Mr K. Parasaran and Mr C.S. Vaidyanathan. Some of the leading Senior Counsels in Supreme Court were sent dockets and some were also briefed, recalled Yogeswaran. The arrow of time moves forward, and by 2019 much had changed, so much so that some of the leading Senior Counsels were directly elevated to the position of Judge of the Supreme Court of India. While change is the only constant, thankfully the evidence, spanning the period from 1 BCE to 1949, remained static.

The problem with evidence was that it instigated thinking minds to ask questions. Thousands of pages had to be kept within sight for reference and easy access, and working towards this day since 2010 was Mr C.S. Vaidyanathan. His readings had given him a good grip of history and archaeology, so he was able to understand the illustrations, site maps and reports pertaining to the evidence for the Ram Janmabhoomi excavations and drive home several points. Every lawyer from Ram Lalla's side acknowledged his extraordinary effort, as well as the hard work that the lawyers from the other side would also put in. This case was to bring forth the artistry of legal thought in the courtroom that can only accrue through the sheer quality of work put in by each side. Only by respecting the industry of the other side, would the other be able to give a fitting reply to their arguments.

Mr Vaidyanathan had the onerous task of not only covering

the entire case, including the voluminous evidence, but also of backing up for Senior Parasaran. He was the ideal partner to the nonagenarian—discussing, suggesting, assisting, and visiting Mr Parasaran whenever required. He was to cover generally the following points:

1. How and why did the archaeological excavation come to be carried out by the Archaeological Survey of India (ASI) at Ram Janmasthan?
2. What was found during the archaeological excavation by ASI? What period of use of land, if any, did ASI reveal in its excavation?
3. What would be the effect of the various discoveries and findings made by ASI in the archaeological excavation?
4. Was there any parikrama in the Ram Kot area by Ram bhakts?
5. Was there parikrama also of the land in dispute?
6. What does the parikrama on land establish?
7. What is the evidence of worship and practice by Ram bhakts in the past?
8. What is the evidence of the practice of faith by Ram bhakts from 1528 to 1885?
9. Was the presence of inscriptions and Hindu divinity on the walls of the mosque/disputed structure noted in the court commissioner's report of 1950? (A court commissioner can be any person tasked with giving the court a finding on the actual position of the land, or, on any question of science, art, etc.)
10. Does the law make any provision for relying on documents such as gazetteers and travelogues, which capture history?
11. What is adverse possession? Can anyone claim adverse possession of the disputed land? Was the disputed land in public land or private land?

Many answers to these questions relied upon historical events and texts, for travelogues and other historical evidence had much to reveal. Mr Vaidyanathan focused first on establishing the practice of faith and belief of Hindus at the disputed site as seen by foreign travellers before the British got the iron grill erected, and later when the iron grill was present. Secondly, the travellers' narratives also identified Lord Ram's birthplace as per the practice of faith and worship within the disputed site. Thirdly, there were several records of people of the time that a temple was destroyed and a mosque was erected at that site. This was what the travellers had heard about. Fourthly, it was important to present what the inhabitants of Ayodhya, even till modern times, maintained about the practice of belief, faith, and worship at the disputed site.

As recalled by the team, in his arguments, Mr Vaidyanathan relied upon the travelogues of Joseph Tieffenthaler along with those of other authors/travellers/gazetteers. These not only gave insight into the history of the times but some of them also revealed how English words were spelt then. Joseph Tieffenthaler wrote his travel account in Latin, which was translated into French as *Description Historique et Géographique de l'Inde.* Tieffenthaler was a Jesuit missionary, reportedly proficient in Arabic, Persian and Sanskrit, and visited India in 1740. He lived and worked in India from 1743 to 1785. His visit to Ayodhya is described in French, the text of which was made available during the trial. An English translation was furnished by Government of India in pursuance of an order of the High Court. Tieffenthaler's account talked about both, the practice he saw himself at the disputed site as well as the story of the demolition of the temple as he had heard, describing Vishnu as *Beschan* in the account. Tieffenthaler's account of the ancient city reads thus:

> *'Avad called as Adjudea by the educated Hindus, is a city of very olden times. Its houses are (mostly) made up of mud only; covered with straw or tiles. Many (however), are made*

of bricks. The main street goes from South to North and it has a length of about a mile. The width (of the city) is a little lesser. Its western side and that of North as well, are situated on a mud hill. That of north-east is situated on knolls. Towards Bangla it is united [...]

'Emperor Aurangzeb got the fortress called Ramcot demolished and got a Muslim temple, with triple domes, constructed in the same place. Others say that it was constructed by "Babor". Fourteen black stone pillars of 5 (/) span (4) high, which had existed at the site of the fortress, are seen there.

'On the left is seen a square box raised 5 inches above the ground, with borders made of lime, with a length of more than 5 ells and a maximum width of about 4 ells. The Hindus call it Bedi i.e., the cradle. The reason for this is that once upon a time, here was a house where Beschan was born in the form of Ram. It is said that his three brothers too were born here. Subsequently, Aurengzeb or Babor, according to others, got this place razed in order to deny the noble people, the opportunity of practising their superstitions. However, there still exists some superstitious cult in some place or other. For example, in the place where the native house of Ram existed, they go around 3 times and prostrate on the floor. The two spots are surrounded by a low wall constructed with battlement. One enters the front hall through a low semi-circular door. Not far from there is a place where one digs out grains of black rice, burned into small stones, which are said to have been hidden under the earth since the time of Ram. On the 24th of the Tschet month, a big gathering of people is done here to celebrate the birthday of Ram, famous in the entire India [...]'

Earlier to Tieffenthaler, William Foster[62] edited *Early Travels in India (1583–1619)* which gives narratives of seven Englishmen,[63] including William Finch, who travelled in western and northern India during the reign of Akbar and Jahangir.

According to the submissions, the significance of the account of William Finch, who visited Ayodhya between 1608 and 1611, was the absence of any building of importance of Islamic origin. The expression 'ruines (ruins) of Ranichand(s) castle and Houses' has been appended in a footnote stating, 'Ram Chandra, the hero of the Ramayana'. The reference is to the mound known as the Ram Kot or fort of Ram. There is a reference in the travels of William Finch to Ayodhya:

> *To Oude (Ajodhya) from thence are 50c; a citie of ancient note, and seate of a Potan king, now much ruined; the castle built four hundred yeeres agoe. Heere are also the ruines of Ranichand(s) castle and houses, which the Indians acknowled(g)e for the great God, saying that he took flesh upon him to see the tamasha of the world. In these ruins remayne certaine Bramenes, who record the names of all such Indians as wash themselves in the river running thereby; which custome, they say, hath continued foure lackes of yeeres (which is three hundred ninetie foure thousand and five hundred yeeres before the world's creation).*

Robert Montgomery Martin wrote *The History, Antiquities, Topography and Statistics of Eastern India* in three volumes. Martin, born in Dublin in 1801, was an Anglo-Irish author and

---

[62]Foster, William, *Early Travels in India*: 1583–1619, London, 1921, p. 176; also referred to in Para 560 of the Judgement of the Supreme Court of India, and Para 88 of Addenda to Judgement.

[63]Ralph Fitch (1583–91); John Mildenhall (1599–1606); William Hawkins (1608–13); William Finch (1608–11); Nicholas Withington (1612–16); Thomas Coryat (1612–17) and Edward Terry (1616–19). Among them, William Finch arrived in India in August 1608 at Surat with Captain Hawkins.

civil servant.[64] He spent 10 years in medical practice in Shillong, East Africa and New South Wales, besides working as a journalist in Calcutta where he established *The Bengal Herald*. Martin, too, commented along the same lines:[65]

> *The bigot by whom the temples were destroyed, is said to have erected mosques on the situations of the most remarkable temples, but the mosque at Ayodhya, which is by far the most entire, and which has every appearance of being the most modern, is ascertained by an inscription on its walls (of which a copy is given) to have been built by Babur, five generations before Aurungzeb.*

P. Carnegy, who was posted as Officiating Commissioner and Settlement Officer, Faizabad, wrote the *Historical Sketch of Faizabad with Old Capitals Ajodhia and Fyzabad*(1870).[66] Carnegy underscored the importance of Ayodhya to the faith of Hindus and talked about the practice of faith in the entire area of the disputed structure:

> *—Ajudhia—Ajudhia, which is to the Hindu what Macca is to the Mahomedan, Jerusalem to the Jews, has in the traditions of the orthodox, a highly mythical origin, being founded for additional security not on the earth for that is transitory, but on the chariot wheel of the Great Creator himself which will endure for over [...]*
>
> *The Janmasthan marks the place where Ramchandar was born. The Sargadwar is the gate through which he passed*

---

[64]Robert Montgomery Martin (c. 1801–68), biographical details, British Museum; also referred to in the judgement of the Supreme Court of India.

[65]King, F.H.H., *Survey our empire! Robert Montgomery Martin (1801–1868): A Bio-bibliography*, 1979; also referred to in Para 562 of the judgement of the Supreme Court of India.

[66]Carnegy, P., *Historical Sketch of Faizabad with Old Capitals Ajodhia and Fyzabad*, Oudh Government Press, 1870; Carnegy's work is referred to in the judgement of the Supreme Court of India.

> *into Paradise, possibly the spot where his body was burned. The Tareta-Ke-Thakur was famous as the place where Rama performed a great sacrifice [...]*
>
> *It is remarkable that in all the copies of Babar's life now known the pages that relate to his doings at Ajudhia are wanting. In two places in the Babari mosque the year in which it was built, 935 H., corresponding with 1528 AD, is carved in stone, along with inscriptions dedicated to the glory of that emperor. If Ajudhia was then little other than a wild, it must at least have possessed a fine temple in the Janmasthan; for many of its columns are still in existence and in good preservation, having been used by the Musalmans in the construction of the Babari Mosque. These are of strong close-grained dark slate-coloured or black stone, called by the natives Kasoti (literally touchstone) and carved with different devices. To my thinking, these strongly resemble Buddhist pillars that I have seen at Benares and elsewhere. They are from seven to eight feet long, square at the base, centre and capital, and round or octagonal intermediately [...]*
>
> *It is said that up to that time the Hindus and Mahomedans alike used to worship in the mosque-temple. Since British rule a railing has been put up to prevent disputes, within which in the mosque the Mahomedans pray, while outside the fence the Hindus have raised a platform on which they make their offerings.*

There were other accounts too for the court's consideration: Edward Thornton's *Gazetteer*, first published in 1858[67]; Surgeon

[67]Thornton, Edward, 1799–1875, *A Gazetteer of the Territories under the Government of the East-India Company, and of the Native States on the Continent of India*, W.H. Allen, London, 1854.

General Edward Balfour's *Cyclopaedia*[68]; the compilation[69] and the *Gazetteer of Oudh* (1877) by Alexander Cunningham, who was Director General of the Archaeological Survey of India. Then there was A.F. Millet's *The Report of Settlement of Land Revenue, Faizabad District* (1880); H.R. Nevill, I.C.S., compiled and edited the works titled *Barabanki: A Gazetteer* being Volume XLVIII of the *District Gazetteer of the United Provinces of Agra and Oudh*; and *The Imperial Gazetteer of India, Provincial Series, United Provinces of Agra and Oudh*, Vol. II (Allahabad, Banaras, Gorakhpur, Kumaon, Lucknow and Faizabad divisions and the native states). The arguments made in respect to these texts raised a lot of questions from the judges of the Supreme Court. *The Hindu*[70] covered the submissions of Mr Vaidyanathan and the queries answered:

> *The Hindu parties involved in the Ayodhya title appeals received a barrage of questions from the Constitution Bench, including whether there is any evidence on record to show that the first Mughal emperor, Babur, ordered the building of the Babri Masjid.*
>
> *While Justice S.A. Bobde asked about when the structure, demolished by kar sevaks on December 6, 1992, began to be called 'Babri Masjid', Justice D.Y. Chandrachud reflected on historical texts to point out that Ayodhya and the disputed area seemed to have been a confluence of several religions, including Buddhism, Jainism and even Islam.*

---

[68]Balfour, Surgeon General Edward, *Cyclopaedia of India and of Eastern and Southern Asia, Commercial, Industrial and Scientific: Products of the Mineral, Vegetable, and Animal Kingdoms, Useful Arts and Manufactures*, Third Edition, Bernard Quaritch, London, 1885.

[69]Cunningham, Alexander, *Four Reports Made During the Years 1862-63-64-65*, Archaeological Survey of India, Volume I, Government Central Press, Simla, 1871.

[70]Rajagopal, Krishnadas, 'Ayodhya hearing: Supreme Court poses queries to Hindu parties' counsel', *The Hindu*, 14 August 2019, https://tinyurl.com/3jshedm3. Accessed on 18 January 2025.

> *Responding to these questions and observations from the Constitution Bench led by Chief Justice of India Ranjan Gogoi, senior advocate C.S. Vaidyanathan on Wednesday relied on travelogues and personal accounts of foreign travellers to India to show that the belief among the local people that Ram Janmabhoomi was divine remained unshakeable for centuries all together.*

Mr Vaidyanathan emphasized that travelogues of foreigners, such as the Christian missionary, Joseph Tieffenthaler, and others like Robert Montgomery Martin and William Finch, about the historical belief in Ram and the existence of the ruins of a temple in Ayodhya showed that the belief of the people about the holiness of the place remained undisturbed despite various invasions and other influences and happenings. As foreigners were under no compulsion to lie, Vaidhyanathan articulated that these accounts could be accepted as credible. The article from *The Hindu*[71] continued:

> *At this point, the Bench intervened to point out that Tieffenthaler seemed [to] have two varied accounts of the demolition of a temple in the area—one, that it was destroyed by Babur, and the other, that it was razed by Aurangzeb much later.*
>
> *But Mr. Vaidyanathan contended that it did not matter who destroyed the temple as long as the missionary's accounts go to prove the existence of a temple and that it was demolished before 1786. 'Who demolished the temple would not matter for [sic] us as it proves that the temple existed. What is important about the document is that it identifies the JanamAsthan and that a mosque was put up at the site of the Ram temple,' he submitted.*
>
> *Mr. Vaidyanathan said the first use of [the] name 'Babri*

[71]Ibid.

Masjid' traced back only to the 19th century. 'Nothing before that to show it was called Babri Masjid,' he contended. He said even the memoirs of Emperor Babur were 'silent' on his stay in Ayodhya.

But Senior Advocate Rajeev Dhavan clarified [...] that Baburnama is silent about Babur's visit to Ayodhya. 'Baburnama says about Babur crossing the river to Ayodhya. Two pages of his stay in Ayodhya are missing. That cannot mean he did not visit Ayodhya,' he said.

But Mr. Vaidyanathan repeated that the intent of his arguments was to only show that there was [a] temple in the area and the people associated [a] certain divinity to the place. 'There is archaeological evidence to show there were temple ruins' [...]

For some, archaeology was a system of study that revealed mysteries hidden deep below the surface of the earth, or maybe not so deep. Yet, it did reveal secrets and mysteries of ancient eras. It also proved that everything and everyone was dispensable. However, what was to be discovered was the antiquity of the city of Lord Ram for it was not in dispute that Lord Ram was born in Ayodhya.

Mr Vaidyanathan's submissions brought forward the plea which was also accepted by the Allahabad High Court in its judgement in 2010 that preponderance of probabilities was the key to the evaluation of evidence. It was a settled law by the Supreme Court of India.

The Allahabad High Court, which first confronted the issue, admitted the gravity of the situation:

To our mind, instead of puzzling ourselves in so much literature etc., certain aspects which emerge from whatever we have mentioned above may be summarised which probably may give some idea as to how the questions are to be answered. The antiquity of Ayodhya is not disputed. It is also not disputed that Ayodhya is known as the principal place of religion and is mainly concerned with Vaishnavites, i.e. the followers of Lord Rama. Lord Rama was born in Ayodhya and ruled thereat. The religious texts like Valmiki Ramayana and Ramcharitmanas of Goswami Tulsidas and others like Skandpuran, etc. mention that Lord Rama was born at Ayodhya, and it is his place of birth but do not identify any particular [precise] place in Ayodhya which can be said to be his place of birth. On the one hand, we do not get any idea about the exact place or site but simultaneously, we can reasonably assume that once it is not disputed that Lord Rama was born at Ayodhya, there must be a place that could be narrowed down to the site of his place of birth. It is true that a search for a place of birth after a long time, even today, may not be very easy if one tried to find out in this regard just three or four generations back. Therefore, making such an inquiry in a matter of such antiquity is almost impossible. But when a dispute in such a manner is raised, then we go by the well-accepted principle, in the law of evidence, particularly as applicable in civil cases, i.e., the preponderance of probability.[72]

Preponderance of probability was and is the only way to solve such issues under the civil law of India. This standard is sometimes also described as a balance of probability or the preponderance of evidence. A process is followed to reach the answer in a case where it is questioned how the conclusion should be reached based on the preponderance of probabilities. First, the subject matter of a dispute is to be analysed. For example, is the dispute old, centuries-old, or historical? Then what can be an impossibility is discarded and one moves to

[72]Ayodhya Sri Ramajanmabhoomi Case Records, *Vada Prativada*, https://tinyurl.com/bdz98ynh. Accessed on 18 January 2025.

the possibilities and then to more probable and then to most probable. If, therefore, the evidence is such that the court can say, 'We think it more probable of any event taking place rather than not taking place', the burden is discharged (or there is probable proof). The court can then favour one party as probabilities have tilted the balance to one side. However, if the probabilities are equal and the balance does not tilt towards one, then the scales remain equal.[73] In civil cases, therefore, the evidence need not reach absolute certainty but must display high probability. Proof beyond reasonable doubt does not mean proof beyond the shadow of a doubt:

> *The impossible is weeded out at the first stage, the improbable at the second. The court often has a difficult choice to make within the wide range of probabilities, but it is this choice that ultimately determines where the preponderance of probabilities lies. Important issues affecting the status of parties demand closer scrutiny [...]*[74]

Archaeological evidence was next to be submitted to the court which had its own share of contest and controversies. The judges on the bench too had their own set of questions dug deep.

[73]*Phipson on Evidence*, 16th Edition, pp. 154–155, formulates the standard also followed by the Supreme Court of India, in *M. Siddiq (D) Thr Lrs v. Mahant Suresh Das & Ors*, Civil Appeal No. 10866–10867 of 2010, p. 112.

[74]*Dr. N.G. Dastane v. S. Dastane* (1975) 2 SCC 326.

13

Archaeology and the Temple: Evidence from 1 BCE to 1528 CE

Undoubtedly, for team Ram Lalla, the archaeological evidence was a salient feature of the case. The burden of dealing with the archaeological aspect of the case lay singularly on Mr Vaidyanathan's shoulders. Though Yogeswaran and Bhakti did brief him, it was Mr Vaidyanathan who had to dig deep. For some time, the scene of operations shifted from Senior Parasaran's office to Mr Vaidyanathan's office for Sridhar, Bhakti, and Yogi. Mr Vaidyanathan's arguments were to be followed by other counsels for the side of Hindus, and then Mr Jain would argue for Nirmohi Akhara.

Senior Parasaran used this interval to attend hearings, take notes, and do some work in the morning and evening. If he could wrap up by 8 p.m., he could get some rest. This was also the time to fine-tune the submissions on Juristic Person and sort out differences within the team—yes, these still festered, anticipating the arguments that the Sunni Waqf Board would make on this point. Mr Parasaran would hold some discussions with Anirudh every day on the issue of Juristic Person, and some discussions with Aditi and Ashwin on limitations and the findings of High Courts, etc. This was also the time when Mohan Parasaran could get back his associates Aditi and Ashwin from what his father termed as 'misappropriation'.

Mr Vaidyanathan was a veteran of many important cases. Apart from archaeology and all other aspects of the case that Senior Parasaran was covering, he was also covering the point as to whether Ram bhakts were continuously using the land for devotional purposes.

The reins were now in Mr Vaidyanathan's hands who led with the point that Ram bhakts were always present, and had never abandoned the disputed land; therefore, the other side had no claim of adverse possession of the land. Adverse possession refers to the unchallenged claim of an illegal occupant of land for a continuous period of 12 years. An adverse possession gives the ownership right of the land to an illegal occupant and seeks to destroy the rights of the true legitimate owner. In that manner, adverse possession places a premium on the illegitimate act of encroachment. This illegal occupation must be in a manner hostile to the rest of the world and must be within the knowledge of the true legal owner. With no challenge to illegal occupation, the squatter continues to be in unchallenged, peaceful possession and perfects his claim after 12 years, i.e., becomes the owner of the land. If the possession of the illegal occupant is not peaceful or is challenged, the squatter fails in his effort to claim the land. If the illegal occupation and possession continue unchallenged peacefully, only then is there conversion of his illegal status to legal status, and the squatter becomes the owner. Mr Vaidyanathan tried to establish that there was never a period when Ram bhakts did not lay claim on the land. Their claim on the land remained intact. This repelled any claim of adverse possession.

1. The question was: 'To establish the claim of adverse possession, what did the illegal encroacher have to prove?' The answer to this question was that the encroacher had to prove the following:
2. That the occupier/encroacher/squatter of the land threw out from the land the owner of the land as well as any other parties or claimants to the land.
3. The illegally encroaching party should have enjoyed the benefits of the land for a period of 12 uninterrupted years peacefully, without the original owner protesting at all.

4. That the illegal encroacher declared themselves to be the owner and excluded every one of the other parties totally from the land.

Yogeswaran, though thorough with facts, was in the habit of doubting himself. Lawyers in the case knew the weight of history that it carried. Sometimes, Yogi would double-check that the historical evidence, apart from rebutting the claims of adverse possession of the land by the Sunni Board, would also establish the continued presence of Ram bhakts. Though there was other evidence, the historical evidence was indeed important. It had to prove that Ram bhakts had never been thrown out from the disputed site.

Bhakti was more detailed and focused than Yogeswaran. He would point out that the travelogues of the foreigners, like the ones written by the missionary Joseph Tieffenthaler, and others like William Finch, Robert Montgomery Martin, etc., about the history of Ram and the ruins of a temple in Ayodhya show that the belief of the people about the holiness of the place has remained undisturbed despite various invasions and other influences and mishaps. As delineated in the factual matrix, these travelogues and gazetteers were dated both before and after 1855. These submissions helped establish the continued presence of Ram bhakts, their prayer and practice of faith, and the archaeological evidence establishes this faith and negates the claim of the other side.

Mr Vaidyanathan and Senior Parasaran would discuss what was to be submitted to the court. When it came to archaeological evidence emanating from the excavation conducted by the Archaeological Survey of India, it was a comprehensive report running into ten chapters:[75]

[75]Archaeological Survey of India (ASI) Report, VOL I & II, *Vada Prativada*, https://tinyurl.com/3e647h4y. Accessed on 18 January 2025.
Also *see*: Written Submission No. A104, The Submissions on behalf of Plaintiffs in Suit 5 by Mr. C.S. Vaidyanathan, Sr. Adv., *Vada Prativada*, https://tinyurl.com/5a4xzr69.

Chapter I: Introduction
Chapter II: Cuttings
Chapter III: Stratigraphy and Chronology
Chapter IV: Structure
Chapter V: Pottery
Chapter VI: Architectural Fragments
Chapter VII: Terracotta Figurines
Chapter VIII: Inscriptions, Seals, Sealings and Coins
Chapter IX: Miscellaneous Objects
Chapter X: Summary of Results
(*See images of archaeological findings in photo inserts.*)

Mr Vaidyanathan was to concentrate on the recoveries made during the excavation and the various periods of time which had seen the occupation of this site for human public use and as a public temple. He was to inform the court about the recovery of a place for the Shiva Linga, etc. His arguments would traverse from 1 BCE to the late Mughal period. Excavation results went back to nearly 2,500 years to disprove the claim of the Sunni Board that the land on which the disputed structure stood was unoccupied.

Outside of the lawyers' offices, the question often asked was, 'What all did the excavation reveal?' According to Yogeswaran and Bhakti, the ASI report revealed a deep treasure of history. The report of the excavation had resulted in recoveries which showed the presence of human occupation and use of objects such as ear studs, animal figures in terracotta, terracotta figurines of female deities, iron knives, glass beads, and bone points, among others. It also showed the presence of the Brahmi script dating earlier to even 2 BCE, although no structural activity of the time was encountered in the area excavated. The earliest

---

Accessed on 18 January 2025.
Also *see*: Written Submission No. A116, The Submissions on behalf of the Appellants by Mr. C.S.Vaidyanathan, Sr. Adv., *Vada Prativada*, https://tinyurl.com/46m8kj96. Accessed on 18 January 2025.

recoveries date back to 13 BCE. As per the radiocarbon dating of the pottery, human presence was found easily up to 1000 BCE.

Excavations also pointed to constructions below the disputed site starting way back in the 2nd or 1st BCE. According to the Hindu side's case, terracotta artefacts of the mother goddess, and human and animal figurines representing the cultural matrix typical of pre-3rd-century era (Sunga Period) were also found at the site. Rich deposits of pottery of the following Kushan period dating from 1st to 3rd century era were also found there.[76]

The Gupta Period pertaining in particular to the 4th–6th-century era marked its presence at the site through terracotta figurines and a copper coin. A subsidiary shrine belonging to the 7th–10th-century era (post-Gupta–Rajput period) was also discovered at the site. The circular shrine discovered in this period was given much importance after a thorough analysis.

Excavations also revealed a thick floor made of brick crush to have been attached to a wide and massive-looking north–south-oriented brick wall, markedly inclined to the east. Floors with varying thicknesses, calcrete stone blocks have been noticed in formation which could have been of large dimensions. It was over the top of this construction that the disputed structure was constructed during the early 16th century. This floor had a relation to the 11th–12th-century era (medieval Sultanate period).

From the end of the 12th- to the beginning of the 16th-century era (medieval period), a massive wall in the north–south orientation was found. A floor of lime mixed with fine clay and brick crush, over which a column–based structure was built with evidence of pillar bases, was also discovered. The existence of a circular depression, facing the central part of the disputed structure over which Ram Lalla/Deity was enshrined was found

[76]Written Submission No. A104, The Submissions on behalf of Plaintiff in Suit No.5 by Mr. C.S. Vaidyanathan, Sr. Adv., *Vada Prativada*, https://tinyurl.com/5a4xzr69. Accessed on 18 January 2025.

to indicate that it was a place of importance. In a later sub-period, the findings included foundations to support pillars or columns.

Constructions from the Mughal period, as well as the late and post-Mughal periods, were also discovered, wherein the north–south wall of the earlier period was retained as the foundation for the later structure. The late and post-Mughal levels saw two successive floors, the addition of another platform to the east, forming a terrace, and subsequently, the erection of two successive enclosure walls.

Chapter IV of the ASI report was important, as it dealt with structures. A significant aspect of this chapter was a section titled 'The Massive Structure Below the Disputed Structure'. It gave penetrative insights.

From the excavation, it could be inferred that there were 17 rows of pillar bases from the north to the south, each row having five pillar bases. Due to the restriction of the area and a natural barrier, the pillar bases in the central part occupied by the makeshift structure on the raised platform could not be located. Out of the 50 pillar bases excavated, only 12 were completely exposed, while 35 were partially exposed and three could be traced only in sections.

A decorated octagonal sandstone block was found. It was on pillar base 32 with floral motifs on the four corners in trench F7 in the southern area—a unique example at the site, which as per the ASI report belonged to 12 CE, as it is like those found in the Dharma Chakra Jina Vihara of Kumaradevi at Sarnath, which belongs to early 12 CE.

The Case of the Circular Shrine

The ASI report contained an analysis of an east-facing brick shrine. It stood as a circular structure with a rectangular projection in the east. It had a circular outer face as a *pranala* (water chute), which was a distinct feature of contemporary temples already known from the Ganga-Yamuna plain—to drain out water, as is the case after the '*abhisheka* (ritual bathing) of the deity which is not present in the shrine now'. This brick circular shrine was stated to be similar to the Shiva temples near Rewa in Madhya Pradesh at Chandrehe and Masaon, belonging to 950 CE, a Vishnu temple and another temple without a deity at Kurari, and a Surya temple at Tinduli in Fatehpur district. ASI has drawn an inference that on stylistic grounds, the circular shrine dates to 10 CE. On a comparative basis, ASI had inferred that the circular shrine could be dated to 10 CE. It was noted as per the submissions that though the structure stood damaged, the other wall still retained a provisional pranala.

The ASI report noted that there was sufficient proof of existence of a massive and monumental structure having a minimum dimension of 50m x 30m in the north–south and east–west directions, respectively. The area below the disputed site remained a place for public use for a long time till the disputed structure came about.

It was a happy discovery to know that lawyers were not alone in using words which common folk found difficult to use in their everyday existence. Besides medical experts, engineers and many others, archaeologists and historians also use technical language. The conclusion of the ASI report in the language of archaeologists read as follows:[77]

> Viewing in totality and taking into account the archaeological evidence of a massive structure just below the disputed structure and evidence of continuity in structural phases from the 10th century onwards up to the construction of the disputed structure, along with the yield of stone and decorated bricks, as well as mutilated sculpture of divine couple and carved architectural members,

[77]Archaeological Survey of India (ASI) Report, VOL I & II, *Vada Prativada*, https://tinyurl.com/3e647h4y. Accessed on 18 January 2025.

> including foliage patters, *amalaka* (structure found on temple tops), *kapotapali* doorjamb with semi-circular pilaster, broken octagonal shaft of black schist pillar, lotus motif, circular shrine having *pranala* in the north, 50 pillar bases in association of the huge structure are indicative of remains, which are distinctive features found associated with the temples of north India.

During the hearing, Mr Vaidyanathan covered all the above points. He highlighted the fact of the presence of a non-Islamic religious structure in the archaeological report, topping the evidence with the recording of gazetteers of English times, and of the site being the site of the practice of faith, as highlighted by the given evidence. He reiterated the points considering the fact of parikrama by the devotees, wherein the disputed structure lay in the path of the parikrama. Going deeper into evidence, Mr Vaidyanathan brought out the report of factual findings as was sought by the court back in the 1950s, for which the court had appointed the court commissioner. The court commissioner had taken photographs and submitted them in his factual report. Mr Vaidyanathan also took the court deep into archaeological material. He then lightly touched on what is prohibited in a mosque to corroborate it in sync with the discoveries in the ASI report. The *Supreme Court Observer*[78] followed the arguments of Mr Vaidyanathan and the day's proceedings:

> *2.18 Archaeological evidence shows that Babri Masjid was built on a temple*

---

[78]'Day 28 Arguments, Ayodhya Title Dispute', *Supreme Court Observer*, 16 August 2019, https://tinyurl.com/5ysy52ky. Accessed on 18 January 2025.

Also *see*: Written Submission No. A104, The Submissions on behalf of Plaintiff in Suit No.5 by Mr. C.S.Vaidyanathan, Sr. Adv., *Vada Prativada*, https://tinyurl.com/5a4xzr69. Accessed on 18 January 2025.

Also *see*: Written Submission No. A116, The Submissions on behalf of the Appellants by Mr. C.S.Vaidyanathan, Sr. Adv., *Vada Prativada*, https://tinyurl.com/46m8kj96. Accessed on 18 January 2025.

Sr. Adv. C. S. Vaidyanathan resumed by taking the Bench through a map of the site. He explained that the path of parikrama shown on the map is a little different from what the oral evidence indicates.

Repeating himself, he referred to photographs of inscriptions, which are allegedly evidence of a temple pre-dating Babri Masjid. He highlighted a stone slab with the inscription 'Janmabhoomi'. He substantiated his position by referring to the Allahabad High Court's interpretation of the photographs.

2.18.1 Idols cannot be present in a mosque

He argued that the photographs show that the site was not a mosque, where prayers were offered. Justice Bobde stated that there is a distinction between whether a structure was built as a mosque and whether it is being used as a mosque. Vaidyanathan responded that images of human beings or God can never be inside a mosque, and hence, the site could not be a mosque.

Justice Bobde asked Sr. Adv. C. S. Vaidyanathan which hadith he was referring to. Loosely referring to the Shariat, Sr. Adv. C. S. Vaidyanathan submitted that while namaz can be offered anywhere, a mosque requires certain conditions to be met. He said that it is against the tenets of Islam to have images of idols present in a mosque […]

Senior advocate Rajeev Dhavan, who represents the Sunni Waqf Board, interjected to say that it was offensive to say namaz can be offered anywhere. He submitted that Justice Sharma, in his opinion (2010 Allahabad High Court Judgment) had stated that prayers can be offered anywhere, and attributed it to Dhavan. Dhavan questioned whether this was a correct interpretation of Islam and denied making the statement.

C. S. Vaidyanathan continued, showing the court a photograph of the Garuda idol and stating that it shows that the site could not be a mosque. Justice Bobde inquired when the photo was taken. Justice Bhushan stated that it would be helpful to present photographs in the period prior to 1950 and explained that after 1950, the structure was evidently used as a temple. He recalled the mention of a collection of photographs in the court commissioner's report. Chief Justice Gogoi read out the mention of 13 photographs taken by Basheer Ahmed […]

2.18.3 Relevance of ASI report to the dispute

[…] Rajeev Dhavan clarified for the court that only organic matter can be carbon dated. He submitted that steel, iron, and bricks could not be carbon dated. He inquired whether the idols had been carbon dated. C. S. Vaidyanathan said no, only the surrounding materials had been carbon dated.

[…]Justice Bobde asked Sr. Adv. C.S. Vaidyanathan to clarify the relevance of the report to the current dispute. He stated that the report appears to apply to many areas in the region, and is not specific to Ayodhya. Vaidyanathan stated that the report demonstrates that a public structure, such as a mandapa or temple, was likely in place since the 2nd century BCE. Justice Bobde was not satisfied, and again asked Sr. Adv. C. S. Vaidyanathan to clarify how this fact relates to the dispute.

Justice Chandrachud directed Sr. Adv. C. S. Vaidyanathan to page 59 of the report, which describes a circular depression apparently made by cutting a large brick pavement. Vaidyanathan suggested that it was a place of importance, as it faced the central structure where the Lord Ram idol is kept. He posited that it was used to drain out water after the abhisheka of a deity […]

Often, after the arguments at court, a few journalists would walk up to Senior Parasaran and Mr Vaidyanathan. None spoke to the media. It was clear that they weren't going to make any statement for public consumption. However, if a fresh young journalist wanted to clear his doubts, this was allowed by the team. No sound bites, but answering queries after the arguments was allowed to help someone clear doubt about the arguments.

The questions centred mainly on the submission as to whether, as per Islamic law, there was a distinction between a structure built as a mosque and whether it is being used as a mosque. The answer to the question was that it was the duty of the Muslim side to prove that. The other issue for them to prove was whether the building was used for prayers after 1528, as the Ram Lalla side was showing that Ram bhakts used it for prayers. So, another question arose: Who did the government records consider the title owners of the land? In the revenue records, the land was shown as government land. However, the government let the courts decide whom the land should go to between the contesting communities.

It was clarified to those who queried—young lawyers, interns, journalists, or lawyer friends who wanted an update about the hearing—what the senior counsels for Ram Lalla were trying to establish. Based on travelogues, gazetteers, ASI reports and oral evidence, the presence of Ram bhakts was established on the disputed land from pre-Islamic and pre-Buddhist India, and certainly from 16 CE. The ruins of the building as discovered by ASI also suggested that the land was put to public use, and not private use. Mr Vaidyanathan surmised, based on the ASI report, that it was a case of public land and public temple. An interesting question raised was whether public land can be claimed by one party as his or her own exclusively, and sold as a general commercial transaction of land?

Mr Vaidyanathan further argued that if any piece of land belongs generally to the public and is put to public use or public religious use, then no individual or private party can claim possession of that public land. Moreover, in Ayodhya, the land itself was a deity. This land from pre-Buddhist days was one such land. The *Supreme Court Observer*[79] reported:

> *2.25 No private party can claim possession of a public temple*
>
> *[...] He then cited case law to submit that no private party can claim possession of a public temple, as this would alter its religious nature. He argued that the temple at the disputed site is a public temple. Hence, he submitted that it is res extra commercium—meaning that none of the parties could claim the right to the property title [...]The disputed property is a deity (a Juristic Person) and external ownership cannot be claimed [...]*
>
> *Justice Bobde and Justice Chandrachud directed C. S. Vaidyanathan to cite case law in support of his arguments that the property of a deity is inalienable. He cited a Privy Council judgment.*
>
> *Next, he added that the property cannot be claimed by adverse possession, since the deity is a perpetual minor in law.*
>
> *Justice Bobde asked if claims of adverse possession can exist if the property is owned by a lunatic and whether it could be alienated.*
>
> *Justice Nazeer asked if adverse possession could be claimed over a property owned by a Waqf.*

---

[79]'Day 29 Arguments, Ayodhya Title Dispute', *Supreme Court Observer*, 20 August 2019, https://tinyurl.com/3he3w7us.Accessed on 18 January 2025.
Also *see*: Written Submission No. A104, The Submissions on behalf of Plaintiff in Suit No.5 by Mr. C.S. Vaidyanathan, Sr. Adv., *Vada Prativada*, https://tinyurl.com/5à4xzr69.Accessed on 18 January 2025.
Also *see*: Written Submission No. A116, The Submissions on behalf of the Appellants by Mr. C.S.Vaidyanathan, Sr. Adv., *Vada Prativada*, https://tinyurl.com/46m8kj96. Accessed on 18 January 2025.

C.S. Vaidyanathan argued that the court in Ismail Faruqui held that the law of limitation would apply to Waqf property. He added that no party can claim possession of the land which itself is a deity or is owned by a deity.

Chief Justice Gogoi summarised C. S. Vaidyanathan's position as: 'The disputed property is itself a deity and hence it cannot be possessed nor have its title claimed.'

[…] He submitted that the site is a public temple because devotees have historically performed worship there. He said that it was, hence, not subject to private title claims. He argued that a mosque was illegally constructed at the site, and that this could not grant the Sunni Waqf Board any claims, since the character of the deity and the sanctity of the deity is perpetual and indestructible.

Justice Chandrachud sought clarification and asked whether there was authority to substantiate that the assumed temple was res extra commercium and could not be subject to possession claims. C.S. Vaidyanathan submitted that no one can destroy the character of a temple or an idol. Justice Chandrachud then asked whether this simply amounted to his first argument, namely that no one can claim possession of a deity. Vaidyanathan submitted that it was a different argument about the character of a temple […]

The character of the temple and idol was to be taken care of by the counsels of Ram Lalla when they were to present their detailed arguments on the Juristic Person of land as janmabhoomi. But for now, in limited time, Mr Vaidyanathan had given an extraordinary presentation of his client's case, while a divided team Ram Lalla debated what line to take on the issue of the land (janmabhoomi) being a Juristic Person.

14

History, Evidence and Parikrama

The Archaeological Survey of India (ASI) report presented to the Supreme Court as evidence generated a great deal of curiosity among the many who were pursuing the case. In an age of digitization, procuring a copy was not difficult. Orchestrating the findings of the report to further lawyers' arguments in favour of their client was the test of skill.

Other than the ASI report, other documents were also presented, as were pleadings from both sides, which were relevant so long as other evidence and the oral testimonies, which witnesses give in the court's witness box, supported them. In fact, oral testimonies often reveal the hidden truths of a transaction, or, of a case.

The cases where practices would have their inception in antiquity were a different ball game altogether. The oral testimonies, therefore, had to be of the elders. Consistent with this perspective, Mr Vaidyanathan ventured into oral evidence primarily to establish continuous worship and practice of faith and belief of Hindus at the disputed site. The identification of the exact site of birth, though not required from the submission of Ram Lalla's counsels, was yet to be proved. Parikrama, the practice of circumambulation of the birthplace of Lord Ram could clarify the position. What could parikrama prove? For some, it could certainly prove what devotees identified as the exact spot of Lord Ram's birth. As the case went on, there was an interesting exchange between the judges and Mr

Vaidyanathan captured by the *Supreme Court Observer*[80] as Mr Vaidyanathan brought out what Hindu as well as Muslim witnesses deposed in their oral testimonies on some issues, including the practice of parikrama, and how important Ayodhya was for Hindus:

> *A 90-year-old witness (Mahant Sri Ramchandra Das) who gave evidence on 22 December 1999, stated that Hindus worshipped at the site because they thought it was Ram's birthplace.*
>
> *An 85-year-old witness born in 1917, who moved to Ayodhya in 1938, recounts worshippers offering darshan and performing parikrama (circumambulation) at the site. Further, he stated that his grandfather and father told him it was where Vishnu was reincarnated as Ram [...]*
>
> *Justice Chandrachud asked Sr. Adv. C.S. Vaidyanathan whether Hindu worship remained continuous when access to the site was restricted by the State. Sr. Adv. C. S. Vaidyanathan submitted that worship never ceased.*
>
> *At this point, Sr. Adv. C. S. Vaidyanathan began taking the court through the Plaintiff witness statements. Relying on the statement made by Mohammed Harshim (PW1), he submitted that Muslim witnesses also refer to the site as a special place of worship for Hindus. Mohammed Harshim (PW1), in his statement, described Ayodhya as a Hindu Mecca.*
>
> *Continuing, Sr. Adv. C.S. Vaidyanathan read out Muslim witness statements describing lakhs of Hindus descending upon the disputed site to perform parikrama around it. He used this as an opportunity to reiterate his argument that*

[80]'Day 29 Arguments, Ayodhya Title Dispute', *Supreme Court Observer*, 20 August 2019, https://tinyurl.com/4kjbx9vj. Accessed on 18 January 2025.

> *the Ram Janam Asthan extends beyond the central dome. Multiple witness statements describe the performance of parikrama around the entire site.*
>
> *Finally, he summarised his interpretation of the documentary and oral evidences. He argued that the evidences demonstrate that Hindus believe the site is the Ram Janam Asthan. He argued that worship never ceased, even when a mosque was built at the site. He said that the presence of the deity is in perpetuity.*
>
> *He clarified that he had not dealt with the oral evidence tied to the ASI report. He said he would submit such evidence if the other parties questioned its evidentiary value.*

Mr Vaidyanathan had for the team Ram Lalla successfully achieved what he wanted to. He repeatedly pointed out in his submissions the recovery of figures and figurines by ASI from the disputed site, and linked them to the question of whether such artefacts are found in a mosque or a temple. He tried to establish that the same place is called Ram Janmabhoomi by Hindus and Babri Masjid by Muslims, even from the witnesses of the opposing side, and in the submission, Muslim witnesses agreed that just like Mecca is sacred to Muslims, so is Ayodhya to Hindus.[81]

The faith of Hindus always worshipping at the disputed site and reinforcing their belief in the disputed site being the Janmasthan, the case was now being deliberated at the

---

[81]Ayodhya case (Day 8): "'Existence of 12th-century temple is proved" Senior Advocate Vaidyanathan submits', *Latest Laws.com*, 20 August 2019, https://tinyurl.com/3ey7p8xm. Accessed on 18 January 2025.

Also *see*: Written Submission No. A104, The Submissions on behalf of Plaintiff in Suit No.5 by Mr. C.S. Vaidyanathan, Sr. Adv., *Vada Prativada*, https://tinyurl.com/5a4xzr69. Accessed on 18 January 2025.

Also *see*: Written Submission No. A116, The Submissions on behalf of the Appellants by Mr. C.S.Vaidyanathan, Sr. Adv., *Vada Prativada*, https://tinyurl.com/46m8kj96. Accessed on 18 January 2025.

highest level. This understanding that the presence and continued worship of Ram Lalla at the site was sufficient to establish the case was also based on the faith and belief of the lawyers who were Ram bhakts themselves. As far as what constituted a mosque and the practice of the other side, only essential requirements were being advanced. Caution was being exercised so that one would not venture deep into the practices of other faiths and religions. However, what could one do if it became unavoidable or if the judges themselves asked any question in which you had to go into the testimony of witnesses of the other side or even the stand of the other side? Well, yes! Testimonies of the other side/Muslim witnesses were also delved into. After all, it could not be denied that this was a case between two communities trying to establish their claim on a property. Though only a property dispute, it was a property dispute between two communities which had elevated the case to the status of being contentious. Hence, even the judges asked pertinent questions on the practice of faith and belief. As Mr Vaidyanathan submitted, the floor of the disputed structure building was constructed over the floor of an earlier structure that was a massive Hindu temple. A website, latestlaws.com[82], reported:

> *[...] Mr. Vaidyanathan submitted that terracotta figures of animals like crocodile, tortoise were discovered at the disputed site, and as per the archaeologists' disposition, animal figures are never seen in any mosque.*
>
> *[...]*
>
> *Justice Chandrachud asked the counsel to state references that show that the earlier structure was of 12th Century.*
>
> *Mr. Vaidyanathan stated that a stone slab was recovered, which contained an inscription in Sanskrit from the 12th*

[82]Ibid.

Century. He said that when the mosque was demolished in 1992, the slab was among various items which were recovered. It had medieval text, which mentioned about the King Govinda Chandra who ruled Saketa Mandala from 1114–1155 AD, of which Ayodhya was the capital. The verses said a big Vishnu temple was built there. Mr. Vaidyanathan submitted that this Vishnu temple is the structure that was excavated by the Archaeological Survey of India.

Justice Chandrachud asked whether the translation of the Sanskrit text or if its authenticity were challenged [...]

Mr. Vaidyanathan answered that there was no challenge to the translation of the contents of the slab and the authenticity of the inscription. He said the challenge was with respect to the fact whether it was recovered from the disputed area or not.

[...]

Mr. Vaidyanathan read out depositions by various witnesses who used to visit the disputed site.

Ramnath Mishra (OPW5) had stated that Ayodhya was in a festive mood every day; thousands of devotees used to come every year for the darshan of Lord Ram, and it is believed that Ram was born under the central dome. The testimony also stated if keys of certain portions were kept in possession of Nirmohi Akhara [...]

[...] Another witness (PW7) said that the inner portion was locked and barricaded, but even then, people used to worship from a distance. Justice Ashok Bhushan observed that there was a difference between south India and north India on the degree of access which devotees had to the temples. In most of the temples in south India, only the priest had access to the sanctum sanctorum. That might not be the case in north India.

> *Justice Bobde pointed out that Mr. Vaidyanathan said that none of the Hindu witnesses saw namaz being offered there; he asked 'were there Muslim witnesses who said that they offered namaz?'*
>
> *Mr. Vaidyanathan then read out the evidence given by Muslim witnesses. Mohammad Hashib (PW1) had stated that the place attached is called Ram Janam Bhumi by Hindus, and Babri Masjid by Muslims. Just like Mecca is important for Muslims, so is Ayodhya for Hindus.*
>
> *Another Muslim witness (PW4) stated that a mosque cannot be built on a forcibly occupied place. If it is proved that a temple was demolished and a mosque was built there, then Muslims will not consider it as a mosque.*
>
> *One Muslim witness has said that Hindus believe that the Janam Asthan is where Lord Ram was born, and worship the place, while people greet each other by saying 'Jai Ram ji'.*
>
> *Mahant Bhaskar Das (PW23) had stated that he had been visiting the disputed site and performed worship as a priest. He said that the idols were placed inside the disputed structure even before 1934, and continued to remain there till 1992 […]*

The combined evidence, be it travelogues or gazetteer reports, the ASI report, depositions, had to be analysed in totality. The stone slab which had an inscription that on translation talked about a Ram temple in Ayodhya in the 12th-century CE was just one of the pieces of evidence. The translation of the inscription on the slab was not doubted by the other side. However, the opposing side highlighted that there was no reliable proof to substantiate that the stone slab was recovered from the same site.

Issues of Concern

As the case went on, while things seemed to be falling in place at an ostensible level, back at the chambers, there were issues of concern. As the hearing on evidence continued, Senior Parasaran's persistent habit of taking notes and trying to be present in court throughout the case, without missing a single hearing, took its toll. One morning, he had to leave for the court before 9 a.m., and was found to be in court running a high temperature. Now his health was getting to be a matter of serious concern.

Doctors were consulted. Proper and adequate sleep was advised, apart from other steps to get over extreme fatigue, which any human being at the age of ninety-two would feel because of arguing while standing for three straight days, and then coming back to work in the office. A compromise was reached between the doctors and a reluctant Senior Parasaran. He would desist from reading for a few days and only take briefings.

For one night, this rule was followed. But guess what? Now Anirudh, Ashwin or Aditi had to read judgements and he would listen and dictate notes from bed. Most of the time, he kept his promise of giving his eyes adequate rest by keeping them closed. Sometimes, the exasperated look on his family members' faces said it all. They did their best to hide it, but quite often they failed. Senior Parasaran tired and exhausted was not a good sight to behold for either the family or the assisting team. Yet, even in this condition, his mind was totally immersed in the case. He would go to court, maybe return a bit early and then, instead of resting, take stock of the case.

One fine day, while Bhakti and Yogeswaran were briefing Senior Parasaran on the archaeological evidence, the nonagenarian felt rejuvenated enough to share the complete story of his association with Ram to his anxious but appreciative team. The fact is, Mr Parasaran wore his spiritual leanings on his sleeve.

When asked why he preferred to read the Ramayana every day over other religious and spiritual texts, he had even told the court that he was appearing in the case 'as a client'.

For him, Ram was like no other. Ram always stood at the highest pedestal. He looked at the life of Ram as always fulfilling his duties towards others. A teenage Ram was sent with Rishi Vishwamitra to fight demons; Ram never complained. After getting married, he was banished to the forest; Ram never complained. He loved Sita enough to search for her everywhere possible, cross over to Lanka and get her back. He performed his duties and never complained. When he sent Sita to the forest bound by his duties as a king, not as a husband, he never remarried. Ram just performed his duties.

Then came Senior Parasaran's advice. He believed that in all religions, in some manner or the other, some chants exist. Chanting is good for everyone. But for young people, reading the Ramayana is highly beneficial and they should remember that reading the Ramayana changes one's life for good.

Now Senior Parasaran was praying to Ram for strength to see the case through. Nirmohi Akhara, though, was bringing in another challenge and literally in third dimension.

15

Nirmohi Akhara's Challenge

The Supreme Court Bench had granted time to Nirmohi Akhara to present its evidence. And Nirmohi Akhara had to also firm up its thoughts. It had opposed the plea of Ram Lalla Virajman in its written submission and opposed the maintainability of the suit of Ram Lalla on the ground that only Nirmohi Akhara could maintain or initiate a suit, and not Ram Lalla or Ram Janambhoomi. For team Ram Lalla, the key question was 'Can a *sevak*/servant/manager/employee oppose the suit of one's own god, that he/she is meant to serve?' Does the opposition to Ram Lalla by Nirmohi Akhara not itself prove that the case of Ram Lalla would not have been effectively and efficiently represented by Nirmohi Akhara had Ram Lalla and Ram Janmabhoomi not themselves approached the court?

Well, proving the presence of Ram Lalla and his worshippers (which could include Nirmohi Akhara as well) was one challenge. Proving the title/right of ownership of Nirmohi Akhara from documents of title or any other evidence was another. Presence on the land itself does not make a party the owner of the land. Detailed notes would be written down by the counsels and the team assisting them when the arguments would go on. You need to see how good lawyers and judges are at taking notes to believe it—it's an art in itself. Just from their notes, judges can pinpoint with accuracy what was argued on an earlier date. Judges also have phenomenal memories. The amount of reading done by a judge is phenomenal. Members of the bar almost universally agree that the workload of a judge is quite punishing. With all the justified criticism with respect to pendency of cases, one must also look at the workload that the Supreme Court judges have to take on. There are two sides to every coin.

Incidentally, jotting notes is a similarity between journalists and law graduates too.

Coming back to the case, so, what had Nirmohi Akhara argued? A short list of answers would be[83]:

1. *Ram Lalla's suit is not maintainable and should be dismissed. That is Suit 5.*
2. *Idols were present under the central dome before December 1949. Nirmohi Akhara was in divergence with Ram Lalla's suit as it did not say that idols were always present under the central dome. It differed.*
3. *Nirmohi Akhara did not support the point that the land, Ram Janmabhoomi can be a Juristic Person. Later a conditional agreement was given. Nirmohi Akhara would agree to this point only if all other Hindu sides support their case and accepted them as the shebait and not otherwise.*
4. *Nirmohi Akhara would not exclude others from worship if they got the land. It would allow all to worship.*
5. *They also relied upon travelogues and refer to Carnegy's report.*
6. *Nirmohi Akhara talked about Hindus offering prayer from the iron railing.*

The *Supreme Court Observer* covered this point:

> *1.24 Nirmohi Akhara's historical presence (cross-examinations and law lectures)*
>
> *Sr. Adv. S. K. Jain presented additional historical documents to show the presence of Nirmohi Akhara and their*

[83]'Day 31 Arguments, Ayodhya Title Dispute', *Supreme Court Observer*, 22 August 2019, https://tinyurl.com/bdfkzsyt. Accessed on 18 January 2025.
Also *see*: Written Submission No. A26 on behalf of the Appellant Nirmohi Akhara by Mr. S.K. Jain, Sr. Adv., *Vada Prativada*, https://tinyurl.com/6tkk6scr. Accessed on 18 January 2025.

management of the temple and idols [...] (Presence of Nirmohi Akhara not disputed after 1950).

The bench noted that devotees were only allowed to give prayers at the railing, and the dome was locked. Sr. Adv. S. K. Jain submitted that Nirmohi Akhara has the keys to the dome, referencing witness testimony stating that the locks were in control of Nirmohi Akhara.

Sr. Adv. S. K. Jain argued that management of the Akhara cannot be disputed and stated that even if Nirmohi Akhara permitted access to other Hindus to access the site, it would not forfeit its management rights.[84]

7. *The Sunni Board has/had no interest in the land and the place always was and is a temple. Therefore, the disputed site can only be given to Hindus.*
8. *Since Nirmohi Akhara is the valid shebait, the disputed land could be handed over only to Nirmohi Akhara among Hindus and all the other claims of all other Hindu parties had to be rejected.*

Their case was that the disputed site was a place of Hindu worship and must be handed over to them. They have been there on the site for a long time and have always worshipped Ram Lalla at the site.

Following the arguments keenly, during the team Ram Lalla meetings, Senior Parasaran would emphasize that Nirmohi Akhara, like Ram Lalla's side, had referred to historical accounts as well. It was clear that there were no two views on the fact that the Nirmohis were genuine Ram bhakts. The historical accounts of P. Carnegy on this matter were used, and Nirmohi Akhara had successfully emphasized its historical presence at the disputed spot. However, the crucial point was their submission of offering

[84]'Day 33 Arguments, Ayodhya Title Dispute', *Supreme Court Observer*, 26 August 2019, https://tinyurl.com/29sturz4. Accessed on 18 January 2025.

prayers from the railings towards the central dome post-1857–1858. Nirmohi Akhara was on the same page as Ram Lalla's case on this point.

With Nirmohi Akhara having completed its turn, a stock-taking exercise became imperative. What had the Akhara gained—or lost—through its arguments? Senior Parasaran was carefully reviewing his notes to ensure no point had been overlooked. However, intermittent watering of his eyes made it difficult to jot down everything. When he addressed his team, he began by acknowledging these physical constraints as the reason for the imperfections in his notes—almost like a pupil explaining to a watchful teacher why his notebook was less than perfect.

Senior Parasaran could not see much of a reason why the Akhara should oppose Suit 5 of Ram Lalla Virajman. 'What do they gain by it?' He was perplexed that the Akhara stood its ground and did not change its stand unconditionally.

Ashwin and Aditi pointed out that the oscillating stand of Nirmohi Akhara seemed to leave even the judges a bit confused as to the direction in which the Akhara's case was heading. Bhakti added that what Nirmohi Akhara would gain by opposing Ram Lalla Virajman's suit and Ram Janmabhoomi as a Juristic Person was unfathomable.

The Ram Lalla case was such that Nirmohi Akhara could not succeed if the claim of Bhagwan Ram Lalla itself is defeated. How can there be a serviceman/manager or a shebait without a lord or deity?

Senior Parasaran had a probing question: 'What was the documentary evidence that Nirmohi Akhara presented to substantiate their claims even before the Allahabad High Court? In the whole bunch of evidence that Nirmohi have [sic] submitted, I do not remember any document saying much. Bhakti was the only person uniquely placed in the team to answer such issues dealing with [the] Allahabad High Court and was the right person to conform [sic] that no documentary evidence was produced even before the Allahabad High Court by Nirmohi Akhara.'

Ashwin joined in with a pointed intervention: 'What Nirmohi Akhara claimed was that they do not oppose the deity, but they oppose the "next friend" of the deity. So, Suit 5 is not maintainable, and that all their evidence got stolen in a dacoity.' Everyone then turned toward Senior Parasaran, eager to hear his opinion. 'See, I could not hear and note down that their documents were stolen. I totally missed it. I will be careful with my hearing aids,' he confessed sheepishly.

The moot issue, however, was of the shebaiti rights of Nirmohi Akhara. Merely doing puja, *arati* (ceremonial worship of a deity with a lamp) does not make for a shebait. Therefore, the issue that arose was, apart from asserting performance of puja and arati, what else did Nirmohi Akhara undertake to establish that they are the shebait? If there was nothing more, then their case ended. If they had proved that they were the shebait, they would get the exclusive rights to file a suit and then Suit 5 of Ram Lalla and Ram Janmabhoomi would have been dismissed. There are conditions one must fulfil to be declared a shebait. The question was, did Nirmohi Akhara assert that it fulfilled all the conditions required to be a shebait, and did it adduce evidence to fulfil all the conditions?

Senior Parasaran wanted to know the opinions of others on how the hearing of Nirmohi Akhara went and what he had missed due to trouble with his hearing aids. In the court, Mr Jain had to face a lot of questions. This was well reflected in the media; the ringside action was as follows:

> *Mr. Jain stated that the shebait is like the Karta of a family. He relied on witness testimonies to submit that there were no allegations that Nirmohi Akhara misused its rights or did anything adverse to the deity, which were the only grounds on which Shebaitship rights can be taken away. Justice Bobde sought clarification on the issue that since the Nirmohi Akhara*

was not claiming ownership, only management rights, what all did they manage? To which, Mr. Jain replied that conducting puja-aarti at the disputed site was done and controlled by them. Justice Chandrachud then observed that the job of Nirmohi Akhara seemed simply to ensure that puja is done, and offerings are received as per rituals and traditions.[85]

Relying on oral evidence, Mr Jain stated that nobody has disputed their Shebaitship and possession of over 150 years, of both the inner and outer courtyards.

Justice Chandrachud observed that the job of Nirmohi Akhara is simply to ensure that puja is done, offerings are received as per rituals and traditions.

Mr. Jain said that giving 1/3rd of the disputed property to Ram Lalla and Sunni waqf board was 'wrong', he said that they cannot be given possession, decree should have been passed in favour of Nirmohi Akhara only.

He went on with submissions stating that when digging was by the Archaeology Department, under the chabootra another chabootra was found exactly beneath it. Relying on witness testimonies he submitted that the disputed structure was never used as a mosque till 1856-57, and no historic evidence has been found to show that namaz was offered there.

Justice Bobde told Mr. Jain to focus on those evidences which support his case and prove his right of Shebaitship.

Mr.Jain stated that "There were tons of documents establishing the right of shebaitship, but in dacoity they all have got stolen."

[85]Ayodhya Case (Day 12): '"In the suits in which deity is vitally interested, it has to be heard" Justice Chandrachud says', *Latest Laws.com*, 26 August 2019, https://tinyurl.com/78hmdvvf. Accessed on 18 January 2025.

After quoting a number of witness testimonies, Mr. Jain submitted that presence of Nirmohi Akhara and its possession has never been doubted, there is no dispute about it. He stated that the Allahabad High Court has also recognised in its impugned judgement that Nirmohi Akhara was managing the affairs even after idols were placed under the central dome of the disputed structure.[86]

God and His Servant

There was an interesting contest between the right of Ram Lalla Virajman as well as Ram Janmabhoomi to initiate Suit 5. The stand of Nirmohi Akhara oscillated. An interesting point was whether the case of the manager of God/Nirmohi Akhara would have any meaning if the case of God failed. The exchange between the counsel for Nirmohi Akhara and the judges brought out the interdependence between the case of the shebait and the case of God. *Latest Laws.com* covered this part of the exchange.

Justice Chandrachud told Mr. Jain that he has categorically denied that Plaintiff No. 1 and Plaintiff No. 2 in Suit 5 are juridical persons, however in his oral submissions he says that they are juridical persons, but the moment he accepts that they are juridical persons, they have right to be represented by counsels.

Justice Chandrachud asked him that if the suit of the deity fails, who will he be shebait for? "You stand together, you fall together" Justice Chandrachud added.

Mr. Jain said that his only endeavour it to get his suit accepted. This prompted Justice Bobde to ask, "Should we take it then that you are not seeking dismissal of Suit 5?" Mr. Jain

[86]Ibid.

stated that in this regard he will be able to make a statement tomorrow.

Justice Chandrachud told Mr. Jain that there is no boundary between his claim as a shebait and claim of Plaintiff No. 3 as next friend, because even if the case is decreed in their favour, Nirmohi Akhara can independently claim shebaitship.

Justice Chandrachud further explained that the moment he said that Plaintiff No. 1 and Plaintiff No. 2 are juridical persons, there is no conflict between his suit and their suit, and even if the suit is decreed in their favour, he will still be entitled to assert his cause of action.

Justice Chandrachud told him that he is unnecessarily entering an area of conflict which does not belong to him, it belongs to Sunni Central Waqf Board.

Mr. Jain was further told Justice Chandrachud that his case is that Suit no. 5 cannot be maintained, then the only consequence would be dismissal of the Suit, and if the Suit no. 5 is dismissed, he should consider what the consequences would be for him, he cannot be shebait for a mosque.

Justice Chandrachud said that his submission should be to independently accept his suit, without opposing to Suit no. 5.

Agreeing, Mr. Jain submitted that his endeavour is this only, but the possession has to be handed over to him.

Quoting from precedents, Mr. Jain stated that an idol is certainly a juridical person, who can hold property, has power to sue, be sued in respect of the property, but its personality is linked with physical personality of Shebiat.

Relying on caselaws, Mr. Jain further submitted that it has been held that shebait can maintain a suit on behalf of the deity in his own name and need not implead the deity as a party to any case.

> *Justice Chandrachud pointed out that in the suits in which deity is vitally interested, it has to be heard. Mr. Jain said that the personality of idol is merged with the shebiat, and the shebiat is suing on behalf of the deity. However, Mr. Jain said that plaintiff in the suit of next friend has mentioned that Shebiat is not acting in the interest of deity.*
>
> *Justice Chandrachud explained that if a claim is brought by debtor or there is a suit for recovery of property belonging to the deity, then you will not implead the deity, because in such a situation shebait may represent the deity, but in a situation where it has to be established whether a person is his or her shebait, then the deity clearly has right to implead and ascertain whether this person has the Shebaitship.*[87]

Such was the interest in the battle in court that many a time, reports, especially on web portals, were presented to Senior Parasaran to show how the media was reporting court exchanges in detail. For Mr Parasaran, it was indeed a revelation how the reporting was so detailed and live—a new trend in the field of law in India. For a media-shy person, he probably looked at it with horror and some contemplation. 'We may soon have what they call live telecast of court cases in India, won't we?'

Senior Parasaran was also of the opinion that the prayers at the railing, and the parikrama undertaken by the devotees around the disputed site were very important pieces of evidence, which Nirmohi Akhara too relied upon, but he still wondered: 'What does Nirmohi Akhara want? Nirmohis were trying to give fatal blows to Ram Lalla's case while also proving worship of Ram Lalla at the same site. Even after the judges having grilled them, Nirmohis perhaps didn't realize that they must sail with Ram Lalla Virajman or else they sink.'

Nirmohi Akhara's challenge was keeping the team on their toes. Additionally, their concern about the health of their Senior

[87]Ibid.

kept growing. It was a strange dilemma—Senior Parasaran had to press on, yet he was in dire need of rest as well.

Despite his painfully red eyes, Senior Parasaran would work as usual even against medical advice. Fortunately, his turn to appear before the court was some days away and, therefore, it was fervently hoped by his team, family and well-wishers that his sleep could be regulated through the pills prescribed by his doctors, and he could get some rest. Eventually, the team would discover that the *Supreme Court Observer*[88] had reported the Akhara's days in court as follows:

> *1.23 Reference to P. Carnegy to establish historical possession of Nirmohi Akhara*
>
> *Sr. Adv. S. K. Jain described how British archaeologist Patrick Carnegy wrote a report in 1870 that referenced Nirmohi Akhara. Justice Chandrachud directed Sr. Adv. S. K. Jain to present documents directly relevant to the Akhara's shebait claim.*
>
> *However, Sr. Adv. S. K. Jain returned briefly to P. Carnegy's work, referencing a 19th-century sketch of Faizabad to establish that Nirmohi Akhara's name has continuously been included in historical records. Further, he read out accounts that referenced Nirmohi Akhara in gazetteers.*
>
> *Justice Bobde stated that these historical accounts did not conclusively establish the Akhara's shebait rights. Sr. Adv. S. K. Jain argued that the accounts established the Nirmohi Akhara's possession of the site. He submitted that references to a 'property Hindu' should be read to mean the Nirmohi Akhara.*
>
> *Sr. Adv. S. K. Jain referenced a historical agreement executed in 1900, whereby Nirmohi Akhara took responsibility for*

[88]'Day 33 Arguments, Ayodhya Title Dispute', *Supreme Court Observer*, 26 August 2019, https://tinyurl.com/29sturz4. Accessed on 18 January 2025.

> *providing water to travellers. Sr. Adv. S. K. Jain argued that this was an example of the Nirmohi Akhara performing its duty as the shebait.*

The facts were becoming clearer now that Nirmohi Akhara was establishing the claim of performing prayers at the disputed site. The effect of Nirmohi Akhara's presence would bolster the claims of Suit 5 of Ram Lalla on facts, yet on the grounds of law, they opposed Ram Lalla's suit and challenged the maintainability of Ram Lalla's suit which could destroy the whole claim of Ram Lalla Virajman. That, in short, was Nirmohi Akhara's case.

Mr Ranjit Kumar sought to bring in a dimension of the position of Ayodhya in 1949-50. He referred to a total of 14 affidavits, including that of Jan Mohammed, Abdul Sattar, Abdul Gani, Rojid, Hosaldar, Ramzan, Gulle Khan, Md. Ismile Abdul Sakoor, Abdul Razaqe, Naseebdar who, in their respective affidavits, all dated 16.02.1950, had stated that the Babri Mosque was erected by demolishing Ram Janmabhoomi Temple but in spite of the erection of said mosque, Hindus did not give up their possession and Hindus were all along worshipping their idol therein. Muslims were able to offer prayer therein only on Fridays with the help of the forces of the nawabs. These affidavits also seemed to support the contention that Muslims of Ayodhya who deposed had no problem if the land was given to Hindus and they believed that the disputed site was not the appropriate place in religion for offering their prayers.

An important aspect of the statements of these witnesses was that they were never cross-examined and the admissibility of these statements as evidence was under a cloud. However, Mr Kumar submitted that these affidavits were looked into by the Civil Judge in the case when the order of injunction/stay was confirmed on 3 March 1951, wherein it is noted:

> *[...]it further appears from the copies of number of affidavits of certain Muslims residents of Ayodhya that at least*

from1936 onwards the Muslims have neither used the site as a mosque nor offered prayers there.

This order of the learned Civil Judge was confirmed by the High Court in the appeal on 26April 1955.

The court then heard Senior Advocate P.N. Mishra for Shankaracharya connected to the Janam SthanPunroddhan Samiti—Shankaracharya Surupananda Ji Maharaj of Dwarka Pith, Defendant 20 in Suit 4.

Mr P.N. Mishra raised questions on what could be considered a valid mosque and what could not be considered one? He went into the issue of establishing a valid mosque as laid down in the Holy Koran and Hadith, and valid or invalid Islamic practices. A few other counsels followed.

However, the focus of the case and the evidence centred majorly around Ram Lalla and Nirmohi Akhara's suits.

Dr Rajeev Dhavan had made a few interventions when the Hindu side was arguing. Dr Dhavan's journey from Allahabad to some of the top universities of the world was very well known. As a scholar, he required no introduction. Additionally, he was the author of several books. As an academician, he had taught and lectured at several universities across the world. His present status as one of the leading names in the Indian bar was also well known. Dr Dhavan's commitment to this case and his contribution to the development of the law of the land were evident to all. One could deduce that he was passionately involved in the case. He was leading the Muslim side and was the most important pillar of the case from the opposing side.

SECTION III

THE OPPOSING SIDE

16

The Opposing Side

The court is an interesting place—a modern-day arena where great minds battle it out. Lawyers contest cases for their clients, often fighting their way out of tight corners on behalf of their clients. However bitter the contest, it is left behind as the battling lawyers step out of the courtroom, often to share tales over a cup of tea or coffee. If you were a fly on the wall, you may even hear them support or oppose each other's clients, and sometimes even jointly oppose or jointly support an objective. The line in the sand for lawyers is that the case ends in the court itself. After that, it's a new day, rather a new moment, a new contest, and a new tale to tell. A lawyer may have an adversary for today with whom he can discuss and share information for tomorrow's common client. As Senior Parasaran would often say, 'Do as adversaries do in law, strike mightily but wine and dine together.' There was, however, no denying that there were moments of intense conflict too.

Dr Rajeev Dhavan started his submissions for the Sunni Board on 2 September. At the very outset, he stated that Zafaryab Jilani, Meenakshi Arora and Nizam Pasha would follow him. Dr Dhavan was assisted by an affable and ever-pleasant Advocate-on-Record, Mr Ejaz Maqbool. Every day, before the hearing, Dr Dhavan would greet the sadhus and Mr Champat Rai from the Vishwa Hindu Parishad present in the court as well as those involved with the Ram Lalla side or Nirmohi Akhara side. He would go on to exchange greetings and pleasantries with Senior Parasaran or exchange a few notes and anecdotes or chat till the legal contest began.

The suit of the Sunni Board made for an interesting read on the history and legal jugglery that all lawyers engage in, and that characterizes every suit. Some more, some less. In this case, none of the suits could be decided in isolation as all the suits were heard together, evidence was analysed in the totality of all the five suits filed, and then, judgement was rendered by the Allahabad High Court. Therefore, it would be necessary to go over what the Sunni Board said then, in Suit 4.

Suit 4 was instituted on 18 December 1961 by the Sunni Central Waqf Board and nine Muslim residents of Ayodhya. It was stated that the suit had been instituted on behalf of the entire Muslim community, and the entire Hindu community was made opposing parties to the suit. The suit was based on history, asserting the existence of a historic mosque known commonly as the Babri Masjid which was constructed by Babur more than 433 years ago following his conquest of India and the occupation of its territories. The pleadings further stated that the mosque was built for use as a place of worship for Muslims in general, and for the performance of religious ceremonies. The main construction of the mosque was depicted by the letters A B C D on the plan annexed to the plaint of the Sunni Board.

The presence of a graveyard adjoining the land was also stated. The Sunni Board had stated that as per their religious belief, both the mosque and the graveyard stood already vested in the Almighty, and since the mosque's construction, it had been used by Muslims for offering prayers while the graveyard had been used for burial. In this context, it was averred that a cash grant was paid from the Royal Treasury for the upkeep and maintenance of the mosque, which was continued by the Nawab Wazir of Oudh.

After the annexation of Oudh, the British Government continued with the cash *nankar*s (grants) until 1864 in the form of revenue-free grants in the villages of Sholapur and Bahoranpur in the vicinity of Ayodhya. The plaint also referred to the riots of

1934 and to the restoration work of parts of the mosque that were damaged in the riots, at government expense. According to the Sunni Board, following the enactment of the UP Muslim Waqfs Act 1936, an inquiry was conducted by the commissioner of waqfs, and the commissioner's report was published in the official gazette. The plaint claimed that Muslims had been in peaceful possession of the mosque which was used for prayer until 23 December 1949 when a crowd of Hindus entered the mosque and desecrated it by placing idols inside.[89]

The suit then stated that the title was vested in the Sunni Board through possession of the disputed land for a long time. In legal language, the Sunni Board also claimed adverse possession. It stated, assuming without admitting, that even if there had existed a Hindu temple as alleged by Hindus on the site on which the mosque was built 433 years ago by Emperor Babur, Muslims, by virtue of their long, exclusive, and continuous possession, commencing from the construction of the mosque which continued till 1949, had title/ownership by adverse possession.

There was another specific part of pleading mired in history which would create a flutter later.

The suit gave a history of other suits and the orders through which Hindus had been permitted to perform puja of the idols placed within the mosque. The plea also stated that Muslims have been prevented from entering the disputed site.

The suit was amended following the demolition of the Babri Masjid to place on record subsequent facts and events. According to the Sunni Board, a mosque did not require any particular structure and even after the demolition of the mosque, the land on which it stood continued to remain a mosque in which they were entitled to offer prayers. The pleadings stated that the cause of action for the suit arose on 23 December 1949 when Hindus

---

[89]Para 6 of Supreme Court Judgment, *api.sci.gov.in*, https://tinyurl.com/mr2arh5b. Accessed on 18 January 2025.

were alleged to have wrongfully entered the mosque.[90]

As Dr Dhavan continued his arguments, the rigours of the profession, that of taking notes, now fell on the assisting team of the temple side. Team Maqbool was now neck-deep in work while the lawyers for the Hindu sides found themselves relatively relaxed, focusing on listening to the arguments presented by the other side and taking notes. The notes of Senior Parasaran's team would reflect the salient points of Dr Dhavan's submissions for the Sunni Board side:

1. Suit 5 of Ram Lalla is not maintainable and liable to be dismissed. The land Ram Janmasthan as titled in the suit cannot sue or maintain a case in its own name. Ram Janmasthan cannot be a Juristic Person.
2. Placing of idols in a mosque is illegal usurpation of the property.
3. The parties supporting Ram Lalla's case cannot succeed in the present dispute. Hindus must identify the exact birthplace of Lord Ram with accuracy and not a particular area. They must prove that Lord Ram was born under the central dome of, where lay The Babri Masjid. Suit No.5 as well as other suits do not advance sufficient evidence to identify the exact birthplace of Ram and fail to prove that Ram was born under the central dome.
4. Belief of Ram bhakts alone is no proof or evidence to declare Ram Janmabhoomi/Janmasthan as a Juristic Person. Belief alone cannot establish Juristic Persons.
5. Faith and religious scriptures are irrelevant to adjudicate such disputes as the present one.
6. Evidence of the Hindu side is unreliable and do [sic] not pass the scrutiny of law. No pointed or reliable evidence has been advanced to point out that parikrama routes delineate the boundaries of Ram Janmabhoomi. Ram Janmabhoomi also does not fulfil the test and criteria of a swayambhu deity.

[90]Ibid.

7. The disputed site is subject to Quranic law. Just because historical texts do not mention mosques, it does not mean no mosque was present at the disputed sites.
8. India's modern legal system began in 1858 and Vedic law cannot be relied upon. The principles of justice, equity, and good conscience[91] were relied upon in the 19th century by the British and inherited by Indian legal system and that only shall apply.
9. Ram Lalla Virajman cannot sue or maintain a case in his own name. Only a shebait has the right to sue for the deity/God which suit has already been filed by Nirmohi Akhara. So that ends the case of Ram Lalla Virajman.
10. It was argued that the judgement of Justice Sudhir Agarwal of the Allahabad High Court was based on 'conjectures or preponderance of probability'. Dr Dhavan raised a point—how do you do a preponderance of probability of historical dates? His point was that the court was being urged to do guesswork.

Among all these submissions opposing Ram Lalla's suit, the tangent of Nirmohi Akhara kept haunting the parties.

It seemed that the Sunni Board was supporting Nirmohi Akhara, but to what effect? A particular submission by the Sunni Board created a huge flutter. Those following the case scrambled to ensure that what they heard and understood was right. This also led to many consultations within the side of Ram Lalla. It was, therefore, imperative to see what reporters captured. The *Supreme Court Observer*[92] reported on the 2 September hearing about Dr Dhavan's submission:

> *7.1.1 Cannot rely on Vedic law*
>
> *He submitted that India's modern legal system began in 1858 and argued that vedic law cannot be relied upon. 'What is the*

[91]A42 Submission No.1 by Dr. Rajeev Dhavan, Sr. Adv., *Vada Prativada*, https://tinyurl.com/3p5p4ujn. Accessed on 18 January 2025.

[92]'Day 38 Arguments, Ayodhya Title Dispute', *Supreme Court Observer*, 2 September 2019, https://tinyurl.com/2b4juyws.Accessed on 18 January 2025.

law that Your Lordships has inherited? The law we follow is not Vedic law. Your Lordships' legal system starts in 1858,' he submitted.

Providing a genealogy of contemporary Indian law, he referred to Hindu law as Anglo-Hindu law. He submitted that interpretations of Hindu law are dependent on British law.

7.1.2 Hindu parties' evidence is unreliable

He disputed the nature of evidence being relied upon by the Hindu parties, Ram Lala in particular. He submitted that the parikrama (circumambulation) performed at Ram Jamnabhoomi cannot be treated as evidence. Recall that CS Vaidyanathan relied on the area of the parikrama to demarcate the area which belonged to Ram Lala. Rajeev Dhavan made a similar claim about the swayambhu (manifestation of idols).

[…]

7.1.4 Cannot use historical texts to frame negative inferences

He defined the limits of historical accounts in so far as they can be used to deduce material facts. He argued that historical texts cannot be relied upon to make negative inferences. In other words, if something is not mentioned in a historical text, like the presence of mosque, one cannot reliably infer that it did not exist.

7.1.5 Ram Lala's suit is not maintainable

He questioned the maintainability of Ram Lala's suit, emphasising that no Hindu party rebutted the Nirmohi Akhara's stand.

He challenged the deity's right to sue as a juristic person, highlighting various cases. He argued that Ram Lala's suit was not maintainable as the deity lacked locus standi. He argued that only the shebait has the right to sue for the deity.

He concluded the morning session by stating that the secular fabric of the Constitution is under threat if the rights of Muslims are ignored.

For 4 September 2019, the *Supreme Court Observer* recorded, among other issues, that in Dr Dhavan's submission, there was lack of integrity in the Faizabad officials, especially in 1949, when the idols were allegedly placed below the central dome. It was argued that Dr Dhavan's clients were not the favoured ones for the officials and the Hindu side were the favoured ones by the officials during various time spans.

Dr Dhavan further stressed that the maps relied upon by Ram Lalla's side were not reliable and janmasthan and janmabhoomi were not the same:[93]

7.3.4 Hindu parties' maps are based on surmise

He disputed the maps relied upon by Ram Lala, Nirmohi Akhara and other Hindu parties, arguing that the division of land proposed is based entirely on surmise. He submitted that their land claims rest on the 'Swayambhu' (divine self-manifestation) arguments, which do not justify any claims on 'other composite' areas.

Rajeev Dhavan submitted that the Ram Janmabhoomi and Ram Janmasthan are not synonymous. He requested the court to keep this mind when considering the prayers of individual plaintiffs.

The Sunni Board's attack on the submissions of the counsel for Hindus side was pointed and in-depth. Dr Dhavan was trying to build a convincing case of lack of evidence. He took a holistic view of the case and presented the Sunni Board's attack on Suit 5 as well as on Suit 3. The suit of Ram Lalla had advanced historical evidence in the form of travelogues, gazetteers, ancient texts and then the ASI report.

[93]Ibid.

Any holistic reply to Suit 5 had to consider the historical facts of neutral parties against whom no bias had been alleged, and then the court appointed the ASI's report. Dr Dhavan was negating the use of any history or historical evidence which was pre-1858 in deciding the case. He meant that all historical evidence pre-1858 had to be discarded. He disputed the presence of any massive ancient structure pre-1528 at the disputed site and discarded the effect of the presence of symbols such as a lotus or a peacock as symbols which would identify the disputed structure as a Hindu structure.[94]

But would abandoning history prior to 1858 not affect the Sunni Board's own case adversely too? This was to be tested, but for now, history was being shown its limitations. A reply giving the overall theme of the Sunni Board's case was covered in various reports. One report which was later discussed among the team Ram Lalla members was *The Indian Express*[95] report of 3 September. It carried the line of attack on archaeology and the historical evidence that Ram Lalla's side had sought to advance, and matched their notes. Senior Parasaran and Mr Vaidyanathan though did not bother much about the reports; the team didn't see any harm either in sometimes reading them. The report, while discussing Dr Dhavan's submission, read as follows:

> *[...] There was no massive structure at the site and no Hindu motifs. Just because there is a peacock or lotus does not mean they are Hindu," Senior Advocate Rajeev Dhavan, appearing for the main appellant M Siddiq, told a five-judge Constitution [...]*

---

[94]'Ayodhya [Day-18] Idols Surreptitiously Put inside Babri Masjid at Ayodhya in 1949, Muslim Parties tell SC', *Live Law*, 3 September 2019, https://tinyurl.com/yc7hb573. Accessed on 18 January 2025.

[95]'Counsel for Babri Masjid side: There was no massive structure, Hindu motifs at site, SC told', *The Indian Express*, 3 September 2019, https://tinyurl.com/4n4xve8h. Accessed on 18 January 2025.

[...] Dhavan was referring to the arguments of the temple side that the recovery of lotus and peacock motifs discounted the claim that it was a mosque. 'The Roman empire had every possible animal,' he said. Denying that there was a massive structure at the site, the counsel pointed to flaws in the methodology adopted by the ASI.

Disputing the argument that the presence of a 'parikrama route' around the structure could be considered as proof of a temple in the middle, Dhavan said, 'Parikrama (circumambulation) is not an Ashwamedha sacrifice where a horse runs around and all that territory belongs to the king... parikrama is only a form of worship, it is not a form of evidence', and asked 'does a parikrama entitle you to actual title of the place?'

Dhavan said that it will create difficulties if Hindu-Muslim issues were to be decided on the basis of such evidence given by persons. 'The important question is with whom was the title of the place when the sovereignty of this part of the country passed on to the British,' the senior counsel said, adding there is proof that it was a mosque. He contended that as far as a civil suit was concerned, there was no question of relevance of historical facts, and if they were relied on, it would lead to erroneous conclusions.

Dhavan argued that the judgment of Justice Sudhir Agarwal of the Allahabad HC was based on 'conjectures or preponderance of probability'. 'How do you do a preponderance of probability of historical dates?' he asked, adding that 'your Lordships (are) being urged to do guess work.'

Referring to arguments that some foreign travellers before the reign of Mughal emperor Aurangzeb had not mentioned the mosque in their travelogues and that this was because it did

> *not exist there at the time, Dhavan said Marco Polo had not seen the Great Wall of China but this could not be argued to contend that the wall did not exist.*
>
> *Taking the court through the problems of relying on what historians had said in support of the temple, Dhavan said, 'Mughal historians will have a different version,' and asked, 'are we going to play amateur historians?' He said the court was being asked to draw a negative reference from the fact that since one of the travellers had not seen the mosque during Babar's time, it must have been built during Aurangzeb's reign.*
>
> *At this, Justice Chandrachud pointed out that such an argument not to rely on historical evidence would also affect his case, which was built on the 'positive case' that the Babri Masjid was built during Babar's time and the reference to inscriptions which were based on history. Agreeing, Dhavan said there was no need to go into such historical evidence and the only proof to be taken into account is from 1858. He claimed that Hindus followed 'yuga' and asked how that can help determine dates [...]*

Hence, according to Dr Dhavan, 1858 was to be the cut-off date for evidence to be considered by the court. It was clear that Dr Dhavan, Ejaz Maqbool and the team were putting in humungous effort into building their case. The industry and the thought going into building the case was extraordinary and not surprising as it came from a team helmed by a top academician-cum-top-lawyer. Without doubt, it created some sense of unease in those following the case and supporting Ram Lalla's case. The impact that Dr Dhavan made right at the inception was such that concerns and questions started reaching the team. It was natural that discussions on Dr Dhavan's argument and the impact he made would follow.

Dr Dhavan's submissions laid a great emphasis on the

principles of justice, equity, and good conscience. He had traced out the history of the adoption of the principles of justice, equity and good conscience from Impey's Regulation of 1781, and the regulations for the administration of justice in the courts of Dewanne e Adaulut (Divani Adalat or Civil Court) of the provinces of Bengal, Bihar and Orissa, also dated 1781, onwards to Mussalman Wakf Validating Act, 1913, until the Hindu Gains of Learning Act. If the counsels of Ram Lalla's side relied upon old case laws, so did Dr Dhavan, and he went back to cases like the *Collector of Masulipatnam v. Cavaly Vencata Narrinappa*[96] decided in 1860, and Re Kahandas Narrandas[97] decided in 1881, holding that in all matters of trust, Hindus in India must resort to English law to *Khushro v. Guzder* (AIR 1970 SC 1468) where after Independence, the Supreme Court of India held that in a case of a suit seeking damages, old English law as compared to recent development should be applied as it was closer to the principles of justice, equity and good conscience.

The depth of research in Dr Dhavan's submission was remarkable. Though team Ram Lalla had its holes to punch in Dr Dhavan's submissions, as colleagues at bar, the team was overawed by the sheer industry and academic inputs in the submissions. Such remarkable effort required an equally remarkable team. The team composition of Dr Dhavan and the work put in was later revealed by Mr Ejaz Maqbool.[98] Ten of his staff members including four juniors—Akriti Chaubey, Qurratulain, Kunwar Aditya Singh, and one Esha Meher—were completely devoted to Dr Rajeev Dhavan's office. Their work schedule used to stretch late into the night and went up to 2 a.m. or 3 a.m.in the morning. Besides them, two junior lawyers—

[96]A43 Submission No.1A by Dr. Rajeev Dhavan, Sr. Adv., *Vada Prativada*, https://tinyurl.com/4c9d9p5n. Accessed on 18 January 2025.

[97]1881 ILR 5 Bom.154.

[98]'The Supreme Court has rewarded someone's illegal actions, Advocate Ejaz Maqbool on the Ayodhya Judgment', *Bar and Bench*, 20 November 2019, https://tinyurl.com/bdc87cww. Accessed on 18 January 2025.

Pervez Dabas and Uzmi Jameel—from the office of Mr Shakeel Ahmed Syed also worked with Dr Dhavan on the case. Further, Dr Dhavan's junior Ms Siddhi Padia was also a part of the core team. It had taken them almost two months to prepare the matter before the hearing started. Many a time, the written submissions were finalized at 2 a.m., after which Mr Maqbool's team compiled 35–40 copies of the same by 10.30 a.m. the same day.[99]

Mr Maqbool, often in interactions with the Ram Lalla team over coffee in the Supreme Court cafeteria, shared what assisting counsels in Ram Lalla team also felt—in his thirty-two-year career, never had he come across a case of such magnitude and volume.[100] The voluminous nature of the case had made all seniors', juniors', and clerks' work onerous. One could well imagine what it would have done to the court staff, and the judges too. Or maybe, even the mediation panel had an onerous workload themselves. As the case was reaching its crescendo, on 18 September 2019, the court passed an order allowing the parties to once again engage in mediation with the help of the earlier court-appointed mediation panel under strict confidentiality. The court was latching on to any chance of finding an amicable settlement as this property dispute, of course, had religious sentiments attached to it. However, Gopal Singh Visharad, an original claimant who filed a title suit in 1950, through his survivor Rajendra Singh and counsels for Ram Lalla indicated that they were no longer optimistic about mediation.[101] Hence, only the court could resolve this issue.

---

[99]Ibid.

[100]Ibid.

[101]'Ayodhya: SC says parties can go for mediation if they want to', *The Economic Times*, 18 September 2019, https://tinyurl.com/5xk5dndf. Accessed on 18 January 2025.

17

Of 'Rights', 'Wrongs', 'Belongs To', and 'Threats'

Dr Dhavan took the battle right to the opposition camp, so vehement were his arguments. One of his major contentions was that no advantage could be claimed by a party based on an illegality or a wrong perpetrated by that party itself. He had raised the issue that the idols were placed inside the building and below the central dome illegally and surreptitiously only on 22–23 December 1949.[102] Before this date, Hindus would have to prove what rights they had inside the building, which was part of the inner courtyard after the British erected a railing. The point he made was—can any right be claimed based on wrongs/illegalities? Two wrongs were specifically highlighted, the first being the surreptitious placing of the idol inside the building and second being the demolition of the mosque. It was submitted that wrongs cannot be the basis of any rights in favour of anyone.

Dr Dhavan relied on a detailed flow of events that led to the placing of the idols inside the sanctum sanctorum. The case of the Sunni Board was that tensions were already growing in Ayodhya around the disputed premises at the time of Independence. Moreover, the events preceding and following the incidents of placing the idols inside the sanctum sanctorum had to be viewed in a composite manner which would reveal the illegalities committed. The following were some of the salient

[102]Para 6 of Supreme Court Judgment, *api.sci.gov.in*, https://tinyurl.com/mr2arh5b. Accessed on 18 January 2025.

points argued by Dr Dhavan, as noted by team Ram Lalla:[103]

1. *Tensions and threats around the disputed site had led to the posting of a police picket on 12 November 1949, followed by a letter dated 29 November 1949 of the Superintendent of Police, Faizabad, to K.K. Nayar, Deputy Commissioner and District Magistrate, apprehending that Hindus were likely to force an entry into the mosque with the object of installing the idols of the deity. The letter in parts read as follows:*

   I visited the premises of Babri Mosque and the JanmAsthan in Ajodhya this evening. I noticed that several—Hawan Kunds have been constructed all around the mosque. Some of them have been built on old constructions already existing there.

   [...]

   I found bricks and lime also lying near the JanmAsthan. They have a proposal to construct a very big Havan Kund where Kirtan and Yagna on Puranmashi will be performed on a very large scale. Several thousand Hindus, Bairagis and Sadhus from outside will also participate. They also intend to continue the present Kirtan till Puranmashi. The plan appears to be to surround the mosque in such a way that entry for Muslims will be very difficult and ultimately, they might be forced to abandon the mosque. There is a strong rumour that on Puranmashi, Hindus will try to force entry into the mosque with the object of installing a deity.[104]

2. *A report dated 10 December 1949 of the Waqf Inspector Mohd. Ibrahim also reported that Dr Dhavan's clients were being harassed by Hindus and Sikhs with a view to prevent them*

[103]'A68 Note and Caselaws on Illegal Acts Cannot be the Foundation or Rights', by Dr. Rajeev Dhavan, Sr. Adv., *Vada Prativada*, https://tinyurl.com/5xuvv926. Accessed on 18 January 2025.

[104]Supreme Court Judgment, *api.sci.gov.in*, https://tinyurl.com/mr2arh5b. Accessed on 18 January 2025.

from using the mosque when they sought to pray in the mosque for Namaz Isha;

3. *Dr Dhavan submitted that Mr K.K. Nayar was biased in favour of Hindus. Contrary to ground realities, a communication dated 16 December 1949 was sent by the Deputy Commissioner and District Magistrate Mr K.K. Nayar to the Home Secretary, Government of Uttar Pradesh requesting the State Government not to give credence to the apprehensions of Muslims regarding the safety of the mosque. This was contrary to the letter of the Superintendent of Police. Mr Nayyar's letter narrated the theory of a temple built by Vikramaditya at the site and the building material of the temple being used in the construction of the mosque and that after eclipse of a long-time gap, Hindus were restored to the possession of the site. The letter recorded some happenings of 1949:*

> *[...] Sometime this year, probably in October or November, some grave-mounds were partially destroyed apparently by Bairagis who very keenly resent Muslim associations with this shrine. On 12.11.49, a police picket was posted at this place. The picket still continues in augmented strength. There were since other attempts to destroy grave-mounds. Four persons were caught and cases are proceeding against them but for quite some time now, there have been no attempts. Muslims, mostly of Faizabad, have been exaggerating these happenings and giving currency to the report that graves are being demolished systematically on a large scale. This is an entirely false canard inspired apparently by a desire to prevent Hindus from securing in this area's possession or rights of a larger character than have so far been enjoyed. Muslim anxiety on this score was heightened by the recent Navami Ramayana Path, a devotional reading of Ramayana by thousands of Hindus for nine days at a stretch. This period covered a Friday on which Muslims who went to say their prayers at the mosque were escorted to and from safely by the Police. As far*

as I have been able to understand the situation, Muslims of Ayodhya proper, are far from agitated over this issue with the exception of one Anisur Rahman who frequently sends frantic messages giving the impression that the Babri Masjid and graves are in imminent danger of demolition.

4. *On the night intervening 22/23 December 1949, about fifty to sixty persons belonging to the Hindu community placed idols of Ram Lalla and his brothers inside the Babri Mosque below the central dome.*
5. *An FIR was therefore lodged after the incident of 22/23 December 1949 detailing the placing of idols of Ram Lalla and his brothers below the central dome.*
6. *Dr Dhavan also relied on the letter dated 26 December 1949 of K.K. Nayar, District Magistrate, to the Chief Secretary, expressing surprise over the incident which had taken place. He stated that the events of 22/23 December were 'unpredictable' and 'irreversible'. Though the State Government had ordered the idols to be removed from the mosque, the District Magistrate declined to carry out the orders stating that 'If Government insisted that removal should be carried out [...], I would request to replace me by another officer.'*
7. *A letter dated 27 December 1949 of K.K. Nayar was further relied on stating that Nayar would not be able to find any Hindu who would undertake the removal of the idols. He further proposed that the mosque should be attached by excluding both Hindus and Muslims. Only exception of a minimum number of pujaris should be made and the parties should be referred to the Civil Judge for adjudicating of rights.*
8. *The matter finally went to court and a preliminary order was passed in pursuance of which the government took charge through a receiver on 5 January 1950 and made an inventory of the attached property. Dr Dhavan's contention was that it was through an illegality of placing idols surreptitiously, that Ram Lalla's idol continued to remain below the central dome*

of the disputed property and Hindus continued to worship the deities there.

9. *Even after the orders of status quo by the civil court were operational and assurance was given to the Supreme Court of India about the safety of the mosque, the mosque in a completely illegal act was demolished. This was another major illegality after 1949 whose benefit cannot be granted to any party to the suit. Therefore, Hindus cannot take benefit of either of the two illegalities.*
10. *Dr Dhavan's submission was that the Hindu case seeks to take benefit of these two major illegalities, which cannot be granted to them: (1.) Of placing the idols inside the sanctum sanctorum (2.) Of demolishing the Babri Mosque. He also brought forward the point of Hindu-Muslims riots of 1934 in Ayodhya in which some parts of the Babri Mosque were damaged and Hindus were held accountable for the damage.*

The Sunni Central Board had contended even in their plaint in Suit 4 that on 22/23 December 1949, the mosque was desecrated by the installation of idols of Lord Ram and his brothers under the central dome of the mosque. The plaint also stated that the whole area of the disputed premises of approximately 1,500 sq. yd constituted the mosque, and Hindus because of the illegalities committed on 22/23 December 1949 were able to pray below the central dome. They cannot claim any right or advantage arising out of such illegality perpetrated on 22/23 December 1949.

It must be underlined that there was no acrimony between the sides as the case progressed. Instead, mutual professional courtesy existed among the lawyers as well as the clients. The dispute was only legal and not personal in court. It was a property dispute between two communities and not a religious dispute between communities and that is how it mostly panned out. This did not mean that there was no point of conflict either. Dr Dhavan had raised his objections on certain evidence and certain general explanations advanced by the counsels of Ram

Lalla which he termed as irrelevant stories. This had quite upset Yogeswaran. While inside the court, Yogi was ready for a legal war if the need arose, outside the court he received compliments from the opposition, as it were. While the team members of Ram Lalla were standing outside the court during many of the breaks, Dr Dhavan complimented Yogi on his thoroughness in the case and even gifted a book titled *The Hindu Laws of Endowment* by Pandit Prannath Saraswati, in appreciation of his commitment to his client.

The arguments on illegalities and the impressive opening of Dr Dhavan were giving everyone much food for thought. And then, in the middle of the case which was igniting emotions, came an unfortunate piece of news. One retired professor had sent a letter in the poorest of taste to Dr Dhavan, cursing him with most unpleasant consequences for opposing the plea of Ram Lalla. The news was reported everywhere by the press. A contempt of court petition was moved by Dr Dhavan. Thankfully, the gentleman realized his mistake and tendered an apology. While the gentleman had certainly lost his balance, the freedom of speech and expressions and the social networking sites were also put to full misuse.

Another, incident allegedly took place *on the 22nd day of hearing* as reported by *Outlook India* a week or so later.

> *Dr Dhavan mentioned to the Court that he had received a threat message on Facebook and yesterday his clerk was assaulted by few other persons in the apex court premises, he expressed his concern that it is not the right atmosphere conducive for hearing, He submitted that one word from the Court would be enough on this issue.*[105]

But what happened finally? What did these deviations from the

[105]'Ayodhya Case: "Threats Continue, Clerk Assaulted in Court Premises,' Lawyer Rajeev Dhavan tells SC"', *Outlook India*, 12 September 2019, https://tinyurl.com/y55h2y6u. Accessed on 18 January 2025.

subject matter finally result in? The court deprecated such events in no uncertain terms. *Live law*[106] reported a final denouement to this episode and such other episodes, and carried a report, parts of which are reproduced below:

> *The Supreme Court on Thursday closed the contempt case against Chennai-based Professor Shanmugham, after he expressed regret for showering curses on Senior Advocate Rajeev Dhavan for representing Muslim parties in the Ayodhya-Babri Masjid case.*
>
> *The 88 year old Professor tendered unconditional apology for writing the letter to Senior Advocate Dhavan.*
>
> *Senior Advocate Kapil Sibal, representing Dhavan, submitted that the contempt petition was not pressed in view of the regret expressed by the octogenarian. Sibal said that the petition was meant to send out a message that no one should intimidate a counsel directly or indirectly for taking up a brief.*
>
> *Before dropping further proceedings, the CJI-led bench admonished the Professor for his letter and said that such conduct by anyone will not be tolerated in future.*
>
> *Dhavan filed the contempt petition stating that Shanmugham in his letter had asked how could Dhavan 'betray his faith' by appearing on behalf of Muslims for 'their so called right in Ayodhya'. Shanmugham said Dhavan that he will 'pay for his blasphemy' and cursed him with severe physical maladies.*
>
> *The 'intimidating letter' interfered with the course of administration of justice by threatening an advocate for discharging his duties, and hence will amount to 'criminal contempt', stated the petition.*

---

[106]Livelaw News Network, 'Professor Who Cursed Sr Adv Dhavan For Representing Muslims In Ayodhya Case Offers Apology; SC Closes Contempt Case', 19 September, 2019, https://tinyurl.com/59afuj2b. Accessed on 19 September 2025.

On September 3, the Constitution Bench hearing the Ayodhya case issued notice on the contempt petition.

With such deviations taken care of by getting the court's notice to such gross acts, the case could normally proceed. However, the case of Nirmohi Akhara like a double-edged sword always hung over both the sides.

One could simply not ignore Nirmohi Akhara. So, Dr Dhavan also attacked Nirmohi Akhara's case. He contested the claim of Nirmohi Akhara over the disputed property both inside the iron railing set up in 1858 as well as outside the iron railing—the inner courtyard, and the outer courtyard. He read out the Akhara's plaint to make out a case that Nirmohi Akhara never claimed ownership of the land but only rights to access the land for prayers. So, at best Nirmohi Akhara's case was of accessing the land and not of ownership of the land. Therefore, if Nirmohi Akhara did not claim ownership and, according to Dr Dhavan, Ram Lalla's suit was not maintainable and was to be dismissed, then the disputed land was to be under exclusive possession and ownership of the Sunni Board.

Further, the historical timeline of Babur getting the mosque constructed in 1528 had not been disputed by Ram Lalla's case. What Ram Lalla's side asserted was that it was not a valid mosque, and that the prayers and offering to Ram Lalla was made inside the building that had been a mosque but was used as a temple by worshippers and had Hindu figures and motifs found in Hindu temples. It was only the suit of Nirmohi Akhara which said that the building remained a temple all throughout and was never a mosque.

There was emphasis on the use of the words *'belonging to'* in the plaint of Nirmohi Akhara in Suit 3 which had claimed that the building was always a temple and never a mosque. Yes, such simple English language phrases such as 'belonging to' used in a case can have varied meaning for lawyers. Such wordplay keep lawyers in business. A term from smart draftsmen of statutes or laws should be such that it should be simply understood and not be left open to interpretation. The text and context must be clear. If the draftsman makes the mistake of having a statute or law which is not clear in the text and context, and requires interpretation, then a lawyer must burn the midnight oil to help a client. In this case, the words 'belonging to' got much attention, even though they didn't arise from a statute or a law but from the suit of Nirmohi Akhara which reads as follows:[107]

> *2. That Janma Asthan now commonly known as Janma Bhumi, the birthplace of Lord Ram Chandra, situate in Ayodhya belongs and has always belonged to the plaintiff no. 1 who through its reigning Mahant and Sarbrahkar has ever seen been managing it and receiving offerings made there at in form of money, sweets, flowers and fruits and other articles and things.*

The counsel of Ram Lalla had attacked Nirmohi Akhara on the grounds that they were not the legal manager or shebait of Ram Lalla. On the contrary, even if they were the shebaits, they had claimed title and ownership of the land Janmasthan and, therefore, were acting against the ownership rights of Ram Lalla himself. This was based on the simple logic that a person who is merely manager of a deity's land cannot claim to be the owner of the land. If the manager claimed himself to be the owner, then the deity's interests were not safeguarded. Therefore, there was no one to safeguard the interests of Ram Lalla. There were a few instances where managers had claimed the deity's property as their own. Hence, to protect the interests of Ram Lalla and ultimately the interests of Ram's devotees, Suit 5 was moved.

Dr Dhavan, to the surprise of team Ram Lalla, supported the case of Nirmohi Akhara. Dr Dhavan's case was that the relief as sought by Nirmohi Akhara was for management and

---

[107]Nirmohi Akhara O.S. NO. 3 of 1989, Reg. Suit no. 26 of 1959, *Vada Prativada*, https://tinyurl.com/57bz8vny. Accessed on 18 January 2025.

charge of Lord Ram Lalla. Claim of Managerial Rights could not be equated to a claim of ownership. This was so because the relief sought by Nirmohi Akhara was only with respect to management and charge of the idols of Lord Ram. The case of Nirmohi Akhara stood on the basis that there was deprivation of Shebaiti rights by an order of attachment by the government in December 1949. The claim of Nirmohi Akhara was against the order of attachment and against the State for possession of the land and to restore Shebaiti rights to serve Ram Lalla. In short, Dr Dhavan argued that words such as 'belong' or 'belonging to' will have a flexible meaning for which he brought to the notice of the court previously decided judgements. However, in its plaint, the Akhara had claimed that the Janmasthan *'belongs'* and has always *'belonged to it'* and the use of these terms in a generic or loose sense may, in a given context, be inferred as *'possession'*, *'ownership'* and *'implied title'*. But that was not the case here as *'belongs to'* and *'belonged to it'* in the Nirmohi Akhara plaint must be read only in the context of managerial and management rights that as a shebait, Nirmohi Akhara could claim.

If Nirmohi Akhara had claimed title/ownership of the land for itself, then it would stand at odds with the suit of Ram Lalla. Dr Dhavan, therefore, clarified that Nirmohi Akhara merely claims to serve the idol and is not claiming the land of the idol itself. Nirmohi Akhara was claiming a duty and not the right to ownership and title. This was the defence of Nirmohi Akhara that was advanced by Dr Dhavan.

But then had Dr Dhavan accepted that Nirmohi Akhara were the shebaits? The team Ram Lalla members asked each other to confirm if they had understood it right. If yes, nothing less than a tectonic shift had happened for the team and the case.

18

A Tectonic Shift

Nirmohi Akhara's suit had always appeared as a perplexing riddle. On a few points, the suit of Nirmohi Akhara, if successful, could destroy the case of both the Hindu and Muslim sides. Therefore, an earnest and persistent effort had to be made to keep a check on which side Nirmohi Akhara's arguments were damaging at any given moment. Every support or opposition given to Nirmohi Akhara had to be strategically weighed. In essence, Nirmohi Akhara's case was that it was present at the site for worshipping Ram Lalla. If Nirmohi Akhara's presence were to be proven, it would automatically prove the presence of Ram Lalla's idols and the presence of worship of Ram Lalla at the site because the Akhara claimed to have acted as a pujari or a shebait or manager of Idol Ram Lalla. The manager or shebait being a religious servant of God could not have had an existence independent of the god it was to serve. Leave aside a shebait, for any regular worship by anyone of Ram Lalla's idol the idol had to be present there.

Had the Opposition Accepted This?

Nirmohi Akhara had claimed the whole premises to be a temple. They had contested the theory of Babur having had any mosque constructed at all on the site, and that the disputed structure was only and only a temple and was never a mosque. All the Hindu sides had averred to the claim of Ram Chabutra, Sita Rasoi, and the disputed structure were one composite whole and did not accept the division by the British into two different units—

the outer and inner courtyards. But then what was the case of the Sunni Board? Did it look at the whole site as one composite whole in its suit or did it claim the land to be divided into outer courtyard and inner courtyard?

The vehemence with which Dr Dhavan had attacked the temple case in his opening arguments followed by his strident arguments of illegalities in the placing of the idols below the sanctum sanctorum were still ringing in the minds of those following the case. Those without access to the evidence of the case were now waiting for more incisive arguments. For some, Dr Dhavan had made a huge impact. Such a strategy, however, could be more nuanced, as events would reveal. But in this offensive, perceptive ears heard something amazing. Before coming to the issue of '*belonging to*', Dr Dhavan's submissions had caused, albeit stated dramatically, an earthquake for those following the case. *For the first time*, the Sunni Board had conceded in effect some crucial points of Nirmohi Akhara's stand. These were:

1. Nirmohi Akhara were indeed the shebaits of Ram Lalla and had been praying to Ram Lalla at Ram Chabutra within the disputed premises which the Sunni Board claimed as a mosque.
2. Idols of Ram existed within the disputed premises, evidence of which can be traced back to 1858.

It, therefore, meant that a fundamental aspect of the case around the question of whether there was prayer for Ram Lalla inside the disputed portion of the land (now left as less than 1,500 sq. yd incorrectly reported as 2.77 acres) was not disputed. *Both sides agreed to this bare minimum fact.* And this fact could have significant and deciding ramifications on the case. Every step from here had to be carefully followed to see how it would unfold further. However, Dr Dhavan's use of the erection of iron railings over the land in 1857-1858[108] by the British brought in another legal argument worth engaging in. The argument simply put was:

1. By erecting iron railings over the land, the British had partitioned the land in 1858 into an outer courtyard and an inner courtyard as evident in the map. The inner courtyard had the disputed structure/mosque within it.
2. After the division, the inner courtyard had been handed over to Muslims; Muslims had exclusive possession of the inner courtyard.
3. After the division, the Hindu worship was limited only to the outer courtyard which had Ram Chabutra and Sita Rasoi. This was conducted by Nirmohi Akhara. Hindus were kept out of the inner courtyard where the disputed structure stood.
4. Both the parts, the inner courtyard and outer courtyard, would have to be looked at distinctly and not as a composite whole.

As the case progressed, there was greater reliance on the division/distinction between the inner courtyard and outer courtyard after the erection of the iron railings as stated by Dr Dhavan. His continued emphasis was that post-1857, only his clients, Muslims had possession of the inner courtyard. This was a game laid out to ensure possession of that area where the idols of Ram Lalla had been installed, for his clients. But what about the other areas? *What about the bombshell that was dropped which seemed impossible till even a day before?* Remember, both sides had laid claim to every inch of the disputed area.

Another point that was recurring in everyone's mind was how would the Sunni Board handle Nirmohi Akhara? But the

[108] 'Day 47 Arguments, Ayodhya Title Dispute', 18 September 2019, *Supreme Court Observer*, https://tinyurl.com/2wmtkvmx. Accessed on 18 January 2025. 'Day 48 Arguments, Ayodhya Title Dispute', *Supreme Court Observer*, 19 September 2019, https://tinyurl.com/2s8p78p8. Accessed on 18 January 2025.

tectonic shift in the Sunni Board's stand meant that the media had got its scoop. The media went on to report how Dr Dhavan tried to meet the challenge of Nirmohi Akhara's pursuits. Having accepted the presence of idols on the spot, the reaction of the judges to this fact led to a few questions being put to Dr Dhavan. In the assisting team, deeper discussions would go on to somehow protect the Janmabhoomi land. Someone or the other would lay their hands on some important news report, or some follower of the case would send them the report. The question was: could the Sunni Board ever abandon its claim over any part of Ram Janmabhoomi land? Publications covering the case ran interesting reports, *India Today* reported[109].

Ayodhya case in Supreme Court:
How Sunni Waqf Board has left many confused

> Senior Advocate Rajeev Dhavan, appearing for the Sunni Waqf Board, has conceded to the shebait right of the Nirmohi Akhara. But he has contested the claim of deity and title claim of Akhara.
>
> *[...] On Wednesday, Dhavan told the Supreme Court that the Sunni Waqf Board agreed to 'shebait' right of the Nirmohi Akhara. Shebait, literally meaning a devotee, refers to an entity—which could be a person, group or another body—entrusted with the management of affairs of the deity.*
>
> *The stand left the bench a bit perplexed. 'You do not dispute their shebaiti rights,' the bench asked Dhavan, who replied saying, 'No. I do not.'*
>
> *The bench then told Dhavan, 'If you accept that Akahara as 'shebiat' then do you also accept that it was in possession of*

---

[109]Dutta, Prabhash K., 'Ayodhya case in Supreme Court: How Sunni Waqf Board has left many confused', *India Today*, 6 September, 2019, https://tinyurl.com/2b5fxhur. Accessed on 19 September 2025.

> *the outer courtyard.' Dhavan contested saying Akhara's claim as shebait over the area known as Ram Chabutara may be fine but not as title holder of the land.*
>
> *The Supreme Court bench remarked that by accepting Akahara's right as shebait, 'you (the Muslim side) are necessarily giving up your claim over Ram Chabutara and Sita Rasoi of outer courtyard. Therefore, the outer courtyard cannot be a mosque.'*
>
> *Dhavan replied saying, 'Technically, your lordships can say that some portion may be given' to the Hindu side.*
>
> *The bench reminded Dhavan that the Sunni Waqf Board in its pleadings in the lawsuit has claimed title over the entire disputed land.*

Mala Dixit's take in her book was: The moment Dhavan stated this, the judges on the bench posed a series of questions. The court said: if you are accepting the right of Nirmohi Akhara to serve and worship, then you admit that there existed a temple along with a mosque. When Rajeev Dhavan saw that he was getting in a fix with this line of argument, he stated that Nirmohi Akhara used to worship outside on the Chabutra only, not in the inner courtyard. Muslims had the right in the inner courtyard. Chief Justice Ranjan Gogoi, in order to clarify Dhavan's argument, pointed out that while he was accepting the right of Nirmohi Akhara to perform worship, at the same time he was saying that worship was done in the outer courtyard, that there was an idol there.[110]

The Times of India quoted Dr Dhavan as *stating: '...deity was there. The idols were there. We cannot pretend the idols were not there. But [...] Hindus' right to worship was granted but their claim to title was denied.'*[111]

---

[110]Dixit, Mala, *Ayodhya se Adalat Tak Bhagwan Shri Ram*, pp. 56–57, Namyapress.com.
[111]'Ayodhya: Muslim Parties Ready to Coexist with Hindus', *The Times of India*, 5

Mala Dixit further reported Justice S.A. Bobde as saying that the Akhara was the sevadaar of the temple. To this, Dhavan said that there was an idol on the Ram Chabutra in the outer courtyard, which was worshipped by Nirmohi Akhara and those idols were placed inside on the night of 22–23 December 1949. Despite this clarification given by Rajiv Dhavan, the judges on the Bench continued to question him. Justice D.Y. Chandrachud said, 'Sunni Board has made two prayers in its suit. One, it should be declared a mosque; second, ownership rights should be given over the entire area as per the given map ABCD.' Justice Chandrachud told Dhavan that his second prayer included the entire area but if he was accepting the right of Nirmohi Akhara to serve and worship, then he was giving a part of it to them (Nirmohi Akhara). Dhavan replied that Nirmohi was only asking for the right to serve and worship. They were not asking for ownership rights on the land.[112]

Dhavan said that Nirmohi Akhara used to worship there under the right of convenience, i.e. easement right, but the ownership right of the mosque was with the Waqf Board and the Muslims only. On this argument, Justice Chandrachud responded that Nirmohi Akhara might have had an easement right, but the right of the deity (Ramlala) installed there was greater than that. The right of the deity was greater than the right of the sevadar. Dhavan said that his argument was that the deity would have limited rights. Also, the sevadar (Nirmohi Akhara) could not claim ownership rights.[113]

Dhavan said, 'If we look at the facts of the case, then Hindus used to worship from outside the railing. Some people can say that they used to even go inside also but that does not give them rights there.' Justice S. Abdul Nazir asked Dhavan to explain the beliefs of India and Arabia on the presence of a temple-mosque

---

September 2019 https://tinyurl.com/s43b9n7b. Accessed on 10 September 2025.

[112]Dixit, Mala, *Ayodhya se Adalat Tak Bhagwan Shri Ram*, pp. 56–57, Namyapress.com.

[113]Ibid.

jointly at one place. Dhavan stated that this was the case in many places in India, including in Mathura.[114]

Amidst the arguments, Justice Chandrachud again came to the main issue. He told Dhavan that his case was that he was accepting the presence of both (Hindus-Muslims) together but was claiming ownership over the entire land. Dhavan stated that his case was about the claim of Waqf property on the basis of use by people. If understood in the language of law, it was called waqf by user. Dhavan, while claiming ownership of the entire land, stated 'we can be together' and that other people could use the property, but they could not be the owner.[115]

[…]

Questions began pouring in from those interested in getting clarity in the case. Was it too early to react? Bhakti and Yogeswaran's smiles were tinged with an air of victory, but they were restrained at least in public, limiting their responses to 'one of the points in the case is whether there was worship by Hindus in the disputed premises.' As usual, Yogi was excited, 'Our case is that throughout, Hindus worshipped at the disputed site. Dr Dhavan on behalf of the Sunni Board has accepted that from 1858, there has been worship by Hindus in the disputed structure, but he regards the time before 1858 as irrelevant.' Sridhar, a while later, was seen articulating the import of the said submission is that we have entered the outer court yard, another step towards the janmasthan. The other point that required clarification was—why had Dr Dhavan accepted Nirmohi Akhara as the shebait if the Sunni Board sought title of ownership over the complete disputed land of 1,500 sq. yd? The answer was it was done to get rid of Suit 5 of Ram Lalla Virajman and Ram Janmabhoomi.

The sight of Senior Parasaran struggling with poor health prompted Dr Dhavan, Mr Jilani and Meenakshi Arora to

[114]Ibid.
[115]Ibid.

enquire about his health quite regularly. Mr Parasaran's fever refused to abate, and the redness of his eyes was not lessening either. Fortunately, there was a five-day break from the hearings, and availing of this opportunity, his doctors summoned the nonagenarian to Chennai much to the relief of Mohan Parasaran. However, Mr Parasaran wasn't going anywhere until he had marshalled his team and led a detailed conference. The discussions that ensued were tinged with optimism and caution.

Bhakti seemed happy that from a position of exclusivity, Dr Dhavan's submission had come around to accepting the presence of Ram Lalla within the disputed premises. The Sunni Board had accepted that worship had been taking place within the disputed land. Ashwin brought out that even the judges confirmed from the Sunni Board that they are not seeking exclusive rights to the site. They can't say they have exclusive possession. At best, their case can be only of sharing with admission of this fact.

Sridhar optimistically stated that 'after this concession, our clients can never be out of the suit land.' Aditi was more cautious, only accepting that the right to worship within the premises has been accepted as per what she had followed, and that too has been camouflaged as merely an easementary right only in the outer courtyard and not for the inner courtyard, as Dr Dhavan was harping on that distinction. Yogeswaran being the most optimistic, would add that one must read archaeological evidence, travelogues, gazetteers, and this concession, and 'the case is won.'

After much thought, Senior Parasaran gave his view that what has been argued is the practice of our faith. Not merely faith. Continued practice of faith through neutral sources as pointed out by Mr Vaidyanathan was substantiated by this submission of Dr Dhavan that the idols have been present within the disputed site and worshipped within the disputed site. Further, Mr Parasaran was of the opinion that oral evidence from Hindu witnesses as well as Muslim witnesses had already been brought forward by Mr Vaidyanathan to establish the practice of faith, worship, and right to worship.

Finally, Senior Parasaran would pose a question: 'So legally speaking, is it a matter of faith or of hard law? The right to worship or the presence of idols?'

Sounding a note of caution, Senior Parasaran would go on to point out that now, no one must let their guard down, more so because of his vision being disrupted, he would require help. 'Everyone has to keep working, merely because part of the case of the presence of idols being accepted within the disputed site does not rule out new points being argued against Ram Lalla's case. Dr Dhavan's case being that he recognizes the idols' presence giving only easementary rights through which you can enter to perform worship may be a double-edged sword. Tomorrow a new point against you may be argued,' was his constant caution.

Many questions and debates arose among those following the case as to what would emerge next from the Sunni Board's support of Nirmohi Akhara. But in the first instance, why did Nirmohi Akhara get support from the Sunni Board? If Nirmohi Akhara's suit was allowed, then the Sunni Board's side does not get anything either. The witnesses of Nirmohi Akhara had stated quite a lot in their testimonies. If those testimonies sailed through, the Board would be totally out of the disputed land. How long could the Board support Nirmohi Akhara?

The Sunni Board wanted to establish Nirmohi Akhara as the shebait so that the suit of Ram Lalla Virajman and Ram Janmabhoomi would get knocked out of the reckoning. The grounds had been prepared that if a valid shebait enters, and the valid shebait moves a suit, then no one else can move another suit for the same deity or Ram Lalla, which was the correct position in law and was not disputed by anyone. Further, the point that would be urged was that if an established shebait is there, Ram Lalla's Suit 5 cannot be there since all of Ram Lalla's rights already stand represented by the shebait. The presence of the shebait ensures that there cannot be any suit on behalf of Ram Lalla or Ram Janmasthan. Once Dr Dhavan manages to get Suit 5 of Ram Lalla Virajman knocked out, the Sunni Board would then handle Nirmohi Akhara's suit on other grounds and get it dismissed as well—primarily on the ground that the suit was time-barred or beyond the period of limitation—an interesting legal manoeuvre.

Yet, the hurdle before them was that Nirmohi Akhara had yet not been declared as shebaits, as Yogeswaran would constantly remind the others. The case of the lawyers for Ram Lalla was that Nirmohi Akhara, by asserting that the land '*belongs to*' them, had claimed ownership of the land and had, therefore, destroyed its case as the land can never belong to the servant/manager/shebait. It can only be owned by God, Ram Lalla himself. Moreover, Nirmohi Akhara has made a claim which is time-barred.

The team went through the suits and the pleadings of all parties with a fine-tooth comb to check for any pleading claiming the inner courtyard and outer courtyard as not being a composite but two disjoint independent units. While the rest only gave objective answers to Senior Parasaran's queries, a prod from Bhakti or Sridhar would get Yogeswaran going. Yogi answered passionately and even beyond the points enquired about. A sample of an answer to this simple query of checking pleadings concerning the inner courtyard and outer courtyard being a composite unit or not, would be: 'This point of looking at the inner courtyard and outer courtyard disjointly is never pleaded by any party in their suit. Further Sir, we have prayed through the railings to the inner courtyard and there is evidence that Ram bhakts made attempts to enter the inner courtyard as well. It is totally unfair for the Sunni Board to take such new pleas at this stage.' As Yogi finally paused to inhale, Bhakti, the absolute contrast of the passionate Yogi would politely point out that even the judges reminded Dr Dhavan that the Sunni Board in its pleadings in the lawsuit has claimed the title over the entire disputed land. Now they are themselves partly abandoning their claims.

Dr Dhavan had further argued that Nirmohi Akhara's suit was not maintainable, and they had sued the wrong party. The prayer in Nirmohi Akhara's suit sought to assert a right against the Faizabad magistrate who issued the 1949 order attaching the inner courtyard area of the disputed property. Nirmohi Akhara's suit has not claimed title of ownership against any party to the suit or against the Sunni Board. Ram Lalla's suit was the problem that claimed the title ownership over the land against all, including the Sunni Board. If Dr Dhavan's incisive arguments were accepted and Ram Lalla's suit was dismissed, Ram Janmabhoomi would be out of the reach of Ram bhakts forever.

Dr Dhavan's Sunni Board's strategy now seemed to secure the minimum. The hope was that even if all Dr Dhavan's other arguments were not accepted by the Supreme Court, the title ownership to the inner courtyard could be handed over to Dr Dhavan's clients and only the outer courtyard could be handed over to Ram Lalla or Nirmohi Akhara separately. The inner courtyard was the place Hindus claimed was the exact birthplace of Lord Ram. Implicit in this point was that in terms of possession and use of the land, the disputed 1,500 sq. yd of land cannot be said to be one composite unit. Even when the judges had questions to put on the concession about Nirmohi Akhara and Ram Lalla's idols being present at Ram Chabutra and the adverse effect of accepting the presence of Nirmohi Akhara on the case, many of the explanations of Dr Dhavan came through the distinction between the inner courtyard and outer courtyard. Another point recurring in everyone's mind was how would the Sunni Board handle Nirmohi Akhara's presence which the Board itself was accepting? The case Dr Dhavan sought to advance would meet the challenge of the unguided dimension of Nirmohi Akhara's case. The essence of those answers by the Sunni Board was, that a party had to prove its presence in the outer courtyard separately, and in the inner courtyard separately, and not at the site as a composite whole. That was the case which Dr Dhavan sought to advance.[116]

But the main attack was yet to come from Dr Dhavan. The main attack of course was on Suit 5, and then, in the opinion of team Ram Lalla, Nirmohi Akhara would be easy to handle for the Sunni Board. The history of India and the case was yet to be put on trial. The historical evidence was yet to be debated. But the case of history was more of a civilizational challenge.

[116]Dixit, Mala, *Ayodhya Se Adalat Tak Bhagwan Shree Ram*, Namya Press, New Delhi, 2020.

19

On Whose Side Was History?

History had to be decoded only after analysing what had happened in 1885. Ram Lalla's counsel had also brought in various historical accounts. Dr Dhavan had raised pointed doubts on the reliance of evidence from the Hindu sides, such as travelogues and gazetteers. His written submissions accentuated his attacks, and he suggested that if read from a different perspective, these documents prove the Sunni Board's case rather than that of Ram Lalla's side. Dr Dhavan, to rebut the contention of the plaintiffs in Ram Lalla's Suit 5, led a detailed analysis of these documents. Counsels for Ram Lalla had apart from other pieces of evidence heavily relied upon the *Skanda Purana*, travellers (travelogues) and gazetteers to support the arguments that, a) the birthplace of Lord Ram can be traced to the site of the Babri Mosque, b) the Babri Mosque was built after demolishing a previous temple built on the disputed site itself. Dr Dhavan submitted[117] that there were doubts in the mind of the Allahabad High Court itself:

> *The antiquity of Ayodhya is not disputed. [...] Lord Rama was born at Ayodhya and ruled thereat. The religious texts like Valmiki Ramavan and Ramcharitmanas of Goswami Tulsidas and others like Skandpuran etc. mention that Lord Rama was born at Ayodhva and it is his place of birth but do not identify any particular place in Ayodhva which can be said to be his place of birth.*[118]

[117]System of oral and written submissions followed by Dr Dhavan.

[118]Written Submission No. A76, Note on Proof of Belief-I (*Skanda Purana*, Travelers,

In this light, what needed to be analysed was on whose side was history. Which side was historically correct? To mitigate the reliance on the *Skanda Purana* by the counsels for Ram Lalla, Dr Dhavan pointed that even the judgement of the Allahabad High Court observed that no exact place of the birth of Lord Ram could be traced within religious texts like the Valmiki Ramayana, the *Ramcharitmanas* of Goswami Tulsidas or in other scriptures like the *Skanda Purana*, etc. No evidence exists that suggests that any place in Ayodhya was associated with Ram's birth either in the 11th century or even in the 17th century. As per Dr Dhavan's submissions, the first identification or suggestion in any documents came only from the late 18th century onwards when the disputed site first became associated with the birth of Lord Ram. Dr Dhavan submitted that the location given in the various Mahatmyas in the *Skanda Purana* does not tally with that of the Babri Masjid.[119] He also stated that hearsay evidence, which, as per general law of evidence, was not reliable in the writing of travellers and gazetteers as was the direct evidence of facts which the travellers had seen for themselves, which was more reliable. Such hearsay evidence should be held as tales, stories and folk tales.

Mr Vaidyanathan had relied upon Father Joseph Tieffenthaler's *Description Historique et Géographique de l'Inde* to show that the disputed site was worshipped as the birthplace of Lord Ram. Dr Dhavan pointed out that it was also recorded that Aurangzeb demolished the fortress called Ramcote and erected a Mohammedan temple with a triple dome. It was submitted by Dr Dhavan that the source of this information from Tieffenthaler himself was local belief which itself is hearsay evidence. More so, Tieffenthaler talked about the demolition of the fortress and not a temple. Tieffenthaler's information about who was the demolisher was also not specific and hence not reliable. It was

Gazetteers) by Dr. Rajeev Dhavan, Sr. Adv., *Vada Prativada*, https://tinyurl.com/wu344m4c. Accessed on 18 January 2025.

[119]Ibid.

also pointed out that he also mentions a bedi and states that it was on this where Beschan (Vishnu) was born in the form of Ram. The statement about the bedi had to be read, as per Dr Dhavan, with the statement of the witnesses who stated that Ram Chabutra was also called bedi. This was relied on to show that the Hindu belief was that Lord Ram was born on Ram Chabutra and not below the central dome. The statement of Dr T.P. Verma (an expert witness—epigraphist and historian) was also pointed out as being relevant to prove that the best case was Lord Ram was born at Ram Chabutra/bedi and not under the central dome as claimed by the Hindu side. Dr Verma was a witness who had deposed on behalf of Ram Lalla's side in Suit 5. He has stated that this bedi must have been kept above this Chabutra.[120]

For team Ram Lalla, the Sunni Board's submission was a double-edged sword. The Board was clearly trying to shift focus from the area below the central dome of the disputed structure to Ram Chabutra. This shift of focus nevertheless identified Lord Ram's birthplace within the disputed site of around 1,500 sq. yd. which was a composite unit as pleaded by both Ram Lalla's side and the Sunni Board. While team Ram Lalla attempted to prove that the birth spot was below the central dome, Dr Dhavan's arguments denying the claim, were in themselves identifying the birth spot at Ram Chabutra. While on one hand, it was being pleaded that the documents proved that there was a mosque and it was constructed by Babur, the travelogues also suggested the destruction of Lord Ram's abode. Further, the documents were also being rejected as recording hearsay accounts.

Dr Dhavan's take was that history suggests Inner Courtyard was a Mosque and the Outer Courtyard was Ram Chabutra. Edward Thornton's *The Gazetteer* (1858) was relied upon by Ram Lalla's side to prove that the mosque was built after demolishing the temple. *The Gazetteer* stated that 'a quadrangular coffer of

---

[120]Ibid.

stone—whitewashed, five ells long, four broad, and protruding five or six inches above ground is indicated as the cradle in which Rama was born as the seventh avatar of Vishnu and is accordingly abundantly honoured by the pilgrimages and devotions of Hindus.' It was submitted by the Sunni Waqf Board that this cradle was at Ram Chabutra which, though within the disputed structure, was in the outer courtyard and was not below the central dome which was in the inner courtyard. The statements of Dr T. P. Verma, witness for Ram Lalla's side and another witness who appeared on behalf of Nirmohi Akhara were relied on to point out that the cradle lay on top of Ram Chabutra.[121] Again Ram Chabutra was brought into focus and the area below the central dome was not being identified with Lord Ram.

The systematic deconstruction of evidence placed by team Ram Lalla continued. The Archaeological Survey of India reports by Alexander Cunningham, (1862–63–64–65) were relied on to show that King Vikramaditya had rebuilt a temple on all the holy sites of Ayodhya and had restored all temples, and at some point, had referred to the existence of a Janmasthan temple. Cunningham's version was also sought to be rejected as unreliable evidence. It was submitted that the source of information is popular tradition which itself is hearsay evidence. Cunningham did not mention the demolition of the Janmasthan temple and the construction of the mosque. It was further pointed out that the Janmasthan temple mentioned by Cunningham stood about one-quarter of a mile away from Lakshman Ghat and that the Babri Mosque is at least 5 miles away from Lakshman Ghat. Therefore, there was a possibility that Cunningham was referring to another temple altogether and not the one that housed Ram Chabutra.[122]

The case of the Sunni Board as understood by team Ram Lalla was that while Ram Lalla's side relied upon the afore-

---

[121]Ibid.

[122]Ibid.

mentioned travellers, the travellers themselves had seen the mosque and its inscriptions. Some of the travellers after 1857, had even witnessed Muslims offering prayers in the inner courtyard inside the mosque and Hindus worshipping outside in the outer courtyard at Ram Chabutra. Since these travellers presented their eye-witnessed accounts of the existence of a mosque, these can be relied upon concerning the case of the Mosque alone, and had proved the Sunni Board's case. At the same time, the notings in these same travellers' accounts as well as the gazetteers about the mosque having been built after the destruction of the temple are mere hearsay and hold no value. The birth spot is also not identified as being below the central dome of the mosque and hence Hindus had no claim to the inner courtyard. Janmasthan was at best identified in the outer courtyard within the disputed site but then these also revealed the story of a time period before 1885.[123]

Similarly, P. Carnegy's book *Historical Sketch of Tahsil Fyzabad, Zillah Fyzabad* (1870) had also been relied on to show that Babur built a mosque on the site of the erstwhile Janmasthan temple. Carnegy had, inter alia, recorded that: a) Babur built a mosque at the Janmasthan, b) the mosque bore the name of Babur and there were two inscriptions, c) till 1855, Hindus and Mohammeddans alike used to worship in the mosque-temple, and d) since British rule, a railing had been put up to prevent disputes. It is within this railing that the mosque exists and that is where Muslims pray. Whereas Hindus pray outside the fence where they have raised a platform.[124] Again, Carnegy's account was sought to buttress the claim that the Hindu side has failed to justify its claim concerning the land below the central dome. The Hindu sides' evidence pointed only towards Ram Chabutra.

W.C. Bennett's *The Gazetteer of the Province of Oudh* which had been relied upon to show that the Janmasthan temple

[123]Ibid.

[124]Ibid.

existed on the place where Lord Ram was born was rejected by Dr Dhavan as the source of information was *locally affirmed* which was heard by the author and was not Bennett's own observation. It had recorded that since British rule, a railing has been put up to prevent disputes. It is within this railing that the mosque exists and that is where Muslims pray. Whereas Hindus pray outside the fence where they have raised a platform and so the Hindu rights must be restricted only to the outer courtyard if any. However, like Carnegy's document, Bennett's document too indicated that till 1855, Hindus and Mohammeddans alike used to worship in the mosque-temple. Similarly, the case of the Sunni Board was sought to be built through other recordings of travellers and gazetteers in the same manner. It was highlighted that a number of these travellers noted both the iron grill/ partition erected after 1857, the structure built by Babur, the presence of Hindus only in the outer courtyard and the presence of the mosque in the inner courtyard.[125]

As Ram Chabutra was drawn more and more into focus, one of the striking arguments of Dr Dhavan was that the Chabutra could have pre-dated the installation of the iron railing. He rejected the claim of the Hindu parties that Ram Chabutra came into existence after the installation of the iron railings by the British as a result of which, Hindus were displaced from the inner courtyard in 1855.[126] This argument was backed by the accounts of Tieffenthaler, the 18th-century Jesuit missionary. Dr Dhavan had sought to establish that the missionary describes a possible precursor to the Chabutra. Tieffenthaler had described a small bedi in the approximate location of the Chabutra.[127] The effect of this argument was to highlight that Ram Chabutra already existed as the birthplace of Lord Ram, and the central dome and

---

[125]Ibid.

[126]Ibid.

[127]'Day 48 Arguments, Ayodhya Title Dispute', *Supreme Court Observer*, 19 September 2019, https://tinyurl.com/2s8p78p8. Accessed on 18 January 2025.

the area of the building of the mosque were not relevant to the case of Lord Ram.

To challenge the location of Lord Ram's birthplace as lying below the central dome, the historian's report to the nation was brought in to stress the point that the location described in the 'Ayodhya Mahatmya' of the *Skanda Purana* did not match with the present-day location of The Babri Masjid. The report had been prepared by R.S. Sharma, M. Athar Ali, D.N. Jha, and Suraj Bhan. The submission was that the 'Ayodhya Mahatmya' uses the terms 'Janamsthan' and 'Janambhoomi'. If both these are to be taken as the same place, the resultant place does not match with the site of the Babri Masjid.[128] The Allahabad High Court had not considered the report as 'tenable' under the Indian Evidence Act, 1872 and had hence rejected the report.[129] The report had inter alia concluded:

1. *No evidence exists in the texts to indicate that before the 18th century, any veneration was attached to a spot in Ayodhya as being the birth site of Lord Ram.*
2. *There are no grounds for supposing that a temple of Lord Ram, or any temple, existed at the site where the Babri Masjid was built in 1528–29.*
3. *There is no mention of the Babri Masjid in Ramcharitmanas composed in 1675–76.*
4. *The legend that the Babri Masjid occupied the site of Lord Ram's birth did not arise until the late 18th century, and that a temple was destroyed to build a mosque was not asserted until the beginning of the 19th century.*
5. *The full-blown legend of the destruction of the temple at the site of the birth of Lord Ram and Sita Ki Rasoi dates back to 1850, after which there is a progressive reconstruction of imagined history, based on faith.*

---

[128]Written Submission No. A76, Note on Proof of Belief-I (*Skanda Purana*, Travelers, Gazetteers) by Dr. Rajeev Dhavan, Sr. Adv., *Vada Prativada*, https://tinyurl.com/wu344m4c. Accessed on 18 January 2025.

[129]Ibid.

6. *No stone pillars or architecture of roof material of a temple were found in the debris of the trenches where the pillar bases stood.*
7. *The brick bases found in the excavation conducted by Professor B. B. Lal in 1979 were mentioned by him only in 1990, though several papers had been published by him.*
8. *The carvings on the pillars of the mosque do not indicate a Vaishnavite association.*
9. *There is no basis in the Skanda Purana ('Ayodhya Mahatmya') to indicate the site of the Babri Masjid as the birthplace of Lord Ram.*

The Sunni Board stressed that top historians had authored the report, and one of them was an archaeologist. Therefore, the report was multi-disciplinary and ought to have been given due weightage as expert evidence. But then, did all the participants sign the report? How are such reports prepared? What is an 'on-the-ground study' or was a 'field study' done? Were complete materials of earlier field studies/archaeological excavations by Dr B.B. Lal taken into account or not? Were the authors of the report brought before the court as witnesses? Did the experts have any knowledge of the Puranas? Did the experts have sufficient time or was there pressure to somehow prepare some kind of report? These questions were relevant as the report had made significant observations which had to be backed by evidence. Such questions were also posed by the court as reported by *The Times of India*.

> *The bench [...] peppered senior advocate Rajeev Dhavan with questions on the evidential value of the historians' report and said, 'At the highest, this report can be taken as an opinion.'*[130]

However, only a minuscule part of the cross examination of

[130]Mahapatra, Dhananjay, 'Historians' Report on Babri Mosque Mere 'Opinion': SC', *The Times of India*, 18 September 2019, https://tinyurl.com/ybzapw99. Accessed on 22 July 2025.

Mr Suraj Bhan, one of the four historians who had authored the report, was referred to in the news report. The part cross-examined in detail and the observations of the Hon'ble Allahabad High Court are reflected as follows[131]:-

NOT SIGNED BY ALL FOUR HISTORIANS

3611. This document, though claimed to be written by four historians, but as a matter of fact, it was not signed by Sri D.N. Jha, as admitted by Sri Suraj Bhan (PW 16), as expert witness.

DID ALL FOUR VISIT AYODHYA FOR STUDY?

3615. The following part of his statement is relevant to ascertain sincerity, genuineness and correctness in the alleged research of the witness and his statement:

Only Sharma and myself had gone to Ayodhya at time of Ayodhya research." (ETC)

EDUCATION & PROFESSIONAL BACKGROUND

3613. 'I got my graduation degree from Delhi University. In graduation, my subjects were Economics and Sanskrit besides English and Hindi. History was not my subject in B.A. […] I did my M.A. in Sanskrit from Delhi and later in archaeology and culture from M.S. University Baroda.' (E.T.C.)

'I am an M.A. in Sanskrit language. I can not speak Sanskrit, and since I have not used it for quite some time, I face difficulty in reading as also in following it.' 'I did my B.A. in 1953. Sanskrit and Economics were my subjects in B.A. English literature, too, was my subject […] I did not study history and archaeology as subjects up to B.A. I passed the M.A. Examination with Sanskrit and also with Archaeology

---

[131] Allahabad High Court Judgment Para 3611-3615, https://tinyurl.com/5n86hy5z. Accessed on 22 September 2025.

and Culture […] I only remember that ancient history and early medieval history were not in my course. The said two parts of history was of India only.' (E.T.C.)

RECORDED HISTORY AND THE STUDY

'I did not make any study of any recorded history with regard to the disputed subject.' (ETC)

'I did not make any excavation at the site, nor was it a part of my investigation.' (ETC)

'Recorded history, too, was not my subject, nor am I its specialist. I am also not a specialist in art history but I have general understanding of it.' (ETC)

ON SPECIALISATION IN FEATURES OF MOSQUE

3614. 'I have knowledge of post-Qutbuddin Muslim history but not in its minute details; I do not have any study on it.' (page 42) 'I did not read what features a mosque may not have.' (page 75) 'I am not a specialist in epigraphy and numismatics.' (page 82) (E.T.C.)

'I am not a geologist.' (page 95) 'I am not a student of Geology […] It is correct that I have not studied paleology as a subject, nor do I have its knowledge.' (page 110) 'Since construction of mosques after demolishing temples is not the subject of my research, so I did not make an endeavour to make study of those places. Otherwise also, I am not a historian with regard to medieval period.' (page 127) 'I did not read Skandha Purana […] I did not think it to be necessary to read other Puranas also as their study was not my subject.'

'But it is true that I am not a specialist in history.' (page 169) 'I did not do any research work after making excavations in Uttar Pradesh. I did not make any excavation in Bihar.' (page 170) 'I did not do any research work with respect to ancient

archaeological buildings, nor did I write a book in this respect.' (page 179)

WAS THERE ANY PRESSURE?

'We were given only six weeks' time for the entire study. Pressure was being repeatedly exerted; so, we submitted our report without going through the record of the excavation work by B.B.Lal.' (ETC)

'It is true that constructions going on a particular time are influenced by the circumstances prevailing at that time. As a historian I have seen a mosque in Benares which is built by demolishing a temple to half its size.' (ETC)

Senior Advocate Dhavan also brought to the court's attention the testimony of historian Suvira Jaiswal, who had deposed before the High Court. She had testified that there was no archaeological evidence demonstrating that the site was Ram's birthplace. Justice Agarwal in the Allahabad High Court had analysed the evidence of Suvira Jaiswal, formerly a professor at Jawaharlal Nehru University. Suvira Jaiswal stated that her knowledge about the destroyed site was based on newspapers or the work of other historians and not her own study. It was also a fact that Suvira Jaiswal was supporting the report of her own guide Professor R. S. Sharma who was a co-author of the Historian's report to the nation.[132] Suvira Jaiswal was a doctoral student under his guidance. She was not accepted as an expert witness. Ultimately, Justice Agarwal in the Allahabad High Court concluded that the report had not been signed by all the four historians (Professor D.N. Jha not having signed it) and the opinion of an alleged expert (Suvira Jaiswal) was not based on her study and research but a reflection of what others had written. Accordingly, Justice Agarwal had held that it was not credible evidence under Section

[132]Para 3618 of Justice Sudhir Agarwal, Allahabad High Court Judgment, *elegalix.allahabadhighcourt.in*, https://tinyurl.com/ytwedray. Accessed on 18 January 2025.

45 of the Indian Evidence Act, 1872.

Now the Supreme Court had to decide why two communities were fighting for a piece of land since at least 1855–1858, the timeline when Dr Dhavan drew the boundary for evidence to be considered. The court had to consider why there were riots in the 1800s. What drove Ram bhakts in hordes to the disputed site as recorded by gazetteers and travellers? What importance was to be given to the recordings from the days of Father Joseph Tieffenthaler (1770) and Edward Thornton (1858), that pointed out the belief as well as the practice of belief that within the disputed structure lay the birthplace of Ram?

The court also had another issue to resolve—the submission of Dr Dhavan in the arguments that the inner courtyard and outer courtyard had to be treated as two separate units because the British had erected iron railings and restricted Hindus to the outer courtyard where lay Ram Chabutra, and Muslims to the inner courtyard where lay the Babri Mosque, and that is how it should be worked out by the Supreme Court as well. Hindus should be restricted to the outer courtyard, at best.

While the team calibrated Dr Dhavan's submission and the possible replies to such submissions, Senior Parasaran could get adequate rest. The court break of five days allowed him to travel to Chennai, where to his discomfort, he was not told many charitable things about his eyes. He returned from Chennai, more cautious and a bit more accommodating of the concern expressed by his doctors and family members. Of course, terms like 'a bit more', and 'a little bit more', are subjective. No one has had an objective assessment of these values, but more rest for the eyes and body was required. 'A bit more' has no fixed definition similar to terms like 'belong', 'belonging to' and 'ownership'. Hard-working lawyers serving their clients know the meaning can change with the context. For Bhakti, Mr Parasaran was participating in the Ashwamedha of Ram. But then, was the horse of Ashwadhama halted? If yes, what happened in 1885 that halted it?

20

A Stumbling Block or an Ashwamedha?

Counsels from both sides were burning the midnight oil. It was not a client's case. For most, it was cause lawyering pro bono. And all were setting health-related obstacles aside. Mr Zafaryab Jilani, a senior advocate appearing for the Sunni Waqf Board, was also suffering from physical disability. He was much younger than Senior Parasaran, and thus suffered from a lesser number of age-related ailments, but like Mr Parasaran, he too was struggling to read. Mr Jilani had also postponed the advised medical procedures, as also did Mr Ranjit Kumar, prioritizing the case for Ram over personal health. During lunch recess, these senior counsels were seen exchanging notes on eye surgery. Such is life when you become a 'Senior Citizen'. Dr Dhavan was the youngest and fittest among the seniors in Mr Parasaran's opinion. This was based on Mr Parasaran's assessment of Dr Dhavan's work which was of sterling quality and reflected his commitment to the case. The banter of the seniors was interesting. Mr Parasaran tried his best to convince everyone around him about how ugly, bald and old he looked, and how handsome and young Dr Dhavan in his seventies was with lots of hair on his head.

In the Supreme Court, behind every case is an Advocate-on-Record (AOR). If the side of the Ram bhakts had Yogeswaran and Bhakti, then the other side had Mr Ejaz Maqbool. Maqbool's office presented elegant compilations, notes and tabulations.

The Supreme Court Bar has several distinguished women members who add great value to the proceedings, at par with their male counterparts. Several such accomplished and competent lady Advocates were part of the case representing different parties in the historic case. The younger members of the Bar also prioritized their professional work over personal life.

But what if matrimonial ceremonies were also being deferred to concentrate on the case?

Yes! It was whispered in court among lawyers that one of the lady advocates had even postponed her marriage to concentrate on the case. Dhananjay Mahapatra of the *Times of India*, as usual, investigated into it with the world coming to know about it later. A report in the newspaper narrated the humble background of lawyers like Yogeshwaran who came from a small village in Tamil Nadu, and the fact that Akriti Chaubey had lost her father when she was in class five. Akriti with her mother's help worked her way up in the profession. The report was kind and accurate, even mentioning the effective assistance being provided by Akriti and Qurratulain to the Sunni Board side which made it possible for Dr Dhavan to present their case. However, the most striking part in the *Times of India* report was the following:

> *Advocate Akriti Chaubey, advocate Ezaj Maqbool's junior, sacrificed much on her personal front to delve deep into the case. Chaubey was to get engaged [...] Chaubey decided that her engagement could wait as the case couldn't.*[133]

This presents the reader with two teams led by two sets of committed Senior Counsels and a number of assisting counsels. The case which had succeeded before the Allahabad High Court was Suit 5 of Ram Lalla Virajman. Suit 3 of Nirmohi Akhara as well as Suit 4 of the Sunni Board had not succeeded though they were granted one-third of the disputed land. If Suit 5 of Ram Lalla was the stumbling block for one of the sides, then it was Ashwamedha for the other. Hence, an attack on Suit 5 was

---

[133]Mahapatra, Dhananajay, 'Ayodhya verdict: Lawyers slogged without a break, a junior put off her engagement', *The Times of India*, 10 November 2019, https://tinyurl.com/yn9hutv4. Accessed on 18 January 2025.

necessary for those for whom it was a stumbling block. The points of attack against Suit 5 by the Sunni Board side were:

1. Lord Ram could be represented by only one party. Nirmohi Akhara (Suit 3) as shebait had already presented its suit, hence Ram Lalla's case (Suit 5) was not maintainable.
2. The purpose of Suit 5 was to take away Shebaiti rights from Nirmohi Akhara, take over the land from them, destroy the old building, and construct a new temple.
3. Suit 5 was moved only in 1989 at a much belated state and as such, the claim was time-barred, stale and beyond limitation.
4. Suit 5 was a vehicle to destroy and remove the existing structure.
5. The strongest attack came on the point that Ram Janam Bhoomi, the land itself, was not a Juristic Person like a company or bank against whom cases could be filed.

The threat from Ram Janmabhoomi, the land itself being declared a Juristic Person, was that if Ram Janmabhoomi was a Juristic Person in itself, then no possession of the land could be claimed by the other side. The land itself would exist as a composite whole and would have a personality in the eyes of the law in the same way as a company or a cooperative society or a bank does.

Therefore, if the land became one composite personality like a company, the land could not be divided at all. It could not be occupied or captured or claimed by anyone, neither could it be divided into parts on the ground that a personality cannot be divided, and in the present case, divinity cannot be divided. While faith of course is intangible, was something tangible required to confer the status of a Juristic Person on a place of belief or faith? Or were faith and belief sufficient to confer the status of Juristic Person to a land?

Dr Dhavan's case was that the objective, physical manifestation of divinity in a form on the land was necessary to confer the status of a Juristic Person. The land, Ram

Janambhoomi, as canvassed, lacked any material objectification, and mere land cannot be a Juristic Person in the eyes of the law. The presence of some symbol on the land was necessary. Only showing belief in the land being the birthplace was not sufficient; further, worship based on that belief had to be shown. Dr Dhavan, contested the belief, arguing that there was a complete absence of reliable evidence to hold that there was belief that Lord Ram was born under the central dome. The moot proposition was belief and the active practice of belief for the Hindu side. Dr Dhavan, however, insisted on some material manifestation, even if belief existed. The game laid out by the two legal greats, Lal Narayan Sinha and K. Parasaran, concerning Janmabhoomi as a Juristic Person was being played out. The Sunni Board had to lay out the contours of Hindu belief. However, 'belief' itself can be an issue which can be proved by evidence.

Such propositions necessarily result in some probing by the judges. The media too reported the attack on Suit 5 extensively. *Livelaw.in*[134] reported the exchange between Dr Dhavan and the judges as follows:

> *[…] Senior Advocate Rajeev Dhavan resumed his arguments on the Juristic personality of the Janmasthan. He urged the bench that there must be an objective manifestation of a belief to confer the status of a juristic person to that belief. 'At what point does a belief translate into something objective and when does that objective form transform into a juristic person?' Dhavan asked the bench, and further stated that there has to be consecration of an idol.*
>
> *While Justice Ashok Bhushan distinguished the concept of idol from that of Janmasthan, saying the latter was based on epics, Justice D. Y. Chandrachud threw light on difference between*

[134]Chaudhary, Nilashish, 'Mere Belief That Lord Ram Was Born At The Site Will Not Confer It Juristic Personality, Argues Dhavan', *Live Law*, 23 September 2019, https://tinyurl.com/368sr7ka. Accessed on 18 January 2025.

Swayambhu, consecration of idol and juristic person. There are times when it is about belief, but sometimes it needs more than belief to make it juristic personality, he added.

Dhavan further submitted that belief was tenuous, and even if he conceded to the belief, objective manifestation of that belief had not been shown. His argument was that the Janmasthan could be much larger in area as compared to the exact spot claimed, and such a large area could not have juristic personality. […]

Justice Chandrachud then stated that Dhavan's first argument that belief is tenuous was an evidentiary issue, however, sought clarification regarding his second argument that a manifestation of the belief was required. 'What is the object of the manifestation of belief that is required?' he asked. 'Worship is good enough, but they've shown belief, not worship,' replied the senior advocate. […]

[…] Moving on, Rajeev Dhavan stated that the purpose of plaint 5 was to destroy the shebait, make a new temple and take over. Reiterating his allegation that, as per that suit, the existing structures are to be destroyed and new temple is to be constructed. He submitted that Suit no.5 was 'simply a vehicle to destroy, to remove'.

They have only mentioned Lord Ram was born there, without establishing contours of the area, he added. Referring back to his original argument of juristic personality, Rajeev Dhavan submitted that he agreed that 'Lord Ram was born here but that does not make it a juristic personality [...] only after 1989 was it claimed that the place is a juristic personality.' To this, J Bobde asked why should anyone have to prove there's a divine character? [...]

Coming to the question of title, Dhavan then argued that only the Ram Chabutra can be shown as the place of offering

> *prayer, and discussing parikrama, it was asserted that parikrama itself cannot create title.*

The Sunni Board had merely agreed that the Ram Kot area in Ayodhya could be the birthplace of Lord Ram, but he stuck to the earlier stand that there had to be positive evidence adduced by the side of Ram Lalla that the birthplace was below the central dome. As per Dr Dhavan, only belief concerning the area below the central dome was brought as evidence and not evidence of worship. But then where was the place for the offering of prayers?

In Senior Parasaran's chambers earlier as well, the discussion had centred on the concept of Juristic Person in Hindu Law. Mr Parasaran had deliberated with his team on various propositions. Would a water tank, established for the purpose of providing drinking water to the poor, qualify as having a purpose significant enough to be recognized as a Juristic Person? Could a scenario be envisaged in which a water body, constructed on two acres of land and dedicated by a public-spirited individual for common and general use as a means of accruing *punya* (spiritual merit), be deemed a Juristic Person? The man who dedicated the water body is no longer the owner as he has already gifted it to the general public. The water body now belongs to everyone. Who takes care of it? Who owns it? Is it not serving the whole of society? To protect the water body and the pious object of service of all mankind, will you not treat it as a Juristic Person? How will that water body be protected when someone encroaches on its land when the man who dedicated the water body for public use is no longer alive? Who can file a case to protect the water body as its owner? The water body has no owner now. But shouldn't the water body be protected for the good of all living creatures? Should all that is required to be done not be allowed to be done out of necessity to protect the water body? The water body and the pious purpose in the water body get elevated to the status of a Juristic Person, to safeguard it.

Another stream of questions had to be answered: 'What all

is worshipped in Indian tradition from ancient times? What can Hindus worship or worship as of now?' The answers to these questions were based on belief. These discussions arose from the fact that Hindus had diverse forms and methods of worship, and were flexible in their worship. Various entities, as per Hindu belief, were worshipped. So, can the land on which Shri Ram took birth be holy or not for someone who is a bhakt?

Of course, it can be, and the test will be belief-based. A seasoned lawyer like Dr Dhavan would take his call and bring his perspective to the table. Dr Dhavan had his questions. Will all the land that Ram walked over from Ayodhya to Sri Lanka will be holy or not? What about lands that the Buddha or Krishna walked over? Dr Dhavan, therefore, posed questions that had valid ramifications.

These are instances where legal issues got entangled: What lands could be a Juristic Person? That the birthplace is certainly more special than any other place, and that the Janmabhoomi was special were undisputed. But then what all pieces of land where Ram, the Buddha and Krishna walked over across India could be a Juristic Person? All, or some? What would be the test? There was a lot of research and chiselling down of the proposition between Senior Parasaran and Anirudh on the point of Juristic Person. The decision of the master for the pupil was to wait and watch and keep working.

Much depended on the other side's answer to the question 'What all can Hindus worship?' When someone opposed the plea of Ram Janmabhoomi being a Juristic Person and being divine in itself, one will have to answer what all can be divine for Hindu worship and what all cannot be divine. Is the worship of an animal, an idol, the *shiva in the form of a shivling*, and a *shaktipeeth*, a reality in India? Then why not worship of that piece of land where God himself took birth?

As expected, Dr Dhavan did give insight with examples of the width of the flexibility of Hindu worship. Dr Dhavan's submissions veered around the point that there are two kinds of Juristic Personalities[135] in Hindu Law:

1. Swayambhu or self-revealed areas in nature (e.g., lingam in Kailash, undulating land in Kedarnath, and so on)
2. Human-created artificial idols

In both the systems of swayambhu as well as idols, firstly, there existed some form of manifestation/identification. Secondly, there existed continuity of practice, overt religious act as well as belief. Though it was accepted that parikrama is a form of practice, but it is not a claim of ownership or domain as in ashwamedha. While natural manifestations like the one at Amarnath could be recognized as swayambhu. A mere piece of land could not be conferred divinity or status of a Juristic Person without there being manifestation in the material form of a lingam or any other form. Dr Dhavan gave an illustrative list of temples in India with no idols. It read:

1. *Thillai Nataraja Temple, Chidambaram, Tamil Nadu: No idols; a curtain is raised and people worship the notional linga behind the curtain.*
2. *Pakshi Mandir, Sabarkantha District, Gujarat (part of khedroda group of monuments): No idols; birds are carved on the walls and are worshipped.*
3. *Male female temples, Nilgiris, Tamil Nadu: No idols; male and female powers are worshipped.*
4. *Patal Mandir, Bhuvaneshwar, Odisha: No idols but has natural formations in the form of Sheshnag (five-headed serpent); belief is that the cave is placed on the spine of Sheshnag.*
5. *Kamakhya Temple, Guwahati, Assam: No idols; a yoni-like stone with a natural spring flowing over it is worshipped.*

---

[135]Written Submission No. A81, The Note on Juristic Personality of Idols and Areas by Dr. Rajeev Dhavan, Sr. Adv., *Vada Prativada*, https://tinyurl.com/4apyy4a5. Accessed on 18 January 2025.

6. *Alopidevi Temple, Allahabad, Uttar Pradesh: Worship is in swing.*
7. *Raja Rani Temples, Bhubaneswar: Images of Shiva and Parvati, though no idols.*
8. *Hadimba Temple, Manali, Himachal Pradesh: No idols; devotees worship two large footprints.*

Unconventional Temples

9. *Dog Temple in Channapatna, Karnataka: This unconventional temple was established in 2009 to respect dogs and their quality of faithfulness. Two dog faces act as idols within the temple. Villagers believe that the deities in this temple will stop any wrongdoing in the area.*
10. *The Om Banna Temple, better known as the Bullet Baba Temple, near Jodhpur, Rajasthan: No idols, no pictures; the deity in this temple is a 350cc Royal Enfield Bullet motorcycle.*

Dr Dhavan's submission was that it is relevant to note that in each of the afore-mentioned temples, though there are no idols, there is either a natural manifestation of an image, a formation or a temple entity that is worshipped.

Considering the afore-mentioned, Dr Dhavan reiterated that without any manifestation, the land Ram Janmabhoomi could not be looked at as divinity in itself and, therefore, could not be a Juristic Person in law.

Dr Dhavan then also attacked the submissions made by the counsels of Ram Lalla on the grounds of lack of evidence. He submitted that the mere existence of parikrama would not concertize the Hindus claim over the disputed land. Parikrama of the Janmabhoomi did not identify the spot of the birth of Lord Ram. He attacked historical documents like the Gazetteer cited by the counsels for Ram Lalla on the grounds that such documents do not constitute proof in themselves and have only secondary or tertiary significance in corroborating facts. Dr Dhavan's point was that these are merely like stories. Neither parikrama nor the historical documents were hard evidence. On the contrary, the argument was historical texts cannot be relied upon to deduce negative inferences. If the presence of a mosque is not mentioned in a historical document that Mr Vaidyanathan relied upon, it did not prove that the mosque did not exist.[136]

As important points arose, there were also discussions between the Senior Counsels. It was either Senior Parasaran calling up Mr Vaidyanathan or Mr Vaidyanathan calling up Senior Parasaran to discuss the line to be taken for an important proposition, or to discuss some issues of facts. This happened even during court hearings. Lunch recess was used by the seniors to discuss and fine-tune their points and strategies. Many a time, Mr Parasaran and Mr Vaidyanathan were joined by Mr P.S. Narasimha and Mr Ranjit Kumar. On important issues, strategies were discussed and propositions chiselled. 'Juristic Person' was one such issue.

However, the idea was to first wait for the other side to end its arguments on this point. As Yogeswaran, Bhakti and Sridhar got busy, sometimes briefing Mr Vaidyanathan and other counsels, and Ashwin and Aditi got busy with conferences with Mr Mohan Parasaran, Anirudh relished his time with the living legend and his guru Senior Parasaran; his fan boy moment continued. Ashwin did give him some competition for the fanboy spot, yet Anirudh was in the lead. Every member of team Ram Lalla had to thank their colleagues and friends who backed them up and helped them with their private clients. Some private clients even delayed filing some matters of their own to help the assisting team concentrate on the Ram Lalla case.

The arguments of the Sunni Board challenged the presence of evidence of practice of belief. For team Ram Lalla, further discussions centred around the point that worship at the site

[136]Written Submission No. A76, Note on Proof of Belief-I (*Skanda Purana*, Travelers, Gazetteers) by Dr. Rajeev Dhavan, Sr. Adv., *Vada Prativada*, https://tinyurl.com/wu344m4c. Accessed on 18 January 2025.

had to be analysed from two perspectives to get a complete picture: (1) worship within the premises of the land in dispute, and (2) worship of Ram bhakts of the land from outside the disputed area. Such an approach could clarify not only the point of the practice of faith but also the dimensions that the two points would unfold. These points also perfectly mingled with the accounts of Christian missionaries and non-Hindu foreign travellers as well as gazetteers to reveal the truth of the Janmabhoomi.

Senior Parasaran could delve into some cases on the Chidambaram Temple to explain, if need be, the concept of Hindu worshipping a formless deity—as in Chidambaram, only a blank open space is worshipped. At the same time, the assisting team was ready with cases to show how international courts had viewed temples and Juristic Persons, including a court of appeal case from England dealing with an abandoned temple/a temple in ruins viz. the concept of a Juristic Person. There was even a case from the International Court of Justice. The story of a temple that English and Canadian courts discussed, gave new insights while many lawyer colleagues were surprised to discover that nations went to war over a temple land or a land having a temple.

The case had now opened up. The secrets in the closets of history regarding 1885 were yet to be unravelled. What happened in 1885 was the key. No less important was the new focal point of the case. The centre of gravity had shifted to a new geographical location within approximately 1,500 sq. yd of the disputed area. The new focal point was the key to unravelling the secrets of 1885. 1885 was haunting everyone.

SECTION IV

1885

21

The Focal Point

Why did Ram Chabutra become the focal point after 1855? The case was to be governed by the rules of a civil suit. A civil suit mandates that parties cannot travel beyond what they pleaded in writing when they first filed their case. In essence, this simply means that if you state that you have bought the house with your father's income, you cannot turn around and state later that you bought the property from your mother-in-law's income or its self-acquired. What you state at the first instance binds you and that crystallizes your case.

All the parties wanted the entire 1,500 sq. yd of land as one composite unit, and there was no prayer for the division of the land. (*See maps in photo inserts.*) All the parties in their pleadings were unanimous that the Hon'ble High Court of Allahabad had erred in partitioning the land where no point on the partitioning the land was ever pleaded, no question of partitioning the land ever arose or was argued, no issues concerning the partition of land were ever formulated and none of the parties in their suits prayed for the partition of land either into half or three. All the parties had vehemently pointed out these facts. Consequently, what should have happened, and happens in such cases, is that either a party proved its title based on the preponderance of probabilities and got the complete land or it did not get any piece of land. There was a no deviation from this rule as per the counsels of Ram Lalla too. The partition of land was not pleaded for, the partition of land was not prayed for, and the partition of land was not argued for, yet the partition of the Janmabhoomi was the final consequence.

Reverting to the evidence, what argument was advanced? Since neither science nor faith allowed for witnesses either from 1 BCE or 16 CE to be summoned in person, and thankfully so, the case was bound to be proven in the manner allowed to prove historical facts and historical practice of faith. The parties had to prove that they had a better case based on the preponderance of probabilities to establish their title.

Dr Dhavan was unequivocal in his submissions that the disputed site was subject to Quranic law.[137] His propositions were emphatic that once a land has been dedicated to the Almighty and therefore made a *waqf* with complete detachment of the owner from the land, it will always continue to be a waqf. To put it in simple terms, once a mosque always a mosque[138]; even if the building of the mosque gets demolished, the mosque continues to be a mosque.

Dr Dhavan relied upon the report dated 3 August 1950 submitted by Mr Basheer Ahmad Khan, Pleader Commissioner to counter the claim of Nirmohi Akhara that the building was never a mosque, while the case of Suit 5 of Ram Lalla and some other parties was that Babur got a mosque constructed over Ram Janmabhoomi. However, this mosque was never dedicated as a mosque, never used as a mosque and where Hindus continued their prayers, and the disputed building continued to have figurines of Hindu gods and goddesses. Hence, these submissions did not bother Ram Lalla's case much. Basheer Ahmad Khan's report contained a total of thirteen photographs. Photograph 1 depicted the word 'Allah' inscribed in Arabic above the arch of the main gate outside the disputed structure. Photograph 8 contained three inscriptions of Allah in Arabic characters. It was taken from the courtyard of the building of the middle arch in the eastern wall while Photograph 10 was of the mimber or

[137]Written Submission No. A123, The Note on the Issue of Wakf by Dr. Rajeev Dhavan, Sr. Adv., *Vada Prativada*, https://tinyurl.com/5y9urtrr. Accessed on 18 January 2025.
[138]Ibid.

pulpit. The Commissioner's report[139] inter alia stated:

> *Photo No.1 is the Photograph of the disputed building from outside, of the main entrance. A little above the arch of the main gate towards the right and left there are small circles in which the word 'Allah' is written (inscribed) in Arabic. A little above it there now hangs a picture of Hanumanji. (Beneath the frame of the picture 'Allaho Akbar' is inscribed in the wall in the Arabic characters). This inscription has been covered by the said picture and, therefore, it is not visible in the Photograph, and as the photo of this portion could not be taken without the removal of the Picture of Hanumanji, I am making it clear in my report, I did not insist on the removal of the Picture with a view to avoid any trouble or ugly situation that might have arisen.*
>
> *Photo 8 contained three inscriptions of 'Allah' in Arabic characters. It was taken from the courtyard of the building of the middle arch in the eastern wall.*

The Commissioner's report stated:

> *No.8 is Photo taken from the Courtyard of the building in suit of the Middle Arch in the eastern wall. A little below the top of the arch at three places—'Allah' in Arabic characters is inscribed. Below the 'Allah' in the middle, the inscription 'Toghra' (...) is blurred in the photo (but at the spot it can be read).*

Photograph 10 was of the mimber or pulpit in respect of which the Commissioner's report states:

> *No.10 is the Photo of the pulpit (Mimber) on which the idols*

[139]Supra 13.
Also *see*: Written Submission No. A54, Note of Mr. Bashir Ahmad Khan, Pleader Commissioner, dated 03.08.1950, along with 13 photographs, Dr. Rajeev Dhavan, Sr. Adv., https://tinyurl.com/mpn8jt6d. Accessed on 18 January 2025.

> *are placed. On the left side of the mimber there is a Persian inscription which is blurred in the Photo.*

Dr Dhavan further submitted that the argument of un-Islamic features present in the mosque, such as the decorative depiction of animals, decorative inscriptions, the instalment of fourteen kasauti pillars and the images of lions as referred to by Mr Vaidyanathan did not indicate that the structure was not a mosque. The structure continued to be a valid mosque. Dr Dhavan's case was that the Nawab of Oudh may have not acted as per the Quran in some respects but that did not deny the existence of a mosque.

Back in office, questions were buzzing in the minds of those supporting team Ram Lalla. The foremost query was who proves that a mosque stands validly dedicated? Who proves that there was prayer at the mosque? What if you concede that it was a prayer place for someone else also who did not pray in a mosque? What about the fact that a non-Islamic structure already stood identified below in the excavations? Yogeswaran, as usual, was quite emphatic about these points. In contrast, the quiet and steady Bhakti was ready to point out more evidence till the time Senior Parasaran would politely intercede saying, 'Yogeswaran and Bhakti, Vaidyanathan is looking after this particular part of evidence. He has already placed the evidence and whatever more is required, he will do the needful, Vaidhyanathan and I will discuss these.'

What worried Yogeswaran was the submission of the Sunni Board that the inner courtyard was used exclusively by Muslims after 1857 and should exclusively be a mosque. The Senior Counsels for Ram Lalla were not worried. They were emphatic: 'It's a property dispute. Dispute of title. Either the property goes to one party or to another party. The case might have religious overtones, but it is not a religious dispute inside the courtroom. The property cannot belong half to one person and half to someone else. Even the Sunni Board has not pleaded for that.'

Mr Parasaran would listen to all the points and even at the cost of repetition, rewrite the points given by his briefing counsels and, of course, dish out a fresh version of the notes. Mr Vaidyanathan, in contrast, would grapple with his thoughts by himself as Aditi would wrestle with the task of proofreading and correcting late into the night, the new versions of Mr Parasaran's notes. The only lady in the team was thought to be most reliable for such a tedious job by Mr Parasaran who found the men to be less emotionally intelligent. That included him as well when he compared himself to his wife. Mr Parasaran held the same view when he compared his daughters-in-law with his sons.

Yogeswaran was also concerned that the basis of Dr Dhavan's submission went in favour of Nirmohi Akhara. Dr Dhavan had submitted that Nirmohi Akhara and the idols of Ram Lalla had been present at the disputed site. However, Yogi's worry was that Dr Dhavan had said that the Ram bhakts were present only outside the railings put up by the Britishers in 1857–58.

On several occasions since the hearing began, Senior Advocate Dr Rajeev Dhavan maintained that the prayers of Ram bhakts/Hindus were limited to the outer courtyard, at Ram Chabutra, before 1949. He seemed to suggest that no prayers were ever held in the inner courtyard by Hindus, even prior to 1857–58 when there was no partition through the iron railing. The court on 18 September 2019 had sought clarifications from Dr Dhavan regarding the place where Hindu prayer was offered. What happened to the Hindu mode of worship after the iron railing were erected by the British?[140]

What would have been the case if no iron railing was there in 1858? Why was the iron railing required at all to keep Hindus

[140]'Day 48 Arguments, Ayodhya Title Dispute', *Supreme Court Observer*, 19 September 2019, https://tinyurl.com/2s8p78p8. Accessed on 18 January 2025.
Also *see*: Rajagopal, Krishnadas, 'Ram "Chabutra" becomes the focal point in Ayodhya hearing', *The Hindu*, 3 December 2021, https://tinyurl.com/mr34xubh. Accessed on 18 January 2025.

out? What exactly did the iron railing and worship at Ram Chabutra within the premises of the disputed area signify? Did it signify that Hindus believed that this was the actual site of the Ram Janmasthan or Ram Janmabhoomi? After all, it was no longer debated that worship did take place within the disputed structure, be it the inner courtyard or the outer courtyard.

Undeniably, Ram Chabutra was a place of worship within the disputed site. Now the iron railing and Ram Chabutra became the focal points of the case. The court exchanges between the judges and the counsels as reported by the media also focused on this point. *The Hindu*[141] carried this report and recorded some questions put by the Bench:

> *[...] The observation from the judge is significant as the Allahabad High Court, in its 2010 judgment, took a 'leap of faith' and deduced the space under the central dome of the masjid, demolished by kar sevaks in 1992, to be the exact birthplace of Lord Ram.*
>
> *Justice Chandrachud, one of the five judges on the Constitution Bench led by Chief Justice of India Ranjan Gogoi, began his remarks by observing that it was 'coincidental' that Ram Chabutra came up along with the construction of the railing by the British following an armed clash between Hindus and Muslims in 1855. Prior to that year, both Hindus and Muslims entered it for prayers.*
>
> *After the violence, Muslims entered the mosque and Hindus prayed at the Chabutra, a platform erected merely 50 yards away from the mosque's central dome.*
>
> *'After 1855, Ram Chabutra was erected just outside the railing. It in fact came up along with the railing. So it must*

---

[141]Rajagopal, Krishnadas, 'Ram "Chabutra" becomes the focal point in Ayodhya hearing', *The Hindu*, 3 December 2021, https://tinyurl.com/mr34xubh. Accessed on 18 January 2025.

be that worshippers believed that praying at the "chabutra" meant actually praying at the central dome[...] They actually went to pray at the central dome,' Justice Chandrachud observed.

Justice Ashok Bhushan intervened to say, 'They went to the railing because they believed that birth happened there [under the central dome].'

Justice Chandrachud observed, 'Why do you need to pray at the railing? You go to the railing to look beyond the railing.'

The Senior Advocate for the Sunni Waqf Board, Dr. Rajeev Dhavan, had dismissed the judge's reasoning as mere 'conjecture'. Justice Chandrachud had shot back, saying it was a 'preponderance of probabilities', which the court could indulge in.

'Why did the chabutra become the focal point after 1855? Prior to 1855, both Hindus and Muslims went in [...] All this upsurge happens after the railing comes up. Why? It may be because of a sense of exclusion among the Hindus. This not just conjecture, but preponderance of probabilities,' Justice Chandrachud addressed Mr. Dhavan.

Mr. Dhavan responded that the 1850s was a time of inter se conflict and conquest. 'The context of the time was that of a riot situation. British may have come and said, "enough of this nonsense." But the context then was that of a riot situation. Not just riot, but internecine conflict,' he submitted. He said that Justice Chandrachud was 'adding something' not in the case records. 'Where is it said from the records that they [Hindu worshippers] prayed to the inner dome from the chabutra? This is conjecture within the meaning of unreasonable probability [...] I go till the railing outside the lion's den knowing it is dangerous beyond that,' he argued.

> *Dr. Dhavan reiterated that the Hindus had no claim over the inner courtyard as the inner courtyard was in exclusive possession of the Muslims where only they had the right to pray; the Hindus worshipped only in the outer courtyard.*

The questions now were: Was there was some evidence with respect to Ram bhakts' belief that the premises below the domes also constituted Ram Janmabhoomi. Were Hindus still looking towards the domes beyond the iron railings for spiritual and religious succour? All these were delicate issues that had bearing on the case. To top all this was the following question: Was it believed that below the central dome existed the exact birthplace of Ram?

While the Sunni Board argued, team Ram Lalla and the senior counsels, Senior Parasaran, Mr Vaidyanathan, Mr Ranjit Kumar, and Mr Narasimha calibrated the response. Now, there was no dispute that Ram bhakts were praying all these years within the disputed area at Ram Chabutra. This was leading to the legal battle of 1885.

There was serious dispute between the two sides on the issues. Dr Dhavan's assistance was sought to this line of questions, and the media which wanted answers to these focal point questions, was eager to lap up every word of the exchange in court. It seemed that the newspapers had a story they loved. *The New Indian Express* reported: 'Ayodhya Dispute: Muslim Parties' Lawyer Rajeev Dhavan Loses Cool, Terms Judge's Tone as "aggressive"',[142] but the team didn't bother about the tag line. Dr Dhavan did have a personality which did get worked up but it never took away anything from the respect for his industry and erudition. The team knew that the media was leaning in favour of sensationalism. The team, however, did bother about some

---

[142]'Ayodhya dispute: Muslim parties' lawyer Rajeev Dhavan loses cool, terms judge's tone as "aggressive"', *The New Indian Express*, 20 September 2019, https://tinyurl.com/59pku5pd. Accessed on 18 January 2025.

of the questions asked by the judges and the responses to them to calibrate its stand, not with respect to sensationalism but on issues of evidence. Vartha Bharati report captured the happenings in court in its report as follows:

> *Losing his cool, a senior advocate for Muslim parties in the Ram Janmabhoomi-Babri Masjid land dispute case in the Supreme Court, told a curious judge [Bhushan] Friday that he was seeing 'some kind of aggression' in his tone.*
>
> *[...] The bench was earlier questioning senior advocate Rajeev Dhavan, appearing for the Sunni Waqf Board and others including original litigant M. Siddiq, about the testimony of a witness who had visited the disputed site in 1935, and had deposed before the Allahabad High Court in 2000.*
>
> *The bench, also comprising justices S. A. Bobde, D. Y. Chandrachud, Ashok Bhushan and S. A. Nazeer, asked Dhavan to read some other portions of the testimony of witness Ram Surat Tiwari dealing with prayers offered by the Hindus at the railings on the disputed site.*
>
> *'This witness said that he had gone there (site) in 1935. Read his statement; whether we believe it or not is something else,' Justice Bhushan asked Dhavan.*
>
> *'I can see some kind of aggression in My Lord's tone,' Dhavan said, adding, 'If lordships are saying that I am twisting the evidence, then I will read that out.'*
>
> *'This is not about twisting; the point is whether certain facts are there or not,' the judge said.*
>
> *Senior advocates C. S. Vaidyanathan and Ranjit Kumar objected to the assertions of Dr Dhavan who quickly apologized to the bench.*
>
> *'My apologies. Sometimes, I am taken aback. I get frightened.*

What should I do? When there is a hearing which is going on for this long, we sometimes get carried away,' Dhavan said.

'Dr Dhavan, people who come from the North West Frontier do not get frightened. We are impressed by the history,' the CJI observed with a smile."[143]

On the following days as well, Dr Dhavan termed the Supreme Court's observation that the belief of Hindus of the prevalence of some divinity in the central dome of the disputed structure at the site made them offer prayers at the railings put up by the British in 1858, was conjecture.

At times, interactions between the Bar and the Bench do throw up heated moments. The court and every lawyer must come back to the facts of the case and the legal regime governing the case. Every lawyer weaves in a world of anecdotes, stories, idiosyncrasies and then, comes back to the facts and the law of the case. The Sunni Board, after accepting the presence of Lord Ram Lalla's statues and his worship within the disputed site at Ram Chabutra, had to build a case where they could state the difference and dichotomy between the inner and outer courtyards which were brought into existence by the iron railing partition after 1857. He tried to discard the versions of Hindu witnesses for the purpose and started bringing in the card of 1885 with the focal point being Ram Chabutra. *Vartha Bharati* further reported Dr Dhavan's interaction with the Bench:[144]

He referred to the suit filed by Nirmohi Akhara's Mahant Raghubar Das in 1885 and said that it was constructing a temple at 'Ram Chabutara' in the outer courtyard of the site.

---

[143]Infra.

[144]'Babri Masjid land dispute: Muslim parties' lawyer loses cool, terms judge's tone as "aggressive"', *Vartha Bharati*, 19 September 2019, https://tinyurl.com/yfkz44b7. Accessed on 18 January 2025.

The Sub-Judge, Faizabad, did not allow the petition and there was a finding that Muslims were praying inside and Hindus were offering puja in the outer courtyard, he said.

He again responded to yesterday's observation of the apex court that 'Ram Chabutara' was set up in the close proximity of the railing because Hindus believed of some divinity in the central dome and this is the reason they were praying at the railing.

There was no evidence that Hindus prayed at the railings or grilled wall, Dhavan said.

He then dealt in detail with the evidence of Tiwari as the top court wanted him to read the testimony in totality to have the clear picture.

He said Tiwari had visited the place with his uncle in December 1935 when he was 12–13-years-old and said that he had seen one idol and one photograph there at the site.

Dhavan said the witness stated he was an atheist and believed that Lord Ram took birth inside the central dome and described the details in the court in 2000 about what he saw in 1935.

There were many discrepancies in Tiwari's testimony and he is not able to remember anything, he added.

However, the bench said that there was evidence that he had seen the idols inside the central dome before 1949, the year when it was alleged that the idols were placed inside surreptitiously.

All this evidence came after 1989 when the lawsuit on behalf of the deity was filed, and these are no credible proofs, Dhavan said, adding that after the 'rath yatra' and demolition of the structure, the Ram Janmbhoomi had become a bigger

> *issue and such testimonies were recorded after these events.*
>
> *He also referred to principles of law on evidence and said with the 'deepest respect' the statements of the witness cannot be regarded as credible proof [...]*

Dr Dhavan was constructing his case of evidence and was attempting to establish that the Hindu case had no evidence of worship beyond Ram Chabutra. There was no evidence of worship below the central dome.

The case was now reaching its zenith. History, evidence, law, and advocacy were all playing out at their best. But 1885 held the key. The events of 1885 had a huge bearing on the case from either side. It was, therefore, no surprise that the Sunni Board, right from its plaint in Suit 4, was relying on the judgement in the Suit of 1885, and for the same reasons, every lawyer from Ram Lalla's side was careful of the point: How would Dr Dhavan play on 'What happened in 1885?' The answer was awaited.

22

The Riddle of 1885

History is riddled with controversies. Certainly, analysis of some events can be controversial. Thankfully some points are not disputed, for instance, the fact that Lord Ram was born in Ayodhya. But events around undisputed facts are often challenged. If it was not disputed that Lord Ram was born in Ayodhya, then where was he born in Ayodhya was the question. Was there any alternative theory that the opposing side to Ram Lalla's suit wished to proclaim about the birthplace of Lord Ram?

If yes, then where, according to the opposing side, as per their records or their version was the birth site of Lord Ram? What was the relevance of the Suit of 1885 concerning the location of the birth site of Lord Ram? These were the searching questions to be answered; the riddle to be solved.

The Suit/Case of 1885 had a huge bearing on the case as pleaded by the Sunni Board. The Suit of 1885 also had a bit of history. Disputes between the two communities over the issue of the Janmabhoomi had started arising just after 1857, which required the intervention of the authorities. If the British had thought that erecting an iron railing which resulted in the creation of the inner and outer courtyards in 1858 would prevent any further law-and-order problems, they were mistaken. If these steps were taken according to the British divide-and-rule game, then the game was a stupendous success. The controversies and the divide kept growing, and Hindu-Muslim riots were not uncommon in that era. These disputes were also highlighted later by the Sunni Board to state that they were in possession of the disputed land throughout. Hence, the disputes had to be revisited even at the cost of repetition.

The first dispute that required authoritative intervention after the installation of the iron railing, arose when a Nihang (Nihang Singh Faqir) entered the inner courtyard. The Nihang had entered the disputed structure/Babri mosque, placed a picture of the idol of Lord Ram Lalla inside the mosque, and conducted puja along with lighting a fire. The Nihang had also gone ahead and written the words 'Ram Ram' with coal on the walls of the mosque/disputed structure and raised the Nishan Sahib—the Sikh flag. This prompted Syed Mohammad Khatib (Moazzin of the Babri Masjid)[145] to file a complaint on 30th November 1858, which was known as Case Number 884. An inquiry by then Thanedar, Sheetal Dubey, confirmed the presence of the Nihang and the version of the Moazzin.

Consequently, an order dated 5th December 1858 was passed which mandated that the Nihang must leave the spot, or he must be arrested and presented in court. The order was complied with, and the Nihang was presented in court and the flag uprooted.[146]

History took another turn on 5 November 1860 when one Mir Rajjab Ali complained about a new chabutra being constructed. His application prayed for the demolition of the newly built chabutra. The application further alleged that when the muezzin recited the *azaan* (call to prayer), the opposite party started blowing the conch and ringing bells. It prayed that an undertaking/bond should be given by the opposite party that they will not unlawfully and illegally interfere in the masjid/ mosque and will not blow conch shells at the time of azaan.[147]

Proceedings kept multiplying. On 12 March 1861, in continuation of the application filed on 5 November 1860, another application was filed by Mohd. Asghar, Rajjab Ali, and Mohd. Afzal again complaining about a chabutra being erected

---

[145]Supra 13 [Part O (ii)(b)].

[146]Supra 13.

[147]Ibid.

by a Sikh, who had illegally occupied the land, and the chabutra had been erected without permission near the Babri mosque. Finally, on 18 March 1861, the Subedar tendered a report on the eviction of the Imkani Sikh and the demolition of his hut. The hut had become an issue of concern. Whenever a Mahant would go to stay in the hut, some dispute would arise.[148]

Another proceeding and another order were passed against one Tulsidas and other Bairagis on 26 August 1868 by Major J. Reed, Commissioner, Faizabad. This was on an appeal moved by Mohd. Afzal, *Mutawalli* (Manager/Administrator), the Babri Masjid, where the allegation was that a *kothri* (small room)had been newly constructed for placing of idols, etc., inside the door of the mosque where the Bairagis had constructed a chabutra, and had also attempted to construct a *Shivalaya* (Shiva Temple). The prayer was made that the mosque may be protected from the Bairagis and an order for dismantling the kothri may be passed.[149]

A dispute then again arose in the year 1873 due to the placing of an idol on the 'platform' of the Janmasthan. This resulted in an order dated 7 November 1873, in the case of *Mohd. Ashgar v. Mahant Baldeo Das*, directing the removal of the *Charan Paduka* (symbolic footprints of the deity). This was followed by another order dated 10 November 1873 by the Deputy Commissioner to remove an image placed on the Janmasthan platform. Though Baldeo Das was not found, the order was explained to other priests who refused to carry it out. The Charan Paduka and the image continued to occupy their place.[150]

In 1877, once again there was a controversy, this time due to the growing rush of devotees at the Ram Janmasthan. Hindus requested the opening of another gate within the disputed premises. This led to an order being passed by the Deputy Commissioner, Faizabad. On 3 April 1877, permission was

---

[148]Supra 13 (Para 684–685).
[149]Supra 13 (Para 687).
[150]Supra 13 (Para 689).

granted to Hindus to open a new door in the disputed premises. This permission was challenged by Mohd. Asghar and finally, on 13 December 1877, this challenge was dismissed on the ground that the outer door was in the interest of public safety. The order allowing the opening of another door within the disputed premises was based on the report of 14 May 1877 of the Deputy Commissioner which relied upon the fact that there was a huge rush in the premises on important days, and that if the door was not opened, human life would be endangered in the rush.

These historical facts made Senior Parasaran feel a bit younger. A wry smile would be followed by an admission from the nonagenarian: 'I like judgements of old decided cases and historical facts.' Both Mr Parasaran and Mr Vaidyanathan laid much stress on the 1877 proceedings. In 1877, there was a heavy rush on religious days. Idols of Ram Lalla were already there. The rush was such that human life was threatened. What more proof was required of this land being worshipped as Janmabhoomi? But the hurdle of further historical facts stood in the way.

If all these conflicts between the parties were not enough, Mohd. Asghar again moved Suit no. 374/943 of 1882 against Raghubar Das, claiming rent for the use of the chabutra and *takht*, describing that the chabutra was situated near the door of the Babri Mosque or before the Babri Mosque. The suit was dismissed on18th June 1883 by Sub-Judge Faizabad. Dr Dhavan's claim concerning these proceedings was that though the suit was dismissed, Mohd. Asghar's capacity as Mutawalli of the Babri Mosque was not challenged.

These disputes, as per the Sunni Board's case, proved the exclusive possession of the Board over the inner courtyard, and the title over the whole of the inner and outer courtyards. Dr Dhavan was also making his point that all claims and ingress of Ram bhakts in the inner courtyard were repelled. Dr Dhavan further submitted that these contests went in favour of proving the title of Muslims. A few other disputes arose and finally came the Suit of 1885 (numbered as Original Suit no. 61/280 of 1885) which was moved by Mahant Raghubar Das who claimed himself to be the Mahant of the Janmasthan.

Of course, as the proceedings progressed, the assisting team notes became peppered with highlights while Senior Parasaran's files comprised three to four rounds of highlighting, and his comments as he would be reading and re-reading, at midnight, early morning, or whenever possible. The concern was now over the Sunni Board raising the issue that the Suit of 1885 had already decided the case in favour of Dr Dhavan's clients and against Hindus. If the Sunni Board side succeeded in demonstrating that the claims and counterclaims of ownership of the disputed property between Hindus and Muslims stood already decided in 1885, then the case of Ram Lalla's side would be over.

Mr Jilani mostly concentrated on the factual aspects and evidence while Dr Dhavan took the holistic view of the case. For team Ram Lalla, they were proving to be as difficult as any opposing team could possibly be. Mr Jilani had very pointedly raised the following points before the Suit of 1885 would start showing its true colours:[151]

1. *Though the Hindu belief concerning Ayodhya being the birthplace of Lord Ram is not challenged, the Scriptures do not contain a reference to the site. Neither in the Ramayana nor in the Ramcharitamanas,* there stands any mention of Ram Janmabhoomi. There stands nothing to verify the belief that the Ram Janmabhoomi is the birthplace of Lord Ram.
2. *The theory of existence of any ancient temple is totally false.*

[151]'Day 50 Arguments, Ayodhya Title Dispute', *Supreme Court Observer*, 23 September 2019, https://tinyurl.com/42bfwkby. Accessed on 18 January 2025.
Also *see*: Supra 13 (para 554).
Also *see*: Written Submission No. A88, The Note on Historical Documents & Gazetteers etc. by Mr. Zafaryab Jilani, Sr. Adv., https://tinyurl.com/4yyaa9yv. Accessed on 18 January 2025.

There is also no reference of any Janmabhumi Temple or Janmasthan Temple anywhere in the ancient scriptures.

3. *There is absence of evidence of belief, an absence of evidence of worship, and also the absence of evidence that Lord Ram was born below the central dome. Historical books, gazetteers and travel accounts fail to establish that the birthplace of Ram is at the disputed site.*
4. *No Hindu worship took place under the middle dome (of the Babri Masjid) prior to 1950. It is just a belief that gained currency in recent times that worship took place below the middle dome prior to 1950.*
5. *The courts in 1885 had already denied Hindus the right to construct a temple at the disputed site.*

The case hung there, on what the 1885 Suit decided, and could have been decided. The legal field has always used slightly different terms than those used in common parlance. Even in 1885, it could be assumed that legal language was legal language. Mr Jilani brought in the issue of 1885 in his arguments. For the sake of history, some parts of the plaint of 1885 had to be read as per the legal language in 1885 which is otherwise difficult to follow. Even at the cost of repetition, it may be taken that the legal language was still legal language in 1885.

IN THE COURT OF MUNSIF SAHIB BAHADUR

Mahant Raghubar Das
Mahant Janmsthan
Situated at Ayodhya
Plaintiff

versus

Secretary of State for India in the Session of Council

Defendant

The plaintiff above named submit as under:

Suit for grant of permission for construction of Mandir, i.e., prohibition to the defendant that plaintiff should not be restrained from construction of Mandir on chabootra janmashtan situated at Ayodhya, North 17 feet, East 21 feet, South 17 feet, West 21 feet and the value of the suit cannot be fixed as per market rate therefore as per Item No. 17, paragraph 6, Appendix-II, Act, 1870, court fee was affixed and the position of the site can be known very well from the attached map/sketch.

Section 1: That the place of janmsthan situated at Ayodhya City, Faizabad is a very old and sacred place of worship of Hindus and plaintiff is the Mahant of this place of worship.

Section 2: That the chabootra janmasthan is East-West 41 feet and North-South 17 feet. Charan Paduka is fixed on it and small temple is also placed which is worshipped.

Section 3: That the said chabootra is in the possession of the plaintiff. There being no building on it, the plaintiff and other faqirs are put to great hardship in summer from heat, in the monsoon from rain and in the winter from extreme cold. Construction of temple on the chabootra will cause no harm to anyone. But the construction of temple will give relief to the plaintiff and other faqirs and pilgrims.

Section 4: That the Deputy Commissioner Bahadur of Faizabad from March or April 83, because of the objection of a few Muslims opposed the construction of the mandir, this petitioner sent a petition to the local government regarding this matter where no reply was received about this petition. Then the plaintiff sent a notice as required under Section-444 of the Code (of Civil Procedure) on 18th August, 1883 to the office of Secretary, Local Government but this too remained unreplied. Hence the cause for the suit arises from the date of prohibition at Ayodhya under the jurisdiction of the Court.

> *Section 5: That a well-wishing subject has a right to construct any type of building which it wishes as the land is possessed and owned by it. It is the duty of fair and just government to protect its subjects and provide assistance to them in availing their rights and making suitable bandobast for maintenance of law and order. Therefore, the plaintiff prays for issue of the decree for construction of temple on chabootra—Janmasthan situated at Ayodhya North 17 feet, East 41 feet, South 17 feet and West 41 feet and also to see that the defendant does not prohibit and obstruct the construction of mandir and the cost of the suit should be ordered to be borne by the defendant [...]*

Let's get back from the legal language of lawyers to how the case actually panned out. Mr Jilani read out witness statements to buttress his claims that the exact birthplace of Lord Ram cannot be traced. Out of the three possible theories of the existence of the disputed structure, the first was that Babur demolished a temple to build a mosque which some Hindu sides claimed; the second was that Babur built a mosque on the ruins of a temple; the third was that Babur built a mosque on barren land. Mr Jilani advocated the third line and also referred to *Ain-i-Akbari* and other historical reports to point out the absence of any mention of Lord Ram's birthplace in the book. It was submitted that a few pages of *Baburnama* were missing.

Therefore, arose the question: Was the Babri Masjid an important mosque, or just another mosque, or a mosque that wasn't so important? It was a matter that only the Sunni Board could answer. Not surprisingly, this question came up during the hearing. Babur was an emperor. Any construction by an emperor who is the law unto himself would be important and a celebrated place would have been recorded, wouldn't it? But what about 1885?

There was a view in the public domain that the Sunni Board had conceded the case and accepted that Lord Ram's birthplace was within the disputed land. Was the Babri Mosque important to worshippers?

An Alternative Birthplace?

With all these issues of controversies being debated, 24 September 2019 was a day of controversies if the media reports were anything to go by. The controversies of that day and the next day arose, thankfully, without Ram Lalla's side even opening its mouth or *making any submissions.* Newspapers and news portals reported all the controversial takes. *The Indian Express*[152] reported an issue of this controversy as if the case has been conceded by the Sunni Board:

> *The Sunni Central Wakf Board on Tuesday accepted that Ram was born at the spot known as Ram Chabutra which is in the outer courtyard of the disputed site in Ayodhya, even as the Supreme Court questioned why the 16th-century Ain-i-Akbari was silent on an 'important' mosque like the Babri Masjid.*
>
> *Senior advocate Zafaryab Jilani, representing the Board, told a five-judge Constitution bench hearing the Ram Janmabhoomi-Babri Masjid dispute case that it had accepted the Chabutra as the birthplace of Ram as the Faizabad district judge had held that the spot—60–65 feet from the Babri Masjid, which was demolished in 1992—was worshipped by Hindus as Ram's birthplace.*
>
> *Jilani was responding to Justice S. A. Bobde who asked, 'You don't dispute Chabutra as the place of birth?'*

---

[152]G., Ananthakrishnan, 'Ayodhya hearing in SC: Wakf Board accepts Ram was born at Ram Chabutra', *The Indian Express*, 25 September 2019, https://tinyurl.com/bdrmvr2a. Accessed on 18 January 2025.
Also *see*: 'Day 50 Arguments, Ayodhya Title Dispute', *Supreme Court Observer*, 23 September 2019, https://tinyurl.com/42bfwkby. Accessed on 18 January 2025.
Also *see*: Rajagopal, Krishnadas, 'Muslim side accepts Ayodhya as Lord Ram's birthplace', *The Hindu*, 25 September 2019, https://tinyurl.com/yb4ch4xm. Accessed on 18 January 2025.

The counsel replied, 'Earlier we had. But the district judge said it was worshipped believing it to be the birthplace.' His reference was to the 1885 decision rendered by the Faizabad judge dismissing a suit filed by Mahant Raghubar Das seeking permission to construct a temple over the Ram Chabutra.

[...]

The bench also sought to know why Ain-i-Akbari—written in the 16th century, the period when the Babri Masjid was allegedly constructed—did not mention the mosque.

Jilani had sought to rely on the book to establish the claim that no temple was demolished in Ayodhya to construct the Babri Masjid. He said the late historian Jadunath Sarkar had said that Ain-i-Akbari, written by Akbar's court historian Abu'l-Fazl ibn Mubarak, recorded the minutest details. 'If there was any demolition of a temple in 1528 in Ayodhya, it would not have been missed in the book,' Jilani said.

Justice Bhushan told him that the Hindu side's contention was that it did not have all the details. Jilani replied that it only had the important details.

'Are you saying the mosque is not important?' asked Justice Bhushan. Jilani said, 'It became important only now. Then (in 1528), it was just another mosque.'

Intervening, Justice Bobde asked, '[...] If a mosque was built by an emperor, how can you say it is of no importance?' Jilani replied that it was not built by Babur in person but by his commandant Mir Baqi.

Justice Bobde said that if it was on the instructions of Babur, then it was important. Jilani contended that it was the case of the Hindu parties that it was built by Babur, to which Justice Bobde said, 'It could be wrong'. Jilani said in that case their suit must be dismissed, but Justice Bobde replied that a suit

'*Bhishma Pitamah*' of the Indian bar and his team: (*From L-R*) Bhakti Vardhan Singh, Aditi Anil Dani, Sridhar Potaraju, P.V. Yogeswaran, former Attorney General K. Parasaran (*seated*), who represented the deity Ram Lalla Virajman in the Ram Janmabhoomi-Babri Masjid title suit, Anirudh Sharma, Mohan Parasaran and Ashwin Kumar D.S. at senior Parasaran's chamber on 16 October 2019—the final day of hearing of the Ram Janmabhoomi-Babri Masjid land dispute.

Breakfast brainstorm: Former Additional Solicitor General P.S. Narasimha (*seated second from right*) in an animated discussion with K. Parasaran in Chamber 92 of the Supreme Court. Also seen are Vishnu Mohan, Bhakti Vardhan Singh and P.V. Yogeswaran.

Key excavation finds: (*Left*) An ornamental female figurine made of terracotta, and (*right*) a human head adorned with a large earring.

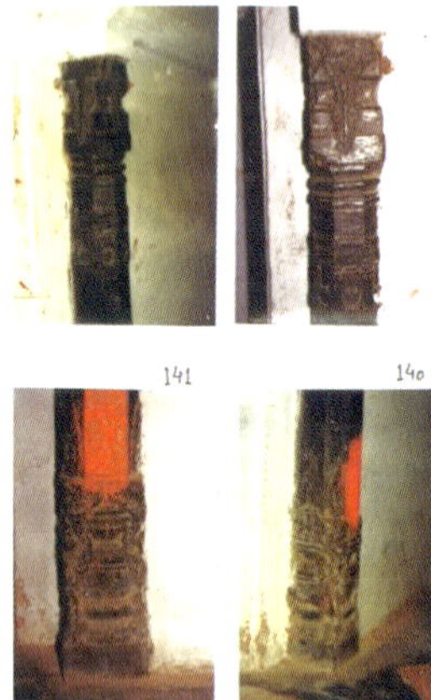

Foundation of evidence: Multiple *Kasauti* pillars made of black stone on which the disputed structure rested. This was presented in court as evidence of the original temple.

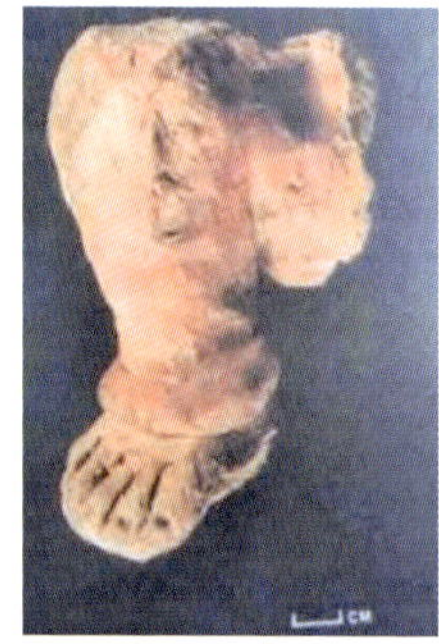

Timeless journey of terracotta legs: On the left, a leg resting on a pedestal, and on the right, a human leg; both were unearthed during excavation and recorded in the ASI report.

Foliage in stone: An architectural clue

Evidence that spoke: Excavation site images reveal the depth of structures predating the disputed site and the artefacts recovered.

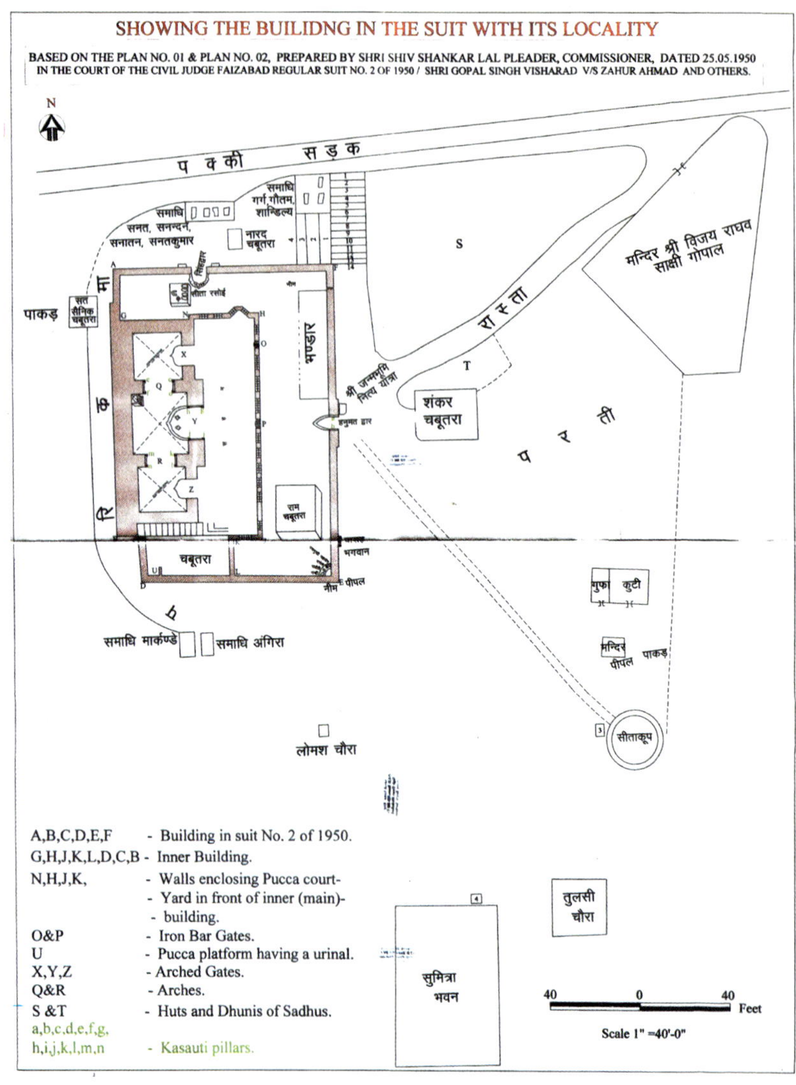

Tracing boundaries, tracing history: Site map in Suit No. 2 of 1950 shows the disputed structure and some area around the disputed land.

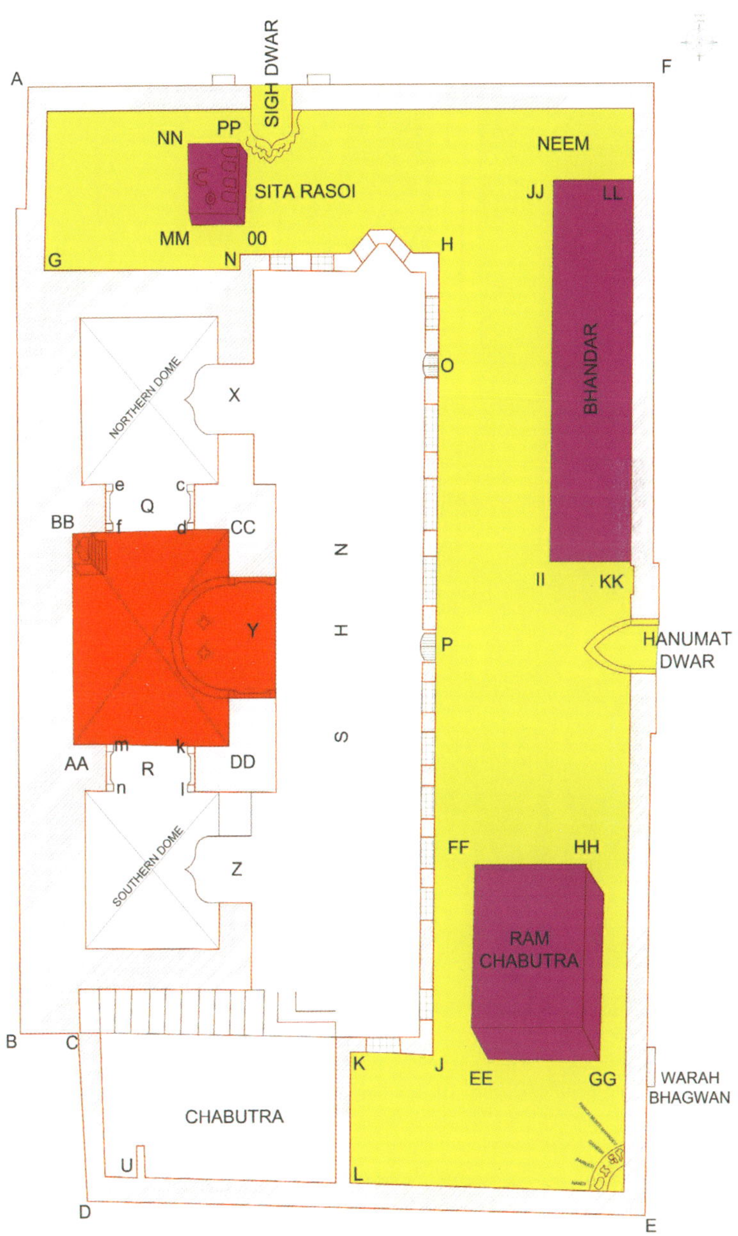

1,480 square yards on trial: Colour map of the disputed property submitted by K. Parasaran on 8 August 2019. Prepared at short notice by architect Meetu Goel, it formed part of the official case record, with the marking A6 showing the site plan of the disputed 1,480 sq. yards.

Top: (*Left*) **Camaraderie beyond the courtroom:** Advocate-on-record Ejaz Maqbool, who represented the Jamiat Ulema-e-Hind, shares some anecdotes with K. Parasaran as they walk back together post-lunch to the CJI's courtroom in October 2019. Advocate Sridhar Potaraju follows behind. (*Right*) **All in a day's work:** Former Solicitor General of India Ranjit Kumar (*second from right*) poses with (*from left*) Anirudh Sharma, Niharika Singh, Ankita Sharma and Sridhar Potaraju in the corridors of the Supreme Court.

Bottom: (*Left*) **When legends meet:** K. Parasaran (*on the left*), senior Advocate for the Hindu side, waited nearly 15 minutes in the Supreme Court parking to be photographed with Rajeev Dhavan, advocate for the Muslim parties in the case, after the judgement was reserved on 16 October 2019. (*Right*) **Moments before the verdict:** (*From left*) Advocates-on-record for Ram Lalla Virajman Bhakti Vardhan Singh and P.V. Yogeswaran are seen here with K. Parasaran outside the Supreme Court chambers.

From airport to courtroom: K. Parasaran meets Rajya Sabha MP and counsel for Ram Lalla since the 90s, Bhupender Yadav (*left*), in Chamber 92 at the Supreme Court on the morning of 9 November 2019, the day the Supreme Court delivered its judgement. Parasaran reached directly from the airport, preparing to receive the judgement.

Before the gavel falls: Tushar Mehta, Solicitor General of India (*second from right*), walks with K. Parasaran in the court premises on the same day. Also seen are Sridhar Potaraju, Anirudh Sharma and Nachiketa Joshi.

The final shot! (*Standing from left*) Harish Vaidyanathan, P.S. Narasimha, C.S. Vaidyanathan, K. Parasaran, Tushar Mehta, and other advocates share happy moments in front of the CJI's court after the judgement is pronounced.

Lawyers line up for Parasaran: For the first time in Supreme Court history, K. Parasaran is swarmed for a photograph—lawyers had to be arranged on the stairs for this historic shot. The crowd was so large that multiple group shots became necessary.

cannot be dismissed just because some part of it is wrong.

The Wakf Board counsel said that 'since the entire case is based on faith, we have to ascertain whether it is borne out by the facts.' Pointing to the Ramcharitmanas composed in 1574 and Valmiki Ramayana, he said these texts mention Ayodhya as the birthplace but do not specify any particular spot as the Janmasthan.

Justice Chandrachud said this argument would amount to assuming that all the information about the Hindu faith was contained in these two texts.

Jilani said 'there was a temple which was called the Janmasthan Temple to the north of the disputed structure' which the Hindus believed to be the birthplace.

Justice Chandrachud drew attention to witness testimonies that Skanda Purana had put the spot of Ram's birth at about 200 paces west of 'Sita koop', a well. Jilani said the same Hindus had believed that the Janmasthan temple was the place of birth.

To this, Justice Bhushan said the Allahabad High Court had held that the Janmasthan temple he was referring to was a recent one. But Jilani said the HC was wrong as there was mention of it in a book published about 150 years ago.

Justice Bobde also referred to a witness testimony about the place of birth being in Dashratha Palace and asked if such a palace exists. Justice Chandrachud pointed out that various spots identified as the birthplace were in 'close proximity' to the disputed site. Jilani, however, contended that there was 'no witness from whom anything can be inferred about the exact place of birth.'

Mr. Jilani leveraged the point that though Lord Ram's birthplace was within the disputed premises, there was no evidence that the exact spot was below the central dome. Ram Chabutra was the birthplace as identified and the Hindus, therefore, had no claim over the inner courtyard of the disputed premises. It was evident even before there was any news reporting that the day's proceedings would make quite a stir. However, another controversial part was more striking but without any evidence or basis. The submissions were concerning Lord Ram's alternative birthplace. The Supreme Court Observer reported the submission of Mr. Jilani that Lord Ram's birthplace was 'actually located north of the disputed land.'[153]

Back in conference mode and making further preparations, Senior Parasaran moved from being a lawyer to a bhakt and from a bhakt to being a lawyer. The assisting team too had to adjust according to this changing status. It was getting challenging to figure out when the bhakt would pop up and when the lawyer would be in charge. Mr Parasaran would often ask, 'If all throughout, Ram bhakts believed in Ram and worshipped Ram, then how could they have abandoned Ram's birthplace? If it is not disputed that Lord Ram was born in the vicinity, then is faith alone not sufficient to point out the place of birth?' The judgements of 1885 and 1887 have to be understood together.

Thankfully, when the bhakt took over, there was the evidence to bring back the lawyer. Yogeswaran and Bhakti would remind the nonagenarian that here was a case where both evidence of worship as well as historical documents were there to prove that within the premises of the disputed structure lies Lord Ram's birthplace. The alternative theory that the birthplace is somewhere else had no basis in the mind of the team, no evidence to stand on. No serious attempts were even advanced to substantiate with evidence that the alternative site was the real

[153]'Day 50 Arguments, Ayodhya Title Dispute', *Supreme Court Observer*, 23 September 2019, https://tinyurl.com/42bfwkby. Accessed on 18 January 2025.

birthplace. The focal point had already moved to Ram Chabutra.

However, such theories got the team to re-evaluate the evidence. Is there any evidence of worship at the disputed site? Had the Christian missionaries of those times pointed out such facts? Why then did riots take place in British India because of this disputed place and not some alternate structure? Why was an iron railing, separating the inner and outer courtyards, installed at this place way back in 1857? The team could have answered such questions easily by now. But the important aspects of the issue that lay ahead were: What was decided in 1885? Against whom did the case go in 1885? And in whose favour was the case decided in 1885? History could not be ignored in this case.

23

Who Won in 1885?

A new dawn can usher in new beginnings. Or perhaps tumultuous beginnings? The newspapers on 25 September 2019 suggested that concession had been made by the Sunni Board concerning Lord Ram's birthplace. The next day brought some confusion and once again, controversies abounded. Although Senior Parasaran and Mr Vaidyanathan expected the case to take such turns, the team was grateful that all this happened without anyone from the Ram Lalla side making any submission that they were preparing to advance. But now there was a concern—was there a retraction of the admission by the opposition that Ram's birthplace was inside the disputed premises of Ram Janambhoomi/The Babri Masjid? Did the Sunni Board completely retract its stand or had the Board indulged in some verbal jugglery and there was no admission or concession at all? This was the latest controversy. What did the Sunni Board state or mean? *The Indian Express* reported:[154]

> *The Sunni Central Wakf Board clarified on Wednesday that it had not accepted that Ram was born at the spot known as Ram Chabutra but brought to notice that it had not challenged the Faizabad court's 1885 finding that Hindus had worshipped it as his birthplace.*
>
> *[...]*
>
> *On Tuesday, senior advocate Zafaryab Jilani, representing*

---

[154] 'Ayodhya hearing: Didn't accept Ram Chabutra as Ram's birthplace, clarifies Wakf Board', *The Indian Express*, 25 September 2019, https://tinyurl.com/tnaz56d9. Accessed on 18 January 2025.

the Board, told a five-judge Constitution bench that it had accepted the Chabutra as the birthplace of Ram after a Faizabad district judge in 1885 held that the spot was worshipped by Hindus as Ram's birthplace.

[...]

During the hearing [on] Tuesday, Justice S. A. Bobde had asked Jilani, 'You don't dispute Chabutra as the place of birth?

To which, Jilani replied, 'Earlier we had. But the district judge said it was worshipped believing it to be the birthplace.

What was decided in the Suit of 1885 about Mahant Raghubar Das had surely tied both parties in knots. Mr Jilani was not the only person trying to unravel what happened in 1885. Mr Naphade was to argue on the 1885 Suit and its judgement on behalf of the Sunni Board. But what did the controversy of 1885 finally decide? Why did Mr Jilani also have to rely on the1885 Suit and then state that the judgement did indicate that the Faizabad court held that Ram Chabutra was being worshipped as Lord Ram's birthplace within the disputed land? Only the judgement in the case of 1885 could solve the riddle. Though it seemed at first blush that the Suit of 1885 was going in favour of the Sunni Board, it was Ram Lalla's side that was reading, re-reading and analysing the suit. The number of times Mr Parasaran and his team had read those judgements concerning 1885 was now uncountable. Sometimes they would read only to themselves, sometimes to each other and sometimes collectively with Mr Parasaran.

The suit went through three stages. First to the Sub-Judge at Faizabad, then to the District Judge, and then to the Judicial Commissioner.

One view was that the Sub-Judge at Faizabad, in his judgement on 24 December 1885, had accepted the possession and ownership of the Ram bhakts of the area surrounding the wall of the masjid while also accepting the Muslim prayers within the premises.

The Sub-Judge inter alia held:

> *—Over and above this, on the temple situated on the chabootra an idol of Thakurji is kept which is being worshipped. The chabootra is in the possession of the plaintiff and whatever is offered on it is taken by the plaintiff.*
>
> *[...] The possession of plaintiff is proved by the witnesses of the plaintiff and railing wall separating the boundary of Hindus and Muslims exists from a long period[...]*
>
> *[...] It is evident that before this controversy arose that both Hindus and Muslims offered worship on the place. In the year 1855, after the quarrel between Hindus and Muslims a wall in the form of the railing was erected to avoid controversy. So that Muslims may worship inside it and Hindus may worship outside it. So, the outside land with chabootra which is in the possession of the plaintiff belongs to Hindus [...]*
>
> *[...] Taking into consideration the special situation of the place, the prayer for construction of the temple is at the place where there is only one way to the Masjid. Though the place where Hindus worship, they hold its possession since old because of which there cannot be objection to their ownership, and the area surrounding around the wall of the Masjid and on the outer door the word 'Allah' is engraved [...]*
>
> *[...] Therefore, this Court is also of the opinion that permission for construction of a mandir/temple is tantamount to laying the foundation of a war and mischief between Hindus and Muslims [...]*

Therefore, on the grounds of apprehension of a serious breach of law and order, the Suit of 1885 was dismissed but finding of facts like accepting possession and ownership of Hindus, having very serious ramifications, were part of the judgement. An appeal was placed by Mahant Raghubar Das before the District Judge, Faizabad. On 18/26 March 1886, the District Judge *inter alia* held that:[155]

> *It is most unfortunate that a Masjid should have been built on land specially held sacred by the Hindus, but as that event occurred 356 years ago, it is too late to remedy the grievance; all that can be done is to maintain that parties in status quo.*

The District Judge noted on a site inspection that the Chabutra had been occupied by Hindus on which there was a small wood superstructure, in the form of a tent. The Chabutra was said to indicate the birthplace of Lord Ram. While maintaining the dismissal of the suit, the District Judge came to the conclusion that the observations on possession and ownership in the judgement of the trial judge were redundant, and hence, were to be struck off. He finally held that 'the only question decided in the case is that the position of the parties will be maintained.' This meant that the District Judge said that no rights have been decided and that the site will remain as it is.

The judgement of the District Judge was further carried in appeal before the Judicial Commissioner, who affirmed the dismissal of the suit on 2 November 1886. The Judicial Commissioner observed:

> *—The matter is simply that the Hindus of Ajudhia want to erect a new temple of marble [...] over the supposed holy spot in Ajudhia said to be the birthplace of Sri Ram Chandar. Now this spot is situated within the precincts of the grounds surrounding a mosque constructed some 350 years ago owing to the bigotry and tyranny of the Emperor Baber who purposely chose this holy spot according to Hindu legend—as the site of his mosque.*

---

[155]Supra 13 (Para 46).

> *The Hindus seem to have got very limited rights of access to certain spots within the precincts adjoining the mosque and they have for a series of years been persistently trying to increase their rights and to erect buildings over two spots in the enclosure.*
>
> *(1) Sita ki Rasoi (2) Ram Chandar ki Janam Bhumi.*
>
> *The executive authorities have persistently repressed these encroachments and absolutely forbid any alteration of the status quo.*
>
> *I think this a very wise and proper procedure on their part and I am further of opinion that Civil Courts have properly dismissed the plaintiff's claim.*
>
> *[…]*
>
> *However, I approve of their final conclusion to which it has come and I see no reason to interfere with its order modifying the wording of part of the judgment of the Court of First Instance. There is nothing whatever on the record to show that plaintiff is in any sense the proprietor of the land in question. This appeal is dismissed with costs of all Courts.*

The opposing side, therefore, was repeatedly caught by the judgements in the Suit of 1885 recording Lord Ram's birthplace as being within the disputed site. Mr Jilani's submission now, to the understanding of the assisting team, was that he was merely restating what the judge who dealt with the Suit of 1885 had recorded. It was recorded there that Ram Chabutra was the birthplace, therefore, the birthplace was within the disputed land for team Ram Lalla, and now there was no doubt as far as legal evidence was concerned. Lord Ram's birthplace as a matter of common ground was within the 1,500 sq. yd of the disputed land.

Did Ram Bhakts Win or Lose in 1885?

Once a suit is decided, it means that for all times to come, the suit is decided between the contesting parties. This norm of common sense is termed by lawyers as 'res judicata'. With so much at stake within the 1885 Suit, the proceedings had to enter the territory of res judicata. Res judicata further meant when any issue or controversy between two or more contesting groups is finally decided for once, it shall not be re-opened. A duel of wrestling, once over, is final. For the rule of res judicata to apply, it is imperative that (1) the contesting parties should in essence, directly or indirectly, be the same or claim through the same representatives before the court; (2) the dispute should be the same, for example, for the same piece of land both in the earlier and later suits directly and substantially; and (3) the issue should have been the same which should have been contested and finally decided by the court in the earlier suit.

Mr Shekhar Naphade argued on the point of res judicata from the Sunni Board's side. The submission of res judicata was directed against all Hindu parties including Nirmohi Akhara. The pleading was that Mahant Raghubar Das had filed the 1885 Suit as the Mahant of Nirmohi Akhara. The whole controversy was boiling down to the fact of whether the Mahant was representing the whole of the Hindu community or not and whether all Hindus were aware of such a legal contest or not? Was he even representing Nirmohi Akhara or was he contesting the suit only in his personal capacity? If Mahant Raghubar Das was indeed representing the whole of the Hindu population, then the danger of the argument that Ram Lalla's suit was over would make sense. Mr Naphade's main submissions in short were:

1. The title or ownership of the property claimed by Hindus in both suits, that is, 1885 and Ram Lalla's Suit 5, stand the same. It is the same property as in 1885 which is under contest.
2. In the proceedings of 1885, final adjudication was given and

the right to construct a temple at the site was not recognized. This has acquired finality. That Hindus lost the right to construct a temple cannot be contested again by Ram Lalla's suit. The temple side's claim of ownership and possession was rejected in 1885.

3. The cause of action, that being the main grievance in the proceedings of 1885, and the proceedings now are the same.
4. In the earlier proceedings of 1885, it was clearly held that a mosque exists on the site and that Hindus have limited rights and are attempting to increase their rights.
5. The plaintiff Mahant Raghubar Das in the Suit of 1885 represented all Hindus, and Mohd. Asghar, the Mutawalli of The Babri Masjid, represented all Muslims. The parties now are also the same. It was a case of Mahant vs. Mutawalli, hence it was a representative suit for all practical purposes between Hindus and Muslims. So, both the 1885 Suit and the present suit are between same parties.
6. The adjudication to title/ownership of the property shall not be dependent on whether the full property or only a part of the property was claimed in the Suit of 1885.
7. The proceedings of 1885 were to the knowledge of all Hindus of the area concerned and all Muslims of the area concerned. It was a proceeding of a public nature and was not directed against any particular person. Now the judgement operates against all Hindus and not only against the Mahant. As stated in legal language, the 1885 Suit was in rem (against a thing) and not in personam (against anyone identified person), hence it bound all Hindus.
8. In light of the afore-mentioned points, the role of res judicata in all its form and vigour applies to the present dispute as in law, the claim of the temple already stood resolved by the 1885 Suit and the Suit of Ram Lalla and Nirmohi Akhara are therefore barred in law, and the suits of Hindus must be dismissed on this account alone.

The reaction of the court to these points was to test the basic propositions/principles of res judicata. So, the question was, were the contesting parties in the Suit of 1885 and the present suits the same? The reports of various media portals gave the story.

The court seemed to be in disagreement with the plea of the Muslim parties that the 1885 suit barred Hindus parties supporting the erection of a temple from filing any case later in time. This meant that Nirmohi Akhara suit filed in 1959 and the suit of Ram Lala filed in 1989 were not maintainable. The observations of the Bench were reported as follows:

> *[…] The issue whether mahant Raghubar Das was shebait on behalf of Nirmohi Akhara was not an issue in the 1885 suit and hence, the concept of res judicata does not stop Hindus from filing another case.*[156]

> *Sr. Adv. Naphade proceeded to dispute the Allahabad High Court's findings on the res judicata issue. The High Court had held that res judicata did not apply, as the 1885 suit did not adjudicate on the title dispute, but rather 'refused to decide the controversy' in favour of maintaining the 'status quo' […] Sr. Adv. Naphade disputed this, submitting that the Mahant's plaint stated that it was filed on 'behalf of the Hindus'.*[157]

> *Justices Bobde and Chandrachud observed that the 1885 suit could not be considered a representative suit if it failed to follow the appropriate procedural requirements defined in the CPC. In particular, they observed that public notice should have been issued in the 1885 suit. Sr. Adv. Naphade argued that it was safe to assume that the public at the time was*

[156]'Ayodhya hearing in SC; Birthplace of Lord Ram also a juristic entity capable of filing lawsuits, Hindu party tells apex court', *First Post*, 1 October 2019, https://tinyurl.com/4djcv884. Accessed on 18 January 2025.

[157]'Day 54 Arguments, Ayodhya Title Dispute', *Supreme Court Observer*, 27 September2019, https://tinyurl.com/52yjjbeh. Accessed on 18 January 2025.

aware of the legal dispute due to the prevalent law and order situation. He argued that the Bench should adopt a purposive interpretation (i.e. consider the reasons behind the framing of the relevant CPC statutes) and hold that public notice was in effect issued.[158]

Therefore, when it is claimed that title/ownership of a piece of land stands already decided between the parties, some important questions arise. In the discussions with Senior Parasaran, the res judicata plea qua 1885 Suit filed by Mahant Raghubar Das and opposed by Mohd. Asghar, the Muttawali of the Babri Masjid, had forced the team long back to think about certain questions and facts. For the team, the pointed issues were:

1. Who were Mahant Raghubar Das and Mohd. Asghar, the Muttawali of the Babri Masjid, representing? If either of them was not representing the whole of their community, then the Suit of 1885 does not bind the communities.
2. In what capacity was the Suit of 1885 filed by the Mahant? A suit can be filed by a person in his individual capacity as well as in the capacity of a representative of a legal entity, like a partner of a firm, head of a Hindu family, as the Head of a Math or institution, as a Muttawali of a mosque, or as a representative of an entire community.
3. What was claimed in the suit and what was contested and what was proved? Was ownership of the whole disputed area claimed or only a part of it was claimed and contested?
4. Was the case filed on behalf of the whole of the contesting communities? Did the law in 1885 allow for a representative suit where public rights like the right to worship of a community could be contested? If not, then how can the Suit of 1885 decide a community's public right to worship?
5. Can one busybody or any non-serious person file a claim on behalf of the community without informing the whole

[158]Ibid.

community and defeat the community's rights or must the whole community be informed before an issue is decided?

All these questions were taken into consideration. As the team of assisting lawyers seemed sure about the success on the point of res judicata going by the court's reaction, Senior Parasaran and Mr Vaidyanathan were quick to point out that nothing can be taken for granted: 'Don't be sure about a judge's mind until the judgment is out.' Mr Parasaran was back to work, dictating his points. With his memory back, he started shooting off one decided case law after another, with the team diligently keeping pace. The main points, however, were, that between the Suit of 1885 and the present suits, especially Suit 5, there were crucial differences, so there was no way that the suit in favour of Ram Lalla's side was barred by res judicata:

1. Parties are different, neither the Janmasthan nor the Sunni Central Waqf Board were parties to the Suit of 1885;
2. The Suit of 1885 was instituted by Mahant Raghubar Das in personal and not representative capacity.
3. The suit was merely for asserting a personal right to construct a temple on the Chabutra. The Suit of 1885 did not reflect the community claims of Hindus.
4. Neither the Ram Janmabhoomi nor Ram Lalla Virajman nor the Hindu public claimed any right through Mahant Raghubar Das in 1885. In fact, the Mahant did not even state that he is representing anyone other than himself. He did not mention even Nirmohi Akhara.
5. If the community has to be represented, then the community has to be made known of the legal contest through newspaper advertisement or other reasonable means. One member of the community cannot privately represent the community.
6. The Plaintiffs in Suit 5 of Ram Lalla and Janmabhoomi will never be bound by the 1885 verdict as their rights

were unrepresented and never put to contest. There was no adjudication of the title of Ram Lalla and Ram Janmabhoomi, which has to be decided now for the first time.

7. The Suit of 1885 was against the then Government (Secretary of State for India), for permission to construct a temple while the present property dispute pertains to the character of the property: whether it is a public mosque or a place of public worship for Hindus.
8. Whether Asthan Ram Janmabhoomi is a juridical personality is an issue, which goes beyond the scope of the Suit of 1885. The Suit of 1885 was limited only to the construction of a temple in 1885.
9. In the Suit of 1885, the subject matter was only the Chabutra measuring 17x21 feet, while in the present proceedings, the suit property in both Suits 4 and 5 comprises the whole area of approximately 1,500 sq. yd consisting of the inner and outer courtyards.
10. In the Suit of 1885, only a private right was sought to be enforced, whereas in the present proceedings, a public right to the worship of a community is sought to be enforced.
11. In 1885, there was no provision in law to represent public rights in a representative suit as it is now available since 1908. Public rights were added only in 1908.

Lawyers often juggle words. A word added or subtracted may result in substantial difference in its meaning. This is what had happened qua the law as applicable in 1882 and as changed in 1908.

The bare reading would show the absence of public rights in the wordings of the relevant law CPC in 1882 and the addition of public rights in 1908. This absence and presence of public rights would make a significant difference.

Section 13 CPC 1882	*Section 11 CPC 1908 Explanation V–Explanation VI*
1882 *Where persons litigate bonafide in respect of a private right claimed in common for themselves and others, all persons interested in such right shall, for the purpose of this section, be deemed to claim under the persons so litigating.*	*1908* *Where persons litigate bonafide in respect of a public right or of a private right claimed in common for themselves and others, all persons interested in such right shall, for the purpose of this section, be deemed to claim under the persons so litigating.*

Save for a handful of veterans of the bar, most professionals associated with the case would not have known the difference in the language used in the 1882 CPC and 1908 CPC. This is where Senior Parasaran revels with his profound knowledge of not only the law but also the history and evolution of the law. He had worked on the language of the 1882 CPC which defined 'res judicata' and the difference in the language in 1908 CPC. Once this difference was brought on record, the contention but had to wither away.

1885 was an issue of history, but now that it had been covered, the next issue which had caught the attention of the people was archaeology. What would be the challenge of the Sunni Board to ASI's excavation report? It was the first time, in the knowledge of the lawyers associated with the case, that in a case of this magnitude, archaeological evidence was being scrutinized.

24

The Worth or Worthlessness of Archaeology: Reply to ASI Report

Meenakshi Arora's response to archaeological evidence relied upon by Mr Vaidyanathan was not only a targeted attempt to punch holes in the contents of the Archaeological Survey of India (ASI) report, but was extended to questioning the authenticity of the ASI report itself. Mr Vaidyanathan of team Ram Lalla had built a convincing case, placing reliance on archaeological evidence. Ms Arora, to begin with, argued for the entire ASI report to be ignored. Not merely was the report attacked but an alternative theory as to what lay below the disputed structure was advanced. It was argued that what lay beneath was not at all concerned with religions that have temples.

Mr Vaidyanathan, had relied upon the ASI findings while representing Ram Lalla, to rebut the claim made in Suit 4 by the Sunni Board that a mosque stood erected on a vacant piece of land that had never ever been used earlier. He also attempted to substantiate *from his perspective* that a temple stood below the land and that the structure below had no connection with Islam. Before the ASI's report, the report of the Court Commissioner was available. Dr Dhavan had earlier referred to it and so had Mr Vaidyanathan. Since the ASI's report was an expert's report, it would be apt to bring out how the archaeological survey had been conducted, and what was sought to be known from the exercise.

The Allahabad High Court had initially only ordered a Ground Penetrating Radar (GPR) Survey or Geo-Radiology Survey, on 1 August 2002; it would give a sort of an X-ray position of the site. Till this time, even prima facie, no one knew whether traces of any past building existed below the disputed structure except *Sruti* (what has been heard) and *Smriti* (what has been remembered) of the beliefs for generations about the existence of a temple and its demolition. Legally speaking, there were only claims and counter-claims. The High Court, by its order dated 23 October 2002, explained the purpose and object of a Ground Penetrating Radar Survey. In essence, the High Court had stated that:

> *The nature of super structure to a great extent is related to the foundations. [...] If any foundation is existing of any construction, it may throw light as to whether any structure existed and, if so, what would have been the possible structure at that time [...]*

After objections to the proposed directions of the GPR survey were heard, they were rejected by the High Court on 23 October 2002.

The ASI had a survey conducted by a corporate entity called Tojo–Vikas International which submitted its report to the High Court on 17 February 2003. The report found the presence of 'anomaly alignments'. In layman's terms, the report suggested that below the disputed area, there was a possibility of the existence of ancient and contemporaneous structures, such as wall slabs, floorings, and structures of some sort of floorings that could extend over a large part of the disputed site. These patterns gave first-hand indications of successive constructions belonging to varying periods. Therefore, the report was the first-ever document indicating the presence of a structure below, contrary to the claims of the Sunni Board that no structure existed below the disputed site. However, the GPR survey indicated that the exact nature of these could only be determined further, based on archaeological excavations or archaeological trenching. Thus, the findings of the GPR survey were the basis for the High Court to order an excavation. On 5 March 2003, when the High

Court directed the ASI to excavate the site, it was to determine[159] whether there was any temple/structure which was demolished and a mosque was constructed on the disputed site.

Importantly, the direction was to conclude 'whether there was any temple/structure which was demolished' and not whether a Ram temple was demolished. The archaeological excavations were to be carried on even as the place was being used for worship of Lord Ram. It was directed not to disturb the area where the idol of Lord Ram was installed, and an area around the idol to the extent of 10 feet was left out. Further directions were issued on 26 March 2003 for recording the nature of the excavations found at the site, and the sealing of the artefacts found in the presence of the parties and their counsels. Photographs of the findings were permitted to be taken.

To bring objectivity and neutrality to the process as well as to ensure that the parties of the dispute could have confidence in the whole archaeological process, the High Court had ensured that adequate representation of both the communities was to be maintained in respect to the functioning of the ASI team and the engagement of the labourers. To ensure transparency, two judicial officers from the Uttar Pradesh Higher Judicial Services of the rank of Additional District Judge were deputed to oversee the work. The work of excavation and its findings were documented by still and video footage.

The ASI excavated 90 trenches in five months and submitted its report within 15 days of the completion of the excavation. The whole task was carried out in the presence of the contesting communities and their counsel. Excavated material including antiquities, objects of interest, glazed pottery, tiles, and bones recovered from the trenches were sealed in the presence of the parties and their advocates and lodged in a strong room provided by the Commissioner of Faizabad Division. Complete reports

[159]Supra 13 (Para 486).

with day-to-day register as well as videographic records were submitted to the High Court.

Hence, it was a report of an excavation that was carried out by ASI, a body with international repute under orders of the High Court in the presence of judicial officers by experts who were Court Commissioners or Officers of the Court, in legal terms. This was an expert opinion and The Indian Evidence Act, 1872, allowed for such a report to be taken into consideration. Section 45 of The Indian Evidence Act allows for an opinion of an expert in certain circumstances as it could assist the court in forming an opinion on a point of foreign law, science, or art or on the identity of handwriting or finger impressions. An expert opinion is not a judgement in itself. It is not conclusive in itself. It becomes a part of the evidence, and depending upon the facts and circumstances of the case, can have varying impacts on the case.

None of the parties had examined any of the experts who had authored this report. Hence, the version of the experts remained unchallenged. No one questioned the ability or competence of the ASI team. One can of course ask for the experts/authors of any report to be examined/cross-examined before the court and discredit their version. If a party does not exercise its right to cross-examine the expert, then what happens? The expert opinion would normally go through unchallenged. This rule of law concerning the report or evidence of experts in technical terms is also referred to as Order 26 Rule 10 of the Civil Procedure Code.

Now it was time for archaeology as an expert vocation to be tested for its worth along with the ASI report. The High Court had given its ruling against Ms Arora's clients/Mosque side concerning what lay beneath the disputed structure. One part of the ruling observed:

> *The identification and appreciation of the excavated material like human or animal figurines etc. is a matter of experts. None of these eight experts (Archaeologists of the Sunni*

> *Board side) claimed to be the experts in this [...] branch, in archaeology. Even otherwise, their stand in respect to these finds is varying. One witness says that these finds were not at all recovered from the layers they claim while others say otherwise. We have seen photographs of many such artefacts and finds and in generality there is no such inherent lacuna or perversity in the observations of the ASI or other identification which may warrant any [...] comment from this Court or may vitiate their report. It is not in dispute that no Islamic religious artefacts have been found during excavation while the artefacts relating to Hindu religious nature were in abundance. For some of the items, it is claimed that it can also be used by non-Hindu people but that would not be sufficient to doubt the opinion of ASI.*[160]

It came as no surprise that Ms Meenakshi Arora placed her case, attacking the findings on archaeology as made by Mr Vaidyanathan with as much vehemence as possible, being a Senior Counsel of repute. She started by clarifying the points concerning Ram Chabutra which Mr Jilani had advanced. Ms Arora then laid a threadbare attack on the ASI report.

Ms Arora pointed out that the report of the Archaeological Survey of India has to be discarded as only chapters were signed and the final summary of the report was signed by none. Hence, the complete report without the signatures of the members in the final summary could not be considered evidence. On an analysis, the initial challenge was three-fold.[161]

1. The authenticity of the report itself was doubted.
2. The manner in which excavations were carried out was also questioned.

---

[160]Supra 13 (Para 469).

[161]Mahapatra, Dhananjay, 'Ayodhya verdict by November 17 will be a miracle: SC', *The Times of India*, 27 September 2019, https://tinyurl.com/2yxveymp. Accessed on 18 January 2025.

3. The methodology the ASI employed to interpret excavated data was also questioned.

In team Ram Lalla's mind, there were counter-questions. Who could answer why the summary of the report was not signed? Who could explain whether the report was authentic or not? Perhaps only those people who were part of the archaeological team. The response of the judges were simple questions as to why the Sunni Board did not cross-examine the members who authored the ASI report before the High Court and what use was the attempt to discredit the ASI report during the hearing of appeals before the Supreme Court? However, Dr Dhavan as the senior most counsel for the Muslim side, intervened. He said, 'No one is arguing that the report is not authentic.'[162]

Dr Dhavan was of the opinion that there was no ground to challenge the authenticity or the authorship of the report. He was also of the opinion that 'the court may not have the expert eyes to sit in judgement over the experts.' What, however, could be challenged was the content of the ASI report. His point was that all the conclusions drawn must be supported by the report itself, based on consistency, relevance, and probability. He, in effect, submitted that the court must consider the following:

1. Whether the ASI team fulfilled the task given to it by the court to answer the queries/issue referred to it?
2. Whether there are obvious inconsistencies in the ASI report?
3. Whether conditions and limitations have been observed by ASI?
4. Whether the conclusions arrived at by the ASI are in conformity with the discoveries/findings during the excavations at the site?
5. Whether conclusions in the ASI report have been drawn beyond reasonable probabilities?

---

[162]Ibid.

'But there is a big question mark on authenticity of the summary or conclusions drawn by the ASI. The court must consider it,' was Dr Dhavan's point.[163] Both Mr Vaidyanathan and Senior Parasaran agreed with the point that conclusions drawn by a report can always be questioned, and that any party had the right to question such reports. Positions and attacks on merit and findings on the report that Ms Arora may take would have to be met.

For the convenience of the lawyers and perhaps to communicate the mind of the Bench to the bar, the judges clarified[164] what types of arguments the court would be willing to entertain:

1. Disputing whether the ASI's report went beyond its court commissioned mandate
2. Presenting contradictions in the report
3. Contesting the authenticity of summaries of the report

It was stressed that the Bench could not go into the authenticity of the report itself, as relevant evidence should have been used to do so at an earlier stage in the proceedings before the matter reached the Supreme Court. Despite the Sunni Board's failure to do so, the Bench agreed that the Board had not forfeited the right to question the report on the above three issues.

The attack on the merits of the report revealed the painstaking academic work done by Ms Arora. The arguments continued. The grounds of bias against the ASI were, therefore, given up, and the report had to be attacked using the contents of the report itself which Ms Arora had already initiated. If analysed, Ms Arora systematically attacked the ASI report[165] on

---

[163]Ibid.

[164]'Day 53 Arguments, Ayodhya Title Dispute', *Supreme Court Observer*, 26 September 2019, https://tinyurl.com/mv2m8xw3. Accessed on 18 January 2025.

[165]Written Submission No. A94, Reply to the Submissions of Mr. C.S. Vaidyanathan, Sr. Adv. on ASI Report Vol. III (Vol. 85) by Ms. Meenakshi Arora, Sr. Adv., *Vada Prativada*, https://tinyurl.com/4p64hrxv. Accessed on 18 January 2025.

the following grounds: (a) the merits of the process undertaken by the ASI; (b) the discipline of archaeology itself, as archaeology being not fit enough to be relied upon as evidence in a court proceeding; (c) the primary questions referred to the ASI not answered; and (d) relevant materials pointing to the Islamic presence and Idgah, pre-dating the mosque, ignored and inferential findings given. The process undertaken by the ASI was faulted, of which the salient points were:

1. The periodization undertaken by the ASI which characterized periods like the Shunga, medieval period may not be accurate: Soil layers are to be marked immediately on excavation which was not done which can cause the change of colour resulting in the exact periodization not being recorded correctly.
2. The ASI members failed to maintain accurate records of the recovery of artefacts from specific layers and consequently having lost the context; there are fatal errors in the attribution of artefacts to correct periods. Hence the report is unreliable.
3. The bones found during the excavation should have been subjected to relevant scientific tests like C–14, dating paleo-botanical studies, to arrive at better estimates of periods. This was not done. Even the discovery of construction using lime-surkhi which is characteristic of Islamic architecture was not given due consideration.
4. The time frame in which the excavation was carried out was also questioned. The excavation was hurried and there were time constraints. This would have affected the accuracy of the report. The fact that procedures have not been followed is borne out from the report itself which records the unusual conditions of the excavation which are deviations from the usual practice and methods of excavation as per the ASI's own bulletins; for example, the report inter alia recorded: 'On the directions of the High Court, Archaeological Survey

> of India has excavated 90 trenches in a limited time of five months, soon after which the excavation report is required to be submitted within fifteen days. This is an unprecedented event in the history of 142 years of the existence of the survey.'

Such arguments would generally raise queries from the court and force the other side back to the drawing board. While team Ram Lalla calibrated its approach, the alternate theory from the Sunni Board side as to what lay underneath the surface of the disputed site was yet to come. The interaction between Ms. Meenakshi Arora and the Bench also probed the issue of alternate theory as to what lay below the disputed structure acutely. These were work-overload times for Bhakti—being the first line of assistance for Mr Vaidyanathan; he highlighted from the record of what was argued as also what was not argued on the point of archaeology before the Allahabad High Court to undermine, if not discredit, the ASI report.

25

What Do Experts Want? What Do Courts Want?

Justice Nazeer also questioned the claim that the wall was part of an Idgah, and asked if it was so, where was the portion for the Imam to sit?[166]

The aforementioned question was asked in a particular context. For expert evidence to be discarded by a court, the complaining party must discredit the expert report and cross-examine or examine the expert. Specific to the Ayodhya case, it was the Archaeological Survey of India's report that was the target. Who signed the report? Who didn't? Why were the conclusions/summaries not signed when the report which was submitted by the ASI team had every chapter signed by the experts? This was the query that could only be answered by the ASI team. Technical points concerning excavations could only be clarified by the ASI team. The difficulty for both sides in such a scenario was that an expert can improve upon his evidence or clarify his version. In hindsight, with difficulties faced by all parties, none of the claimants decided to take the risk of examining or cross-examining the experts who could clarify their points against any of the parties. But to attack the experts at the level of the Supreme Court in appeal would necessarily result in the question: 'Why did you not question the experts in the first

[166]G., Ananthakrishnan, 'Ayodhya hearing: Supreme Court questions Idgah claim by mosque side', *The Indian Express*, 27 September 2019, https://tinyurl.com/2rx3wp3v. Accessed on 22 September 2025.

instance before the High Court?' This would have allowed the experts to clarify their points. The Sunni Board, and others on their side, argued that archaeology was no evidence at all. The ASI report was worthless and only an opinion. There was serious discussion in the court on this issue. The arguments which went towards pointing out the worthlessness, non-importance, and non-relevance of the discipline of archaeology as evidence in the Supreme Court could summarily be stated as:

1. The report of the Archaeological Survey of India comes only as an opinion of experts which is inconclusive and liable to change in distinction to evidence and witnesses of fact who are not allowed to change their opinion. Hence, such a report cannot be relied upon to conclude facts.
2. Archaeology is a social science which is considered less precise. Archaeology draws from other subjects such as history, sociology and anthropology which are also subjective social sciences rather than a natural science like physics and chemistry, which provide verifiable hypotheses considered to be more objective and accurate, example, DNA testing. Therefore, the ASI report is weak evidence and requires corroboration. In the present case, the ASI report is not corroborated by any other piece of direct or substantive evidence regarding the existence of a temple at the disputed site and, hence, cannot be relied upon by the court.
3. The overall depositions of the expert witnesses who support the ASI report are also merely opinions under Section 45 of The Indian Evidence Act, 1872 and are not substantive evidence, and are based on the ASI report itself. Further, there are inconsistencies and contradictions as well.
4. Objections to the ASI report were filed. The High Court decided that these shall be dealt with when the matter is finally decided, and the ASI report will be subject to objections and evidence of the parties. Objections were not

decided at the time of the final hearings.[167]

As a sequester of arguments being made to dismantle the ASI report, the question arose as to why the experts were not examined/cross-examined? *Live Law*[168] reported the interaction between the Bar and the Bench as follows:

> *Meenakshi Arora went on to discredit the ASI report as an opinion which could not be admitted as evidence. She argued that archaeology is an inexact science, a social science, and not a natural science like physics and chemistry.*
>
> *On being questioned by Justices Bobde and Chandrachud whether the structure was demolished or if it fell on its own, Arora argued that if a structure crumbles and the title holder makes no effort to restore it, and then somebody else builds on the land, after years of it lying unused, the title holder can't make a claim.*
>
> *Asserting that the temple being there was mere conjecture, Arora's next line of argument was that no member of the ASI team had signed the summary of the report. While chapters of the entire report were signed, the authorship of the last chapter (the summary) was unknown. The Bench seemed disinclined to hear this aspect of the argument as such objections must have been raised at an earlier stage, in the High Court. Arora submitted that the objection had been raised, but the court said it would deal with it at a later stage but never did.*
>
> *Justice D. Y. Chandrachud reiterated that 'objections such as chapters being signed, who authored the summary, etc. should*

[167]Written Submission No. A95, The Submissions & Case Laws by Ms. Meenakshi Arora, Sr. Adv., *Vada Prativada*, https://tinyurl.com/4hp55d3c. Accessed on 18 January 2025.

[168]Chaudhary, Niashish, '[Ayodhya Hearing] [Day 32]: ASI Report Contradictory, Not Conclusive Submits Senior Adv Meenakshi Arora for Sunni Board', *Live Law*, 26 September 2019, https://tinyurl.com/55ddcxv7. Accessed on 18 January 2025.

be raised at an earlier stage [...] the Commissioner, who is an officer of the court, should have been examined then [...] as per Order 26 Rule 10 of CPC, ASI report, submitted by the commissioner, "shall" be evidence unless discredited by examining him.'

CJI Ranjan Gogoi then laid out the procedure to raise objections and said by operation of law, the report is part of record. 'If you sought to exclude report from the record, you could have done so but didn't.'

Ms. Arora pointed out that even the structures found below the pillar bases were not in alignment and were of different sizes and shapes and some of them were not load-bearing. She had submitted that the so-called pillar bases, as found by the ASI, could not either have formed a part of a massive temple or supported the alleged massive structure/temple and the pillars do not belong to the same floor.

This was an attempt to refute the claim of the ASI that the disputed structure stood on the remains of a non-Islamic earlier structure. Ms. Arora submitted that even bones found during the excavation and bone fragments were not given due study. Ms. Arora questioned the periodisation (the timelines and periods attached to archaeological recoveries) carried out by the ASI. Relying on witnesses like Jayanti Prasad Srivastav (DW-20/5) who was formerly a Superintendent Archaeologist with the ASI. She stated the need for more clarification: 'Since the term "early Medieval" has got a definite meaning in the chronological sense, I cannot equate it with Medieval-Sultanate level lightly, hence the excavators, who got this chart prepared, are required to clarify the situation before any conclusion is drawn by us.'

For Ms Arora, one of the most important points seemed to be the fact that no finding had been recorded by the ASI on whether there was a pre-existing temple that was demolished for the construction of a mosque. The submissions further attacked the conclusions on points like:

1. The ASI report is hypothetical and based on inferences, interpretations, and conjunctions and cannot be taken as concrete proof as to the existence of any Hindu temple at the disputed site. The objects recovered in the excavations could belong to any other religious or non-religious structure. Consequently, it would be risky for the court to rely heavily on such an opinion to arrive at a finding on the existence of a Hindu temple below the disputed structure. The risk of reliance on the ASI report would be even greater if the court were to decide the title of the disputed site based on the ASI report as it would be tantamount to giving a judgement based on assumptions and presumptions. She relied upon expert witnesses supporting the ASI report like Mr Jayanti Prasad Srivastav, who testified that 'interpretation is an important aspect in excavation.' Witnesses like Prof Shereen F. Ratnagar, retired Professor of Archaeology, Jawaharlal Nehru University, opined in the context of the fact-finding discipline of archaeology that 'what constitutes a fact itself can be disputed. However, if the fact is established, there may be due opinions on the fact by two archaeologists.'
2. Since the historical accounts as produced in books and gazetteers were varied, the Allahabad High Court felt it necessary to direct a scientific investigation. Hence, those cannot be relied upon either.
3. The query put to the ASI by the Hon'ble High Court was only regarding a temple or structure, and not a Ram temple. Therefore, the query itself was framed in such a broad manner that the ASI was not required to give its opinion on whether the temple or other structure was a Ram temple or even a Hindu temple. Eventually, the ASI report only enforced the presence of a North Indian temple at the

disputed site and does not opine on whether this temple was the Ram/Janam Sthan/Hindu temple. Therefore, the ASI report is of no assistance in deciding the fact in issue, that is the existence of a Ram temple at the disputed site.

4. The ASI did not answer the direct, categorical question: Whether a temple was demolished and a mosque built in its place? The ASI report is silent on this aspect. The burden of proof is on the Hindu side to establish in Suit 5 that there existed a Ram Janam Sthan temple at the disputed site and not any Hindu temple. It was also submitted that the archaeological evidence if believed indicated through the presence of the pranala and circular shrine, the presence of a Shiva and not a Ram temple.
5. The ASI report ignores the presence of walls in its report which represent the presence of an Idgah rather than a temple.
6. The bones recovered from the site, and the use of lime-surkhi—all pointed to an Islamic presence at the site.

The effort put in by Ms Meenakshi Arora and her team spoke for itself. She had submitted detailed research, authorities, and her interpretation of the evidence. Academic texts were submitted which included extracts from Sir Mortimer Wheeler's *Archaeology from the Earth* (1954), Colon Renfrew's and Paul Bahn's *Archaeology, Theories, Methods and Practice* (1991), and *An Encyclopedia of Indian Archaeology from the Earth, 2 Vols.* (1989), edited by A. Ghosh.[169]

But Yogeswaran had a counter for every step taken by the other side. Seeing Ms Arora referring to several books and authorities, he decided to unleash his own books. As the hearings went on, a much-hassled Mr Vaidyanathan would find all kinds of archaeological books being arranged on the desk in front of him. He was taken aback by the sudden and magical appearance of

[169]Supra 167.

books in Yogi's hands which, on closer look, were not required. In an aside, he asked Yogi why these books were being brought inside the courtroom and received an epic answer, 'This is not for us, Sir, but to put psychological pressure on the other side by letting them know how many books you have read and how well we have prepared.' All this was happening in the middle of the hearing, while Mr Vaidyanathan was preparing to answer Ms. Arora's submissions. Yogi had again left him speechless. A seemingly smiling Yogi even instructed the understandably taken aback Mr Vaidyanathan to open the books and start reading at least a couple of them. Mr Vaidyanathan was left with no option but to leave his Advocate-on-Record to his own devices. The *Supreme Court Observer*[170], while covering these hearings and arguments of Ms Arora, was oblivious of the little drama being played out around Mr Vaidhyanathan's table. A seasoned and successful Senior Counsel like Ms Arora would, of course, be too busy to even notice what the other side's assisting counsel would be up to.

The *Supreme Court Observer* covered Ms Arora's arguments as follows:

> *7.76.6 Structure Has Islamic Features*
>
> *She reiterated that the structure could be Islamic in nature. Reading out witness statements, she submitted that certain architectural elements had Islamic features. For example, she said that the walls used lime plaster. The Bench asked whether only Islamic buildings of the time used lime plaster, to which she responded that she would compile relevant evidence on the record.*[171]
>
> *7.76.7 Pre-conceived Notion that Artifacts were Hindu*
>
> *She substantiated her argument that the ASI officers suffered*

[170]'Day 53 Arguments, Ayodhya Title Dispute', *Supreme Court Observer*, 26 September 2019, https://tinyurl.com/mv2m8xw3. Accessed on 18 January 2025.

[171]Ibid.

from a pre-conceived notion that the site was Hindu. Taking the court through various artefacts documented by the ASI, she argued that it had reached faulty conclusions. For example, she questioned how a mutilated figure recovered from the debris (i.e. not during excavations) could be assumed to be a divine Hindu artifact. Similarly, she argued that various other artifacts found in the debris had features that could be attributed to any religion. She argued that some artifacts were likely Islamic, such as certain glazed pottery tiles. She submitted that the ASI had chosen not to date them and argued that omissions such as these, skewed the conclusions of the report. The judges required further clarification.

7.76.8 ASI Did not analyse Animal Bones

She concluded the day by pointing out further alleged discrepancies in the ASI's report. She referred to certain artifacts which had been assigned multiple dates by different ASI officers. In addition, she drew the Bench's attention to animal bones found at the site, which had not been dated. She argued that this was significant because animal slaughter is not associated with Lord Ram's worship.

Referring to a witness statement, she submitted that ASI reports usually have a chapter on animal bones.[172]

Justice Chandrachud remarked that while archaeology may be an inferential science, archaeologists are trained experts. Sr Adv. Arora agreed but emphasized that archaeologists often reach divergent conclusions. She submitted that many archaeologists had disagreed with the conclusions reached by the ASI. Justice Nazeer stated that the report must be given greater weight than what Sr. Adv. Arora advocated as it was commissioned by the High Court under Order 26 Rule 10 of

[172]Ibid.

the Code of Civil Procedure.

He stressed that the Sunni Waqf Board should have filed objections at the trial stage. Sr. Adv. Arora responded that several High Courts have held that the findings of a report can be challenged either by filing objections or by presenting opposing evidence.[173]

7.78 Structure Is Not Necessarily 'Hindu'

After clarifying this point, Sr. Adv. Arora substantiated her argument from yesterday that the structure was not necessarily Hindu. Yesterday, she had argued that some of the site's features indicated it was an Islamic site, like the lime-plastered walls. The Bench had asked her to substantiate her claims with evidence. Today, she handed over a compilation of relevant evidence on the record. She stated that the ASI had failed to take into account all the excavated material. She argued that the site had architectural features common to Hinduism, Buddhism and Jainism and questioned why the report assumed the structure was Hindu.[174]

7.79 Archaeology is an inferential science

Sr. Adv. Arora asserted that the ASI report is only advisory in nature. She emphasised that archaeology is not an exact science, but rather an inferential science. Referring to Section 45 of the Indian Evidence Act, 1872, she argued that while the ASI may be an expert body, their report can only be considered an opinion on facts, not a set of conclusive facts. She drew comparisons to handwriting experts and argued that the ASI's report must be considered weak evidence, which must be corroborated by other evidence. She asserted that,

---

[173]'Day 54 arguments, Ayodhya Title Dispute', *Supreme Court Observer*, 27 September 2019, https://tinyurl.com/52yjjbeh. Accessed on 18 January 2025.
[174]Ibid.

> *hence, the report cannot be interpreted to have conclusively determined that a Lord Ram temple existed at the site prior to Babri Masjid.*
>
> *Responding to Sr. Adv. Arora's Section 45 argument, Justice Nazeer questioned how she could simultaneously maintain that archaeology is not a true science and rely on Section 45 to argue that the ASI report is only opinion. Section 45 of the Indian Evidence Act, 1872 applies when the court has to form an opinion on a scientific question. Sr. Adv. Arora reiterated that archaeology is an inferential science, whose findings require corroboration.*[175]

The alternative claim of an Idgah preceding a mosque was argued with vehemence. But this claim of an Idgah was not pleaded in the Sunni Board Suit, therefore it seemed to some that the debate would rest with the issue that the case of the Idgah had never been pleaded. Nevertheless, the court also went into the merits of the claim and the queries were reported by *The Indian Express*:[176]

> *The Supreme Court on Thursday questioned the mosque side in the Ayodhya case over its claim that a wall discovered during excavations by the Archaeological Survey of India (ASI) at the disputed site was part of an Idgah, and wondered why it had not raised such a claim in its plaint.*
>
> *'You said the Mosque was built on barren land. Now you say there was an Islamic structure below it,' Justice Ashok Bhushan, who is part of a five-judge Constitution bench hearing appeals against the September 30, 2010 verdict of the Allahabad High Court, told senior advocate Meenakshi Arora who sought to assail the ASI report.*

---

[175]Ibid.

[176]G., Ananthakrishnan, 'Ayodhya hearing: Supreme Court questions Idgah claim by mosque side', *The Indian Express*, 27 September 2019, https://tinyurl.com/2rx3wp3v. Accessed on 18 January 2025.

[...]

Justice Bhushan's remarks came when Arora said the wall, which dates back to the 12th century AD, was on the western side, away from habitation and had lime-surkhi plastering on the inside which pointed to its Islamic origins and that it may have been part of an Idgah.

Justice Bhushan said, 'But you did not say so in the plaint,' and asked, 'Can you be allowed to develop your case on evidence?'

Arora replied that there was no contention about any pre-existing structure beneath the ground at the time it filed its plaint. She added that the contention of the Hindu side that the wall was part of the temple was only an inference and that being the case, an alternate inference that it may have been part of an Idgah was also possible.

On Wednesday, the Bench had told Arora that she should have taken steps before the trial court to summon the author of the ASI report and examine him if she had problems with its contents.

Intervening, senior advocate C.S. Vaidyanathan, appearing for the deity Ramlalla, pointed out that the wall was older than the 12th century and that part of it was demolished in the 12th century and rebuilt some years later.

Justice Nazeer also questioned the claim that the wall was part of an Idgah and asked if it was so, where was the portion for the Imam to sit.

Arora contended that the pillar bases found by the ASI were in different layers of soil and this showed they were erected in different time periods. She asked how pillars made in different periods could support one massive structure as concluded by the ASI.

> *Joining the issue, Justice Chandrachud said instead of drawing adverse conclusions, these questions should have been put to experts at the trial stage.*
>
> *As Arora sought to question the basis of the ASI's claims, the CJI remarked, 'Why ask us? You should have asked the expert who would have given the answer.'*

Though Mr Vaidyanathan would further reply to the doubts raised by Ms Arora, team Ram Lalla was a bit relaxed as the important issue raised by Justice Nazeer with respect to the place of the seat of the Imam could not be answered. The change of the Sunni Board's stand that the mosque was not built on barren land further left the team astounded. With the debate on the ASI revealing a few points, it was now time to go back to the counsels for Ram Lalla.

SECTION V

THE CASE OF THE TEMPLE

26

The Last Wish

There was a reason why Yogeswaran had accumulated so many books on archaeology. Since 2010, both Yogi and Bhakti had begun assisting Mr Vaidyanathan when he set aside some time for the Ayodhya case. He held intense and in-depth conferences which often continued right through the court vacations. Every year, Mr Vaidyanathan went to Arya Vaidya Pharmacy to recoup from the rigours of a stressful professional life. However, it is doubtful if he had much of a vacation, or if any destressing was possible, whenever Yogi and Bhakti reached there. Bhakti, the gentle equal partner who was playing second fiddle to Yogi, would, of course, have been the soothing balm after an aggressive briefing by a passionate Yogi.

In these discussions, complete facts, including the statement of witnesses and evidence of both sides, were thoroughly vetted. However, the real stress sometimes was on understanding the subject of archaeology for which, not only detailed study had to be undertaken but experts also had to be consulted.

In the initial phases, Yogeswaran and Bhakti were accompanied by Mr Vikramjit Banerjee, Additional Solicitor General of India, but later, when Mr Banerjee was a private practising lawyer, he was no longer able to participate in every conference. Mr Bhupendra Yadav was also part of the team even though he had a very busy schedule, especially after assuming the position of Member of Parliament. Whenever possible, he would make a pointed effort to attend these meetings and conferences. Mr Yadav continued his official association with the case as a lawyer and appeared quite regularly in the courts in this case, and also attended the meetings and conferences. On a Saturday or Sunday, whichever day he was free, Mr Vaidyanathan would dedicate himself to the Ayodhya case. Mr Vaidyanathan's family members looked after the briefing counsels conscientiously.

Mr Vaidyanathan, the lawyer, approached the complex and new subject of archaeology as a student. As Bhakti would cheerfully instruct the other team members to start their new journey as students of archaeology, Mr Vaidyanathan would buckle down and begin his reading to understand the basic concepts of the subject. He consulted professors and technicians in the field for this purpose. Some of the seminal books he read were *Archaeology: A Brief Introduction*[177]; *Archaeology from the Earth*[178]; *Archaeological Research: A Brief Introduction*[179]; *The Archaeology Coursebook: Introduction to Themes, Sites, Methods and Skills*[180]; and *The Oxford Companion to Indian Archaeology: The Archaeological Foundations of Ancient India and Stone Age to AD 13th Century*[181].

Everything case-specific had to be covered and understood. There was a possibility that the archaeology of temples might or might not differ from other sites. Hence, temple architecture specific to temples had to be understood. Help came from a book exclusively on temple architecture in India—*Alayam, The Hindu Temple, An Epitome of Hindu Culture* (2010) authored by G. Venkataramana Reddy. The author, who was a qualified architect and town planner had designed and overseen the construction of

[177]Fagan, Brian M., and Nadia Durrani, *Archaeology: A Brief Introduction*, Routledge, New York, 2012.

[178]Wheeler, Mortimer, *Archaeology from the Earth*, Oxford University Press, London, 1954.

[179]Peregrine, Peter N., *Archaeological Research: A Brief Introduction*, Routledge, New York, 2016.

[180]Grant, Jim, Neil Fleming, and Sam Gorin, *The Archaeology Coursebook: Introduction to Themes, Sites, Methods And Skills*, Routledge, New York, 2015.

[181]Chakrabarti, Dilip K., *The Oxford Companion to Indian Archaeology: The Archaeological Foundations of Ancient India and Stone Age to AD 13th Century*, Oxford University Press, London, 2006.

many temples. Talking to an expert would further bring a clearer understanding, therefore, Chithra Madhavan's help was sought.

Chithra Madhavan was the author of seven books on the history and culture of Tamil Nadu, including books on Vishnu Temples of South India, and Sanskrit education in the ancient and medieval periods. She is also the author of *Srirangam: Heaven on Earth*. Madhavan's rare interest in ancient Indian history was piqued when she was a child. In her own words, she had 'always been interested, even in the junior classes when studying at Sishya.' However, it was in Class VIII that she became fascinated with the Indus Valley Civilization. This was followed by family trips to temples across South India and she was stunned by their architecture. She knew then that this was what she wanted to do.[182] She was also actively writing on temples for *The Indian Express*. Her books *Vishnu Temples of South India* (1905) and *South Indian Heritage: An Introduction* (2005, co-editor) were studied carefully by the team. Discussions with some experts in the field of archaeology were also undertaken. All the books mentioned were deeply analysed by Mr Vaidyanathan. It was only after this elaborate exercise of transforming himself into a student of archaeology that he was confident of handling any query from the judges or meeting any objection of the opposing side.

Mr Vaidyanathan kept preparing his replies as was his style, and perhaps could be defined as a 'ploughing a lonely furrow', despite the available assistance of Yogeswaran and Bhakti who were there to sort out his doubts if any. Meanwhile, a growing interest in Ram's lawyers became evident from the questions that the team members began to receive from young lawyer friends, family members, acquaintances, and of course, the media. Unfortunately, the media rarely reported Mr Vaidyanathan's

---

[182]Alexander, Deepa, 'Wanderlust teamed with academia made Chithra Madhavan take history into the open', *The Hindu*, 16 July 2018, https://tinyurl.com/jrn552f. Accessed on 18 January 2025.

commendable efforts. Just as they missed the efforts of government law officers such as Mr Tushar Mehta and Mr Maninder Singh, who more than once took up the cudgels[183] for final hearings to begin while appearing on behalf of governments. When it came to the merits of the case at the time of the final hearing, the law officers maintained their neutrality as that was the stand of the government all through; the complete burden rested on the shoulders of Mr K Parasaran, Mr Vaidyanathan, Mr Ranjit Kumar and Mr Narasimha. News reports had the spotlight on K. Parasaran's luminous career (*see* Chapter 2). An *Indian Express* article called him the key face in the Ayodhya case,[184] but people familiar with the team were interested in knowing how the case was prepared and how long did the preparation take. Among other things, *The Indian Express* reported:

> *[…] Parasaran started his practice before the Supreme Court in 1958. During the Emergency, he was Advocate General of Tamil Nadu and in 1980 was appointed Solicitor General of India. He served as Attorney General of India from 1983 to 1989.*
>
> *Parasaran often found himself on the other side of Nani Palkhivala on key Constitution cases in the 1970s—Palkivala mostly appearing for private interests challenging tax and administrative laws.*
>
> *Last week, when senior advocate Rajeev Dhavan objected to daily hearings in the Ayodhya case before the Supreme Court, Parasaran said: 'My last wish before I die, is to finish this case.'*

---

[183]'Senior lawyers spar in Supreme Court during Ayodhya case hearing', *Hindustan Times*, 6 April 2018, https://tinyurl.com/vppdnv6s. Accessed on 18 January 2025.

[184]Vishwanath, Apurva, 'At 92, key face in Ayodhya case K Parasaran is a trusted voice of many governments', *The Indian Express*, 12 August 2019, https://tinyurl.com/5x24xn3t. Accessed on 18 January 2025.

This often-stated last wish, though unnerving to the team, was simply an objective observation by Senior Parasaran. It also brought forth regrets. He regretted not spending enough time with his wife. He felt he owed her as much he owed to the divine. Memories of the major contributions to his life by his wife would come flooding in. Mr Parasaran would often remind himself and those around him, 'My success is because of luck; you all won't understand how luck was on my side throughout. Getting a helpful and kind wife or a good wife is in itself a "divine blessing". My wife helped me concentrate on my work for eighteen hours a day.'

If someone pointed out that luck might not have been the only factor, the bhakt would immediately say, 'Yes, I was lucky enough to receive God's blessings and a great helping hand in the form of my wife.' So, God, Luck and Wife kept preceding and succeeding each other in turn as the reason for Senior Parasaran's success. The 'love for law' was not forgotten either. So, it was God, Luck, Law and Wife. Law was always his first love. He accepted his guilt, for he married law after marrying his wife and did not spend enough time with his actual wife.

'She tolerated my bigamous nature; I spent more time with law than with her. I would not even remember the class my younger son Satish was in; she would manage everything on her own—even when finances were less and even when finances were sufficient. We were together in a shed and travelled together to the residence of the Attorney General for India.'

Interestingly, Senior Parasaran's family members would reminisce that whenever VIPs visited him, *badam kheer* (Indian dessert) would be served first to the drivers and workers, and then was offered to the VIPs. The logic given by his wife was that those working in the scorching sun would need such home food, cooked by a housewife, to cool them. The nonagenarian would remember all this with fondness and regret, 'But I kept myself busy with books, cases and clients. Now that she is not there, I miss her.' A few enquiries with those who were junior to Mr Parasaran in the 1970s revealed similar tales about Mrs Saroja Parasaran. She was fondly remembered by these juniors, some of whom were now retired judges. Justice D.V. Shylendra Kumar (retd) of the Karnataka High Court recalled, 'My senior's wife Smt. Saroja, who was popularly known as "Ammayi", was a mother not only to her children but also to all office juniors and all relatives.' Many a time, she would invite the office juniors to take food along with Senior Parasaran before leaving for the court. Mr Parasaran was not just fast but superfast, whether in taking food or in arguing for a case. He would finish his lunch in no time and go sit in the car and wait for the other juniors to finish their food and join him. After a brief wait, annoyance would creep in as it would be getting late for the court. Life in the court was driven by judges, and at home, Mr Parasaran was driven by his wife. Mrs Parasaran's advice to the juniors was not to get perturbed because, according to her, Mr Parasaran was always in a hurry, no matter what.

'He finishes his food in a hurry, you better have the food in a proper manner, slowly, and then go.' That used to be her attitude. In fact, Mrs Parasaran's ability to manage the household was remarkable. On occasions, Senior Parasaran would ask for coffee and snacks for 15–20 people in the office. Justice D.V. Shylendra Kumar (retd) would marvel at her abilities: 'I do not know what magic or superpower my senior's wife had; she would prepare it in no time and send it to the office to be served to seniors, juniors, clients, and the people who were present in the office, including the office staff. Such was my senior's wife's kindness and generosity. No one who approached my senior's wife for help would return empty-handed.' Justice D.V. Shylendra Kumar has passed on; however, his son Ashwin D.S. keeps the family flag flying high.[185]

---

[185]Also part of the unedited part of an article written for *The Hindu*; abridged version by Kumar, D.V. Shylendra, 'K. Parasaran, a man for all reasons', *The Hindu*, 8 December

These stories of good old times and of his wife were often told when Senior Parasaran would have wrapped up the day's work.

The final countdown for the case had begun in the midst of intense media glare, with minute-by-minute reporting on it. Live Law led the way but Senior Parasaran was unaware of this modern trend where the Supreme Court was allowing every word spoken in the court to be in public domain. So, thankfully, media interest in the lead counsel for Ram Lalla went unnoticed by Senior Parasaran, for any media attention made him uncomfortable. At the very sight of a camera, the nonagenarian would turn into an introvert. Thanks to the media, much gossip and many questions started coming up, some of which took even the team members by surprise; for example, did Senior Parasaran turn down the post of Chief Justice of India? The mystery was solved by another news report, this time from 1986.[186] This was the time when the then Chief Justice of India, Justice P. N. Bhagwati, was about to be succeeded by Justice R.S. Pathak, and it was speculated that Justice Pathak would reverse the public interest spirit that the Supreme Court had displayed. It was rumoured that the government was looking at a suitable alternative to Justice Pathak. Guess who was speculated to succeed Justice Pathak? A news report in *India Today* stated the following:

> *[...]*
>
> *The prime minister's office [...] has suggested that Bhagwati be succeeded by Attorney-General K. Parasaran, who enjoys the status of a Supreme Court judge.*

2019, https://tinyurl.com/89vbntsh. Accessed on 18 January 2025.

[186]'Dilemma over choosing successor to Supreme Court Chief Justice P.N. Bhagwati', *India Today*, 31 January 2014, https://tinyurl.com/3awucd5k. Accessed on 18 January 2025. In another instance, Abhinav Chandrachud in his book, *Supreme Whispers: Conversations with Judges of the Supreme Court of India 1980–89* (2018), also talks about Mr K. Parasaran, Fali S. Nariman, and Mr K.K. Venugopal among those who did not accept direct elevation to the Supreme Court of India.

The same article further reported that Senior Parasaran was unwilling to accept such a position and thereby refused to step *'into Bhagwati's shoes [...]'*

Justice R.S. Pathak took over as Chief Justice of India from Justice Bhagwati; more than 30 years have passed since this news item appeared.

At this point, the case was positioned a bit differently from where it had started. Hence, a recapitulation was imperative. At the very least, it was now accepted that Ram bhakts were present within the disputed site since 1857, worshipping at what they believed to be Lord Ram's birthplace as held by the 1885 judgement. It was accepted by the Sunni Board that through a judicial order, Ram Janmabhoomi was within the disputed site of 1,500 sq. yd. The presence of Nirmohi Akhara within the disputed structure and their performance of puja, arati, etc., was not disputed. However, the ownership of the site, with whom lay the possession of the site, and whether Ram Janmabhoomi was a Juristic Person/Juristic Entity or not, were all disputed. It was also disputed whether the area below the central dome was Ram Janmabhoomi.

Could there be a situation, as Dr Dhavan canvassed, where the ownership of the land was with the Sunni Board, yet the worship of Ram Lalla within the disputed site would be allowed; or would there be no worship of Ram Lalla at the disputed site at all? Any eventuality other than the land completely belonging to Ram Lalla knocked the wind out of the team and got Senior Parasaran back to work from whatever medically advised rest he was supposed to take.

Senior Parasaran was overwhelmed by representing Lord Ram almost at the end of his career; he was 'Lord Ram's lawyer', which was above any material possession. While he was reluctant to speak, it was back to more work for him, with the Sunni Board getting over with its submissions. The next round of submissions was going to be highly technical. The time for the history or story of the case was over. Now the nonagenarian had to bring out his arsenal of law. It was time for the best legal manoeuvres from the counsels of both sides.

27

The Test of Indianness

[...] Much of the existing Hindu Law has grown up in that way from instance to instance, the threads being gathered now from the rishis, now from custom, now from tradition [...][187]

Alarming divides had arisen within the team over whether a piece of land could be seen as a Juristic Person. Yogeswaran, Aditi and Ashwin were not in favour of going ahead with this argument as they thought it was a futile point. For Bhakti, Sridhar and Anirudh, on the other hand, it was a point of crucial importance. For Anirudh, working on a difficult point of law was of the most interest. During his interactions with Senior Parasaran, Anirudh understood that many targets were being aimed at with a single arrow. The arguments on land as a Juristic Person might actually prove to be a *divyastra* (divine weapon). Dr Dhavan had already given a list of Hindu temples which established diverse forms of temples and a huge width of religious practices which reiterated that it was the belief of the devotees which could confer the status of a temple at any place.

The reader may recall that disagreements within the team around the legal concept of Juristic Person had begun almost at the inception (*see* Chapter 3). At one point, Yogeswaran and Aditi, the two warriors of the team, saw the quiet and mild Bhakti and Anirudh extremely assertive on this point. In fact, they were taken by surprise by this assertiveness. While Yogi, Aditi

---

[187]The Supreme Court in its Constitution Bench Judgement '*State of West Bengal v. Anwar Ali Sarkar AIR1952 SC 75*'.

and Ashwin opined that stress should be more on evidence of practice of faith, Bhakti, Anirudh and Sridhar were in favour of putting forth the broad dimensions of Hindu Law with respect to temples and worship in analysing the evidence. While the former group thought that this would unnecessarily bring religious issues into a property dispute, the latter group argued that what had already been decided by Indian courts were not issues of faith but judgements by secular courts. While the former group wanted to keep religious beliefs out, the latter group insisted that if practice of faith was evidence, the dimension of this faith too must be clarified. All kinds of academics at both ends led to heated debates within Senior Parasaran's team, until Nandini Parasaran would send some mouthwatering snacks which would ease the tension for the moment, only to be reignited once the food was devoured. Happily, these sharp and heated discussions within the team were sorted out as the case advanced. The debate on the case finally convinced Yogeswaran, Aditi and Ashwin that the issue of land as a Juristic Person had to be argued; in fact, the list of temples given by the Sunni Board side convinced them to change their stand.

The next rounds of arguments were shorter, and therefore, less physically consuming in the courts. However, more work needed to be done by the lawyers in their offices. One cannot plan or perceive in advance what the flow of arguments in a court can be. The entire flow could change course with a single question or suggestion from the judges. The arguments were reported by media houses and by *Live Law*.

> *Senior Advocate K. Parasaran continued arguing his rejoinder on day 35 of the Ayodhya land dispute hearing by citing some shlokas from the Bhagvad Gita and reiterated that the birthplace place must be considered a juridical person. 'If the people believe a place to have supernatural powers, it can be considered to a be a juristic person irrespective of the kind of manifestation of the divine.' He*

> *submitted that all elements—air, water, earth, fire and space—are worshipped. All directions are worshipped and it ends with worshipping the Earth.*[188]

The most important aspect of the case for some was the issue of the land Janmabhoomi/Janmasthan being a Juristic Person. This necessarily required an evaluation of modes of Hindu worship. Hence, back in office, it was all hands on deck. Senior Parasaran and Mr Vaidyanathan prepared the following important questions that had to be raised before the court directly or indirectly:

1. What or who is it that Hindus worship?
2. In how many ways can there be manifestations of the divine as per Hindu thought, belief and practice?
3. What can be called a temple? Can there be a place of worship for Hindus without a temple or even a building?
4. What is the purpose and position of an idol or an image of a deity in Hindu thought?
5. When does an idol or a deity get destroyed? Can it be destroyed at all?
6. Whose interest is to be protected by protecting an idol or a temple?

To a few of these questions, Dr Dhavan had given his reply, but to Janmasthan as a Juristic Person, all these questions necessarily required deep research and understanding of the philosophy and thoughts in Hindu practice. Therefore, it was an asset for the case that the lead counsel was well versed in Sanskrit texts. Not only Senior Parasaran, but the team also had Mr P.S. Narasimha and Sridhar Potaraju who had deep interest in ancient thought and Indic literature and texts. The argument on such a vexatious

---

[188]Chaudhary, Nilashish, '[Ayodhya Hearing] [Day 35]: Hindu Parties Submit Reply Arguments on Juristic Personality and ASI Reports', *Live Law*, 1 October 2019, https://tinyurl.com/4j2bvkhr. Accessed on 18 January 2025.

point of law in the interpretation of philosophy and, in particular, religious philosophy and practice, had to be seen only from the perspective of Indian practice and Indian living, and not from how the rest of the world, or the Western world looked at Indian practices. Since time was of the essence, detailed written arguments had to be readied, and the team was working on this. Mr Parasaran was clear on the point that relying on Western notions without testing those notions through Indian living, Indian thought and Indian ethics was contrary to the law laid down by the Supreme Court of India. He lamented that of late reliance was placed more on Western ethics rather than Indian ethics against which the 13-Bench judgement in the case of *Kesavananda Bharati v. the State of Kerala*[189] had warned, and the views of the Kesavananda Bharati case were binding. However, these binding views were many a time ignored to just ape the Western world view.

'They, the judges in the Keshavananda Bharati case had said that Indian soil is different, Indian ethics are different, Indian thought is different, everyone is bound to follow this test,' Senior Parasaran often stressed. Hence, the base of Mr Parasaran's submission with respect to why the Janmabhoomi should be declared a Juristic Person lay in the authoritative pronouncement of the Kesavananda Bharati case:[190]

> *The seed of the Constitution is sown in a particular soil and it is the nature and the quality of the soil and the climatic conditions prevalent there which will, ensure its growth and determine the benefits which it confers on its people. We cannot plant the same seed in a different climate and in a different soil and expect the same growth and the same benefit therefrom. Law varies according to the requirements of time and place. Justice thus becomes a relative concept*

[189](1973)4 SCC225 @ 614, para 1107.

[190]Ibid.

> *varying from society to society according to the social milieu and economic conditions prevailing therein. The difficulty, to my mind, which foreign cases or even cases decided within the Commonwealth where the Common Law forms the basis of the legal structure of that unit, just as it is to a large extent, the basis in this country, is that they are more often than not, concerned with expounding and interpreting provisions of law which are not in pari materia with those we are called upon to consider. The problems which confront those courts in the background of the state of the society, the social and economic set-up, the requirements of a people with a* ***totally different ethics, philosophy*** *[authors emphasis], temperament and outlook differentiate them from the problems and outlook which confront the courts in this country. It is not a case of shutting out light where that could profitably enlighten and benefit us. The concern is rather to safeguard against the possibility of being blinded by it.*

The law laid down in the Kesavananda Bharati case led to a question as to what would be the test to determine what is worshippable and what is not worshippable under Hindu belief. How will a court determine it? Have courts determined these issues earlier? Won't these issues be intertwined with **Indian ethics and Indian philosophy which have originated in Indian Soil?**

A series of questions would therefore arise: Are only idols that are in human form to be worshipped by Hindus? What yardstick or test will be applied to determine answers to these questions? This brought the nonagenarian to the submission that only Hindu notion and practices are the determining considerations in concluding what is to be the object of Hindu worship and the location of divinity. With Hindu notion as the determining factor, came back old decided cases. In a judgement reported in 1890 by the name of *Jamna Bai v. Khimji*

Vullubdass[191], Sir Charles Sarjeant Kt. CJ., while interpreting a will, gave precedence to local Oriental notions. He held, '[…] Such an object is so frequently the result of charitable intention in Oriental countries, and is so entirely in accordance with the notions of the people of this country.' The Supreme Court of India in the year 1954 gave its stamp of approval to the 'notion of the people' test in the case of *Saraswathi Ammal v. Rajagopal Ammal*,[192] where the Supreme Court approved of the following:

> *What are purely religious purposes and what religious purposes will be charitable must be entirely decided according to Hindu Law and Hindu notions.*

The question of Hindu notions was not simple—it was also intermixed with Hindu Law. Ram Lalla's case, which reached High Court and Supreme Court, had to travel way back to 1952, to the case of the *State of West Bengal v. Anwar Ali Sarkar*[193] where it was observed:

> *[…] Much of the existing Hindu Law has grown up in that way from instance to instance, the threads being gathered now from the rishis, now from custom, now from tradition […]*

Hence the notions of the Ram bhakts and how they pray were to be tested in order to test the legal status of land Janmasthan. With Hindu notions as the guiding light, the submissions moved to examine the characteristic features of Hindu divinity—whether Hinduism believed in the multiplicity of God or the multiple manifestations of *one* God; what was the nature of the Hindu religion?

The submissions of Senior Parasaran and Mr Vaidyanathan

---

[191]ILR (1890) 14 Bom1, also quoted with approval by this Hon'ble Court in *Kamaraju Venkata Krishna Rao v. Sub Collector*, (1969) 1 SCR 624 @ 627–628.
[192]1952 SCR 284 @ 363.
[193]*AIR1952 SC 75.*

moved into a zone of deep Hindu philosophy. The point made was that Hindus do not worship the material body of the deity/ idol/ God made of clay or gold or any other substance. God is formless and shapeless. Hindus worship the eternal spirit of the deity/God or certain attributes thereof in a suggestive form which is used for convenience as a mere symbol or emblem of God. It is the incantation of the mantras, particular to a specific deity, that causes the manifestation or presence of the deity. Mantras, therefore, were important as the source of reaching the divine. In fact, mantras were there before any idol worship started at all, or as some thoughts stated, even before any religion was established. Idols were important but idols were not the only things important.

'God is "*Anoraniyanmahatomahiyan*", i.e. smaller than the smallest, and bigger than the biggest' (*Katha Upanishad*; Verse 20, 79), was quoted. It is difficult to conceive of 'God' in this manner; only *gyani*s or the wise can perceive God of that nature in the absence of any form or idol. For ordinary worshippers, to be able to conceive of the idea of 'God' and concentrate on the deity while offering worship, an idol or image is consecrated and installed in the temple. That was the importance of idols in Hindu thought. The submissions further enunciated this issue and went on to exhort that where an idol or image was consecrated and installed in the temple, it represented the physical manifestation of the formless deity that was sought to be worshipped.

Therefore, devotees would make charities in favour of the divine, and to facilitate the connection of the multitude with the divine, devotees would construct temples or ponds, and donate valuables, jewellery, etc. In such cases, who would hold the property dedicated to the divine? Who would ensure that the property of the idol or temple was not swindled? But, most importantly, to which person would the property then belong? Humans take birth and depart but institutions like temple survive for centuries.

In such scenarios, an idol or image comes to be recognized as the juristic entity, capable of holding property endowed/dedicated to the deity. However, the object of worship was not the idol itself, but the deity/God/divinity which is believed to be manifest in such an idol. This proposition in the submission of Senior Parasaran, was settled by the Madras High Court in the case of *M.L. Hanumantha Rao v. Sri Sai Baba*[194]wherein the issue was whether the idol of Sri Sai Baba could be treated as a deity as the court observed:

> *The legal position, therefore, appears to be this. Normally, the images worshipped by the Hindus are visible symbols representing some form of the three-fold attributes of God based upon the Hindu idea of Trinity, namely, Creator, Preserver and Destroyer. The object of worship is not the image but the god believed to be manifest in the image for the benefit of the worshippers who cannot conceive or think of the deity without the aid of a perceptible form on which they may fix their minds and concentrate attention for the purpose of meditation.* ***According to the Hindu notion, the image itself is not the god but it [is] the visible personified deity manifesting itself to the devotees by means of the image*** *[authors' emphasis]. Where a Hindu dedicates property for the worship of a god by means of an image, the property is deemed to be vested in a juristic or juridical person, the god which is believed too is conferred the status of manifest in the image/idol.*

> *Thus, while God/Deity himself/herself is not a person in law, whatever form he/she is believed to have manifested is a person for the sake of the law. Images and idols would vary from place to place and so would the religious notions. The images and idols may be lost or replaced or damaged with time, but with what repercussions?*

[194](1980) 93 LW 328.

Perhaps team Ram Lalla would or would not succeed on the issue of Janmasthan as a Juristic Person, but that these arguments would certainly help in proving nearly every other issue in the case, was the thought of the Senior Counsels. Even on admitted facts, like the presence within the disputed area of Nirmohi Akhara and the idol of Ram Lalla at least from 1857, or the presence of Ram Chabutra or parikrama, the arguments on Hindu thought, philosophy, worship would have an impact. To add to it, the varying nature of the manifestation of divinity/idols/images and manifestation as in the list submitted by Dr Dhavan—and the latitude in the manner of their worship—would not only help advance the arguments on Juristic Person but also help better espouse the cause of worship at the parikrama and Janmabhoomi at the disputed site.

Dr Dhavan, after deep research, had given a list of deities that could be there in Hindu worship. However, what could count as a temple? The Senior Counsel for the Sunni Board had also referred to the Chidambaram Temple which existed without an idol. The Senior Counsel for Ram Lalla had to build further on those lines. A few questions, however, were staring in the face. What can be said to be a temple? What can be said to be an idol? The veteran lawyer had multiple answers to these questions. The devotee that Senior Parasaran was, he would say, 'Ram and Sita were showing him the way and he was doing nothing and was only a medium, a nimittamatra.' The cause for saying so would be the judgement of the Supreme Court in the case of *Ram Jankijee Deities v. State of Bihar*[195] which held:

> *[...]*
>
> *13. Divergent are the views on the theme of images or idols in Hindu Law. One school propagates God having swayambhu images or consecrated images; the other school lays down God*

---

[195](1999) 5 SCC 50 @ 57.

as omnipotent and omniscient and the people only worship the eternal spirit of the deity and it is only the manifestation or the presence of the deity by reason of the charm of the mantras.

14. Images according to Hindu authorities are of two kinds: the first is known as swayambhu or self-existent or self-revealed, while the other is pratisthita or established. The Padma Purana says: 'The image of Hari (God) prepared of stone, earth, wood, metal or the like and established according to the rites laid down in the Vedas, Smritis and Tantras is called the established images [...] where the self-possessed Vishnu has placed himself on earth in stone or wood for the benefit of mankind, that is styled the self-revealed.' (B.K. Mukherjea — Hindu Law of Religious and Charitable Trusts, 5th Edn.) A swayambhu or self-revealed image is a product of nature and it is anadi or without any beginning and the worshippers simply discover its existence and such images do not require consecration or pratistha but a man-made image requires consecration. This man-made image may be painted on a wall or canvas. The Shalagram Shila depicts Narayana being Lord of the Lords and represents Vishnu Bhagwan. It is a shila—the shalagram form partaking the form of Lord of the Lords, Narayana and Vishnu.

Thus, while God/Deity himself is not a person in law, whatever form he is believed to have manifested in, becomes a person in law. Fictions created by law like conferring the status of Juristic Person on institutions like banks, ships and trusts had made the legal profession omnipresent, whether it be cases of humans, gods, or places of worship. As with idols and images, the position in law concerning temples had to be advanced for consideration by the court. Authoritative pronouncements by the court as to what constituted temples made another interesting read. The first interesting part was the fact that the consecration of an idol was not a requisite or an essential condition for a place to be considered a temple. The Supreme Court had settled this proposition too in its judgement in the Ram Jankiji Deities case:[196]

> *15. It is further to be noticed that while usually an idol is consecrated in a temple, it does not appear to be an essential condition.*
>
> *[...]*
>
> *The presence of an idol, though it is an invariable feature of Hindu temples, is not a legal requisite under the definition of a temple in Section 9(12) of the Act. If the public or that section of the public who go for worship consider that there is a divine presence in a particular place and that by offering worship there, they are likely to be the recipients of the blessings of God, then we have the essential features of a temple as defined in the Act.*

The whole submission was that a temple does not cease to be a temple merely because there exists no structure or building. Some Hindus may be idol worshippers; others may not be. Those Hindu worshippers who treat as divine a place with no idols or structures cannot be treated differently from those who worship at a temple with an idol/image. They must be treated equally. Thus, their interests and religious rights under the Constitution of India had to be guarded. The logic which was the basis of Chidambara *rahasyam* or the secret of Chidambaram was quite revealing. Explaining this secret was the next step so that the religious importance of the land where Lord Ram took birth could be explained.

---

[196]Ibid., pp. 58–59, Paras 15–16.

28

The Form of God: Importance of the Worshipper

The concept of 'Juristic Person' of idols and deities had a purpose. A temple or an idol existed as a tool to connect the devotees to the divine. Donations and charities were only for the benefit of the worshipper so that man and the divine could be connected. The properties of the idol/temple were all for this purpose. Hence, the ultimate beneficiary of the entire exercise was the worshipper, who could connect with the divine.

From the perspective of Indian law, the notion of treating an idol as a Juristic Person stood rooted in the faith of the people—in the 'widespread' and 'deep-rooted' sentiment—that God/deity/divinity has manifested itself in such an idol. Therefore, the name of the deity is capable of holding movable and immoveable property dedicated to it, to create accountability in favour of the worshipper. The worshipper being the beneficiary was a concept settled even by the Supreme Court of India in its judgement in 1956 in the case of *Deoki Nandan v. Muralidhar*[197] wherein it has been observed that '[…] the true beneficiaries of religious endowments are not the idols but the worshippers […]' This aligned with the belief that the divine exists for the benefit of its children and all creatures are God's children in Hindu thought. The provision to identify the deity/idol/temple or a holy land as a Juristic Person in Senior Parasaran's submissions was only to ensure that the rights of the worshippers, as well as the jurisdiction and rights of the deity, are

[197]1956 SCR 756 @ 762.

protected. In the absence of any idol or structure, where worship is offered to a formless deity, if recognition as a Juristic Person was not granted to the object of worship, neither the deity's nor the worshippers' rights could be efficiently protected. The place/ property of divinity, of that formless deity could disappear.

Chidambara rahasyam was similarly placed; a temple where no idol/image was worshipped for centuries was the main shrine in the Chidambaram Temple. The Madras High Court[198] had outlined five temples in India where Lord Shiva is worshipped in five forms, each symbolizing the *panchamahabhutas* (five great elements):

> *[...]*
>
> *'Iswara' as Lord Siva is generally worshipped in a particular form known as 'Linga'. The word 'linga' in Sanskrit means a symbol. If all forms in the creation were put together, that would form an indefinable form which is symbolized by 'Linga'.*
>
> *3. The Vedas reduce all forms to five constituent elements called the 'panchamahabhutas', viz., five great elements, they are 'Akasa-Space; Vayu-Air; Agni-Fire; Apah-Water and Prithivi-Earth'. There are five temples in India where Lord Siva is invoked in each of the five elements. At Chidambaram temple, Lord Siva is worshipped as the element of space. At Kalahasthi temple, in Andhra Pradesh, sivalingam as well as a lamp with a constant flame implying the presence of air is worshipped as element of air. At Tiruvannamalai Arunachaleeswara temple, Lord Siva is worshipped as Agni, fire. At Jambukeswara temple located at Tiruvannaikaval, at Tiruchirappalli, Lord Siva is worshipped as the element of water. At Kancheepuram, sivalingam is made of earth and is worshipped as the element of earth.*

---

[198]*Sri Sabhanayagar Temple, Chidambaram v. State of Tamil Nadu*, (2009) 4 CTC 801 @ 805–806.

The High Court further noted what people can call Chidambara rahasyam:

> *4. The Chidambaram Temple contains an altar which has no idol. In fact, no Lingam exists but a Curtain is hung before a wall, when people go to worship, the curtain is withdrawn to see the 'Lingam'. But the ardent devotee will feel the divinely wonder that Lord Siva is formless i.e., space which is known as 'Akasa Lingam'. Offerings are made before the curtain. This form of worshipping space is called the 'Chidambara rahasyam', i.e., the secret of Chidambaram […]*
>
> *Another instance of a place of public worship where there existed no idol/image, was that of the 'Gnana Sabhai' at Vadalur, taken note of by the Madras High Court in its judgment in the case of Pichai v. Com Mr. HR&CE*[199] *where only a light was worshipped:*
>
> *It is a well-known fact that in South India, in a place called Vadalur, Sri Ramalingaswamigal otherwise called Vallaler had found an institution called Gnana Sabhai where no idol or no picture of any deity is kept. But a light is kept burning perpetually, indicating God as 'jyothi' or light. Daily pooja is performed and the Hindu community congregate in large numbers and offer their prayers and worship in the said Sabhai. Thus, it has become a place of public religious worship.*

For the protection of the rights of the worshippers and properties of the deities, if every religious institution had to have an entity that could be termed a Juristic Person, then the same rule had to apply even to those places of worship where no idol or temple existed or where land only had to be termed as holy. The test was of people's faith as a place of religious significance in that land.

---

[199] *AIR* 1971 Mad 405 @ 407.

It could not be said that the worshippers of the Akasa Lingam at the Chidambaram Temple (where no lingam physically exists but offerings are made to it nonetheless) or worshippers of the Gnana Sabhai (where only a light is kept burning perpetually) or worshippers of the Devi at Sree Kadampuzha Bhagavathy Temple (where only the 'divine presence' is worshipped) are not entitled to protection because no image/idol/tangible entity that may be treated as a Juristic Entity, exists. In simple terms, in the absence of the existence of an image/idol/tangible entity, whatever existed had to be treated as a Juristic Entity. The protection of law to all forms of deities had to be equally extended, whether in material form or in formlessness.

Therefore, in the case of Ram Janmabhoomi, if the land believed to be the birthplace of Lord Ram is treated reverentially by the Hindu public and they have sought to offer worship there because of 'such' belief, such reverence and prayers at the land, elevate the land itself. Consequently, land Janmabhoomi/ Janmasthan may be treated as a Juristic Entity alongside the idol that may be believed to manifest Lord Ram as a deity. A deity that is worshipped in a place of public worship had to be protected to enable worshippers to have access and offer their worship. It had also to be protected regarding rights and the discharge of its functions in the context of areas that are not purely religious, such as the properties endowed to such God in any form or endowed in the name of the temple. It will be anomalous and incongruous to hold that the manifestation of the spirit of God can only be in an idol, in human form, and not otherwise. This will defeat the very fundamental right of religious freedom, viz. belief, faith and worship, as guaranteed by Articles 25[200]and 26[201]

[200]Freedom of conscience and free profession, practice and propagation of religion. (1) Subject to public order, morality and health and to the other provisions of this Part, all persons are equally entitled to freedom of conscience and the right freely to profess, practise and propagate religion.
[201]26. Freedom to manage religious affairs
Subject to public order, morality and health, every religious denomination or any

of the Constitution of India.

The question of just a piece of land to be treated as a Juristic Person was uncharted territory in law. It was thought that various dimensions in law through which land had been evaluated for consideration as a Juristic Entity had to be brought forward before the court. Therefore, a submission was advanced that the land itself had been elevated to the status of a Juristic Entity in other instances of charitable endowments. Judgements of the Supreme Court in cases, such as *Kamaraju Venkata Krishna Rao v. Sub Collector*[202] and *Thayarammal v. Kanakammal*[203], were cited. From these judgements, it could, at the least, be proved that there was no bar till date in declaring land as a Juristic Person if the situation so arose. In its judgement in the case of *Thayarammal v. Kanakammal*, it has been observed:

> *A property dedicated for religious or charitable purpose for which the owner of the property or the donor has indicated no administrator or manager becomes res nullius which the learned author in the book (supra) explains as property belonging to nobody. Such a property dedicated for general public use is itself raised to the category of a juristic person. [...] The religious institutions like mutts and other establishments obviously answer to the description of foundations in Roman law. The idea is the same, namely, when property is dedicated for a particular purpose, the property itself upon which the purpose is impressed, is raised to the category of a juristic person so that the property which is dedicated would vest in the person so created. [...]*

---

section thereof shall have the right—
(a) to establish and maintain institutions for religious and charitable purposes;
(b) to manage its own affairs in matters of religion;
(c) to own and acquire movable and immovable property; and
(d) to administer such property in accordance with law.

[202](1969) 1 SCR 624 @ 628–629.

[203](2005) 1 SCC 457 @ 463.

An Idol Never Dies

Thayarammal v. Kanakammal was a case where the judgement spoke about donating land for a charitable purpose. Such endowed/donated land got elevated as a Juristic Person. The Ayodhya case was distinct as it was dealing with land which was a self-manifestation of God. It had got elevated as divinity itself as Lord Ram took birth there. But this was not all. Some crucial questions were still to be probed by the lawyers. Can divinity die? Can a land considered as divine ever lose its divine character? A land's nature may or may not be changed, but could divinity die? If not, what all could exist in perpetuity?

As per the submissions of Mr Vaidyanathan, the Janmasthan being swayambhu, retained its independent identity and was not capable of being endowed. But if the property endowed for a religious and charitable purpose like a water body could be protected by conferment of the status of a Juristic Entity, a place considered to be and worshipped as a deity must be considered for protecting it as a Juristic Person/Entity. It continues to exist in perpetuity notwithstanding any adverse rights claimed by anybody else who does not consider such land as a deity. Since the deity itself is immortal, its manifestation is also immortal. Substantiating such Hindu practice, the Supreme Court in its judgement in the case of *Thakurji Shri Govind Deoji Maharaj v. Board of Revenue, Rajasthan*[204] had held:

> *It is obvious that in the case of a grant to the Idol or temple, as such there would be no question about the death of the grantee and, therefore, no question about its successor. An Idol which a juridical person is not subject to death, because the Hindu concept is that the Idol lives forever, and so, it is plainly impossible to predicate about the Idol which is the grantee in the present case that it has died at a certain time*

[204](1965) 1 SCR 96 @ 100.

and the claims of a successor fall to be determined.

It was submitted that God stands as *ananta* and *anadi* meaning ever-existing, eternal, with no beginning or end. The divinity and eternal nature of the idol were further explained by the courts in various judgements. In *Mahant Ram Saroop Dasji v. S.P. Sahi,*[205]the Supreme Court has held that 'Even if the idol gets broken or is lost or stolen, another image may be consecrated and it cannot be said that the original object has ceased to exist.' Similarly, Justice Chatterjee's judgement in the case of *Bhupati Nath Smrititirtha v. Ram Lal Maitra*[206] pronounced in 1909, cited by the Supreme Court in the case of Ram Jankijee Deities[207], observed that 'if the image is broken or lost, another may be substituted in its place and, when so substituted, it is not a new personality, but the same deity [...]'

This was the first time that Senior Parasaran would be defending the findings of the Allahabad High Court that Ram Janmasthan could be a Juristic Person; this was after Dr Dhavan had attacked that finding. So, many of Mr Parasaran's propositions were new. His point was, 'Why should I open up something when I succeeded on that. I will defend it when the other side has attacked it.' Dr Dhavan had attacked those findings concerning Juristic Person and now Mr Parasaran was defending it. The judges too had questions—if Ram Lala Virajman was already a Juristic Person, what was the need for Janmasthan also to be declared a Juristic Person? Wasn't one of them as a Juristic Person sufficient enough to protect the rights of the worshippers?

The case was entering its last phase as the lawyers were now treading into deep waters. There were times that they were getting tired, anxious and even losing their cool. There were multiple interventions now, with sometimes heated exchanges

[205](1959) Suppl. 2 SCR 583 @ 596.
[206]ILR (1909) 37 Cal 128 @ 167.
[207](1999) 5 SCC 50.

when the judges had to intervene. The daily reporting too reflected such exchanges as the case progressed towards the culmination of the hearing:

> *K Parasaran gave the example of the Chidambaram Temple, where there is no linga but just a curtain, he stated that, 'it's about Nataraj.' 'When people visit, the curtain is lifted.' As he continued to cite examples of other temples which don't have an idol, Rajeev Dhavan, representing the Muslim side, interjected to state that in each example cited, there was a temple. 'It has manifested in the form of a temple.' Parasaran responded by saying that a place of worship attended by the public with belief can be called a temple. A temple, it was submitted, is a generic term used for a place of worship.*
>
> *[…] Justice Bobde then pointed out that 'usually there is something called predominant deity, though there would be others.' 'Though there is a predominant deity, we have the manifestation of that deity in many forms. We call the court a temple of justice. We have many judges but we call the whole as one institution—court,' came the veteran lawyer's response. J Chandrachud clarified J Bobde's point and asserted that though there may be multiple deities, the juristic personality is attributed to the predominant deity of the temple.*
>
> *Rajeev Dhavan intervened to make his objections known. 'This is an entirely new argument,' he said and added that the matter is not about the nomenclature of the temple. He asserted that this would require him to give a note on these new aspects as there had to be arguments on proof backing their belief and worship. 'Every argument is a new one. I can't understand their objection,' retorted K. Parasaran and made it clear that the court could have objections and question his submissions, but not Dhavan.*
>
> *Parasaran went on to cite case laws and submitted that in*

> *cases of charitable endowments, the court has granted the status of a juristic entity to land on previous occasions. J Bobde then asked whether that would be applicable to every temple in India. 'We could go on a case-by-case basis,' said Parasaran. The Constitution has the right to call a place a temple or mosque.*
>
> *During the time of Babur, the sovereign was above everything. But it's not the case now, 'You can decide whether the place is a temple or not,' he added.*[208]

The judges were cautious. While the lawyer, however eminent, must make submissions, it is the judge who must decide an issue and consider the ramifications of deciding an issue either way. Their concern was that if they considered a piece of land as a Juristic Person, what ramifications will the issue have on other important pieces of land? Declaring merely a piece of land without any manifestation or any other form of symbol would lead to a situation where there could be demands that every place where Ram, Krishna or Buddha would have placed their feet be held divine and that land be declared as a Juristic Person. This was also Dr Dhavan's advice of caution to the court. For team Ram Lalla, such caution was reasonable and a challenge to overcome. This could be done by examining Ram Lalla's case itself. The birth was once. The manifestation as Ram was once. One had to look at it from a case-by-case perspective. Siddhartha was born in Nepal, but he became the Buddha in Gaya; Bihar was where he attained Enlightenment under the Bodhi tree. What would be then the importance of the place of Enlightenment of the Buddha—below the Bodhi tree? Could the devotees treat that place as divine? These were the questions in the mind of Senior Parasaran? The court, however, it seemed, wanted to err on the side of caution.

---

[208]Chaudhary, Nilashish, '[Ayodhya Hearing] [Day 35]: Hindu Parties Submit Reply Arguments on Juristic Personality and ASI Reports', *Live Law*, 1 October 2019, https://tinyurl.com/4j2bvkhr. Accessed on 18 January 2025.

J Bobde advised caution regarding this argument and said, 'Consider the ramifications of considering this argument. You say ascribe divine character to land as there's a belief that an avatar was born there.' Moving forward, J Bobde asked about the existence of any astrological or astronomical text supporting the birth of Lord Ram. After a few anecdotes by Dhavan in response, Parasaran replied by saying, 'His birthday is not celebrated, we go to the temple on Ram Navami.'

[...] Before Parasaran concluded his arguments, J Bobde asked him whether there was a difference between a Janmabhoomi and Janmasthan. Janmasthan is specific, while Janmabhoomi could be much larger. The entire country could be Janmabhoomi, he added.[209]

Back in office, as the submissions were being finalized, certain critical questions needed their answers to be included in the written submissions. So, what happens to a temple which is broken or in ruins, or to a temple which is destroyed or gets destroyed and on which a new place of worship of some other religion is built?

Answering such queries was the next step and a judgement on lost statues and ruined temple could help. There was an interesting case in the International Court of Justice where two countries fought, *literally fought*, to get the land where the 'Preah Vihear' Temple was situated. Then one also had to see what the English courts held, about a 'temple in ruins' and a statue of Nataraja stolen from India. There was enormous legal drama before the statues arrived back home in India.

---

[209]Ibid.

29

The World of Temples and Statues

Mr Parasaran would repeat that God chose a particular land and his spirit and energy became entwined with the land. That land in Ayodhya is the Janmasthan. The contention was that the faith of Hindus is that the spirit of Lord Ram has always existed at the place of his birth, that is, the 'Janmasthan'; and this spirit has existed before any structure was put up. The Janmasthan will continue to be the place where Lord Ram was born. Thus, the construction of any kind of structure over the Janmasthan will not detract from its character as the birthplace, thereby making the land of supreme importance and conferring on it a nature and character of its own, which resulted in the land being a Juristic Person/Entity. Originally, worship at Ram Janmabhoomi was without an idol. Over time, an idol was installed. This cannot detract from the place being worshipped as Janmasthan.

The Sunni Board, in its suit, contended that till the Buddhist period, only the formless God was worshipped, and that idol worship started only after the Buddhist period. It was submitted that the Board had accepted that Hindus also worshipped a formless deity. Therefore, if Hindus continued to worship the formless deity in the post-Buddhist period in a similar manner as in the pre-Buddhist period at the Janmasthan, necessarily the Janmasthan has to be a deity in itself. This was an argument rooted in religious belief. Hence, the extract from Srimad Valmiki Ramayana, Part I, *Bala Kanda*, Canto XV, substantiates that the piece of land was a chosen piece of land by the Lord himself as the place of manifestation, and was thus where swayambhu was relied upon. Translated into English, it reads as follows:

> *Thus extolled (by the gods and others), Lord Visnu, the Ruler of gods and the foremost among them, adored of all the worlds, addressed the assembled gods headed by Brahma (the progenitor of the entire creation), who were all given to piety: 'Give up (all) fear. May good betide you! Despatching on the field of battle in your interests the cruel and formidable Ravana—who is difficult to overpower and is the terror of gods and Rishis—along with his sons and grandsons and including his ministers and counsellors, kinsmen and relations, I shall remain on the mortal plane ruling over this globe for eleven thousand years.' Having granted the aforesaid boon, the high-souled Lord Visnu, the adored (even) of gods, now thought of Ayodhya (the place of His projected Birth) on the mortal plane. Then splitting Himself up into four personalities, the Lord, whose eyes resemble the petals of a lotus, wished King Dashratha to be His father in that descent.*[210]

After attempting to substantiate the importance of land as the chosen place by God himself, arguments moved on to the concept of 'Swayambhu'. In the legal realm, one of the earliest cases to mention swayambhu, wherein the deity by the name of Lingaraj Mahaprabhu at Bhubaneshwar was held to be swayambhu was *Sapneshwar Pujapanda v. Ratnakar Mahapatra.*[211]The Patna High Court had in 1916 observed, 'The Swayambhu Siva is the Siva who is self-existent, whose origin cannot be traced, who is unborn and eternal.'

It was to be pointed out that a consecrated idol is not the only form in which the deity is believed to manifest itself. The deity may be believed to manifest itself in any form, physical or perceived. Such form need not necessarily only be a movable object like an idol, for there is no condition for divinity or a

---

[210]*Valmiki Ramayana*, Balakanda Canto XV, Gita Press.
[211]AIR 1916 Pat 146, p. 147.

deity to limit its manifestation. The deity may also be believed to manifest itself in an immovable object, which, in this case, is believed to be the birthplace of Lord Ram. In simple terms, it is the energy or presence of the divine which can be felt by the devotee. This can happen even on a piece of land. That land must be protected by elevating it to the status of a Juristic Person, so that the land gets adequate protection.

The test was the 'belief' of the worshipper. What the worshipper believed in was the only consideration that mattered. An idol or object in a movable form may be swayambhu and natural formations or land in immoveable form may also equally be swayambhu. What is not owned by someone cannot be owned by anyone else either; it remains free, and the rules of property like adverse possession (where one can become the owner by force or squatting) will not apply to such lands, water bodies, tanks, temples, etc.

Only a property and not divinity is capable of being owned, partitioned, alienated, possessed, etc. Insofar as the Janmasthan was concerned, there could be no 'owner'. An idol is not 'owned' by anyone, nor do believers view it as the material it is made from, be that gold, silver or clay. Believers only see the idol as the manifestation of the deity. Similarly, for believers, the Janmasthan was not merely 'land' but a 'deity' based on the belief that the spirit of Lord Ram remained manifested in the land.

Ram Janmabhoomi was a case, where there was no challenge as to the existence of the belief that the land which is believed to be the birthplace of Lord Ram is sacred for Hindus. It was also not disputed till this stage of hearing after referring to the 1885 proceedings, that the birthplace was within the disputed structure. The dispute was now confined to the exact location of such a birthplace, within the precincts of the disputed structure/mosque. The issues in the case had narrowed down in the minds of the members of team Ram Lalla.

Another point to get over was, 'How does one determine

what are the dimensions of the birthplace in the present case?' The term 'birthplace' or 'Janmasthan' is ordinarily relative. It can mean country, city, or house. It was submitted that the Supreme Court, while applying principles of Hindu Law, may interpret the term reasonably to mean the general area considered physically sacred by Hindus. The cities of Ayodhya, Kashi, Mathura, etc. are considered holy, but worship is not offered to the city by a believer; rather, worship is offered at a well-identified place, generally considered to be of specific religious significance. Hence, what were the identifiers of the Janmasthan land?

An identifier of the Janmasthan land may be considered to be the 'parikrama'. A parikrama by itself may not create any ownership to property, but it identifies the place considered to be of religious significance. The birthplace cannot be pedantically interpreted to be the 'exact' room of the birth, for that may well be subject to difference of opinion. It must be interpreted reasonably, on the facts of the case, to generally mean the place of birth, relative to the larger space (in this case, the city of Ayodhya) within which it is located. What must be seen is that the worshippers have generally considered it to be the birthplace. When one visits a temple to offer worship, it is not merely the sanctum sanctorum which comprises the temple. The area surrounding the sanctum sanctorum is also part of the temple. When one considers a dwelling place as their house, it does not mean only the living room/drawing room of the house, but comprises all such areas one dwells in. The term 'birthplace' must be interpreted in a like manner. That is how the European travellers, Christian missionaries, and even the gazetteers had seen the Janmasthan.

It may also be noted that universal belief as to the precise or exact spot of birth is not a pre-requisite for determining whether the Janmasthan is the 'birthplace' of Lord Ram and is a Juristic Entity. What must be seen is whether generally, Hindus have historically regarded and continue to regard the disputed area to be sacred as already found in 1885. But intriguing and revealing was the case decided by The Privy Council in *Madura Tirupparankundram v. Alikhan Saheb*[212] which held as follows:

> *The Tirupparankundram Temple is one of the famous rock temples of South India. It is situated at the base of a hill some 500-ft. high, and is dedicated to Subramanya, the son of Shiva. The inner shrine of the temple is hewn out of the hill and in it, carved in the rock itself, is the image of the deity. Around the base of the hill is a pilgrim's way, nearly two miles long. This is said to be essential to the worship of the devotees, who perform the ceremony of pradakshinam by going round the image of the deity with the right shoulder continuously presented to him. As the image in the temple is an actual part of the hill, it is obvious that the performance of this rite necessitates the perambulation of the hill itself.*
>
> *Therefore, when the image is believed to be the manifestation of the deity, it is part of a larger natural formation, viz. the hill (immoveable property), and the entire hill becomes a part of the worship. So also, in the Ayodhya case, where the manifestation of the deity is believed to be part of the land, then the land itself becomes a part of the worship, was the submission. Questions on international precedents were raised by the judges. Hence, it was important to present before the judges, international instances where Hindu temples and their areas or their belongings were under consideration. The idea was just to place for the consideration of the judges how foreign courts have looked at issues of Hindu temples.*

This is how the case of Bumper Development Corporation became part of Ram Lalla's submissions as finalized by Senior Parasaran and Mr Vaidyanathan to provide an insight into how a temple in ruins where worship was not taking place was

[212](1931) 34 LW 340 @ 341.

sought to be brought before the court. Bumper also brought in the story of an idol smuggled out of India which was successfully brought back to India. Bumper's case was of extreme importance to decide the point as to how the courts would look at the legal status and longevity of a temple abandoned and in ruins in India. Does a temple in ruins itself have a legal entity and longevity?

What about artefacts, and idols, stolen from a temple in ruins? In August or September 1976, an Indian labourer called Ramamoorthy, who lived near the site of a Hindu temple in ruins at Pathur in Tamil Nadu, was excavating sand or similar material when he hit a metal object. The place of excavation was either immediately adjacent to or formed part of the site of the temple called Arul Thiru Viswanatha Swami Temple. The object which Ramamoorthy struck formed part of a series of bronze Hindu idols later identified as members of a 'family' and was a major idol known as Shiva Nataraja or 'Pathur Nataraja'. It was accepted by all the parties that the temple had lain in ruins and unworshipped for centuries.[213]

Notwithstanding his lowly status, Ramamoorthy realized that he had discovered objects of value. The idols were finally sold to one Hussain, who was a part-time dealer in stolen idols and a local government official, and one Balraj Nadur, who was a major dealer in stolen idols. Of all the objects discovered by Ramamoorthy, the bronze Nataraja attracted particular attention and was last sold to a man called Valar Prakash. The antiquity was traced back to the Chola period or around the 13th century. The bronze statue finally landed in London. Information reached the state officials in Tamil Nadu because of which criminal investigations were started. Statements were taken from Ramamoorthy and the others about the discovery and subsequent history of both the Pathur Nataraja and the Pathur bronze. The statements taken in India formed part of the

[213] *Union of India vs. Bumper Development Corporation Ltd v Commissioner of Police of the Metropolis and others* (Union of India and others, claimants) [1991]4All ER 638.

evidence at the trial which took place in London.

A trial was necessary because on 10 June 1982, Bumper Corporation purchased the London Nataraja from a dealer along with three other pieces of Indian art in good faith, with the philanthropic object of donating all four pieces for display in Canadian museums. The dealer had produced a false provenance of the Nataraja for the purpose of the sale. It was while the Nataraja had been sent to the British Museum for appraisal and conservation that the London Nataraja was seized by the Metropolitan police as part of a policy of returning religious artefacts, which it was thought had been stolen, to their owners in India. Bumper started legal proceedings against the Commissioner of Police of the Metropolis and two of his officers for the return of the Nataraja and damages.

On 3 November 1982, the Government of India, through its High Commission in London, had written to the Metropolitan police alleging that the bronze Nataraja had been stolen from the land belonging to a temple in Tamil Nadu, India, and demanded that the statue be returned to India. Returning to the temple site at Pathur, among the surviving ruins and materials there was a stone object of religious worship known as Shivalingam left unworshipped. There were five claimants from the Indian side. Most importantly, the English courts were to test whether a temple abandoned and in ruins could be a valid party or a Juristic Person. To start with, the Union of India was the first claimant, the State of Tamil Nadu was the second claimant. Thiru Sadagopan had sued on behalf of himself as the third claimant and had made the temple which was in ruins itself as the fourth claimant. The fifth claimant most importantly was the Shivalingam itself at a later stage in the trial. The trial was to centre around an issue, namely: 'Whether the State of Tamil Nadu can prove that it has a title to the bronze which is superior to the title of the Bumper Development Corporation to the bronze?'

The stand of India towards a later stage of the trial was that the statue lay buried under the ruins for centuries. Finally, in 1989, the judgement came in favour of the Indian parties. *It was held that a temple on its own could sue for the recovery of the statue.* The question of whether the Shivalingam could have sued for recovery on its own of the statue was not decided. The reason for that was since the temple was in ruins and left unworshipped, it itself was held to be a legal person/Juristic Person/Entity fit enough to sue and get back the statue. Recognizing the temple as a Juristic Entity had solved the issue and no further issues were gone into. Bumper lost the appeals before the higher forums in England—the Court of Appeal as well as the House of Lords.

The Nataraja was returned to India. The matter did not end there. Canada contacted India concerning Bumper's claim for compensation for its loss of the bronze Nataraja. Therefore, on 5th April 1994, India commenced a legal action in Canada for enforcement and recognition of the judgement passed in London. Bumper also claimed compensation from India for its loss of the bronze Nataraja.

Among various grounds, Bumper took a ground that damages under the judgement in London had been awarded only to the ruined temple which had no status or standing before the court in Canada to enforce its claim for the damages. Bumper argued that merely because the ruins of a temple were entertained as a party in London in the court proceedings, it did not make the ruins of the temple a Juristic Entity or an eligible party in the courts of Canada as well.[214] In Canada too, the judgement went in favour of the ruined temple. The issue sought to be advanced in the Ayodhya case was that even foreign jurisdictions have not shied away from recognizing as Juristic Persons/Entities the 'ruins of a temple' left unworshipped, unclaimed and left to wither away. Even a ruined, unworshipped

---

[214]*Union of India vs. Bumper Development Corporation Ltd* (1996) I.L.Pr.78(1995).

temple was a temple and neither a temple nor an idol could ever die. That was the drift of the discussion in team Ram Lalla.

Additional information came through various research articles. In his autobiography, *Honour Bound* (2020), renowned Solicitor Mr Sarosh Zaiwalla whose firm instructed Mr A. Hamilton, QC, on behalf of the Commissioner of the London Metropolitan Police and other claimants, provided additional information related to this case. He spoke of how, for the idol to be considered a Juristic Personality under Indian law, it had to be proved to have been subjected to an extensive religious ceremony before it attained the status of God. He further states that after joining the temple and Nataraja as claimants, Nataraja himself asserted before the court that as a consecrated idol that had attained the status of a God, he wanted to return to his home, to the temple in India. He also remembers Justice Kennedy's words in the Trial Court judgement: 'The plaintiff at its maximum is God Almighty and at its minimum is a mere stone.' Mr Zaiwalla further recalls how this historic judgement brought various other governments, such as that of Egypt and Greece, to contact his firm, asking if the firm could assist them in getting back antique Egyptian artefacts, the Elgin Marbles, etc. from the British Museum, for which he answered: 'Certainly no because these artefacts and marbles do not have the status of God.'[215]

There was yet another international dispute around a temple to bring to the court's notice. Cambodia and Thailand had entered into a couple of wars to claim the land in and around the temple of Preah Vihear. Preah Vihear is a series of buildings arrayed along a 2,600-foot-long central causeway that proceeds dramatically to the edge of a cliff. The complex is meant to represent Mount Meru, the home of Shiva and other Hindu gods. According to Sanskrit inscriptions at Preah Vihear, the temple's formal origins date back to Jayavarman II's

[215]Zaiwalla, Sarosh, *Honour Bound: Adventures of an Indian Lawyer in the English Courts*, First published 2019; Harper Collins, 2020, pp. 59-61.

son, Prince Indrayudha, who, in 893 CE, installed a fragment from a stone monument called a lingam at the site. Much of the stone construction at Preah Vihear took place in the 11th century, during the reign of King Suryavarman I, a Buddhist who also worshipped the Hindu gods Shiva and Rama, and was tolerant of a wide range of religious practices. By the 12th century, Buddhism had become the Khmer state religion and Preah Vihear became a Buddhist sanctuary. A small Buddhist monastery still exists near the ruins and saffron-robed monks come to the 900-year-old buildings to conduct their spiritual practices.[216] The statue and the antiquities attached to the temple also constituted part of the dispute. Apart from the boundary dispute, the question in this case was concerning the status of an ancient Shiva temple and the antiquities attached to the temple. Can a nation claim ownership of antiquities attached to a temple in a boundary dispute, which have been moved to another country?

Following Cambodia's independence, Thailand occupied the 900-year-old Hindu temple in 1954. The temple and its vicinity had long been a bone of contention between the neighbours in recent years and had led to deadly clashes between them.[217] Cambodia had prayed before the International Court of Justice to (i) adjudge and declare that the Temple of Preah Vihear is situated in territory under the sovereignty of the Kingdom of Cambodia (ii) **adjudge and declare that the sculptures, stelae, fragments of monuments, sandstone model and ancient pottery which have been removed from the temple by the Thai authorities since 1954 are to be returned to the government of the Kingdom of Cambodia by the government of Thailand.**

---

[216]Borrell, Brendan, 'The Battle Over Preah Vihear', *ARCHAEOLOGY Magazine*, March/April 2013 Issue, https://tinyurl.com/memvrasu. Accessed on 18 January 2025.
[217]'UN court rules for Cambodia in Preah Vihear temple dispute with Thailand', *UN News*, 11 November 2013, https://tinyurl.com/yck6cyb4. Accessed on 18 January 2025.

In the June 1962 judgement, the ICJ found that the temple is situated in territory under the sovereignty of Cambodia, and that Thailand is under an obligation to withdraw any military or police forces, or other guards or keepers, stationed at the temple or in its vicinity on Cambodian territory.[218]

In 2007, Cambodia requested that the UNESCO World Heritage Committee inscribe the site of the Temple of Preah Vihear on the World Heritage List established under the provisions of the 1972 Convention concerning the Protection of the World Cultural and Natural Heritage (hereinafter the World Heritage Convention). Cambodia also submitted a map along with its application. On 17 May 2007, Thailand contested the claims of Cambodia as showing in the map more territory than what belonged to Cambodia in the vicinity of the temple and sent its own map to Cambodia and the World Heritage Committee.

Following the temple's inscription on that list, several armed incidents took place in the border area close to the temple. On 14 February 2011, the United Nations Security Council called for a permanent ceasefire to be established and expressed its support for the efforts of the Association of South-East Asian Nations (ASEAN) to find a solution to the conflict. No effective steps could be taken. Subsequently, the Chair of ASEAN, Indonesia, was invited by Cambodia and Thailand to send observers to the affected border areas to avoid further armed clashes. This invitation was welcomed by the foreign ministers of ASEAN and their representatives but was not acted upon. At stake was the survival of a unique holy place that was important to the cultural heritage of both nations. Segments on both sides of the divide made it a burning issue. Preah Vihear could also be an important source of income from tourism for the country's economy.[219]

---

[218]Judgment, ICJ Reports 1962, p. 6.

[219]Borrell, Brendan, 'The Battle Over Preah Vihear', *ARCHAEOLOGY Magazine*, March/April 2013 Issue, https://tinyurl.com/memvrasu. Accessed on 18 January 2025.

On 28 April 2011, Cambodia again moved the International Court of Justice and filed a request for interpretation of the 1962 judgement, together with a request for immediate provisional measures. In its Order of 18 July 2011, the ICJ ordered provisional measures which, in particular, required both parties to withdraw their military personnel from a 'provisional demilitarized zone' around the temple. The final judgement of the ICJ finally cleared the air. It held that the judgement of 15 June 1962 in the case of *Cambodia v. Thailand* decided that Cambodia had sovereignty over the whole territory of the promontory of Preah Vihear and that, in consequence, Thailand was under obligation to withdraw from that territory the Thai military or police forces, or other guards or keepers, that were stationed there.[220] Without any intellectual divergence of opinion, the unanimity of thought in team Ram Lalla was that a temple existed even in the ruins and had a claim over its activities and its land even if it was in ruins. However, the courts were yet to either accept or reject this thought process. Mr Vaidyanathan had to reply to the arguments advanced on archaeology. He had prepared a note point-wise. *Live Law* reported it as follows:

....

Mr. C.S. Vaidyanathan then took over, submitted a note, and rebutted the arguments made by the Muslim side on archaeology. It was further asserted by Mr. Vaidyanathan that the High Court had meticulously examined 25 videos and several photographs of the excavation and found nothing against ASI's findings. Dhavan objected to as being abstract and not on record. Vaidyanathan argued that submissions made by the Muslim side cast aspersions on the Allahabad

[220]Request for Interpretation of the Judgment of 15 June 1962 in the case concerning the Temple of Preah Vihear (Cambodia v. Thailand), Judgment, ICJ Reports 2013, p. 281.

High Court's judgment. To characterize the findings of the High Court as guesswork is unwarranted. Rajeev Dhavan intervened at this point to clarify that it was part of the judgment and not their argument,

'I have not characterized anything, it's part of the judgement.'

They had earlier argued that observations that there was a temple before a mosque was built were never proved, and it was used to target Hindus that an exact place of birth was not known and that there was no idol to prove the existence of the temple.[221]

After an exchange ensued between Dhavan and Vaidyanathan, the latter went on to counter the argument that an exact place of birth was not known and that there was no idol to prove the existence of the temple.[222]

"Once it is proved that Lord Ram was born at the palace that existed at the site, there is no need to show the existence of an idol or deity.' A property acquires juristic personality when it's dedicated to a particular purpose, he asserted while arguing that divinity was not a bar to juristic personality, as it can be secular too. As Justice Bhushan agreed that a long-standing practice is sufficient, Justice Chandrachud asked what if there was no dedication. Vaidyanathan responded by reiterating that the belief that Lord Ram was born there was enough, it did not require dedication. 'The belief that the land is sanctified because of Lord Ram being born there is sufficient,' he added.

When Vaidyanathan moved on to use the findings of the ASI report to counter the existence of an Eidgah mosque, Dhavan

[221]Chaudhary, Nilashish, '[Ayodhya Hearing] [Day 35]: Hindu Parties Submit Reply Arguments on Juristic Personality and ASI Reports', *Live Law*, 1 October 2019, https://tinyurl.com/4j2bvkhr. Accessed on 18 January 2025.
[222]Ibid.

intervened to ask how the question can arise without proper digging.[223]

As team Ram Lalla was close to folding its arguments, a final burst came from Mr P.S. Narasimha, Senior Advocate[224]. The religious importance of the land had to be explained, for a Hindu the ultimate goal in life is not heaven but moksha. A mere visit to the place of birth of Ram would enable the devout to attain moksha was the belief. Mr Narasimha cited a *shloka* (verse) from the *Skanda Purana* in support of the religious belief and practise of the faithful. According to the *Skanda Purana*, the ultimate goal in religion is to attain moksha or liberation, and the shloka 'tells us that moksha is attained by visiting the site which is the birthplace of Lord Ram,' Mr Narasimha said. Asserting the importance of the site, the Senior Advocate submitted that Lord Ram's birthplace is an important place for a Hindu which ordains him to go there to attain moksha. He further added that since the *Skanda Purana* existed in the pre-Muslim era, and it records Ram Janmasthan, it means the birthplace already existed before the establishment of the mosque. Countering Rajeev Dhavan's submission, he asked, 'Before the advent of the mosque, had people not accepted the existence of this place as birthplace?'[225] He concluded his submissions by referring to the travelogue of William Finch, which mentioned the ruins on the land of the disputed structure.[226]

With an international perspective before the court, the judges had to decide on the issue of how to treat the ruins or a structure found below the disputed land. What about the submissions with respect to the *makar* pranala (crocodile-shaped water chute),

---

[223]Ibid.

[224]Now a judge of the Supreme Court of India.

[225]Chaudhary, Nilashish, '[Ayodhya Hearing] [Day 36]: Janmasthan Is Important For Hindus As Visiting It Helps To Attain Moksha, Argues Hindu Parties', *Live Law*,3 October 2019, https://tinyurl.com/5n8vbv35. Accessed on 18 January 2025.

[226]Ibid.

and what the experts in history and archaeology had to say about the presence or absence of a temple before the construction of a mosque at the site, was next in submission for Ram Lalla.

30

Judges—Idgah and Archaeology

'Is it their case that the Idgah was demolished to build The Babri Masjid,' Senior Advocate C.S. Vaidyanathan, appearing for Ram Lalla, told a Bench headed by Chief Justice of India Ranjan Gogoi.

The arguments of the case had just barely entered the last phase, and looming on the horizon was Chief Justice of India, Ranjan Gogoi's retirement—it was just a month away. A serious concern was what would be its impact on the hearings on important issues concerning the case. Would there be a judgement at all? Judges in the case were now moving from the legalistic domain to the domain of experts as they were confronted by arguments related to an Idgah, archaeology and a circular shrine by Mr Vaidyanathan. Was the circular shrine a Shiva shrine or a Shivalinga?

Many in the corridors of the Supreme Court wondered whether the Bench would be able to write and pronounce a judgement in such a short period of time. What people had overlooked was that these judges were professionals, having spent many years on the Bench, and were very experienced. It was commonly discussed among lawyers that a judge in the Supreme Court lives as if 'work is life.' Senior counsels often wondered whether it was a self-inflicted punishment by the judges while taking oath as Judge of the Supreme Court of India. The excruciating amount of work along with constant scrutiny and no right to defend oneself in public makes the life and profession of a judge quite challenging. While on working days, judges would be toiling in the court, they would carry on administrative duties after court hours and then also write judgements and study for the cases listed for the next day. Judgements might be written during weekends. If anyone thinks that judges in the Supreme Court enjoy restful holidays on Saturdays and Sundays, they are clearly mistaken. That the Ayodhya case had kept the judges busy was evident from the number of questions posed by them, which, in turn, was indicative of the intensive study the judges had undertaken. However, to prepare a judgement, a timeline was necessary; therefore, a schedule was laid down.[227] After receiving feedback from the counsels, the Chief Justice of India, recommended the following:

- *By 27 September: Sr. Advs. Meenakshi Arora and Rajeev Dhavan to conclude arguments on pro-temple suits*
- *30 September–1 October: Counsels for pro-temple parties to present rejoinders*
- *2–4 October: Sr. Adv. Dhavan to present arguments on Sunni Waqf Board's Suit*
- *7–11 October: Dusshera Vacation*
- *14–18 October: Unassigned. The court was likely to hear the counsels for Nirmohi Akhara and Shri Ram Virajman respond to each other.*

One of the important arguments from team Ram Lalla was based on the archaeological evidence through which Mr Vaidyanathan had claimed that a temple existed below the structure at the disputed site. The structure was a temple and if not a temple, then certainly the site had no identity of an Islamic structure. To counter this submission of Mr Vaidyanathan, Ms Meenakshi Arora had inter alia pointed out that there was the presence of lime-surkhi building material which, according to her, was indicative of an Islamic structure. Further, the theory of an Idgah being present below the demolished structure was also raised.

[227]'Day 53 Arguments, Ayodhya Title Dispute', *Supreme Court Observer*, 26 September 2019, https://tinyurl.com/mv2m8xw3. Accessed on 18 January 2025.

There were other arguments of Ms. Arora on behalf of the other side as well, which Mr Vaidyanathan had to reply to.

Mr Vaidyanathan submitted that surkhi 'is purely indigenous and was not brought in India from Central Asia.'[228] Mr Vaidyanathan referred to expert witnesses of the other side. He mentioned the deposition of Suraj Bhan who had stated that, 'It is correct to say that lime water was found to have been used in the 3rd Century AD during the Kushana period in Takshashila and Pakistan. Similarly, Dr Jaya Menon also admitted in her testimony that [...] lime mortar was definitely used from the Neolithic period.'[229] The judges had more question on the site and on the lime-surkhi and Mr Vaidyanathan had more answers.[230]

> *[Lime-surkhi] 'It was used in Gangetic plain from the 2nd century BC as shown by excavations in Kaushambi, he said, citing experts. He said some experts had suggested that Surkhi is 'purely indigenous and was not brought in India from Central Asia.'*
>
> *[...]*
>
> *Justice Chandrachud referred to the report finding similarities between an octagonal stone block used over the pillar bases and one used in Sarnath and asked if there was any evidence to show that what was unearthed was not part of a Buddha Vihara.*

---

[228]G., Ananthakrishnan, 'Ayodhya hearing: "Lime-surkhi used in India much before Islamic era"', *The Indian Express*, 4 October 2019, https://tinyurl.com/n5wr6u5a. Accessed on 18 January 2025.

[229]Written Submission No. A104, The Submissions on behalf of Plaintiff in Suit No. 5 by Mr. C.S.Vaidyanatha, Sr. Adv., *Vada Prativada*, https://tinyurl.com/5a4xzr69. Accessed on 18 January 2025.

[230]G., Ananthakrishnan, 'Ayodhya hearing: "Lime-surkhi used in India much before Islamic era"', *The Indian Express*, 4 October 2019, https://tinyurl.com/n5wr6u5a. Accessed on 18 January 2025.

[...] Vaidyanathan said Hindus have for centuries held the place as Ram's birthplace. It was not any place of significance for Buddhists, he said, adding that it was possible to draw a reasonable inference that it could not have been a vihara.

'Faith is one thing, but now we are in the area of evidence,' Justice Chandrachud said.

Vaidyanathan said the temple at Sarnath was constructed by the queen of Garhwal Dynasty during the same time when the temple at Ayodhya was renovated by the king of Garhwal Dynasty. He said he will submit a detailed note to answer the query [...]

The detailed note on the archaeological aspect sought to take care of the attack on the circular shrine[231], which was argued to be a Shivalinga. As submitted during arguments attacking the circular shrine, Ms Arora had submitted that (i) No linga was recovered from the circular shrine. It is too small to be a shrine where *jal abhishek* (holy bath of deity/idol/linga) could have been offered. (ii) Two pillar bases were constructed on top of the circular shrine; thus, it could not be a secondary shrine or a shrine at all. (iii) The closest comparison of the shrine has been done to a Buddhist structure. (iv) No explanation is offered as to why a site supposedly related to Lord Vishnu's avatar would have a secondary shrine dedicated to Lord Shiva. No contemporaneous examples of such a practice and tradition have been stated by the ASI nor argued before this Hon'ble Court.[232]Apart from the Buddhist angle, these points also had to be replied to.

---

[231]Written Submission No. A116, The Submissions on behalf of the Appellants by Mr. C.S. Vaidyanathan, Sr. Adv., https://tinyurl.com/46m8kj96. Accessed on 18 January 2025.

[232]Written Submission No. A117, Reply by Ms. Meenakshi Arora Sr. Adv. to Submissions of Mr. C. S. Vaidyanathan, Sr. Adv. on the existence of temple beneath & demolition thereof for construction of disputed structure, *Vada Prativada*, https://tinyurl.com/yy3hyxdu. Accessed on 18 January 2025.

The reply was detailed, and it stated *inter alia* that the circular structure was found with a well-defined pranala. It is stated that it is too small a structure for a tomb or stupa as from the inside, it is only 4.4 sq. ft. Mr Vaidyanathan submitted that 'the circular shrine was an independent miniature shrine. The architectural features suggest that it was a Shiva shrine. It is unthinkable that despite the clear features of a Shiva shrine, it has been identified as a Muslim tomb or a Buddhist stupa by some witnesses produced by Plaintiffs in Suit4.' Thus, it was submitted that the dimension of the circular structure was too small for a tomb or Buddhist stupa; further, the pranala is never found in tombs or stupas while it is an integral feature of the sanctum sanctorum of Shiva temples to drain out the water poured on the Shivalinga. As far as the objection of a Shiva shrine being present in a Vishnu temple was concerned, Mr Vaidyanath replied, 'There are plenty of examples of miniature shrines/temples around the main temple in temple complexes of temple towns.' It was further submitted that from the perusal of the statements of witnesses, it was evident that it could be neither a Muslim tomb nor a Buddhist stupa. Mr Vaidyanathan relied upon Dr R. Nagaswamy's deposition as follows:

> *That existence of circular shrine with parnala towards north proves existence of Hindu Temple. That the brick circular shrine is circular outside and square on the inner side, with a rectangular projection in the east with entrance, it has a water chute on the northern side which is obviously in level with the floor level of the inner sanctum clearly intended for the abhisheka to be drained. As this seems to be secondary shrine dedicated to Siva in his linga form the shrine is built to smaller dimension. Smaller dimension of subsidiary shrines with just minimum entrance space are seen in some of temples e.g. Manasor, Rajasthan Kumbharia Shantinath Temple. Relevant pages that are photostat copies prepared from those books, are annexed with this affidavit as Annexure*

No. 4, 5 (Temples of India by Krishna Deva, published by Arya Books, New Delhi). The smaller dimension does not preclude the structure being a shrine. The absence of any significant artifacts belonging to other sister faiths like Buddhism or Jainism, precludes this structure being identified with any of those faiths

[...] I do know about the 'Buddhist Stupas'. It is not possible that this circular structure will represent a 'Buddhist Stupa'. For the reason 'Buddhist Stupa' is a solid globular structure in which the relics of either Buddha or great Buddhist monks will be deposited inside and such Stupa will not have an entrance opening and no provision for draining the 'Abhisheka' water or liquid as found in a Hindu temple. There are hundreds of Hindu temples where a central deity is a 'Shi-Linga' for which 'Abhisheka' is performed daily a number of times which requires provisions of 'Parnalas' in the northern direction as found in this circular shrine. There is no doubt whatsoever that this circular shrine is a Hindu temple and not a 'Buddhist Stupa'. No 'Linga' is found here but as I have said in my earlier statement that this site has been attacked by iconoclasts in the 11th century once around 1030 CE and again around 1080 CE. The idols have suffered and disappeared. No icon have been left in the site except a mutilated sculpture called Divine Couple. [...][233]

To Senior Parasaran, such objections seemed trivial. It was always understood that Ram revered Shiva and Shiva revered Ram. Rameshwaram was a classic example of this mutual reverence. The greatest oblations to Shiva started with the invocation of Ram. Shiva was also worshipped by Lord Ram and for Shiva, Ram was the highest. However, law of evidence prevails in secular courts, though the subject may be of profound spiritual significance.

---

[233]Allahabad High Court Judgment, Ayodhya Sri Ramajanmabhoomi Case Records, https://tinyurl.com/5n86hy5z. Accessed on 22 September 2025.

With the case reaching its final lap, and the arguments becoming more incisive and precise, the temperature was rising. Senior Vaidyanathan pointed out that the archaeological excavations were carried out in the presence of witnesses and under the scrutiny of the High Court. The High Court had meticulously examined, videographed and photographed evidence of the excavation site, and found the report of the ASI quite tenable. Then a coloured map was referred to when things were getting a bit challenging.

> *[…] Vaidyanathan then turned the Court's attention towards a coloured map of pillars and wall to discredit a submission that there existed an Eidgah which was a single structure. 'This was not the case,' said Dhavan, 'as it is a hall with various walls.' Dhavan again made his objections known, saying none of what was being shown was excavated. The walls don't merge, said Dhavan, according to the maps and so it was concluded that there were walls. Vaidyanathan pointed out that despite arguing for 3 days to disregard the ASI report, these walls were not referred to.*
>
> *Both sides then attempted to persuade the bench regarding what was excavated and what wasn't. Justice Chandrachud then stated that excavations belonged to different periods and Justice Bobde asked the counsels to produce a map which clearly marked what had been excavated and what had not. Vaidyanathan drew the line by submitting that the disputed 'wall' was not a single structure, but a room. As counsels from both sides got into a debate regarding each other's arguments, CJI Ranjan Gogoi intervened and cracked the whip.*
>
> *'The same thing is being repeated to us over and over again, as if there's no application of mind from this side […] please let him continue,' he urged the Muslim side lawyers.*[234]

[234]Chaudhary, Nilashish, '[Ayodhya Hearing] [Day 35]: Hindu Parties Submit Reply

While the presence of a structure which existed back in history in the first millennia, was established by the ASI, and to the minds of team Ram Lalla, was not being seriously disputed, the nature of the structure as claimed by the ASI and Mr Vaidyanathan was being seriously disputed. In contest was the capacity of the pillars excavated to bear the load. The alignment of the pillars, the length of the pillars, the time span, or the time frame to which the pillars belonged were all in dispute and in debate. There was also controversy concerning the organic materials found. The objections and replies flew thick and fast between the two lawyers as did the questions from the judges while the arguments of all counsels, including Mr Vaidyanathan, were being reported live.[235]

> *The wall dates back to the tenth and eleventh centuries. The 'Makarpranal' which is a part of these remains of the earlier temple is Goddess Ganga's 'vaahan'—'Makar' means crocodile. The contention that this north-south wall is an Eidgah wall and that it was an Islamic structure is not true[...]a part of this structure was not excavated because it was under the main dome. It was discovered till 18 feet but it was not possible to dig further because of the barricades […]*
>
> *[…] Next, he [Mr. Vaidyanathan] proceeded to discuss pillar bases. At this point, Senior Advocate Rajeev Dhavan interjected that these pillars were not found to be load-bearing and they could not have supported such a massive structure. Indicating the 3 layers of the pillar bases of brickbats, concrete and decorated sandstone, and pointing out their depth, Mr. Vaidyanathan insisted that the disputed structure was found to be resting on these pillar bases which*

Arguments on Juristic Personality and ASI Reports', *Live Law*, 1 October 2019, https://tinyurl.com/4cmr3n4x. Accessed on 24 September 2025.

[235]Jain, Mehal, [Ayodhya Hearing] [Day 36]: ASI Survey Leads To Inference That Hindu Structure Used To Exist At The Site, Submits Sr. Adv. C.S. Vaidyanathan, *Live Law*, 3 October 2019, https://tinyurl.com/5n77sk8k. Accessed on 22 September 2025.

are of an earlier period, and that to say that these bases could not support the structure is not true. From the ASI report, the pillar bases were shown to be connected to the top floor of the structure that existed prior to the disputed structure. 'The (earlier) structure may not have been of that much load [...] the existence of the structure beneath the disputed structure is proved beyond doubt,' said Mr. Vaidyanathan.

'46 were found in one floor and 4 in another floor. It is not as if there are different structures [...] First they (the Muslim side) said that there was no structure at all. Then they said that the wall is an Eidgah wall [...] when we say that the temple was demolished, it is evidence by these walls and the pillar bases,' replied Mr. Vaidyanathan.

'How does one say that all the pillar bases are of one time?' asked Justice S.A. Bobde. That 46 belong to one period and four to another period was Mr. Vaidyanathan's answer.

'All the 50 exposed pillar bases are resting on one of the earliest floors. The carbon dating ends it to be from around the 900 to 1300 AD,' asserted Mr. Vaidyanathan. 'Organic material was found there?' asked Justice Bobde. While Mr. Vaidyanathan replied in the affirmative, Dr. Dhavan indicated that the carbon found there was charcoal.

'That there is a Hindu Temple is an inference drawn from the other materials found, that is, a massive circular structure just below the disputed structure. A circular shrine bearing the Makarpranal is indicative of a temple. A massive hall shows that it was a public place, not a private residence,' submitted Mr. Vaidyanathan.

'The circular shrine is from between 900 AD and 1100 AD. Would that structure not be equally consistent with a "vihara"? What is the evidence to show that it is a Hindu Temple?' inquired Justice Chandrachud.

'That Ayodhya was the place of birth of Lord Ram is not disputed. Whether that was 60 places away or here is the dispute. Dashratha's palace is not disputed [...] it is not a place of significance for Buddhists but for Hindus and has been worshipped for centuries. If there is a massive structure here, it is a reasonable inference that it is a temple,' answered Mr. Vaidyanathan.

Mr. Vaidyanathan had to face further scrutiny, with Dr. Dhavan also chipping in with his client's objections.

'We are on core evidence right now. Faith and belief cannot be evidenced or disputed; only the practice of faith or belief can be. What are the material evidences?' probed Justice Chandrachud, with Dr. Dhavan piping in that the pillar bases were actually found to be on top of the circular shrine. 'The ASI does not say whether the structure was demolished and whether the demolished structure was a Hindu Temple. There is no categorical ending on whether the building was razed or collapsed on its own because of natural causes,' he added.

On proof of faith and belief, Mr. Vaidyanathan advanced that it is the Shrutis and the Smritis which are the source of Hindu Law, that come from oral transmission. Traditional law is based on immemorial customs and to say that all of this is hearsay is wrong, he contented. 'Shruti' means that which is heard. 'Smriti' means recollection of what Hindus have believed to be tradition. 'Can this be summarily rejected?' he asked rhetorically.[236]

There were two other issues to reply to. The first being the theory of the Idgah and the second being the issue of the importance of the place below the central dome to the Ram bhakts, and whether prayers were even offered in the inner courtyard despite the Britishers putting Hindus out of the inner courtyard. One of the

[236]Ibid.

issues in discussions with Mr Vaidyanathan during the hearing with Bhakti and Yogeswaran was the complete irrelevance of converting an Idgah into a mosque. Hence the following questions and submissions were made which were covered by *The Indian Express*.[237]

> *The counsel also said that the Muslim side had tried to drag the case, asking a witness during trial questions such as 'where was the labour room where Ram was born?'*
>
> *'Is it their case that the idgah was demolished to build Babri Masjid,' senior advocate C. S. Vaidyanathan, appearing for Ram Lalla, told a bench headed by Chief Justice of India Ranjan Gogoi[...]*
>
> *[...] Vaidyanathan submitted that he was asking this since the Board had not contended anytime earlier that there was any structure beneath the Babri Masjid, and that it was built on vacant land. In contrast, Ram Lalla's 1989 Suit had said that a temple was demolished to build the mosque, he said.*
>
> *The submission invited sharp reactions from senior counsel Rajeev Dhavan, appearing for the Muslim side, who said, 'The question of the idgah could only have arisen after the ASI dig.'*
>
> *But Vaidyanathan continued and said,'Muslims changed their stand' when they realised that a wall had been found as the ASI investigation progressed. He contended that not one witness 'had spoken about an idgah' and added that it was mentioned first by three archaeologists produced by the Muslim side.*
>
> *Vaidyanathan said idgahs are built in areas away from*

[237]G., Ananthakrishnan, 'Ramlalla's counsel: Is Wakf Board saying idgah razed to build Babri?', *The Indian Express*, 2 October 2019, https://tinyurl.com/fr72p8bm. Accessed on 18 January 2025.

local habitation, while the Ramkot area, where the wall was discovered, was 'full of habitation'.

These reports could not and did not capture another point in the dispute with respect to expert witnesses. There was contention on behalf of the Sunni Board that the expert witnesses of the Board did not support the ASI report and/or the ASI report stood negated. This line of argument required a reply from the counsel for Ram Lalla. Mr Vaidyanathan already had an overactive Yogeswaran ready at hand. The following witnesses were relied upon.[238]

P.W. 16, Suraj Bhan: *I agree with the report of ASI about the remains of Temple to the extent that these remains may have been of some temple.*

P.W. 24, D. Mandal: *[...] a decorative stone has been fixed in Wall no. 17. This decorative stone is floral motif, it is used in Hindu Temples.*

[...]

It is correct to say that construction activities had been carried out at the disputed site even before the Mughal Period. [...] As an archaeologist, I admit discovery of structures beneath the disputed structure during excavation.

P.W. 32, Supriya Verma: *I agree with the finding of ASI regarding existence of the structure, but I disagree with the interpretation arrived at by ASI. Further, it is correct to say the disputed structure was not constructed on the virgin land.*

Dr Ashok Dutta: *I agree with the opinion of ASI that there lie a number of structures in the form of walls and floors beneath the*

[238]Written Submission No. A104, The Submissions on behalf of Plaintiff in Suit No.5 by Mr. C.S. Vaidyanathan, Sr. Adv., https://tinyurl.com/5a4xzr69. Accessed on 18 January 2025.

disputed structure. Wall no. 1 to 15 may be related to the disputed structure. Wall no. 16 onwards are walls belonging to a period before the construction of the disputed structure.

The issue of evidence locating the spot of birth of Ram was also to be covered. Dr Dhavan's submission time and again was that the Ram Lalla's side has not been able to prove the exact birthplace of Ram and the practice of the religion and faith of Hindus at the site. Where was the site of birth of Ram as per the practice of Hindu faith? The list of evidence was both documentary and oral that Mr Vaidyanathan referred to at different stages and those went into his written submissions as well.[239]

1. *There is evidence of the Darshan of Lord Ram by Guru Nanak Dev on his pilgrimage to Ayodhya. Guru Nanak started on pilgrimage in 1507 and had darshan of Ram-Janmabhumi Mandir between '1510 & 1511'. In 'Adi Sakhian' (1701) and 'Puratan Janma Sakhi Shri Guru Nanak Dev Ji Ki' (1734), it is recorded that during his pilgrimage Guru' Nanak Dev went to Ayodhya, among other places, and had darshan.* ***[Exhibit 68, Suit-4)*** *'Bhai Bale Wali, Sri Guru Nanak Dev Ji ki Janam Sakhi'.*
2. *Father Joseph Tieffenthaler, who visited Oudh area sometimes between 1766 to 1771, referred to the visit of Hindus and their worship in the disputed site by going for parikrama thrice and prostrating on the ground.* ***(Exhibit133, Suit-5)***
3. *'Gazetteer' of Edward Thornton (1858)* ***(Exhibit 5, Suit-S)****, mentions building of a Mosque after demolition of a temple. Edward Thornton in his Gazetteer mentions that Hindus used to visit the property in suit.*
4. *The Complaint dated 30th November 1858* ***(Exhibit 20, Suit-1)*** *made by Syed Mohd. claiming to be a Khateeb (Moazzim*

[239]Ibid.

Maszid Babri) at Oudh admitted that '[...] Previously the symbol of Janamasthan had been there for hundreds of years and Hindus did Puja [...]'

5. ***Appeal no. 56 (Exhibit 30, Suit-1)** filed against the order dated 3rd April 1877 of Deputy Commissioner Faizabad whereby he had granted permission to Hindus to open a new door in the northern outer wall of the disputed building.*
6. ***(Exhibit 24, Suit-1)** is Suit no.374/943 filed by Mohd. Asghar claiming rent against user of Chabutara and Takht near the door of Babari Masjid for organizing Kartik Mela at the occasion of Ram Navami. It shows worship at the disputed site by Hindus and that since ancient times, Mela Kartiki and Ram Navami was being organized there.*
7. *Other travelogues and gazetteers as mentioned earlier were indicated.*
8. *Finally, even oral testimonies were referred to for establishing the fact that this itself was the site of pilgrimage and no new pilgrimage site was being sought to be created. Ayodhya, it was submitted, was described as first among the 'Saptpuris'; in fact, the **witnesses produced on behalf of the opposing parties have themselves admitted that it was important to Hindus as Mecca to Muslims.***

Mohd. Hashim: *As Mecca holds importance for Muslims, similarly Ayodhya holds importance for Hindus because of Lord Rama.' 'It is true that Ayodhya is a place of pilgrimage for Hindus [...]*

Haji Mahboob Ahmad: *It is true that Ram Chandra's birthplace is Ayodhya. From when this turmoil has erupted, Hindus from nooks and corners of the country call and worship the disputed premises as his Janam Bhumi [...]*

Mohd. Yaseen: *Hindus revere this place as sacred and pious [...]*

Abdul Ajij: *It is true that Ayodhya is a pilgrimage of Hindus. Hindus come here from far-off places.*

Several documents like gazetteers and travelogues were relied upon by the counsel for Ram Lalla.

How these were collected was another story told by Bhakti and Yogeswaran. The effort was led by a person who was popularly known as Surya Prakash Ji. Born on 23 May1934 in Mitungumari, he graduated from Punjab University. It was no secret that he was a *pracharak* of the RSS and also held positions in the BJP. In 1987, he quit the political domain and joined the Ram Janmabhoomi movement to enhance the spread of the movement and to ensure better coordination in it. He got in touch with historians, experts in religious affairs to get academic and historical documents which could be used to further the legal case for a Hindu temple. On his demise, as per his wishes, his eyes were donated to Guru Nanak Eye Centre and his remaining body parts were donated to Vardhman Mahavir Medical College, New Delhi.

Champat Rai ji was another gentleman connected with the Vishva Hindu Parishad, who was coordinating legal affairs.[240]. He was present in every hearing and every conference. While lawyers sometimes got delayed by a few minutes, Champat Rai ji was always present a few minutes before time. In the 1990s, with help of late Mr Lala Ram Gupta, Advocate, the cases of revenue records were sought to be strengthened. Mr M.M. Krishnamani, who was also President of Supreme Court Bar Association for some terms, also appeared on many occasions for some of the Hindu Parties. Mr Krishnamani was the person whose arguments had some bearing on the decision of the Allahabad High Court to accept the excavation report of the ASI as part of records. At different stages, Mr Ajay Pandey, Ved Prakash Nigham and Mr K.N. Bhatt, (Senior Advocate) represented Lord Ram Lala. Mr Madan Mohan Pandey at various times and Mr K.N. Bhatt were pleading the case for the Hindu

---

[240]'All credit for Ram Mandir goes to people of Ayodhya', *Hindustan Times*, 13 July, 2023, https://tinyurl.com/4s4pfe5r. Accessed on 18 January 2025.

side. Bhakti could recall Mr Veereshwar Dwivedi of Faizabad, Rakesh Pandey, Mr G. Rajagopalan represented the parties. The case of one of the parties—Akhil Bhartiya Hindu Mahasabha—was pleaded by Mr Hari Shankar Jain. Lawyers of repute like V.K.S. Chaudhary (former Advocate General of Uttar Pradesh) and Justice Kamleshwar Nath after his retirement were guiding the team at different stages. However, one name continued to appear from 1990s be it for analysing the revenue records in Mr Lala Ram Gupta's office or for consulting Mr K.K. Sood (Senior Advocate)—Mr Bhupender Yadav was coordinating and contributing at all levels.

Back to 2019, Bhupender Yadav was in Senior Parasaran's office discussing points and was looking after the well-being of the team members. His efforts were supplemented and strengthened by two recent lieutenants—Saurabh Shyam Shamshery and Vikramajit Banerjee. Both played pivotal roles in marshalling relevant material and visiting the lead counsels at the stage of trial and final arguments before the High Court. All these names, in the opinion of Mr Parasaran and his team, had contributed immensely and had laid an extremely strong foundation for the case. In fact, the counsels in the Supreme court were short of words in commending their dedication and years of hard work.

31

Juristic Person: Final Round

'[...] all elements air, water, earth, fire and space are worshipped. All directions are worshipped and it ends with worshipping the Earth.[241]'

With all the points converted into written submissions, the last rounds of arguments were also shorter and, therefore, physically less demanding. The senior counsels' arguments on behalf of the Hindu side were flowing smoothly. In team Ram Lalla, there was no Parasaran, Vaidyanathan, Kumar or Narasimha. By now, only the counsels for 'Lord Ram' were there. In fact, from the very first day, the four hands formed a symphony. Mr Ranjit Kumar and Mr Narasimha were also putting in all their efforts and adding to the submissions of Senior Parasaran and Mr Vaidyanathan. The case had been arrayed and presented systematically by this time, and everyone was aware of the impending retirement of the Chief Justice of India. The possibility of not getting a judgement despite such a marathon hearing hung over everyone's head like the sword of Damocles. Back in office, Senior Parasaran's frail health, his last wish and the looming retirement of the Chief Justice were giving bouts anxiety to the team and the family members.

On one side was the constant reminder 'I am ninety-two now' and on the other was a well-rested and rejuvenated K. Parasaran. The other three senior counsels were assisting the

---

[241]Chaudhary, Nilashish, '[Ayodhya Hearing] [Day 35]: Hindu Parties Submit Reply Arguments on Juristic Personality and ASI Reports', *Live Law*, 1 October 2019, https://tinyurl.com/4j2bvkhr. Accessed on 22 September 2025.

giant. The point of the Juristic Person was most contentious and fought for, leading to intense scrutiny by the judges. Senior Parasaran's answers would include an old anecdote or a Sanskrit shloka. One can never plan or perceive in advance what the flow of arguments in a court can be. There can be a question asked or a suggestion made by judges and the whole flow can change. There were interventions by the other side too as Mr Parasaran argued but this point of Juristic Person saw the nonagenarian being grilled by the judges and the Sanskrit shlokas being brought to the fore, impromptu.

What Can Be a Temple? What Can Be a Deity?

The issues of Hindu belief were at the forefront. What would constitute a temple? Will the structure of a temple constitute a manifestation? Will the presence of a temple or deity at a religious site of importance run down the argument that a piece of land can have a divine personality of its own? Juristic Person was again the dominating theme between the judges and the lawyers. It would be apt to recall what the judges had queried

> *Senior Advocate K. Parasaran continued arguing his rejoinder on Day 35 of the Ayodhya land dispute hearing by citing some shlokas from the Bhagvad Gita and reiterated that the birthplace place must be considered a juridical person. 'If the people believe a place to have supernatural powers, it can be considered to a be a juristic person, irrespective of the kind of manifestation of the divine.' He submitted that 'all elements air, water, earth, fire and space are worshipped. All directions are worshipped and it ends with worshipping the Earth.'*
>
> *Giving the example of Chidambaram temple, where there is no linga but just a curtain, he stated that, 'it's about Nataraj.' 'When people visit, the curtain is lifted.' As he continued*

to cite examples of other temples which don't have an idol, Rajeev Dhavan representing the Muslim side interjected to state that in each example cited, there was a temple. 'It has manifested in the form of a temple.' Parasaran responded by saying that a place of worship attended by the public with belief can be called a temple. A Temple, it was submitted, is a generic term used for place of worship.

[...] Justice Bobde then pointed out that 'usually there is something called predominant deity, though there would be others.' 'Though there is a predominant deity, we have the manifestation of that deity in many forms. We call court as temple of justice. We have many judges but we call the whole as one institution—court,' came the veteran lawyer's response. J Chandrachud clarified J Bobde's point and asserted that though there may be multiple deities, the juristic personality is attributed to the predominant deity of the temple.

Rajeev Dhavan intervened to make his objections known. 'This is an entirely new argument,' he said and added that the matter is not about the nomenclature of the temple. He asserted that this would require him to give a note on these new aspects as there had to be arguments on proof backing their belief and worship. 'Every argument is a new one. I can't understand their objection,' retorted K. Parasaran and made it clear that the court could have objections and question his submissions, but not Dhavan.[242]

Mr Parasaran had exercised his right to defend the judgement of the Allahabad High Court concerning Juristic Person since the Allahabad High Court had given a judgement in favour of his clients. Hence, in reply to Dr Dhavan's attack on the judgement

---

[242]Chaudhary, Nilashish, '[Ayodhya Hearing] [Day 35]: Hindu Parties Submit Reply Arguments on Juristic Personality and ASI Reports', *Live Law*, 1 October 2019, https://tinyurl.com/4j2bvkhr. Accessed on 22 September 2025.

of the Allahabad High Court, Senior Parasaran gave his defence of the judgement. Dr Dhavan was right in his objection that some parts of the submissions were coming for the first time. Many old and new judgements were cited[243] including the English case of Bumper and the case of *Cambodia vs. Thailand*.

But the moot issue was how do we locate a Juristic Person in case of land? The answer was the judges must decide case by case. The judges were now treading with caution and considering the ramifications of such an eventuality. Dr Dhavan's point of caution to the judges that all of India where Lord Ram or Gautam Buddha or Krishna have walked through cannot be elevated to the status of a Juristic Person, and divinity itself in the eyes of law, was succeeding. Of course, now we were in times when the rule of law governed land, not a king whose command was the law. *Live Law* continued to report:[244]

> *Parasaran went on to cite case law and submitted that in cases of charitable endowments, the court has granted the status of a juristic entity to land on previous occasions. J Bobde then asked whether that would be applicable to every temple in India. 'We could go on a case-by-case basis,' said Parasaran. The Constitution has the right to call a place a temple or mosque.*
>
> *'During the time of Babur, sovereign was above everything. But it's not the case now. You can decide whether the place is a temple or not,' he added.*[245]
>
> *J Bobde advised caution regarding this argument and said,*

---

[243]Written Submission No. A99, The Compilation of Submissions on Land as a Juristic Entity by Mr. K. Parasaran, Sr. Adv., *Vada Prativada*, https://tinyurl.com/yck36nee. Accessed on 18 January 2025.

[244]Chaudhary, Nilashish, '[Ayodhya Hearing] [Day 35]: Hindu Parties Submit Reply Arguments on Juristic Personality and ASI Reports', *Live Law*, 1 October 2019, https://tinyurl.com/4j2bvkhr. Accessed on 18 January 2025.

[245]Ibid.

> *'Consider the ramifications of considering this argument. You say ascribe divine character to land as there's a belief that an avatar was born there.' Moving forward, J Bobde asked about the existence of any astrological or astronomical text supporting the birth of Lord Ram. After a few anecdotes by Dhavan in response, Parasaran replied by saying, 'His birthday is not celebrated; we go to the temple on Ram Navami.'*
>
> *'A deity could be believed to manifest itself in either a physical or perceived form, it is not required that it must be a consecrated idol,' he added. As Rajeev Dhavan made his objections known again [...]*
>
> *Before Parasaran concluded his arguments, J Bobde asked him whether there was a difference between a Janambhoomi and Janamasthan. Janamasthan is specific, while Janmabhoomi could be much larger.*

No one was in doubt that the reply of Dr Dhavan would be in-depth. Unfortunately, or fortunately, the performance of even top lawyers of high stature could be commented upon by rookie lawyers. They could even judge the judges and give their verdicts—but outside the courtroom. The right to pass verdict on judges is enjoyed from the day a lawyer enrols at the bar, again only outside the courtroom albeit at a fair distance from the judges.

All top counsels as well as rookie lawyers were unanimous in their opinion that Dr Dhavan's arguments in the Ayodhya case were reflections of deep industry and were top-notch.

The submission was that from testimonies, few of which have been quoted earlier, a concrete and reliable *parikrama marg* or path of circumambulation that could identify the exact place of birth could not be pinpointed. Such evidence could not confer divinity to the land or serve as reliable evidence. But for team Ram Lalla, the important point was that everyone said that parikrama as a method of worship was performed in Ayodhya.

Benefits from Point of Juristic Person

As far as arguments concerning Juristic Person were concerned, Dr Dhavan had first made a base with the submissions[246] that in the Vedic period there was no idol worship. However, certain areas were regarded sacred such as tanks, trees and rivers, which were important to livelihood and treated with reverence, not clothed with Juristic Personality (Divinity) but only considered sacred. Though it was conceded by Dr Dhavan that idols of Divinity have Juristic Personalities, their rights are limited, and subject to other property rights including the law of time limits, i.e. limitation of time and the law of adverse possession.

Dr Dhavan's stress was on a fact not disputed by Ram Lalla's side. The concept of a juridical person was advanced for the first time only in 1989. He stressed that it was expected that the Juristic Person argument would enable Ram Lalla's side to claim more rights which effectively amounted to a claim by Ram Lalla's side that:

1. Land of Janmabhoomi could not be sold and was above the concept of sale and purchase of land as property. By being divine, it was inalienable.
2. No rights could be created for any human being in land of Janmabhoomi byway of sale or purchase.
3. The government cannot acquire the property either.

---

[246]Written Submission No. A81, The Note on Juristic Personality of Idols and Areas by Dr. Rajeev Dhavan, Sr. Adv., *Vada Prativada*, https://tinyurl.com/28x5cwrp. Accessed on 18 January 2025.
Written Submission No. A84, The Summary Note on Suit No.5 by Dr. Rajeev Dhavan, Sr. Adv., *Vada Prativada*, https://tinyurl.com/bd47et3v. Accessed on 18 January 2025.
Written Submission No. A86, The Miscellaneous Note on Temples and Sadachara by Dr. Rajeev Dhavan, Sr. Adv., *Vada Prativada*, https://tinyurl.com/ytba6hxk. Accessed on 18 January 2025.

4. The property of Janmabhoomi could not be partitioned as Divinity cannot be partitioned or destroyed.
5. Holding Ram Janmabhoomi as a juridical person having a personality of its own and divinity of its own would mean that the status of the Bhoomi would not change and could not be shifted. That meant that Ram Lalla's side wanted the land to be declared above property laws and divine where no other person could claim any right.
6. No adverse possession could be claimed by anyone on the Janmabhoomi.
7. At any stage, rights in favour of any person could be left redundant even if it could be proved that the Janamasthan stood abandoned, destroyed, or taken over by others even beyond a period of twelve years.

All this led to the submission from Dr Dhavan that proof of the religious claim of the Ram Lalla's side could not be just the belief of devotees, but a physical manifestation and worship of the manifestation of the deity in that form were also necessary.

Dr Dhavan had to tackle the submissions made by the counsels of Ram Lalla wherein various instances were given which included different kinds of temples and worship to substantiate that the Hindu concepts of temple and Divinity were endless and not subject to death. The Chidambaram Temple was one such instance. The judgement in the case of *Thakurji, Shri Govind Deoji Maharaj v Board of Revenue of Rajasthan*[247] was another instance holding that 'an idol which is a judicial person is not subject to death.' The idol does not meet an end, meaning that it survives forever. The judgement in the case of *Ram Swaroop Das v S. P. Sahai*[248] holding that even if an idol gets stolen or broken, the object that the idol signifies continues to exist, was another hurdle before the Sunni Board. Further, the

[247]1965 AIR 906.

[248]1959 AIR 942.

case of *Madura Turupparankundram v Alikhan Sahib*[249] where the parikrama of the entire hill was taken, was relied upon by the temple side. Then cases like *Pichai v Com Mr. HR & CR*[250] where only 'a light' was worshipped and there was no picture of any idol or deity, had to be replied to.

Dr Dhavan made every endeavour to meet every part of the submission[251] by the counsels of temple side. Land as a Juristic Person was a grey area in law, and both sides had enough scope to assist the court in laying down the legal position. Dr Dhavan's submissions also had to be considered in light of Senior Parasaran's argument, which referred to cases like *Thayarammal v Kanakammal* and *Kamaraju Venkata Krishna Rao v Sub-Collector*, where the argument was that Supreme Court had held that land itself could be treated as a Juristic Person when it served a pious purpose.

Dr Dhavan sought to dismantle each and every authority Senior Parasaran relied upon by taking the court deep into the facts of each case. In most cases that Mr Parasaran relied upon, the following points were raised: What can be called a Hindu deity? What can be called a temple? What all could be a juridical person? Dr Dhavan's arguments were that only a general theory was advanced and the breadth of Hindu philosophy was demonstrated. Dr Dhavan brought out the facts that in none of the judgements it was held that land even without any manifestation of a form (like a Shivlingam in case of a *jyotirlingam*) could be said to be a Juristic Person. For a student of law, at any age, the quality of Dr Dhavan's submissions in the case was exquisite.

Every case cited by team Ram Lalla, as per Dr Dhavan, had

---

[249] AIR 1931 PC 212.

[250] AIR 1971 Mad 405.

[251] Written Submission No. A81, Note on Juristic Personality of Idols and Areas by Dr. Rajeev Dhavan, Sr. Adv., *Vada Prativada*, https://tinyurl.com/4apyy4a5. Accessed on 18 January 2025.

some or the other physical manifestation, be it an undulating surface of stone in Kedarnath or footprints of Lord Vishnu in Gaya or the fact of existence of a temple structure in Chidambaram. Holding existence of a piece of land as a Juristic Person in the absence of any dedication to the divine or a pious cause or in the absence of any physical manifestation (like a carving or a Shivlingam) was not possible in law, was the Sunni Board's case. In response to the counsel for Ram Lalla citing judgements laying down the law that a valid temple could exist without a building or an idol, it was pointed out that the law was laid down on distinguishing facts, and these judgements did not lay down an authority for the proposition that belief alone could confer Juristic Personality or belief alone could affect religious endowments. Some of the judgements, it was further argued, were based on the interpretation of the Madras Hindu Religious Endowment Act (2 of 1997) or other statutes/acts/laws, and did not lay down a general law.

Dr Dhavan stressed the points that Ram Lalla's side had to present a decided authority for its claim that belief alone could confer the status to the land equivalent to a juridical person. He stated that none of the judgements cited by Senior Parasaran authoritatively emphasized that belief alone, without any manifestation, could conclude that a particular piece of land could gain the status of a juridical person. The judgement of *Sri Thakur Gokul Nath Ji Maharaj v Nath Ji Bhogi*[252] was cited by Ram Lalla's side to prove that consecration was not required to be proved for an idol, to which Dr Dhavan replied in detail. As per him, this case concerned a self-revealed idol representing God himself, with 300 years of reverence and exclusive properties. On the contrary, Ayodhya was not a case of a self-revealed idol.

All this led to the submission from Dr Dhavan that the proof of the religious claim of the Ram Lalla side could not be just the

[252]Law (1953) All 552.

belief of devotees. More was required. A physical manifestation and worship of the manifestation of the deity in that form were also necessary; not mere worship of the land in the absence of a manifestation. Dr Dhavan highlighted the fact that one must not forget that the claim that land Janmabhoomi itself was a Juristic Person, was an afterthought, and was advanced for collateral purposes.

This is how team Ram Lalla looked at the status of the case.

The link between parikrama, the religious importance of Janmabhoomi and Juristic Person was sought to be developed by team Ram Lalla. The Sunni Board attacked the evidence of the Hindu side with respect to parikrama. Their contention was, parikrama could not be credible evidence and could not delineate the property, and the fact that not one credible united path of parikrama was being identified. But then the Sunni Board's witnesses also came out with revealing stuff. In the game of probabilities, all factors had to be collectively weighed. How parikrama, iron railings and witnesses could make a difference to the case, needs to be told.

SECTION VI

THE SPIRIT OF THE LAW

32

Witnesses and Their Evidence

The submission was that throughout the documents, including the judgements from 1877 to 1885, the birthplace of Lord Ram was identified within the disputed piece of land now restricted to less than 1,500 sq. yd. Ancient scriptures established faith. It was also a case where the practice of religious faith had to be proved. The 1877 and 1885 judgements were also proving that. Oral evidence along with judgements and accounts of travellers were brought in to establish the practice of faith. Mr Narasimha had submitted that the Supreme Court, in a large number of decisions, had taken judicial notice of the scriptures including the Puranas.[253]

Valmiki Ramayana which speaks of the journey of Lord Ram was brought on record in the courts, wherein it mentions Sri Maha Vishnu chose Ayodhya as his birthplace. An extract of the *Skanda Purana*, 'Ayodhya Mahatmya', which extols the visit and darshan of Janamasthan on Ram's birthday, especially for one who observes the vow of Navami and has darshan of Ram Janmabhoomi and is then released from the cycle of rebirth, was relied upon.[254]

Among the modern documents of faith in the case, going back to BCE was *Sikh Itihas Mein Shri Ram Janam Bhumi* (1991) by Sri Rajendra Singh. It speaks of the account of the visit of Guru Nanak ji, as mentioned in *Pothi Janam Sakhi* (1787) by Bhai

[253]*Nar Hari Shastri v. Badrinath Temple Committee* (1952) SCR 849; *Adi Vishveshwara of Kashi Vishwanath Temple v. State of UP* (1997) 4 SCC 606; *Yogendra Nath Naskar v CIT* (1969) 1 SCC 555; *Indian Young Lawyers Association and Ors v. The State of Kerala and Ors* 2018 SCC Online SC 1690.

[254]*Srimad Bhagwadgita* with commentary by Swami Ramsukhdas and *Geetawali* by Goswami Tulsidas were also relied upon.

Mani Singh, at a time when the Ram Janam Bhumi Temple still existed and Babur had not yet attacked India. It says that Guru Nanak reached Ayodhya and said to Mardana, 'Ayodhya is the city of Shri Ram ji. Let us go have darshan.' *Ayodhya* (1986) by Hans Bakker is comparatively a recent publication. This book speaks extensively about the history of Ayodhya through the centuries as the birthplace of Lord Ram and also refers to the different scriptures about the divinity of Ayodhya, was also on record.

One argument of the Sunni Board's counsel was that the birthplace of Lord Ram was not below the central dome of the disputed structure. The Allahabad High Court had given a positive finding that Hindus believed that the birthplace of Ram was below the central dome. In the preponderance of probabilities, both sides relied upon the examination and the cross-examination of witnesses concerning the two issues of evidence which were most contentious, and were interlinked with the rest of the evidence in the final decisions of the Allahabad High Court. These issues were of evidence concerning parikrama and the prayers by Hindus towards the disputed structure, particularly towards the central dome after 1857 when the Britishers had erected an iron railing to divide the disputed site. As Ram bhakts could not cross the iron railing, it was contended that they offer prayers towards the central dome from the iron railing itself. In this regard, Mr Vaidyanathan and Mr Narasimha[255] had advanced submissions. Of course, the Sunni Board's side had its version. Witnesses from both sides had entered into the witness box, but the contest on evidence was still on in 2019.

[255]Written Submission No. A104, The Submissions on behalf of Plaintiff in Suit No.5 by Mr. C.S. Vaidyanatha, Sr. Adv., *Vada Prativada*, https://tinyurl.com/yc2ftn5e. Accessed on 22 September 2025.

Also *see*: Written Submission No. A107, The Submissions on behalf of Defendant No.2 by Mr. P.S. Narasimha, Sr. Adv., *Vada Prativada*, https://tinyurl.com/bcex886j. Accessed on 18 January 2025.

Whose evidence in the totality of documents and the facts of the case was more persuasive in the preponderance of probabilities?

It was submitted that depositions dispelled the doubts raised over the exact identification of Ram Janmabhoomi and what area was considered the Janmabhoomi and the Ram Janmabhoomi Temple. The evidence concerning parikrama and prayers from the iron railing towards the central dome was also crucial. In some depositions came the iron wall/partition and in some came the central dome as one of the identifying factors for the witnesses[256] of the Sunni Board, which gave the identification of the land as Janmabhoomi. A few of the witness depositions highlighted in the submission read as follows:

Mohd. Hashim: *The iron-rod wall adjoined the southern wall of the mosque. We call it a mosque and others call it temple.*

[...] *The place which was attached on 22nd/23rd December 1949 is called Ram Janambhoomi by Hindus and The Babri Masjid by Muslims. In the suit of Gopal Singh Visharad also it has been called Ram Janam Bhoomi by Hindus and The Babri Masjid by Muslims [...]*[257]

Abdul Ajij: *It is true that Ayodhya is a pilgrimage of Hindus. Hindus come here from far-off places. Dispute in this case is over temple or mosque. Hindus worship it taking it to be Shri Ramjanmbhumi Temple.*

Saiyed Ahalaq Ahmed: *I hear that Hindus have the belief that Ayodhya is his birthplace. They believe Sri Ramajanmbhumi at Ayodhya to be his birthplace.*

---

[256]Written Submission No. A107, The Submissions on behalf of Defendant No.2 by Mr. P.S. Narasimha, Sr. Adv., *Vada Prativada*, https://tinyurl.com/3j5vwxmd. Accessed on 18 January 2025.

[257]Supra 12, *M. Siddiq (D) Thr Lrs v. Mahant Suresh Das & Ors,* Civil Appeal No. 10866–10867 of 2010, at page 112, https://tinyurl.com/yb977zr6. Accessed on 24 September 2025.

[…] I have heard that Hindus consider this central part to be the birthplace of Lord Rama &sanctum sanctorum.

Mohd. Qasim Ansari: *It is true that what is termed as Babri Mosque by me, is called Janmbhumi by Hindus.*

The identification of the domed structure was emerging as being Ram Janmabhoomi as well as a mosque through some Sunni Board's witnesses. As the case would depend on evidence from both Hindu as well as Muslim witnesses, a look at the extracts from the deposition of Hindu witnesses would therefore be imperative. What did they say about parikrama, the three-domed structure and worship at the site? Did the devotees show reverence towards the three-domed structure at all? If yes, how?

Harihar Prasad Tiwari: *A circumambulation path was laid down around the Sri Ram Janmbhumi premises. Hundreds of devotees used to regularly perform circumambulation every day.*

There were touchstone pillars in the Garbh-grih structure at the Sri Ram Janmbhumi premises, which had figures of flowers-leaves, Gods-Goddesses engraved over them. The dome structure was the sacred Garbh-grih, where Lord Sri Rama is believed to have descended. Hindu pilgrims, devotees and pilgrims used to offer fruits-flowers-money at Him out of faith.

Ramnath Mishra Alias Banarasi Panda: *As per tradition, elderly persons used to tell that Lord Sri Rama was born as son of King Dashratha on the ground beneath this very central dome. On the basis of this very faith and belief, all Rama-worshipping Hindu public and I also used to have darshan of Sri Ram Janam Bhumi, which used to be regarded as a very holy and revered place.*

On the basis of this very faith and belief, pilgrims and devotees have been coming in lakhs to Ayodhya to do darshan-parikrama of Sri Ram Janam Bhumi and so do they do even now. Outside the main entrance gate is fixed a stone of the English period which has words 'Janam Bhumi Nitya Yatra' and number 'ek' (1) of Hindi written on it.

Dr Rajeev Dhavan in an attempt to discredit the evidence of the witness pointed out the inability of Banarasi Panda to identify whether the photographs which were shown to him pertained to the disputed site. He was shown over fifty photographs and he could not give conclusive answers. The witness stated that in 1990, a monkey caused the collapse of the disputed building.[258] *On the day of his cross-examination, this witness was ninety-one years of age.*

Hausila Prasad Tripathi: *After having darshan, my grandmother and I also did parikrama around the entire premises of Sri Ram Janam Bhumi. Because of her old age, grandmother could do parikrama just once but my father and I did parikrama of Sri Ram Janam Bhumi five times. (Para No. 457(5), Page No. 466, Vol. 1)*

Around Sri Ram Janam Bhumi premises was built parikrama marg through which people did circumambulation.

His evidence was attacked on the grounds that at one place he had called himself an atheist, and in the ten photographs shown to him, he could not identify the parts of the disputed site.

Ram Surat Tiwari: *My elder brother had told that it was Sri Ramjanmbhumi and that from ancient times it was the faith, belief of Hindus and prevalent public opinion that Lord Vishnu had incarnated below the central dome of this structure as Sri Rama, son of King Dashratha and due to this, it was called the 'Garbh-grih' of Lord Rama. After having 'darshan' of Ramchabutara, the pilgrims-devotees used to have 'darshan' of Sri Ramjanmbhumi, the 'Garbh-grih' situated in the three-domed structure through the gate in the iron rod wall and they used to offer flower garland, money-prasad, etc. from there itself towards the 'Garbh-grih'.*

The public considered the land under the central dome to be very pious, sacred and worshipful on account of being the birthplace of Lord Sri Ram.

---

[258]Supra 13 (Para 521).

I came to know from my grandfather and father, from ancient times, it has been the customary faith and belief of Hindus that Lord Sri Ramlala had incarnated under the central dome of the three-dome building situated in Ayodhya, as son of King Dashratha in the Treta Yug, which is calledthe 'Garbh-grih', and it is out of this customary faith and belief that innumerable pilgrims, devotees from country and abroad have been visiting Ayodhya and having 'darshan', offering prayer and circumambulating the Sri Ramjanmbhumi.

Prayer at RamChabutara Sita Rasoi, Shiv Chabutara, the 'Garbh-grih' situated below the central dome of the three-dome building i.e. that place of Sri Ramjanmbhumi whereLord Sri Rama was born, and they performed their circumambulation of the Sri Ramjanmbhumi premises along the circumambulation path adjacent to the outer walls of Sri Ramjanambhumi.

Discrepancies were sought to be highlighted with this witness too.

All these depositions did not exist in vacuum. They were interlinked with all other facts and depositions to determine whose case was stronger, based on the preponderance of probabilities, and also with the events of the year 1950. In 1950, two important events recorded the parikrama route. First, the court-appointed receiver took over and the second was the Court Commissioner's report in April. The receiver took charge on 5 January 1950 and made an inventory of the properties which had been attached. It was recorded that the last namaz offered in the mosque was on 16 December 1949.[259] The noting recorded the locational identity and dimensions of the disputed structure and indicated a parikrama route:

15. Building-Three domed building with Courtyard and boundary wall, which is bounded as under:

---

[259]*Supra 13* (page 79).

North-Premises comprising Chhathi Courtyard and Nirmohi Akhara.

South-Vacant land and parikrama (circumambulation path)

East-'Chabutara' (platform) of Ram temple under possession of Nirmohi Akhara, and Courtyard of temple premises

West-Parikrama (circumambulation path)

16. Small brass glass

On 25 June 1950, the Commissioner submitted a report, together with two site plans of the disputed premises which were numbered as Plan no. I and II, to the Trial Court. Both the report and maps indicated the position at the site and are reproduced below:

> *Plan No. I represents the building in suit shown by the figure ABCDEF on a larger scale than Plan No. II, which represents the building with its locality. A perusal of Plan No. I would show that the building has two gates, one on the east and the other on the north, known as 'Hanumatdwar' and 'Singhdwar'respectively. The 'Hanumatdwar' is the main entrance gate to the building. At this gate there is a stone slab fixed to the ground containing the inscription—Shri Janma Bhumi Nitya Yatra, and a big coloured picture of Shri Hanumanji is placed at the top of the gate. The arch of this entrance gate, 10' in height, rests on two black kasauti stone pillars, each 4' high, marked a and b, containing images of—Jai and Vijai respectively engraved thereon. To the south of this gate on the outer wall there is engraved a stone image, 5' long, known as—Varah Bhagwan.*
>
> *[...]*
>
> *Around the building there is a pucca path known as*

> *parikrama, as shown in yellow in Plan Nos. I & II. On the west of the parikrama, the land is about 20' low, while the pucca road on the northern side is about 18' low. Other structures found on the locality have been shown in Plan no. II at their proper places.*[260]

However, on the issue of parikrama one also had to look at the oral evidence of a few of the Sunni Board's witnesses which were pointed out in the submissions.[261]

1. **PW-1 Mohd. Hashim:** *It is true that Panchkosi Parikrama is at a distance from the disputed property. This parikrama is all around the disputed property. It is a very old circumambulation and Hindus have been used it since my childhood. We are also within this parikrama, and they are doing our parikrama also.*
2. **PW-2 Sh. Haji Mehboob Ahmed:** *Panchkosi Parikrama covers the whole of Ayodhya […] It usually takes place in winters. The parikrama attracts a crowd. A number of people come from outside. A number of people hail from the city.*
3. **PW-4 Mohd. Yaseen:** *In my view, Hindus must have had the darshan of this place as birthplace of Lord Rama. I reside at Ayodhya; so, I meet some Hindus and Pandits (scholarly persons) too. Feasts-dinners are also organized at weddings. It is their belief that it is the birthplace of Lord Rama. (Stated on his own that their belief is their own.). Hindus worship this place taking it to be holy and sacred.*

Mohd. Qasim Ansari had further stated: *The 'Panchkosi' (distance of five kos, one kos being equal to two miles)*

---

[260]Supra 13 (page 14), Report of the Court Commissioner appointed in Suit 1 to prepare a map of the disputed premises, dated 25 June 1950, https://tinyurl.com/5b2es7pc. Accessed on 18 January 2025.

[261]Written Submission No. A107, The Submissions on behalf of Defendant No. 2 by Mr. P.S. Narasimha, Sr. Adv., *Vada Prativada*, https://tinyurl.com/3j5vwxmd. Accessed on 18 January 2025.

circumambulation is performed annually, possibly in the Kartika month, possibly around the Kartika fair. It is true that a very big fair is held at Ayodhya on this occasion. It is true that lakhs of pilgrims come to have darshan [...] lakhs of people perform circumambulation on the Panchkosi Path. It is true that such pilgrims who perform circumambulation, also have darshan of Hanumangarhi, Kanak Bhawan and Ramjanmbhumi [...] I also know about 'Chaudahkosi' (distance of fourteen kos) circumambulation. Ayodhya and Faizabad fall in this Chaudahkosi circumambulation path. It is also true that the Chaudahkosi circumambulation also commences in the month of 'Kartika'. It is also true that lakhs of pilgrims and devotees participate in this circumambulation as well.

Issue of Parikrama

The evidence of parikrama being performed around the Janmabhoomi was sought to be rejected by the Sunni Board. Their point was that parikrama as evidence to prove the divinity of land should be rejected as the witnesses had not given a unanimous description of the parikrama marg—what came out was a rather varied description. It was argued that in the present case, there was no singular common parikrama marg. The objection was also that the issue of parikrama was not raised in the suit of Ram Lalla (Suit 5). In such circumstances, it was contended that merely by the performance of parikrama by devotees, it could not be said that divinity was attached to the land janmabhoomi itself. A challenge was laid about the reliability of witness testimonies. Witnesses were quoted to point out that two types of parikramas were performed in Ayodhya: Panchkosi, five miles, and Chaudahkosi, fourteen miles. Further, it was argued that the evidence of parikrama itself did not bring out any consistent route, and the whole area covered by parikrama was huge. Some of the quoted witnesses had stated inconsistent routes for the parikrama.[262]

Hausila Prasad Tripathi's statement with respect to parikrama was that he had performed parikrama of the entire Janmabhoomi:

> *After having darshan of Shri Ram Janam Bhoomi, I have seen thousands of people doing parikrama of the entire Shri Ram Janam Bhoomi from outside. I, along with my father and grandmother also had parikrama of the entire Shri Ram Janam Bhoomi premises after darshans. Due to old age, my grandmother could do parikrama only once whereas my father and I completed the parikrama of Shri Ram Janam Bhoomi for the five times.*[263]

Ram Surat Tewari's testimony was brought out to highlight that he pointed out a totally different parikrama route. He was OPW 7[264]:

> *.........On the rear side there was parikrama marg in the west—it is wrong to say that the thing which I call the parikrama marg was the pustha of the mosque. There are two types of parikramas—Panchkosi and Chaudahkosi.*
>
> *He had also done the parikrama of Ram Chabutara.*
>
> *Two types of parikrama are performed in Ayodhya known as Panchkosi and Chaudahkosi.*

Then some Nirmohi Akhara witness depositions were attacked on the grounds that they had identified completely different directions of the parikrama route, or on the grounds that they stated that they had performed parikrama of Ram Chabutra. One of the witnesses for Nirmohi Akhara had stated:

---

[262]Written Submission No. A84, The Summary Note on Suit No.5 by Dr. Rajeev Dhavan, Sr. Adv., *Vada Prativada*, https://tinyurl.com/3de38dup. Accessed on 18 January 2025.

[263]Supra 13 (Para 522 at p. 615).

[264]Written Submission No. A81, The Note on Juristic Personality of Idols and Areas by Dr. Rajeev Dhavan, Sr. Adv., *Vada Prativada*, https://tinyurl.com/28x5cwrp. Accessed on 18 January 2025.

DW – 3/6

Parikrama was done only outside the complex.

It is wrong to say that the 'Parikrama Route' but it was the 'pushtha' of the Masjid. Parikrama marg was on all sides of the disputed complex.[265]

While another stated:

Parikrama is inside the temple but some people did it outside the temple.

In civil cases, it is not uncommon to find witnesses contradicting their statements a bit. In cases traversing centuries and where the trial goes on for years and sometimes generations pass by, the preponderance of probabilities is the only way to ascertain whose case is more reliable. It is for this reason that proof beyond reasonable doubt cannot be insisted on in civil cases. On whose case lies the probability becomes the determining factor. Many of these witnesses from both sides were also quite aged. The courts also generally consider the age of witnesses while weighing the contradictions in testimonies.

[265]Ibid.

33

Hair-Splitting Law

Sri Jilani fairly admitted during the course of arguments that historical or other evidence is not available to show the position of possession or offering of namaz in the disputed building at least till 1855 [...][266]

The intense arguments on the point of Juristic Person continued through old decided cases by the Senior Counsels for both sides. Many times, these arguments were also through a note given on a point, apart from oral arguments. If the counsels for Ram Lalla relied upon the judgement of the Privy Council to show that a complete hill can be treated as sacred, Dr Dhavan brought in his concept of the preservation of the mosque. The Madura Case underwent intense scrutiny. It concerned a rock temple where the inner shrine is hewn out of the hill. Then the question arose on what was the actual conflict in Madura. The submissions of the two sides, if analysed, unfolded in their manner. The Ram Lalla side relied upon the judgement in *Madura v. Alikhan Sahib*[267]to show the importance and practice of parikrama of the hill and the parikrama route. The attempt was to show the religious importance of the hill, and from the judgement, the relevant observations were pointed out that the inner shrine of the temple is hewn out of the hill, and in it, carved in the rock itself, is the image of the deity. 'As the image in the temple is an actual part of the hill, it is obvious that the performance of this rite necessitates the perambulation of the hill itself.'

---

[266]Allahabad High Court Judgment, https://tinyurl.com/hazp52zs.

[267](1931) 34 Law Weekly 340 (Privy Council).

Dr Dhavan's submission[268] did not dispute that the Madura case hill had been put to temple use. In fact, he submitted that after examination of all the historical documents, the court affirmed the temple status which was not disturbed in the Muslim invasion and British period. He had an important point to present—the presence of a mosque on the hill, which was on the highest point on the hill and on a part of the hill called Nellitope.

Dr Dhavan's submission stressed on the point that the mosque was exempt from the decision of the suit in favour of the temple. The mosque was allowed to stand.

> *The suit was tried by the Subordinate Judge of Madura. He decided against the Government claim and in favour of the temple, except in respect of the Nellitope, and the actual site of the mosque with its flag staff and flight of steps leading up to it, which he held to be the property of the Mahomedan defendants. The decree of the Subordinate Judge was dated 25th August 1923.*

In the submissions of Dr Dhavan, the parts of the hill where the mosque stood, were excluded. This was affirmed by the Privy Council and unfortunately, it was submitted while reading this judgement. This crucial aspect of the case was not given due attention and brought to the court's notice by counsels for Ram Lalla.

> *On the whole their Lordships are of opinion that the appellant has shown that the unoccupied portion of the hill has been in the possession of the temple from time immemorial, and has been treated by the temple authorities as their property. They think that the conclusion came to by the Subordinate Judge*

[268]"Written Submission No. A81, The Note on Juristic Personality of Idols and Areas by Dr. Rajeev Dhavan, Sr. Adv., *Vada Prativada*, https://tinyurl.com/28x5cwrp. Accessed on 18 January 2025.

was right and that no ground has been shown for disturbing his decree.[269]

Mr Vaidyanthan's reply to Dr Dhavan's pointing fault with the Madura judgement was that it was never a mosque v temple property case. In the Madura case, a portion of the unoccupied hill was given to Muslims as they were worshipping there. Mr Vaidyanathan's submissions pointed out that this aspect of the case stood irrelevant. In its judgement, the Privy Council did not have to go into the question of the area being a mosque or a temple at all because the claim in the case was made only to the base of the hill and not to those parts where the mosque stood. Hence, there was no dispute with the mosque and the only point for which the judgement was relevant was that Hindu worship can be of a hill, and there can be a parikrama marg of the temple's ownership which can establish the divine nature of a deity. The relevant part of the judgements was again quoted to establish that the question claiming the entirety of the hill was never at issue in this case.

Mr Vaidyanathan pointed out: 'In the trial court, the temple, represented by its manager, was the plaintiff. He claimed the whole hill, with the **exception of** certain cultivated and assessed lands and **the site of the mosque, as temple property.** The Mohammedan defendants asserted their ownership of the particular eminence upon which the mosque stands, and of a portion of the main hill known as Nellitope.'

The claim by Hindus in this case was never about Nellitope. The suit was tried by the Subordinate Judge of Madurai. **He decided against the Government claim and in favour of the temple, except in respect of the Nellitope, where the mosque existed.**

A reply also had to be given to the strong objection taken by Dr Dhavan on the issue of reliance on contents as recorded by

[269](1931) 34 Law Weekly 340 (Privy Council).

gazetteers and travelogues as PROOF OF FAITH AND BELIEF. It was submitted that the contention of the Sunni Board that the travelogues and gazetteers recording the faith and belief regarding the place of birth of Lord Shri Ram is hearsay and ought not to be given credence, is untenable. The submission is reflective of the deep-rooted prejudice of Western historians and the rejection of the oral tradition in India and other oriental countries, and even in West Asia and the Middle East, where Islam originated and spread. The recording of history in India, unlike in Europe, is not one of recording dates and events; it is more concerning culture, practices, etc. Documentation of history before the Christian era and even up to medieval times is rare. Transmission of history, tradition, and Dharma has been oral—in poetry, music, shloka, etc. Shruti and Smriti are the sources of Hindu Law. Further, it was a fact that no bias was attributed to anyone recording the travelogues or the gazetteers and these was being relied upon by the Muslim side too, pointing out the worth of these documents. Some inscriptions are found in public places, including temples.

Similarly, archaeological excavations have yielded some other forms of recording. Manuscripts in palm leaves or otherwise are of comparatively recent origin.

On the issue of law, it was submitted that authoritative texts on Evidence Law allow for hearsay evidence to be taken into account concerning historical facts. Books on Evidence Law like John Pitt Taylor's *Law of Evidence* (1872), state that, in many cases, indeed in nearly all cases, after a lapse of years, it would be impossible to give evidence that the statements contained in such documents were, in fact, true, and it is for this reason that such an exception is made to the rule of hearsay evidence. It is in this context that the claim of Dr Dhavan that the recording by travellers that the disputed site was the birthplace of Lord Ram was mere hearsay, has to be evaluated. It was submitted that the Privy Council had already held in *Ghulam Rasul Khan vs.*

Secretary of State for India[270] that in such a case as the present, statements in public documents are admissible/receivable to prove the facts stated on the general grounds that they were made by the authorized agents of the public in the course of official duty and respecting facts which were of public interest or required to be recorded for the benefit of the community.

With arguments in Suits 3 and 5 completed, the focus was now on Suit 4, filed by the Sunni Board. All the suits had been tried together by the Allahabad High Court. Evidences were common in all the suits. The difference between Suit 3 and Suit 5 on the one hand and Suit 4 on the other, was that Suit 4 of the Sunni Board had stated that the disputed site was dedicated as a mosque in 1528, and this was a foundational fact. Hence, for Suit 4 to succeed, it had to prove that it was dedicated as a mosque, as well the site was used as a mosque to offer prayers or namaz.

Team Ram Lalla held its view of the matter as the case had unfolded till now. On its analysis of the submissions, the team had from its perspective concluded that certain points, discussed in the following paragraph, had been proven.

Ram Lalla Virajman was being worshipped within the disputed site itself. The disputes at the site which had been going on since earlier than 1855 had resulted in the riots of 1855. Hence, Ram Lalla's claim existed even then. The disputes and riots at that time resulted in British intervention to separate the two communities and erect the iron railings in 1857–1858 to preserve law and order. The Suit of 1885 conclusively proved that it was the disputed site only which was mentioned as the Ram Janmasthan or Ram Janmabhoomi by everyone even then. There was no dispute left now and everyone was bound by it. In essence, the legal dispute as to where the Janmabhoomi site was situated was decided in 1885 itself. But title or ownership of the land had never been decided to

[270]Written Submission No. A77, The Compilation on law relating to Gazetteers by Dr. Rajeev Dhavan, Sr. Adv., *Vada Prativada*, https://tinyurl.com/4zbuck5v. Accessed on 18 January 2025.

date. For the team, the gazetteers and travelogues were successfully proving the fact that the worshippers were entering the entire disputed site as Janmabhoomi or Ram Janmasthan before the iron railing was erected. But the most important aspects were the ones accepted by the other side itself:

a. The Sunni Board had accepted the presence of Nirmohi Akhara within the disputed site and had accepted that prayers were being offered to Ram Lalla Virajman within the disputed site.
b. The concession, as recorded by the Allahabad High Court, by the Sunni Board was that there existed no evidence indicating any use of the mosque between 1528 to 1855 for offering prayers. The same stand was taken by Dr Dhavan before the Supreme Court too. The High Court had recorded:

   [...] even if for the purpose of the issues in question, we assume that the building in dispute was so constructed in 1528 AD, there is no evidence whatsoever that after its construction, it was ever used as a mosque by Muslims at least till 1856–57. Sri Jilani fairly admitted during the course of arguments that historical or other evidence is not available to show the position of possession or offering of namaz in the disputed building at least till 1855 [...][271]

c. Having taken an affirmative stand that the mosque was constructed on a vacant piece of land, the other side was now contending that the structure found in the excavation was an Idgah and not a temple. The stand amounted to saying that either the Mughals demolished the Idgah, built during the Sultanate period, or the mosque was erected on the ruins of the Idgah. This was totally contrary to the case set up by the Sunni Board.

[271] Allahabad High Court Judgment, https://tinyurl.com/hazp52zs.

Again and again, it was stressed that once it is conceded that Lord Rama was born in the Palace of Dashratha in Ayodhya, and the palace was situated in the Ramkot area where the disputed structure exists, it is unnecessary to identify a particular spot or room as *the* place of birth. The small disputed area of approximately 1,500 sq. yd cannot be partitioned. However, evidence indicated the belief and worship of Hindus even in the inner courtyard below the three-domed structure. The orders passed in 1877 and 1885 had left no shadow of doubt that this land was the 'Janamasthan'.

With the aforementioned aspect arising from Suit 3 of Nirmohi Akhara and Suit 5 of Ram Lalla, the team felt confident of getting over Suit 4. Much of the evidence was gone into, but Suit 4, filed by the Sunni Board, could bring in new perspectives. As the Sunni Board was the plaintiff in the case, Dr Dhavan would start the arguments. He may have held back his best for Suit 4. Dr Dhavan's submissions highlighted a crucial aspect. While Suit 1 of Gopal Singh Visharad was filed solely for claiming right to worship, Suit 3 of Nirmohi Akhara was filed for '*management and charge*' of the alleged temple. It is only in Suit 4 of the Sunni Board and Suit 5 of Ram Lalla that the parties claimed *title* of the disputed site.

An outline of Dr Dhavan's submission for team Ram Lalla pointed to a preliminary conclusion that the primary focus was on the_fact that the Babri Mosque was constructed in 1528 under the command of Babur. The maintenance and upkeep of the mosque were managed by a cash grant payable by the Royal Treasury during Babur's rule. Subsequently, the British continued the grant. Several attempts of trespass and encroachment by Hindus and Sikhs were successfully resisted. Even the state authorities protected the rights of Muslims by directing evictions of both Hindu/Sikh squatters from the mosque, and also removal of any construction made by them.[272]

Dr Dhavan attacked the Temple case vehemently on the point that Hindus based their rights on illegal acts like preventing, and indeed flaunting that they prevented/harassed Muslims when they went to offer namaz in the Babri Mosque and then desecrated the mosque on 22/23 December 1949. Focus was also on the point that the parts of the Babri Mosque destroyed in 1934, were repaired and a fine was imposed on Hindus for destroying those parts.[273]

It was also submitted that the demolition of the mosque on 6 December 1992, was in utter violation of the *status quo* orders of the Supreme Court of India. Dr Dhavan's case was also that there was a general belief of Hindus that at least till 1885, the birthplace of Lord Ram was Ram Chabutra, which of course existed within the disputed site. This was also the case in the Suit of 1885. However, despite noting the belief that Ram Chabutra reflected the birth spot, it was submitted that the Suit of 1885 held that Hindus had no rights of title over the Chabutra and that their rights were, at most, easementary (right to access). Even Hindus have always referred to the disputed structure as the mosque, and have recognized it as such.

Dr Dhavan, after accepting that the Sunni Board had no concrete evidence of any happening before 1857, was now presenting evidence. The case of the Sunni Board now was that Muslims were continuously offering prayers in the disputed structure, as borne out by evidence like:

a) Agreement dated 25 July 1936 for payment of arrears of salary of Pesh Imam
b) Testimonies of witnesses as recorded in the Shia-Sunni Suit/dispute of 1941
c) During the course of arguments, some Temple/Hindu

[272]Supra 13 (Para 786).
[273]Ibid. (Para 782)

> parties agreeing that at least till 16 December 1949, namaz was being offered in The Babri Masjid (the period of namaz agreed upon was 1934–49.)

Given the aforementioned details, it was argued by Dr Dhavan that the disputed structure had always been a mosque which had remained in the possession of Muslims since 1528 till its desecration on 22/23 December 1949.

The submission on illegalities to judge a title suit was, for team Ram Lalla, meant to deflect attention from the lack of evidence to prove title and ownership from 1528 onwards. Ram Lalla's claim was based, at least now, on the admitted fact by the Sunni Board that there were prayers offered to Ram Lalla Virajman within the disputed site at least since 1858. Christian missionaries also talked about the site being believed to be Lord Ram's birthplace both pre- and post-1858. Though the judgement of 1885 did not decide ownership of the land, it held that this site was the birthplace of Lord Ram. Oral evidence of the residents of Ayodhya and, above all, archaeological evidence supported other evidence in favour of the Temple.

For team Ram Lalla, there was apparent conflict in Dr Dhavan's submission. On one hand, he had submitted that evidence should be taken only from 1857 onwards, and then he was asserting construction of the disputed site in 1528. To add to that, it was also submitted that a cash grant was being paid by the Royal Treasury of Babur without any grounding in evidence. There was no evidence either to prove any possession of the disputed site by the Sunni Board from 1528 till 1857. This also applied to the disputed structure. Of course, it was not denied by some counsels for the Hindu side that namaz was offered in the disputed structure between 1934 to 1949, but there existed no proof of dedication of the disputed site as a mosque or of namaz being offered before 1934. A fair question would, however, arise: Why was team Ram Lalla referring to the structure both as a disputed structure as well as Babri Mosque?

The reason was that while it was stated that Babur had a mosque constructed at the site of Ram Janmabhoomi, it was always used as a temple, and prayers were offered there by Ram bhakts. The land was always divine—divinity cannot be destroyed—and it continued to exist, as per the faith, belief and practice of the worshippers. Hence, Suit 4 of the Sunni Board had a specific question framed by the court:

> *Whether the building in question described as a mosque in the sketch map attached to the plaint was a mosque as claimed by the plaintiffs?*[274]

The evidence concerning this question had its own story to tell. This necessarily also meant that the court would have been called upon to answer questions like: Have Muslims had the property in suit from AD 1528 continuously, openly, and to the knowledge of the defendants and Hindus in general? If so, what was its effect? 'Was the building dedicated to the Almighty as alleged by the plaintiffs?' Even after the construction of the disputed building, did the deities of Bhagwan Sri Ram Lalla Virajman and the Asthan Sri Ram Janmabhoomi continue to exist on the disputed property? Does the disputed site continue to be visited by devotees for worship? Was the disputed building landlocked and could not be reached except by passing through places of worship of another religion? These were important questions, and the Allahabad High Court had framed such questions. All the answers to questions like these had to be found in evidence. Hence the evidence as brought in by Dr Dhavan and Mr Jilani was *of course* scrutinized and analysed by team Ram Lalla.

---

[274]Supra 13 (Para 70), *M. Siddiq (D) Thr Lrs v. Mahant Suresh Das & Ors,* Civil Appeal No. 10866–10867 of 2–10, https://tinyurl.com/yb977zr6. Accessed on 24 September 2025.

34

Evidence of the Sunni Central Waqf Board[275]

'What was the relation of Mohd. Asghar and Rajjab Ali with Mir Baqi?'

> *[...] It is not out of context that the story of grant might have been set up by the two persons i.e. father and son for the purpose of obtaining valuable grant from Britishers in their favour [...]*

Submissions advanced by Dr Dhavan were systematic and tried to bring in a holistic perspective of the case. The judgement of the Allahabad High Court was highlighted concerning the issues framed in the suit of the Sunni Board and the three-part division of the disputed site. Analysing the evidence, the three judges of the Allahabad High Court—Justice Khan, Justice Agarwal and Justice Sharma—had reached conclusions that did not favour the Sunni Board's stand of exclusive possession of the disputed land. Hence, Dr Dhavan and Mr Jilani faced the task of attempting to overturn these conclusions.

The three judges of the Allahabad High Court had given three different judgements. Justice Khan had held that since both parties were in joint possession of the disputed property, and both parties were joint title holders of the premises in dispute, the property had to be partitioned. Justice Sudhir Agarwal had

[275]Written Submission No. A120, The Summary Note on OOS 4 of 1989 by Dr. Rajeev Dhavan, Sr. Adv., *Vada Prativada*, https://tinyurl.com/5b7y9u7k. Accessed on 18 January 2025.

held that there is no evidence of possession by Dr Dhavan's clients of the property in suit. They did not have possession of the outer courtyard at least since 1856–57 when the dividing railing was raised by the British, but so far as the inner courtyard is concerned it has been used by both parties.

It was held that Hindus and Muslims both visited the disputed property as worshippers, the only difference being Hindus visited the entire property and Muslims were confined to the inner courtyard. So far as the outer courtyard is concerned, it was held that the Hindu religious structures existed therein for more than 150 years, i.e. a period after 1856–57, and they were being managed and administered by the priests of Nirmohi Akhara.

Justice Sharma had held that Dr Dhavan's clients had not shown exclusive and continuous possession over the suit property from AD 1528, nor have they shown that they were offering prayers in the disputed structure from time immemorial. However, Hindus have proved that they were in exclusive possession of the outer courtyard, and were visiting the inner courtyard to offer prayers.

The first challenge before the Sunni Board was to prove that namaz took place inside the disputed structure. If namaz was offered at the disputed structure, then since when and what was the evidence to prove the offering of namaz? Secondly, the Sunni Board had to prove that possession of the disputed site was exclusive to Muslims. From the perspective of timelines, for the first phase of evaluation of evidence from 1 millennium BC to AD 1528, the Sunni Board did not produce any evidence. No evidence could be produced even in light of the ASI excavations, resulting in a finding that there were structures below the disputed site which were non-Islamic.

When asked about evidence, the evidence for the period between 1528 to 1857 was only a statement that a mosque was constructed in 1528, and prayers were offered there since 1528.

Another point was that for the upkeep, maintenance and other expenses incurred in connection with the mosque, a cash grant was provided and paid for by the Royal Treasury during the rule of Emperor Babur. However, no direct evidence was adduced to prove Babur's grant.

The case for the Sunni Board was to prove the grant of maintenance during Mughal rule through the document advancing cash grant for the upkeep of the building of the mosque/disputed structure. No evidence was brought in. The main evidence of the Sunni Board side came in the form of the grants and recognitions given in favour of individuals for the upkeep of the mosque through documents originating in 1860.

Though no evidence was adduced to directly substantiate the grant of any maintenance amount by Babur, or any document whose antiquity was traced back to a sufficient number of years in the Mughal rule,[276] it was submitted that grants that were originally given during the time of Emperor Babur were continued by the British for the upkeep and maintenance of the mosque.

The case set up was that the structure was specifically recognized as a mosque by the British government. Specific reliance was placed on documents with their origin in 1860 after the British conquest. There was no evidence dating back to the Mughal period. For team Ram Lalla, it was interesting to note the nomenclature the disputed site was given, and whether these documents also stated anything about the now accepted position by all parties that at least since 1858, there was regular worship of Ram Lalla at the disputed site. What was the connection of those documents with the Hindu belief of the land being 'Janamasthan'?

The first document was a copy of some register as noticed by Justice Sudhir Agarwal of the Allahabad High Court. Reliance

[276]Para 2314 of the Allahabad High Court judgement noting the stand of the Sunni Board that there was no evidence to prove if the site was ever used as a mosque between 1528 and 1855. The same stand was reiterated by the counsel for the Sunni Board, Para 678 of the Supreme Court judgement.

was placed on the entries in columns 13 and 14 of the register. This document allowed for cash grants for the upkeep of the mosque. As far as the physical condition of the document was concerned, it was noted that it was an 'extremely torn document' and the contents were 'almost illegible'. In the documents produced by the Sunni Board, what the disputed site was referred to was another discovery. The utility of the document was to show that the Register of Inquiry (14.3.1860) of land records (rent free) showed that Emperor Babur granted a revenue grant/cash grant in the name of Mir Baqi for construction and maintenance of the mosque, namely Babri Mosque, at village Shahnawa. The register recorded:

- The name of the person who made the grant was Emperor Babur.
- The rent-free land was situated at village Shahnawa, and it generated an annual revenue of Rs. 302, 3 *ana* and 6 *pai*.
- This rent-free land grant was given as a waqf at the time of the construction of the Babri Masjid by Babur to meet the expenses of the salary of the Muezzin[277] and Khatib.[278]
- This rent-free grant was given to Saiyed Baqi for his lifetime, and thereafter to his son for his lifetime, and thereafter to Saiyed Hussain Ali.
- The decision of the Board dated 29 June 1880) was that the grant would survive till the continuation of the purpose for which it was given, exempt from land revenue.

As far as the admissibility/reliability of this evidence or document was concerned, the document had to establish the date of the grant, the name of the donor, and the exact order passed during

[277]Person who issues the call to prayer from one of the minarets of a mosque. https://tinyurl.com/bp8nn67b. Accessed on 18 January 2025.

[278]Person who delivers the sermon during the Friday prayer and Eid prayers; usually the prayer leader (Imam), but the two roles can be played by different people. https://tinyurl.com/4rnk4b4a. Accessed on 18 January 2025.

the time of Babur or at any other time. However, the indication that came from the document was that there was no knowledge of the date of the grant, and the name of the donor/grantor was entered based on some testimony. Similarly, it had been stated that based on the testimonies, this land-free grant was given as waqf at the time of the construction of the Babri Masjid at Ayodhya by Emperor Babur for meeting the expenses and the salaries of the Muezzin[279] and Khatib.[280]

The dates and the orders referred to were not known. Hence, legally for team Ram Lalla it was not much of a concern. In fact, it was common ground between the parties that this document did not prove any title (ownership) granted in favour of the beneficiary. Meanwhile, the *Supreme Court Observer* reported[281] the day's arguments of Dr Dhavan, a part of which was:

> *7.85.1 Sunnis have historical possession*
>
> *First, he sought to establish that historically Sunnis possessed the site since Babur's time. He took the Bench through a British grant issued for the upkeep of Babri Masjid. He submitted that the British Government only issued the grant after conducting a detailed enquiry into the history of the site. Justice Nazeer observed that the grant was only for upkeep and did not amount to a title grant. Sr. Adv. Dhavan agreed, but submitted that implicit in a grant of upkeep, is the recognition that there was a mosque at the site.*
>
> *J Chandrachud asked Sr. Adv. Dhavan whether the grant changed the nature of the title, as Babur had initially dedicated the mosque to Allah. Sr. Adv. Dhavan replied that the change in sovereign did not change the nature of recognition—namely a mosque existed at the site.*

---

[279]Supra 278.

[280]Supra 279.

[281]'Day 58 Arguments, Ayodhya Title Dispute', *Supreme Court Observer*, 4 October 2019, https://tinyurl.com/42ua9byc. Accessed on 18 January 2025.

He tried to show Muslim possession of the disputed site, by taking the Bench through several instances where Hindus and Sikhs had allegedly attempted to encroach upon the mosque's land. In particular, he discussed how Hindus had illegally constructed the Ram Chabutra in 1857 during British rule.

The aforementioned observations also related to various other documents presented. Two names, Rajjab Ali and Mohd. Ali, were now to feature quite prominently in these documents. They had their own stories to tell, which shall be discussed shortly.

From another register, extracts were brought in to show that the names of Mohd. Asghar and Mir Rajjab Ali were recorded as names of the persons who were holding the disputed land, which was rent-free land. This was also a register from the 1860s.[282] There was no document for the period before that. Every document produced, raised the following questions: Who among Muslims or Hindus was in exclusive possession? Were Muslims or Hindus, or both, offering prayers? What did these documents prove concerning Hindu or Muslim prayers at the site way back in time? How did Nirmohi Akhara enter into these transactions? The Allahabad High Court had analysed these documents relied upon by the Sunni Board, and had come to the following conclusion and commented on the sharing of rent:

2393. *The above documents show that in order to justify the amount received by Mir Rajjab Ali and Mohd. Afjal and their successors in the form of the grant, they made some expenses on the maintenance of disputed structure and that was shown in the records also, which was inspected and found correct by the Government officials namely Tehsildar, etc. The interesting thing discerned from all these documents is that none of them throws any light on the fact whether the Muslim public visited the disputed premises for offering namaz during all this*

[282]In legal terms, this register was called the excerpts of the 'Register No. 6(e), conditional land revenue exemption of Tehsil Faizabad dated June 29,1860'.

> *period. From the stand taken by Mohd. Zaki before the Waqf Commissioner, it is evident that the grant of the two villages was treated as a personal grant and in one or the other documents, besides the words 'Mutawalli'/'Khatib', it also mentions 'Zamindar' qua the two villages grant whereof was allowed. Moreover, in respect to Hindu fairs at Ayodhya i.e. Ram Navami fair, they shared income of rental when some of the part of the land was allowed to be used by outsiders for keeping shops, with the Priest of Nirmohi Akhara, who were managing and possessing Ram Chabutara and other Hindu religious structures and places existing in the outer courtyard.*[283]

Who prayed at the site was also a material consideration. After all, a land that was referred to as government land in official records was claimed by two groups on the grounds of being in possession, worshipping at the site, and ownership. Who were Rajjab Ali and Mohd. Asghar who featured nearly in every document? Did they have any special connection with history or not? The answer to these questions would soon come to light.

In a few years, the cash grants given by the British were stopped. However, the British stopped taking revenue from these lands and declared the land grants as revenue-free land.

The names of Mohd. Asghar and Mohd. Rajjab Ali came up even in 1964. Land allotted in their names was situated in villages Sholapur and Bahoranpur in the vicinity of Ayodhya through a certificate of grant bearing the seal of the Chief Commissioner. The certificate of grant mentioned that both Rajjab Ali and Mohd. Asghar had received a cash grant of Rs. 302-3–6 in rent-free tenure from the former government. It was further stated that the Chief Commissioner, under the authority

[283]Justice Sudhir Agarwal, Allahabad High Court Judgment, Para 2393, *Vada Prativada*, https://tinyurl.com/54u2ju8u. Accessed on 18 January 2025.

of the Governor General in Council[284] was pleased to maintain the grant for so long as the object for which the grant has been made is kept up, subject to certain conditions mentioned in the certificate.

Dr Dhavan stated that this grant was given after a detailed enquiry. Certain important orders/correspondence during the course of the enquiry, as mentioned, were also brought forward. It was submitted that on 25 August 1863, the Secretary, Chief Commissioner of Awadh wrote to the Commissioner, Faizabad Division, mentioning that the Governor General had sanctioned the Chief Commissioner's proposal for the change from the cash payment of Rs 302–3–6 granted in perpetuity for the support of the Masjid Janamsthan_to the grant of rent-free land near Ayodhya. It was further requested that a provision for the change be made by the grant of some Nazul Land (government land) near Ayodhya.

Then again on 31August 1863, an order was passed by the Deputy Commissioner regarding the rent-free land sanctioned by the government to the Masjid Janamsthan. It was ordered that the map of the proposed land marked for the purpose should clearly indicate the boundaries and be sent by the Deputy Commissioner to the Commissioner.

Thereafter, Dr Dhavan's submission was that several orders were passed to consider which lands were to be allotted for the Masjid (Masjid Janamsthan to Rajjab Ali and Mohd. Asghar). Ultimately on 10 October 1865, it was ordered that possession of the land be immediately given and acknowledgment should be taken. Finally, on 19 October 1865, it was reported that the proceedings regarding the handing over of the land had been completed, and the acknowledgement was also confirmed.

After going through the documents, the Allahabad High Court had analysed the position and had given findings and

[284]As was the practice during British rule.

also gave the history of Rajjab Ali and Mohd. Asghar and the claim of their relation with Mir Baqi, the man who was said to have constructed the Babri Mosque on Babur's orders. The court also analysed whether the authorities under British Rule acted judicially while conducting such enquiries. The High Court also brought out the position that there is a distinction between the existence of a mosque and a building being used to offer namaz. But who were Rajjab Ali and Mohd. Asghar? This question was delved into by the Allahabad High Court in its judgement.[285]

> ***2336.*** *The above documents though show that some grant was allowed to Mir Rajjab Ali and Mohd. Asghar but it does not appear that any kind of inquiry was made by the authorities concerned and if so, what was the basis therefore. According to the claim of Muslims, the Commander of Babar, who was responsible for construction of the building in dispute was Mir Baqi while Mir Rajjab Ali claimed himself to be the son-in-law of the daughter of grandson of Syed Baqi. Mohd. Asghar was son of Mir Rajjab Ali, therefore, the son and father claimed relation with the 4th generation of the alleged original Mutawalli and staked their claim for grant. No material exists to show that earlier such a grant was awarded by anyone though stated by the aforesaid two persons. If we go by the averments of the plaint that the alleged waqf was created in 1528, it is wholly untrustworthy to find out that in the last more than 325 years, it could only be the fourth generation or at the best 5th generation. The authorities in 1860-61 were not under a duty to act judicially in this matter and therefore, might not have given any details of their enquiry as to on what basis the alleged enquiry was conducted. Ex facie, to us, the genealogy of Mir Rajjab Ali commencing from Syed Baki who must have existed in 1528*

[285]Justice Sudhir Agarwal, Allahabad High Court Judgment, Para 2393, *Vada Prativada*, https://tinyurl.com/54u2ju8u. Accessed on 18 January 2025.

is unbelievable. It is not out of context that the story of the grant might have been set up by the two persons i.e. father and son for the purpose of obtaining valuable grant from Britishers in their favour. In any case, these documents only show that a financial assistance was provided by the British Government for the purpose of the mosque in question but this by itself may not be proof that the building in dispute was used by Muslims for offering namaz or for Islamic religious purposes to the extent of ouster of Hindu people or otherwise.

2342. *The above documents refer to the cash grant and thereafter the grants of land in lieu of cash grant to Mir Rajab Ali and Mohd. Asghar. Here also there is nothing to support or even to suggest that the Muslims actually attended the disputed building or site for offering namaz at all.*

2345. *Besides, the grant, no doubt was allowed to them in their names, though for maintaining the mosque in question, but the fact remains that there is not even a whisper in any of the above documents that the Muslims visited the place in dispute and offered namaz thereat. On the contrary, continuous visit of Hindus and worship by them at the disputed site is mentioned.*

To add to the above, the fact of grant of additional land by the British was brought in in 1870, for maintenances of the Janamsthan mosque. Another document dated 1931, recorded the presence of Babri Masjid at Plot No. 583 and noted that it was a 'Masjid Waqf Ahde Shahi'. This document also noted that the Chabootra was famous as the birthplace.

To claim recognition as the mosque built by Babur, application that were filed after the communal riots in the year 1934 in Ayodhya against the Bairagis & Hindus of Ayodhya, was relied upon. Reliance was placed on the fact that in 1934, due to communal riots, the domes of the

> *disputed structure and a substantial part were destroyed. However, it was renovated at the cost of the British Government through a Muslim thekedar (contractor). It was submitted that even the Dy. Commissioner Faizabad had passed an order dated 6.10.1934 allowing compensation to be paid for damages to the Babri Mosque, be recovered from the Bairagis and other Hindu people of Ayodhya. This led to notice being published by District Magistrate, Faizabad. This led to the Order dated May 12, 1934 wherein the work of cleaning of Babri Mosque was allowed, so that it could be used for religious purposes.*

All these submissions were leading to a point canvassed by Dr Dhavan that once a property is a mosque, it will always be a mosque. For Senior Parasaran, going through these documents was like going back in time as a trial court lawyer in Chennai. In fact, it was Mr Parasaran who briefed the briefing team about the effect and relevance/non-relevance of these documents. This happened in many cases. The assisting lawyers who came to brief Mr Parasaran went back after getting a comprehensive briefing from him. Of course, with age not on Mr Parasaran's side, it was Mr Vaidyanathan who was dealing with these aspects. For the Senior Counsels of Ram Lalla, it was unequivocally clear that the documents were also pointing out that the site was Janamasthan because, during the same time frame when the documents relied upon by the Sunni Board originated, prayers and worship were going on within the disputed site by Ram bhakts. The judge in the 1885 Suit had also identified the Janamasthan within the disputed site. However, it could also not be denied that during this period the British had brought in the artificial division of the inner and outer courtyards, and the disputed structure lay in the inner courtyard within the disputed site.

35

Possession, Ownership and Questions[286]

The minimum that was conceded by the other side was that Ram Chabutra was where prayers to the idol of Ram Lalla were being performed within the disputed structure. However, there was no credible evidence of the dedication of the mosque by Babur and consequent prayers in the mosque till 1934, or any direct documentary evidence proving ownership either. It was submitted that the temple side did not have any documentary evidence of title either.

To prove further the case of possession, ownership and title, the Sunni Board submitted that from 1528 to 1857, there was no whisper and/or demand for any place called Sri Ram's birthplace within the precincts of the Babri Masjid. For the first time, a chabutra was illegally constructed in 1857 within the boundary but outside the inner courtyard of the Babri Masjid. This was in tune with Dr Dhavan's submission that evidence ought to be evaluated from the time the British took over the country in 1857. The critical question was, who was in possession of the disputed property in 1857? Starting from 1857, there were several conflicts culminating in legal proceedings as detailed in the segment dealing with 1885.

The controversies starting from 1857 finally led to the case

[286]Written Submission No. A112, Note on title by Dr. Rajeev Dhavan, Sr. Adv., *Vada Prativada,* https://tinyurl.com/muw27vkx. Accessed on 18 January 2025.
Also *see*: Written Submission No. A120, The Summary Note on OOS 4 of 1989by Dr. Rajeev Dhavan, Sr. Adv., *Vada Prativada,* https://tinyurl.com/5b7y9u7k. Accessed on 18 January 2025.

of 1885. Dr Dhavan had his perspective on the case of 1885. In fact, time and again, Ram Chabutra and the case of 1885 came to be the two angles from where the case had to be analysed. Dr Dhavan's submission was that after 1855 attempts were made by Hindus to dispossess Muslims from the disputed site. However, these attempts were successfully repulsed, leaving Dr Dhavan's clients in title and possession, subject to certain easementary/prescriptive rights of Hindus over Sita Rasoi and Ram Chabutra, which also were only recognized in the proceedings of the 1885 Suit.[287]

The Suit of Nirmohi Akhara had to be met by the Sunni Board. The Board had accepted the presence of Nirmohi Akhara and prayers by Nirmohi Akhara within the suit's premises. The Suit of 1885 stated that Mahant Raghubar Das was the Mahant of Janamasthan. Thus, it was argued by Dr Dhavan that the Mahant filed the suit in his official capacity as the shebait of Janamasthan. The suit of Nirmohi Akhara further stated, according to Dr Dhavan, that the Chabutra where the prayers were offered was the place of birth. It was identified as an area of 17 x 21 feet, and it was prayed that a temple may be allowed to be constructed on the Chabutra. The lawyers had to go back to 1885. A commission was appointed by the Court of Faizabad to prepare the map of the disputed site by conducting a spot inspection. The commission report dated 6 December 1885 was submitted along with a map of the disputed site. Dr Dhavan contended that this map also specifically showed the masjid. On 24 December 1885, the Sub-Judge rejected the prayer for the construction of a temple at the Chabutra. The judgement of 1885 had held that Muslims were praying inside in the masjid and Hindus were praying outside at the Chabutra. Between the Masjid and the Chabutra is a wall built with railings.

It was further pointed out that before the controversy had

[287]Written Submission No. A112, Note on title by Dr. Rajeev Dhavan, Sr. Adv., *Vada Prativada*, https://tinyurl.com/muw27vkx. Accessed on 18 January 2025.

arisen, both Hindus and Muslims had been worshipping at the site, and therefore in 1855, a wall in the form of a railing was erected to avoid controversy, so that Muslims worship inside it and Hindus worship outside it. The contention was that it was erroneously recorded in the judgement of 1885 that the Chabutra was in the possession of the Plaintiffs (Hindus) and belonged to Hindus. However, this finding was set aside in the appeal. The 1885–86 judgement records the written proofs submitted by the Plaintiff (Hindus) and those were limited to:

- Copy of the selection of *Gazetteer of Avadh State*, page 7, printed by the order of the Government
- Journal of the Asiatic Society relating to the translation of Ayodhya Mahant

It was thus pointed out that even in 1885, 'when a claim was made over the Chabutra, Hindus had no actual evidence to substantiate their pleas, except two.'[288]

Therefore, it was concluded that there was no evidence to show that the ownership of the land was in favour of the Mahant, who, in the Sunni Board's submissions, was representing Hindus. On the contrary, the presence of the mosque was affirmed.

For the Counsels of Ram Lala, the important aspect was that the Sub-Judge had also recorded while deciding the Suit of 1885, '[…] <u>It is evident that before this controversy arose both Hindus and Muslims offered worship on the place</u>. In the year 1855, after the quarrel between Hindus and Muslims, a wall in the form of the railing was erected to avoid controversy. So that Muslims may worship inside it and Hindus may worship outside it.' Further, the District Judge (in the appeal in the 1985 case) vide judgement dated 18/26.3.1886 had clearly pointed out with respect to ownership and possession that: '*The only question decided in this case is that the position of the parties will be maintained.*'

[288]Ibid.

This was in light of the issues framed in the 1885 Suit: 'In whose possession or ownership are the lands of the Chabutra from "among the parties?"' Finally, the Judicial Commissioner, Oudh (Hon'ble W. Young) in his judgement dated 2.9.1886 held as under:

> *[...] The Hindus seem to have got very limited rights of access to certain spots within the precincts adjoining the mosque and they have for a series of years been persistently trying to increase their rights and to erect building over two spots in the enclosure [...]*

The observation of a limited right to access was sought to be developed by the other side. It was submitted that Hindus have only the right to access and pray on the land in limited areas. Ownership of the land remains in the hands of Muslims. Dr Dhavan laid stress on the proceedings which resulted in the eviction of the Sadhus, Fakirs, and Nihangs from the inner courtyard to claim his client's exclusive possession of the inner courtyard. The claim of illegalities perpetrated by the clients of Senior Parasaran and Mr Vaidyanathan was vehemently argued. Dr Dhavan listed out the illegal acts. It was reported that,[289]

> *The Times of India reported Dr Dhavan stating that '[...] the court should keep in mind the illegalities committed by Hindu parties to prevent Muslims from offering namaz at the disputed structure [...]'.*

Dr Dhavan then pointed out towards the various intrusions into the disputed structure/mosque and the court since 1858, the time when Nihang Singh Fakir Khalsa ruled in favour of removing such illegal entrance from the premises and restricting the Hindus to the outer courtyard at Ram Chabutra since then. As often happens, lawyers for both sides were making every

---

[289]'SC trims time for Ayodhya arguments by a day to October 17', *The Times of India*, 5 October 2019, https://tinyurl.com/yc4twwf2. Accessed on 18 January 2025.

possible attempt to find positive and relevant findings for their clients from the same piece of paper. Dr Dhavan's response to Ram Lalla's side producing evidence with an attempt to prove continuous prayer was with the reasoning that the right to prayer does not entail ownership and absence of prayer does not cause loss in title—this point was made with some emphasis. 'Sr. Adv. Dhavan rhetorically asked whether the right to prayer entitles the Hindu parties to ownership. He asserted that belief and historical texts alone cannot confer the Hindu parties with the title.'[290] On the affirmative side, Dr Dhavan sought to substantiate that his clients had historical possession of the disputed site, and that his clients were never dispossessed from the disputed site prior to the disputed site being placed under the custody of the court-appointed receiver in December 1949.

Several points were raised to show that possession of the disputed property lay with Dr Dhavan's clients before the suits were filed. These documents were also being used to affirm ownership and title by the Sunni Board. The claim was mostly based on events between 1934 and 1949, including the disputes between the Mahants of Nirmohi Akhara and the Shia-Sunni dispute over the disputed land, pre-Independence. The history of the controversy was reiterated.

The first set of evidence for Dr Dhavan arose from the proceedings following the riots of 1934. In 1934, due to communal riots, a substantial part of the disputed structure, including the domes, was destroyed. However, it was renovated at the cost of the British Government through a Muslim thekedar. Further, upon an application moved by Muslims, a fine was imposed on the Bairagis and other Hindu persons of Ayodhya to recover the estimated cost of repairs to the Babri Masjid. This finally resulted in an order permitting the clients of Dr Dhavan to receive permission to get the disputed structures ready for

---

[290]'Day 59 Arguments, Ayodhya Title Dispute', *Supreme Court Observer*, 14 October 2019, https://tinyurl.com/mr34vf7k. Accessed on 18 January 2025.

religious purposes. Following the repairs of the Babri Masjid, there were claims moved by the thekedar who carried out repair works about non-payment of his fees. The thekedar (the then approved contractor PWD) Thavar/Zahoor Khan, pursuant to detailed enquiry first by the assistant engineer PWD and then by another report, recommended the payment of Rs 6,825 for the repair of the Babri Masjid, Ayodhya. There were still some disputes left concerning payment. Documents supporting all these transactions were brought to the attention of the court.

The second set of evidence dealt with the presence of a *Pesh Imam* and the salary paid to the Imam. A Pesh Imam is the one who leads the prayers. These documents showed that after the riots of 1934, the mosque was handed over to Muslims after repairs and that continuous prayers were being held in the mosque. Further, it was submitted that since there were prayers, the need to pay the Imam arose.

The third set of evidence related to the suit filed by Mahant Ram Charan Das against Raghunath Das and Ors, being Regular Suit No. 95/1941, regarding properties of Nirmohi Akhara which included the Chabutra which, according to the submissions, was allegedly described as Janambhoomi Mandir. This suit too, it was contended, accepted the existence of the Babri Masjid. Again, a Commissioner's report came on record which accepted Hindu prayers at the site and the presence of the mosque. The suit ended with a compromise and the presence of the Babri Masjid was again noted.

Shia-Sunni Conflict

The fourth set of evidence emanated from the Shia-Sunni conflict. The Shia Central Board of Waqf, UP, sent a notice to the UP Sunni Central Waqf Board stating that the Commissioner of Waqfs had wrongly included the mosque as a Sunni mosque in Suit No. 29 of 1945. The notification was later set aside by the Supreme Court in 1966, setting at naught the claims by the Sunni Board concerning the notification. However, at that time, the conflict between the Shia and Sunni Muslims seemed to have reached its zenith. A case was thereafter filed by the Shia Central Board of Waqf, claiming rights to the Babri Mosque. Both the Shias and the Sunnis were deposed to have offered namaz at the site.

The suit of the Shia Central Board of Waqf was dismissed and the mosque was held to be a Sunni mosque. The Shia-Sunni conflict originated from the suit filed by the Shias.[291] It read as follows:

> *Para no. 1: That Sayyad Abdul Baqi got constructed a beautiful masjid during era of King Babar, which is situated at Birth place of Lord Ram in Ayodhya, District Faizabad which is known as King Babar.*
>
> *Para no. 5: […] Pucca Masjid, which is known as Babri Masjid, which is situated in Mohalla Birth place of Lord Rama, Ayodhya City, Pargana Haveli, Avadh, Tehsil and District Faizabad.*

But the most interesting was the judgement in this suit. The reason being that the Sunni side had relied upon gazetteers and hearsay evidence in the context of history. Be it a case between Hindus and Muslims or a case between Muslims and Muslims, no God allows for spirits to be summoned in a court of law to give evidence. Not even the lords of laws, the judges themselves take risks to summon spirits. It would be interesting to find out if judges would like to continue as judges if spirits frequented their courts in their full grandeur to give statements on oath. The judge in the Shia-Sunni case too relied upon hearsay of people and recordings of gazetteers, and did not bother to connect directly

[291]VOL-73 (P.V. YOGESWARAN, EXHIBITS) at serial no. 1, https://tinyurl.com/mw8jtaju. Accessed on 18 January 2025.

with the spirits. The judgement dated 30.03.1946[292] held inter alia as follows:

> *The Gazetteer of this district also contains references to this mosque at references to this mosque at Pp 173–174. It shows that according to local affirmations, Babar came to Ajodhia in 1528 A.D. and halted here for a week, during which he destroyed the Janamasthan temple and on its site built a mosque using largely the materials of the old structure. The author then goes on to remark that the record of the visit is to be found in Musalman historians but it must have occurred about the time of Babar's expedition to Bihar. The Ist. settlement report also gives the same history of this mosque and adds that according to soyders (sik) memoirs of Babar, the Emperor encamped about 5 or 6 miles from Ajodhia and stayed for a week, selting the surrounding country, though it was remarkable that his doings at Ajodhia were wanting in his own memoirs (Baharauama) (sik).*
>
> *The history of the mosque in the Gazetteer of the settlement report was also sought to be impugned (sic) on the ground that Babar's visit to Ajodhia was not mentioned in any historical work and the settlement officer was not required to make any such investigation. I am unable to accept these contentions also as the books (sic) are works (sic) of reference and admissible under S.57 of the Evidence Act. Moreover, in dealing with matters like the present when no direct evidence is available, such works based on investigation on the spot and local tradition assume great importance and unless disproved by superior evidence, must be accepted as containing a correct history of the subjects mentioned therein […]*

---

[292] Exhibit A-42 to the Judgment at page no. 2522, https://tinyurl.com/5n6nsewh. Accessed on 18 January 2025.

Finally, the judge held the mosque to be a Sunni mosque. It was noted:

> *Then, there is the admitted fact that within living memory the Imams and the Muezzins in the mosque have been Sunnis, that they have been paid by mutawallis who have been Shias, and that Faranech (sic), which is recited by Sunnis only and not by Shias (amongst whom it is prohibited) has been allowed by the mutawallis and paid for by them. In this connection, I may refer to Ex. A 20 which is a deed executed by H. Zaki in 1936 agreed to pay the arrears to M. Abdul Ghuffer the Imam, and A 11, the accounts furnished by Kalab Husain (P.W.8.). These facts are strongly suggestive of the fact that the founder of the mosque was a Sunni as had he been a Shia, the funds for its maintenance would not have been utilized for Waqf Act.*

Dr Dhavan then relied upon a deed of Nirmohi Akhara which put down in writing the customs of Nirmohi Akhara and documents which sought to change the Mutawalli of the mosque by the Sunni Board. Use of the mosque as waqf was sought to be proved through Income Expenditure accounts. Lastly, he again relied upon surreptitious placing of idols, letters exchanged in 1949 between the then Superintendent of Police, the then Deputy Commissioner and District Magistrate of Faizabad and other position holders in the government, and finally the order of attachment of the property when the receiver took over the property. To add to this, there were oral testimonies of witnesses stating that they had offered namaz in the disputed structure between 1934 and1949. Since some Hindu parties had accepted this fact, hence only for the period of 1934 to 1949, the issue of offering prayers in a mosque where there was no evidence of dedication to the Almighty, prayers in the mosque not being proven to have been offered from 1528 to 1934, was not of much consequence. For the team, the issue of consequence was why prayers in the mosque were not offered, and why no document of title existed in favour of the mosque from 1528 to 1857. There was complete absence of evidence of prayers in the mosque from 1528 till 1934. On the contrary, evidence was submitted for consideration of continued prayers from the railings to the Janamasthan below the central dome and parikrama of the whole site, while Ram Lalla's worship continued within the disputed site at the Chabutra also.

Claims of continued uninterrupted possession and continuously using the disputed site were building into a submission of waqf by user, or into the dedication of the disputed property as a waqf or a mosque by continued uninterrupted prayers automatically and not by purchase of property, ownership or dedication. Justice Agarwal in the Allahabad High Court judgement had held the disputed structure to be a mosque on the principle of waqf by user, while Justice Khan had held the disputed structure to be a mosque as it was considered so for centuries. The case for Ram Lalla was not disputing that there existed a building of mosque with the presence of identities of temple like Hindu motifs and figurines which were standing on old kasauti pillars of a Hindu temple; the team, however, was disputing that any dedication took place of the structure as a mosque, or that even the slightest evidence existed of regular prayers held till the year 1934 which the courts could consider. On the contrary, Ram Lalla's counsels were asserting that in spite of the disputed building being present there, prayers to Ram Lalla never stopped at the disputed site and everyone treated the disputed site as Ram Janmasthan. Dr Dhavan's stress was on the fact that continued possession was evidence of ownership. News reports caught interesting exchange reflecting the sense of the courtroom as the final countdown had started.

> *Justice Chandrachud intervened to ask about the Hindus' possession of the outer courtyard as there was documentary evidence since 1858 showing the setting up of the Ram*

Chabutra. Dhavan responded saying Hindus came in from the eastern gate which was opened for them to pray as the only right they had was the right to pray and nothing else. Justice Bobde then asked if that admission did not dilute his claim of exclusive possession. 'Not at all', responded Dhavan, and submitted that Hindus had only claimed prescriptive rights. Dhavan then asserted that there was nothing on record, no evidence to show the Hindus to be the proprietors of the disputed land. They claimed rights, but were only granted right of prescription by the district court, yet they claim the right to build a temple he argued.

After answering some questions posed by the bench, the senior advocate said he had 'noticed something very interesting during this hearing... All your lords questions have been directed towards me, not them (Hindu parties).'[293]

Taken aback, Justice Chandrachud said Dhavan's remark was 'completely unwarranted'. But Dhavan retorted, 'It is not unwarranted though I am duty bound to answer the questions put by the bench.'[294]

CS Vaidyanathan immediately objected and called the comments 'unwarranted'. 'It's not unwarranted at all...I am bound to answer...But perhaps your lordships could have asked them some questions too', he replied.[295]

This was also the time that things were getting a tad dramatic. Though there had been a bit of exchange between the Bar and

---

[293]Chaudhary, Nilashish, '[Ayodhya Hearing] [Day 38]: 'Belief Will Not Give Title', Submits SR ADV Rajeev Dhavan', *Live Law*, 14 October 2019, https://tinyurl.com/y23dkrf6. Accessed on 22 July 2025.

[294]'Muslim Parties asks SC: Why all questions directed at us?', *The Times of India*, 15 October 2019, https://tinyurl.com/v8dz6bsz. Accessed on 18 January 2025.

[295]Chaudhary, Nilashish, '[Ayodhya Hearing] [Day 38]: 'Belief Will Not Give Title', Submits SR ADV Rajeev Dhavan', *Live Law*, 14 October 2019, https://tinyurl.com/y23dkrf6. Accessed on 22 July 2025

the Bench, which deviated from the absolute courtesy shown to the Bench by the Bar in the opinion of some, no one expected the turn of events that would now unfold. For team Ram Lalla, it could be said that the workload at the time of the arguments between Senior Parasaran and Mr Vaidyanathan was 40:60, though the preparation workload on Mr Vaidyanathan, Mr Ranjit Kumar and Mr Narasimha was hundred per cent. It appeared to team Ram Lalla that Dr Dhavan had taken more than eighty-five per cent of the workload on himself. Dr Dhavan's proposition, his industry, and his academic viewpoints were absolutely impressive, so it must have also been the support he received from Mr Jilani, Ejaz Maqbool, and other team members. Burning the midnight oil would have been an understatement. The assisting team members of Ram Lalla unanimously agreed that Ejaz Maqbool's management of the case as Advocate-on-Record was exemplary. His compilation of documents and submissions was perfect. He was organizing all the documents of the case for the ease of not only his team, but also for the court. He inspired team Ram Lalla to get even better organized. But while lawyers appreciated the ability of the opposing counsels, they also agreed to disagree with each other's submissions barring some points of agreement.

36

The Last Act

For first-time visitors to the court, and even for full-time lawyers, at times interesting questions arise in courts. Can a place become a site of religious importance just by offering prayers over a period? Or is it that a place does not become a place of religious significance merely by offering prayers over a period by some people? Or should people be showing continuous prayers and religious beliefs at a particular place of worship over a long period to claim any religious rights over it? In this case, such questions were posing problems for both sides—perhaps less for one, and more for the other. Team Ram Lalla believed that it had answered the questions and proved its point about the worship of Ram Lalla at the disputed site through the evidence as reflected by travelogues, gazetteers, and the ASI report, and by statements of both Hindu and Muslim witnesses. It was now the turn of the Sunni Board to jump over such hurdles.

Dr Dhavan had interpreted a waqf as an irrevocable dedication to Allah of a property. As per his submissions, the mosque stood dedicated as waqf by continuous use of the land for religious purposes as Dr Dhavan's clients had enjoyed unbroken possession since the construction of the mosque in the 17th century.[296]

---

[296]Written Submission No. A123, The Note on the Issue of Wakf by Dr. Rajeev Dhavan, Sr. Adv., *Vada Prativada*, https://tinyurl.com/5y9urtrr. Accessed on 18 January 2025. Also *see*: Written Submission No. A120, The Summary Note on OOS 4 of 1989 by Dr. Rajeev Dhavan, Sr. Adv., *Vada Prativada*, https://tinyurl.com/5b7y9u7k. Accessed on 18 January 2025.

Also *see*: Written Submission No. A112, Note on title by Dr. Rajeev Dhavan, Sr. Adv., *Vada Prativada*, https://tinyurl.com/muw27vkx. Accessed on 18 January 2025.

Dr Dhavan's case[297] was that the disputed site marked out by the letters A B C D was waqf property, because of the long usage of the property as a site of religious worship by the Muslim community.

He contended that the concept of a waqf had a broad connotation in Islamic Law. Therefore, it was possible that even in the absence of an express dedication of the disputed site as a mosque, the long use of the disputed site for public worship as a mosque gave the property in question the status of waqf by user.

This premise was based on a point of history as claimed, that since the construction of the mosque by Emperor Babur in 1528 till its desecration on 22/23 December 1949, prayers had been offered in the mosque. Hence, the disputed property has been the site of religious worship. Moreover, as contended earlier, Dr Dhavan reiterated that possession of the disputed property continued with his clients and the use of the mosque for the performance of public religious worship substantiated the point. The absence of any concrete evidence of dedication as a waqf by Babur and even the absence of any dedication deed was accepted by the Sunni Board. However, it was submitted that the disputed site had its character as waqf property by long use. The long presence and the alleged use of the property also led to the claim that the Sunni Board by adverse possession had got ownership rights over the property, even if a temple or a non-Islamic structure existed below the disputed structure, since they had absolute control, ownership and possession of the property from 1528 to 1949. The submission affirmatively advanced was 'once a mosque, always a mosque'. Even if proper prayers in a mosque are no longer offered, or it is demolished or abandoned, it remains a mosque and its character does not change.

It was submitted that the performance of prayers in the mosque had to be inferred from the various grants of the British

---

[297]Written Submission No. A123, The Note on the Issue of Wakf by Dr. Rajeev Dhavan, Sr. Adv., *Vada Prativada*, https://tinyurl.com/5y9urtrr. Accessed on 18 January 2025.

which were converted into rent-free land, and the various court orders for eviction of Nihangs, etc., as well as the judgement in the *Shia v Sunni*[298] suit dated 30.03.1946 which accepted the mosques as a Sunni mosque. From 1858, it was argued that there was a continuous official record, like administrative and judicial orders, to show recognition of the building as a mosque. The waqf by user argument was upheld by Justice Khan in the Allahabad High Court, though the two other judges did not agree. In any event, it was submitted that the mosque was being used for religious purposes and thus was a waqf as established by user even if direct evidence of prayers in the mosque till 1934 was not available. Once a building is used as a mosque, it continues to be a mosque. Judgements like *Mehraj Din v. Ghulam Muhammad*[299] were relied upon where the Lahore Court held the land to be waqf by user since Mohammedans had been lighting diyas and saying prayers at the property. Similarly, the judgement in the case of *Abdul Ghafoor v. Rahmat Ali*[300] was used to argue that a waqf may, even in the absence of dedication, be established by evidence of long use. Once established, a waqf is permanent and cannot become private property by disuse. Cases like *N.R. Abdul Azeez v. E. Sundaresa Chettiar*[301] had established the rule that 'once a mosque, always a mosque'. However, the problematic case was the case of *Miru and Ors. Vs. Rajgopal*[302]. The Rajgopal

---

[298]Supra 13.
In 1945, there was a litigation between the Shias and Sunnis in Suit 29/1945 which was decided on 30 March 1946. (Part O - Para 703, p. 815)

[299](1931) ILR 12 Lah 540. Also *see*: Written Submission No. A123, The Note on the Issue of Wakf by Dr. Rajeev Dhavan, Sr. Adv., *Vada Prativada*, https://tinyurl.com/5y9urtrr. Accessed on 18 January 2025.

[300]AIR 1930 Oudh 245. Also *see*: Written Submission No. A123, The Note on the Issue of Wakf by Dr. Rajeev Dhavan, Sr. Adv., *Vada Prativada*, https://tinyurl.com/5y9urtrr. Accessed on 18 January 2025.

[301]AIR 1993 Mad 169. Also *see*: Written Submission No. A123, The Note on the Issue of Wakf by Dr. Rajeev Dhavan, Sr. Adv., *Vada Prativada*, https://tinyurl.com/5y9urtrr. Accessed on 18 January 2025.

[302]AIR 1935 All 891. Also *see*: Written Submission No. A123, The Note on the Issue

case was one of easement rights. The dispute was with a Hindu landlord who had given his land to Muslims for prayers. Later, the Muslims wanted to construct a pucca mosque. What the court held was interesting:

> *Where therefore the Court finds that a mosque or a temple has stood for a long time and worship has been performed in it by the public, it is open to the Court to infer that the building does not stand merely there by leave and license of the site, but that the land itself is a dedicated property and the site is a consecrated land no longer the private property of the original owner.*

For the temple's side, the law as held in the Rajgopal case had clarified that this rule would apply to both temples and mosques. This land of less than 1,500 sq. yd was being used as a temple throughout.

It was in this background that the case entered the final phase for the nonagenarian. Senior Parasaran was quite convinced that Ayodhya was his last case because of the laws of nature. He had already argued Sabrimala once; a judgement had been passed and only a review was pending. He wondered whether he would be able to argue that case or his time would come before that. Every evening, there was a meeting with the team. Rarely did a day go by when detailed discussions on the other side's arguments would not take place. For team Ram Lalla, not a shred of evidence had been produced by the Sunni Board to establish worship at the disputed site, or the Board's possession and control over the disputed property, marked by the letters A B C D throughout from the date of construction in 1528 until the erection of the railing by the British government in 1857, first over a span of 325 years and then till 1934.

As far as the timeline from 1857 was concerned, the

---

of Wakf by Dr. Rajeev Dhavan, Sr. Adv., *Vada Prativada*, https://tinyurl.com/5y9urtrr. Accessed on 18 January 2025.

presence and worship of Ram Lalla was always continuing and going on within the disputed site and was institutionalized within the property marked by the letters A B C D. The construction of the railing in 1857 did not confer any property rights but against the background of the preceding riots, acted as an expedient measure to ensure law and order. Any serious attempt to offer prayers in the mosque was made only in time from 1934 to 1949. There was positive evidence of worship of Ram Lalla also in the period from 1857 to 1887 and later, while the Sunni Board's evidence started to come much later. In the minds of team Ram Lalla, it was not disputed that Dr Dhavan's client did offer prayers in the mosque between 1934 and 1949 when Ram bhakts kept praying within the disputed area at the same time. It was also not disputed by some Hindu/Temple parties that Ram bhakts were carrying out parikrama and asserting title which had resulted in many controversies since much earlier than 1934; the only part of the prayers that was disputed by the Sunni Board was prayers of Ram bhakts from the iron railing towards the central dome from the time the railing was put up. But then why was there an absence of evidence of any offering of namaz from 1528 to 1934?

The courts were closed during Dussehra 2019 for a week, which meant that there was enough time to rest as well as to prepare. A long-time associate and former chamber junior, Anirudh felt a change in attitude and energy level in Senior Parasaran. The nonagenarian was a bit more aggressive in his thoughts as the end of the case was in sight. Anirudh had seen the same energy in Mr Parasaran in his closing submissions for the Nagaraja case. Mr Parasaran, in the Nagaraja case, was defending the insertion of Article 16(4)A in the Constitution of India, enabling reservations in promotions for Scheduled Castes and Scheduled Tribes in government jobs, and Anirudh was assisting him. Even on matters where society had varied viewpoints, and passions could run high, like in interstate water disputes, reservations, or claim to a piece of land having conflicting religious connotations for communities as in Ayodhya, Mr Parasaran believed that if the record of the case allowed for a point to be placed, the court had to be assisted with great endeavour. This also meant that the media would splash headlines.

More often than not, Senior Parasaran would pause for sometime intermittently while discussing his points. The pauses were longer. Anirudh shared his observations about the change in body language with other team members but these were brushed aside. As detailed written submissions were being finalized, Anirudh knew from his fourteen years' association with Senior Parasaran that none of them would be referred to. The morning's handwritten notes would be used instead, or perhaps an extempore. Only Mr Parasaran would know what he would argue, or maybe at that time, Mr Parasaran himself did not know what he wanted to argue.

Next morning again, the change in body language was palpable. Senior Parasaran was trying to walk without support, clearing his voice and staring at blank pages and blank walls while going through his notes. His reams of notes had of course highlighted the order dated 3 March 1951 which stated: *'[...] Moreover, it is a matter of admission between the parties that there are several other mosques in the mohalla in question. The local Muslims will not, therefore, be put to much inconvenience, if the interim injunction remains in force during the pendency of the case.'*

The order of 2 November 1886 was also prominently remembered where the Judicial Commissioner had observed: *'The matter is simply that Hindus of Ajudhia want to erect a new temple of marble [...] over the supposed holy spot in Ajudhia said to be the birthplace of Sri Ram Chandar. Now this spot is situated within the precincts of the grounds surrounding a mosque constructed some 350 years ago owing to the bigotry and tyranny of the Emperor Baber—who purposely chose this holy spot according to Hindu legend—as the site of his mosque.'*

The training and lessons of the nonagenarian for his pupils were unequivocal: there should not be emotional points in a lawyer's submissions but points from the record of the case. Even rhetoric is to be from the records of the case. While all others tried to assist with their points, Anirudh chose discretion and assisted only with what was asked for. He stayed back.

The first point to answer concerned the documents as brought in by the other side. Through the aid of these documents, it was contended by the Sunni Board that the British granted recognition to the mosque and title claims to the mosque of the Sunni Board. The question to be answered was if the British had allowed grants in favour of Dr Dhavan's clients, did the British drive the Ram bhakts out of the disputed site in question, or did they allow the prayers to Ram Lalla Virajman to continue in the same premises?

To address the argument of 'once a mosque, always a mosque', Mr Parasaran's submission was it would be an error to recognize the place as one on which a mosque was constructed, vested in the Almighty, and not test the history of prayers on the spot. Such an approach would result in carving out a particular area conquered by virtue of an act of 'Emperor Babar', and taking it away from a set of Indian citizens and their religious practices. Hence, the entire material on the records of the case had to be examined by the court to reach a decision.[303] The reliance of the Sunni Board was on the cash grant for the upkeep and maintenance of the mosque from the Royal Treasury which was continued by the Emperor of Delhi and the Nawab Wazir of Oudh, and the grant of revenue-free land made by the British Government in the villages of Sholapur and Bahoranpur in the

---

[303]Written Submission No. A125 The Submissions in Re. Suit 4 on behalf of Mr. K. Parasaran, Sr. Adv., *Vada Prativada*, https://tinyurl.com/249nstm4. Accessed on 18 January 2025.

vicinity of Ayodhya. For the Sunni Board, these sufficiently proved the titles.

The cash grant or grant of revenue-free land was not a recognition of the title to the mosque; a decision on the title requires that all competing claims be enquired into which was not done. What kind of enquiry was held? The Allahabad High Court too had come to the finding that no inquiry had been conducted by the Commissioner before any order was issued regarding revenue-free land. Grant of revenue-free land only means that the revenue was not to be deposited to the government but was to be used by those individuals who were made beneficiaries of the grant. The grant for maintenance did prove that a building existed but did not prove that the building was used as a mosque nor did the grant prove that Muslims visited the site and offered namaz there.

With continuous outbreaks of riots like those in the 1850s, 1870s, 1934, etc., and continuous controversies arising, with parties running to various authorities and courts to get the dispute settled, it was contended that the present case was not one where the Sunni Board could claim continuous peaceful possession and, therefore, adverse possession. In light of the afore-stated point, Senior Parasaran who in the suit of the Sunni Board, was representing Mahant Suresh Das (who was supporting Ram Lalla's case) advanced submissions to which media persons gave much attention. The nonagenarian stressed that Babur had destroyed the temple and erected a mosque at the Janamasthan of Ram as recorded by an order dated 2 November 1886, passed by the Judicial Commissioner. Hence, he urged the court to 'right a historical wrong.' Mr Parasaran had the order of 3 March 1951 in his mind. It immediately generated some heated questions and some objections reported by *Live Law*.[304]

---

[304]'Ayodhya [Day-39]: Need to Correct Historical Wrong Committed by Babur, Hindu party tells SC', *Live Law*,15 October 2019, https://tinyurl.com/yppsudt2. Accessed on 18 January 2025.

A 'historical wrong' was committed by Mughal emperor Babur after his conquest of India over 433 years ago by constructing a mosque at the birthplace of Lord Ram in Ayodhya and it needs to be rectified, a Hindu party told the Supreme Court on Tuesday in the Ram Janmbhoomi-Babri Masjid land dispute case.

A 5-judge Constitution bench, headed by Chief Justice Ranjan Gogoi, was told by former Attorney General and senior advocate K. Parasaran, appearing for the Hindu party, that there were several mosques in Ayodhya where Muslims can pray but Hindus cannot change the birth place of Lord Ram.

'Please do the reparation of a historical wrong committed by foreign ruler Babur who came here and said that I am the Emperor and my fiat is the law,' the senior lawyer, appearing for Mahant Suresh Das, who is a defendant in a law suit filed by the Sunni Board and others in 1961, told the apex court on the 39th day of hearing in the case.

'Muslims can pray in any other mosque in Ayodhya. There are 55–60 mosques in Ayodhya alone. But, for Hindus this is the birthplace of Lord Ram[...]which we cannot change,' he told the bench, which also comprised justices S. A. Bobde, D. Y. Chandrachud, Ashok Bhushan and S. A. Nazeer.

'Hindus have been fighting for centuries for the birthplace of Ram which cannot be changed and for Muslims all mosques are equal,' Parasaran said, adding that foreigners like Mughals, Portuguese, French and Britishers came to rich India and plundered it which led this country to poverty.

[...] Parasaran said it has been said that the 'ancient mosque' was built by Babur more than 433 years ago after his conquest of India, and hence the title of the mosque is 'traceable to the conquest and occupation of Emperor Babar' but it has not been proved by the Muslim parties.

He then referred to the findings of a Faizabad court in 1886 on a lawsuit filed by Mahant Raghubar Das and said it was held the mosque was built on the land held sacred by Hindus. 'The burden of proof is on Muslim parties to show that this finding, that the mosque was built on land held sacred by Hindus, is wrong. Even where a case is decided in favour of a party, he can attack findings adverse to him in the appeal filed by the other party,' he said.

While he was making submissions that there was a need to correct a historical wrong, senior advocate Rajeev Dhavan, appearing for Muslim parties, raised objections that Parasaran was entering into new arguments by referring to theory of conquests by Babur. The bench then said that it will allow him to make rejoinder submissions.

Parasaran, along with another senior advocate C. S. Vaidyanathan, said there was a lot of interruption from the other side and the court should set things right as this is the case of public right.

The bench asked several questions to Parasaran on legal issues like law of limitation, doctrine of adverse possession and questions as to how Muslims are ousted from seeking title over 2.77-acre disputed land at Ayodhya.

It asked whether Muslims can seek a decree of declaration with regard to the disputed property even after the demolition of the alleged mosque on December 6, 1992.

'They say, once a mosque always a mosque, do you support this?' the bench asked Parasaran. 'No. I do not support it. I will say once a temple always a temple,' Parasaran replied.

Both sides were now in earnest argument, albeit a tad heated at times. However, it was not that objectivity and humour were being lost in court. As soon as Mr Parasaran said, 'No, I do not support it. I will say once a temple, always a temple,' the contest between 'once a mosque, always a mosque' and 'once a temple, always a temple' had the whole courtroom in splits. The nonagenarian had responded in a split second. His impulsive aggressive tone had brought a big smile even on his face and also on the faces of the other side. Similarly, the court had interesting questions to ask Dr Dhavan about his student days. Dr Dhavan did reveal some stories of his student days, yes with a hearty smile, while others were left for pleasant banter for another day.

> *[...] Parasaran said Muslims have claimed the title under the doctrine of adverse possession as well and it meant that they will have to accept that the temple had the prior title over it.*
>
> *The bench asked whether a person can be granted the title in a case on account of 'long user' if both the parties do not have substantial documents to establish the ownership and said, 'Does the long use fructify into the title?'*
>
> *'This destroys the other person's title,' Parasaran replied. Later, Vaidyanathan commenced arguments for the same Hindu party and alleged that Muslims gave up their arguments of adverse possession and is now seeking the property on the grounds of dedication of property as wakf on account of long user. This led to a verbal duel between Vaidyanathan and Dhavan. The court intervened which led to resumption of the proceedings [...]*[305]

Things alternated between light-hearted banter and heated arguments after 38 days of hearing. For Mr Vaidyanathan, the submission that the Ram Lalla side was claiming rights based on illegalities was mischievous, unfortunate, and intended to promote communally divisive feelings. The illegalities were dealt with as and when they arose, and the claim on the land stood

---

[305]Ibid.

for centuries. Mr Vaidyanathan submitted that the Ram Lalla's side had scrupulously avoided any argument that would incite such communal divide and disrupt amity and peace. Arguments such as wanton destruction of Hindu temples, loss of life, and atrocities committed against Hindus could not decide a property dispute. It could not be denied that duels and exchanges were now taking place at times. But these things do happen sometimes in courts.

Mr Vaidyanathan's submission was that Babur illegally constructed a mosque as the Sunni Board could not discharge the burden of proof that the mosque was constructed on vacant land. His arguments went into the last day of the hearing. The case had stretched for a good time from August to October. It was the 38th day of hearing, and it was creating mental fatigue for those lawyers who were used to being part of a new case each day.

37

Prayers and Oral Evidence

The hearing was to begin on 16 October; there were rumours of some settlement being reached by some of the parties. Not all parties were participating in the mediation. Hence, such claims were not legally tested.[306] Some lawyers for the other side wondered how such a settlement, even if reached, was making its way to the press.[307] Though one of the counsels for the Sunni Board, Sayed Shahid Rizwi, stated that a settlement had been reached, he urged every party to read it and then sign it.[308] Opinions were not unanimous.[309]

In the eyes of the law, even if some of the parties did not agree to the solution, the case had to go on. Hence, written submissions and notes were being filed by both parties to highlight their stands. It was 16 October 2019, and time for Mr Vaidyanathan to reply to Suit 4 of the Sunni Board. He contended that the Sunni Board could not prove that the property was in absolute, continuous, uninterrupted possession and control of the Board, which had to result in the ouster and dispossession of the prior legal owner of land Janmabhoomi. Therefore, there could

[306]Rajagopal, Krishnadas, 'Ayodhya mediation panel files settlement document in Supreme Court', *The Hindu*, 16 October 2019, https://tinyurl.com/2fhjdwfy. Accessed on 18 January 2025.

[307]'Don't accept Ayodhya panel "settlement", shocked at Waqf Board "withdrawing claim": Muslim parties', *The Economic Times*, 18 October 2019, https://tinyurl.com/3vkrjbta. Accessed on 18 January 2025.

[308]'Sunni waqf board counsel favours settlement of Ayodhya dispute', *ANI*, 17 October 2019, https://tinyurl.com/y4cnzrdj. Accessed on 18 January 2025.

[309]'Don't accept Ayodhya panel "settlement", shocked at Waqf Board "withdrawing claim": Muslim parties', *The Economic Times*, 18 October 2019, https://tinyurl.com/3vkrjbta. Accessed on 18 January 2025.

be no claim of adverse possession. By the Board's own admission, there was continuous prayer of Ram Lalla within the disputed site. This would constitute not exclusive possession of the Sunni Board. Possession was also in the hands of Hindus. Finally, while it was accepted that no evidence was led at all of prayers offered till 1934 by any Muslim side, it was submitted that the Sunni Board had brought on record some evidence for the period 1934 to 1949 which was subject matter of consideration by the court.[310] This was the only period for which attempts were made to bring evidence on record with respect to prayers by the Sunni Board. These evidences from the Sunni Board were again disputed by some Hindu sides.

Both sides were making positive averments—for instance, Babur constructed the disputed structure in 1528, and the presence of Ram Lalla and his worship within the disputed site was also common ground between the parties as the case stood on 16 October 2016. As Dr Dhavan had attacked the prayers of Ram bhakts from the iron railing, Mr Vaidyanathan had to go back to the testimonies of witnesses from both the opposing sides.

An admission is the best piece of evidence. Even Muslim witnesses including co-plaintiffs of Suit 4 of the Sunni Board admitted as per Mr Vaidyanathan the continuous faith and worship of Hindu devotees below the central dome as the birthplace of Lord Ram[311]. Therefore, even after the erection of the iron railing in 1857, worship continued towards the central dome. Part of the cross-examination of the witnesses made for interesting reading as Mr Vaidyanathan made an attempt to prove that the area of the disputed structure was only believed to be the birthplace. The case of the temple was sought to be proved

[310]Written Submission No. A104, The Submissions on behalf of Plaintiff in Suit No.5 by Mr. C.S. Vaidyanathan, Sr. Adv., *Vada Prativada*, https://tinyurl.com/4cdy26jd. Accessed on 18 January 2025.

[311]Ibid.

through the Sunni Board's witnesses.[312]

PW-1 Mohd. Hashim: *[...] The place which was attached on 22nd and 23rd December 1949 is called Ram Janam Bhoomi by Hindus and The Babri Masjid by Muslims. In the suit of Gopal Singh Visharad also it has been called Ram Janam Bhoomi by Hindus and The Babri Masjid by Muslims.*

PW-2 Haji Mehboob: *[...] The grilled wall adjoined the wall of the mosque to the south. We call it a masjid and the other party calls it a mandir. The height of the entire boundary was the same. This was a fully constructed building to the west of the courtyard. This was a mosque which others called a mandir [...]*

PW-7 Hasmat Ullah Ansari: *[...] It is true that the place I call Babri Masjid, is called Janambhoomi by Hindus.*

Apart from these admissions of Muslim witnesses as canvassed by Mr Vaidyanathan, there were witnesses brought in to support the case of Ram Lalla too. It could be said that no witness for either side could give a crystal-clear deposition. Most of them were over seventy-five years old, and some impact of fading memory and other effects of old age were apparent. That is where trained judicial minds had to decide based on preponderance of probabilities. Some witnesses of the Hindu side relied upon by Mr Vaidyanathan and contested by Dr Dhavan reflected a classic case of reliance being placed by one side on a witness and the other side punching holes in the witness statement to prove it unreliable. This was done with the testimony of Shri Ram Nath Mishra alias Banarsi Panda. On the day of the testimony, Mr Mishra was ninety years old. A part of his deposition was:

> *The main door in the Lord Ram Janambhoomi premises was from the east which was known as 'Hanumat Dwar'. On both corners of the main gate, black pillars of touchstone*

---

[312]Ibid.

were there with pictures, flowers and leaves and deities. After entering through the main gate, there was a chabutra (platform) towards the south, which was known as 'Ram Chabutra'. On that Ram Chabutra, all the idols of Ram Darbar were there and beneath that was the cave temple (gufa mandir). In the south-east corner of Ram Chabutra, also there were idols under the peepal tree which included idols of Lord Ganesha and Lord Shankar and other deities. Inside the main gate towards the north, there was a huge chhapar (thatched enclosure) which was known as bhandar (store) and in which were kept food grains, utensils, containers, karahi (wok) etc. for cooking purpose. Inside the barred wall towards the west of Ram Chabutra and the bhandar, there was the 'Garbhgrah' (sanctum sanctorum) temple covered by three gumbads (domes). According to elderly people, it was under the central dome that Lord Ram was born as the son of King Dashratha. It was on the basis of this faith and belief that I and all the Hindu devotees of Lord Rama used to have the "darshan" of Sri Ramajnam Bhoomi. It was considered to be a sacrosanct place and a place worth worshipping [...]

Inside the Sri Ram Janambhoomi premises in the domed 'Garbhgrah' 'there were pillars of black touchstone which had images of kalashs (earther pots), flowers and leaves and of deities. Between the years 1928 and 1949, I had seen the picture of Lord Ram hung inside the 'Garbhgrah'. The idol of Lord Rama was there on a slab in the corner of the wall. I had seen this idol placed there till 1949.

In the barred wall, there were two doors, which used to remain locked and those doors were opened and closed by the 'pujaris' of the 'Nirmohi Akhara'. The same very 'pujaris' used to offer prayers and perform 'aarti' at Ram Chabutra and Sita Rasoi etc. We used to arrange 'darshan' of the 'Garbhgrah' for

> *the pilgrims from the railing itself. A donation box was also kept there [...]*

Dr Dhavan's submission attacked this testimony as not reliable as the witness in cross-examination could not reply to photographs shown by the cross-examiner and had stated:

> *'In 1990, I heard that a monkey had caused the collapse of the disputed building whereas that building was so solid that thousands of people also won't have been able to raze it within months even if they wanted to. I do not recall now whether this incident of razing the disputed building took place in the year 1990 or 1992 when monkeys demolished the disputed building. Mulayam Singh was the Chief Minister. At the time, there was firing and curfew was clamped. This building was razed not by two or three monkeys, but only by one monkey. The whole building was razed by just one monkey in three to four hours.*
>
> *That monkey could not be caught and his photograph was published in Janamorcha which was published from Ayodhya. Perhaps it was the government of Shri Kalyan Singh when this building was razed.*[313]

But for team Ram Lalla, his statements about the worship from the iron railing towards the three-domed structure and the faith and belief of Ram bhakts were consistent, which could not be broken.

Similarly, witnesses like Mahant Paramhans Ram Chandra Das who was ninety years old at the time of his deposition, Harihar Prasad Tewari who was eighty-five years old on the date of his deposition, and Devki Nandan Agarwal who was eighty years old at the time of his deposition and deposed that

[313]Summary of deposition, https://tinyurl.com/mr2arh5b. Accessed on 18 January 2025. Para 514 onwards and depositions, *Vada Prativada*, https://tinyurl.com/4aj3fctw. Accessed on 18 January 2025.

with locks being placed on the gate of inner premises, Hindu devotees offered worship from outside since the police did not permit entry into the inner courtyard, proved the point against Dr Dhavan's clients. Devki Nandan Agarwal's deposition also met with an interesting challenge.

The cross-examination of Agarwal was not completed due to the death of the witness; nonetheless, it was put in issue. Dr Dhavan had adverted to the testimony of late Mr Agarwal particularly in regard to the association between the Vishva Hindu Parishad and the Ram Janmabhoomi Nyas. Moreover, in regard to the shifting of the idols, Dr Dhavan in his note of submissions[314] highlighted the following facets pertaining to the evidence of the witness:

> *1. The vigrah (idol) of Ram Lalla was seated in a cradle and installed on Ram Chabutra. This vigrah was movable and therefore in accordance with the wishes of the devotees, it was shifted from Ram Chabutra and installed under the central dome.*
>
> *2. Till December 22, 1949, the idols were not inside the disputed building.*

Late Mr Agarwal was also one of the plaintiffs in Suit 5 of Ram Lalla. In his deposition,[315] he had stated that he was a Vaishnavite and a Hindu and that he was suing as a next friend of Ram Lalla Virajman and Ram Janmabhoomi, with no personal or vested interest, but with an intent of service to the deity.

He had stated that during 1932–34, whenever he went to the disputed place with his mother, he saw the worship of the idol of Lord Ram at Ram Chabutra, saw a picture of Lord Ram inside the disputed structure and the priest taking flowers and garlands from worshippers and offering them from a distance. But the

[314]Ibid.

[315]Ibid.

most relevant part was with respect to prayers from the iron railing:

> *There were two pillars of touchstone at the gate of the disputed structure, which were used for its construction after demolishing the temple which earlier existed there. There were two similar pillars also inside the structure, which could be seen from a distance. But two locks were affixed on the gate of the inner premises of the disputed structure and because of them, the police did not allow anybody to enter inside and worship etc. of Bhagwan Shri Ram Lalla, who was Virajman inside, was done from outside the gate, and non-stop recitation and chanting of name of Lord were being continuously done in the outer premises.*

But the real attack on the testimony of Late Mr Agarwal was on the grounds which went to the root of the matter—he did not worship idols and there was no puja *sthan* (place) in his house; he was unable to state the name of the idol or the number of times he had obtained darshan in 1984–85; his statement regarding his belief that the 'Garbh Griha' was situated at that place where the temple had been demolished was hearsay.

> *During the period from 1932 to 1960, Sanatan Dharma did not influence me, because I had no spare time from studying and thereafter from the practice of law. After 1932, I passed. B.A. in 1940. Then after an interval of 12 years, I again took admission in the University in 1952 and passed the law examination in 1954. Between 1932 and 1940, I did not study any religious book. From 1932 to 1940, I did not hear any discourse, etc. of any saint, mahatma or guru. I did not listen to any discourse of Ramcharitmanas or Bhagwat during this period. Ayodhya Kanda of Ramcharitmanas, written by Tulsidas, was part of the syllabus of subject of Hindi in B.A. examination. Some verses of Kabir Das Ji and Surdas Ji were also included in the course. I cannot say whether I got some*

knowledge about Tulsidas Ji or Kabir Das Ji at that time. At that time, the character of Bhagwan Ram did not have any effect on me in spite of my studying Ayodhya Kanda.

During the period between 1940 to 1952, I did business of brick kiln and also worked as a contractor. I did this work till 1954 during my studies also. During the period from 1940 to 1954, when I was doing business, I had no time to take interest in religion. I never did idol worship. Then Volunteer: that his mother used to worship idols. My wife also used to do idol-worship.

The same went even for witnesses of the Sunni Board. Mohd. Hashim was a witness who was stated to be about seventy-five years of age on the day of the deposition. This witness had sought to prove that *Tabari* was read only in the Babri Masjid and that at times he had offered prayers in the mosque five times, and the prayers of Jumme and Tabari in the disputed structure. He claimed to have read the last prayers on 22 December 1949. In his cross-examination, the witness stated that it was in 1938 that he first went to offer prayers. He further had stated in his cross-examination that prayers were offered five times daily at the disputed site. But what in the opinion of any person cross-examining him would make his testimony unreliable would be the following part from his cross examination:

[...] I do not remember that I mentioned my age 55 years in the affidavit submitted in 1986 with Writ Petition.' (The Affidavit of the Writ Petition was shown to the witness). He said: There are my signatures and thumb impression and age has been written as 55 years [...]

I was married twice. I do not remember when I was married first. I do not remember the year when I was married for the second time. My first wife did not beget any child. My second wife gave me two children, a son and a daughter. I do not remember what is the age of my daughter. My son is in the age group of 25–30 years. My daughter is elder to him. I do not know what was my age at the time of my daughter's birth and son's birth.

[...] It is correct that my memory is weak due to old age but our advocate may be knowing about it [...]

The Sunni Board too relied upon multiple witnesses, and like those witnesses testifying for Hindu parties, even the Sunni Board's witnesses did not give a full-proof account. This is what happens in civil cases and that is why preponderance of probabilities is the norm. A comprehensive view of all the evidence of the case is taken in such cases. The case was on its last stretch when an event took place which took the attention away from the hard toils which all the lawyers, clerks, court staff had put into the case.

Dr Dhavan's submission in rejoinder[316] relied upon the documents of the British period which facilitated grants in favour of the mosque. He read it with the statement of some Hindu parties which accepted submission of evidence of prayers offered in the mosque/disputed structure after 1934 to argue that the disputed site was recognized as a waqf. The stand of the temple side was these documents of the British era were merely grants for maintenance and upkeep of the mosque, and not documents proving title. Dr Dhavan replied that implicit in the grant for maintenance and upkeep of the disputed structure was the British recognition of a mosque and a waqf. Dr Dhavan's contention was that when Babur marched towards India, no unified India existed and it was a fact that there were massive conquests of each

[316]"Written Submission No. A123, The Note on the Issue of Wakf by Dr. Rajeev Dhavan, Sr. Adv., *Vada Prativada*, https://tinyurl.com/5y9urtrr. Accessed on 18 January 2025.

Also *see*: Written Submission No. A120, The Summary Note on OOS 4 of 1989 by Dr. Rajeev Dhavan, Sr. Adv., *Vada Prativada*, https://tinyurl.com/5b7y9u7k. Accessed on 18 January 2025.

other by rulers within India, even of the same faith. There were thousands of such conquests in recorded history—like that of Ashoka. Hence, when India was many sovereign political entities, the argument of invaders attacking India could not be sustained, and therefore, Mr Parasaran's argument of 'historical wrong' could not be relied upon.

Dr Dhavan interpreted the 1886 judgement (Suit of 1885) differently from Senior Parasaran. It was his contention that any ownership rights of Hindus were specifically negated by the 1886 judgement. Since the 1886 judgement negated Hindu contention, Muslims did not file any appeal on mere observations, which was used by Ram Lalla's counsels to argue that Babur built a mosque at the Janamasthan. Dr Dhavan also claimed title by virtue of adverse possession. It was also contended that the premises belonged to his clients; what was destroyed belonged to his clients and his clients were entitled for restoration. The property belonged to the waqf and the whole area including Ram Chabutra was prayed for declaration as a public waqf. The proceedings were reported as follows:[317]

> *On Day 40 of the hearing in the Ram Janmabhoomi-Babri Masjid dispute, Senior Advocate Rajeev Dhawan submitted that the mosque was devoted to God, that even the graveyard was in use and the mosque was a place of peaceful worship by the Muslims till it was torn down by a mischievous crowd. 'The burden of proof [of title] is on the Hindus,' he argued on behalf of the Sunni Waqf Board. 'If Hindus are claiming title from before 1855, we are entitled to it by virtue of adverse possession for 2 centuries. The premises are ours. What was destroyed belonged to us. We are entitled to restoration. We had sought the relief of restitution. The bricks are still there*

[317]'Breaking: After 40 days of hearing, SC Reserves Judgment On Ayodhya-Babri Masjid Dispute', *Live Law*, 16 October 2019, https://tinyurl.com/yc852r8e. Accessed on 18 January 2025.

> *[...] The property belongs to the Waqf [...] We are claiming the whole area as being part of the mosque, including the 'chabutra' (which he claimed is in the outer courtyard) [...] And we are not praying for title alone. The declaration is for a public waqf,' he argued.*

The focus of the day had shifted to a controversy which should not have erupted. And then what followed was a topic of standalone coverage in some newspapers. *The final day of the hearing witnessed some dramatic moments with Dr. Dhawan tearing up in court certain maps and other documents sought to be relied on by Senior Advocate Vikas Singh to show the point which the Hindus have believed to be Lord Ram's place of birth.*[318]

Though Mr Vikas Singh stated that the map did not constitute evidence in law, as per media reports Dr Dhavan still had some objections.

> *The CJI told Dhavan: 'Since the Hindu party is not relying on the map, and if you [Dhavan] find it irrelevant, then you can tear it off.*[319]

Live Law further reported

> *The final day of the hearing witnessed some dramatic moments with Dr. Dhawan tearing up in court certain maps and other documents sought to be relied on by Senior Advocate Vikas Singh to show the point which the Hindus have believed to be Lord Ram's place of birth.*
>
> *'You can shred it more', Chief Justice Ranjan Gogoi had commented.*
>
> *With this incident having been widely reported and trending*

---

[318]Ibid.

[319]Mahapatra, Dhananjay, 'In latest theatrics, Rajeev Dhavan shreds "Ram birthplace" map', *The Times of India*, 17 October 2019, https://tinyurl.com/2fe6c4cx. Accessed on 18 January 2025.

on social media, Dr. Dhawan subsequently suggested that he had intended to throw away the papers and proceeded to tear them only when the Chief Justice said so. 'It was with the court's permission'. The Chief Justice also agreed that he had said that the Senior Counsel may tear up the documents.[320]

[...] When there were more interruptions, the CJI said it would be impossible to continue and the Bench would rise if the parties didn't behave.[321]

During the post-lunch session, Dhavan told the Bench: 'There is a controversy that I tore papers in the court on my own [...] I think I asked if I can throw it away, and the CJI told me I can tear it if I want. So I tore it.'

The CJI had a smile when he replied: 'Yes, you are right [...] you can say the CJI told Mr. Dhavan that if it's tearable, you can.[322]

This was the last day of hearing. The court rose on 16 October 2019 itself while it had planned to continue hearing till 18 October. To ordinary people, it would have seemed that the flustered court had got up in a hurry. However, the hearing was complete and the credit for completing the hearing went as much to Dr Dhavan as to all other counsels. The Senior Advocates had filed written submissions for the convenience of the court which had the court move faster with the case than it would have otherwise. With this, the second longest hearing in the history of the Supreme Court of India concluded in a case which perhaps was causing maximum contestation among the citizens outside the court too.

[320]Jain, Mehal, 'After 40 days of hearing SC reserves judgment on Ayodhya-Babri Masjid Dispute', *Live Law*, 16 October 2019, https://tinyurl.com/5949rdx5. Accessed on 22 September 2025.
[321]G., Ananthakrishnan, 'Ayodhya hearing: Drama in SC, Rajeev Dhavan tears Lord Ram's "birthplace" map', *The Indian Express*, 17 October 2019, https://tinyurl.com/tx8pj43p. Accessed on 18 January 2025.
[322]Ibid.

After the hearing concluded, as the counsels were leaving the court premises, Senior Parasaran stopped. He was mobbed by some law students, lawyers and even clerks for pictures. He asked for a picture with all his assisting counsels but Bhakti and Yogeswaran were not around. They were busy managing the case records. One expected the tired nonagenarian to leave. Yet, he waited. He waited for Dr Dhavan, the lead counsel for the Muslim side, to arrive. He told his team. 'I want to meet Dhavan, congratulate him on his submissions and have a picture with him. The judgement of the case will come, but I respect his intellect and hard work.' The nonagenarian waited for 15 minutes standing in the car parking, had a chat with Dr Dhavan, and requested him for photographs which would be splashed across the newspapers the next day. Perhaps a senior citizen from pre-Independence India who had lived through a crucial period of post-Independence India wanted to send a message to the citizens of the country, especially on the extreme fringes of the divide: 'It has all ended in the court itself, and what the court decides will have to be followed and will be final. The streets cannot be the forum for adjudication of a property dispute in a democracy.'

38

The Judgement

The judgement had to be delivered latest by 17 November when the then Chief Justice Ranjan Gogoi was due to retire. It had become a trend that judges on the day of their retirement or a couple of days earlier would pronounce landmark judgements. Hence, it was expected that the judgement would be delivered in the last week of Justice Gogoi's tenure as Chief Justice of India—between 12 November 2019 and 15 November 2019.

On 8 November 2019 evening, Senior Parasaran was in Chennai. As Mr Parasaran planned an 'early to bed, early to rise' schedule for himself, he along with the whole of India learnt that the judgement would be pronounced on Saturday 9 November 2019. This was a first—a judgement being pronounced on a Saturday. With no flights available from Chennai which would ensure that the nonagenarian would be inside the court on time, frantic efforts were made to arrange a chartered flight. Two attempts ended in failure, one due to some technical snag in the plane and the second due to some obscure reason.

Believing he had no chance of reaching Delhi in time for the judgement, Senior Parasaran decided to retire for the night when he was informed of a flight having been made available for him. On the third attempt, a chartered flight had successfully been arranged. For a lawyer of Mr Parasaran's stature, surprisingly this was the first time he was taking a chartered flight. The flight could take off only in the early hours of 9 November 2019.

Mr Parasaran, accompanied by his grandson Vishnu Mohan, finally arrived in Delhi on the appointed day for the judgement of the case in which he was serving his Lord. Sleepless and tired, Mr Parasaran was tired and exhausted, as his grandson gathered his stuff. Vishnu was the fourth generation of lawyers in Mr Parasaran's family. In a lighter vein, with the stress of an impending judgement bothering people, it was said that 'Vishnu has come to receive Ram Lalla's judgement.'

While travelling to the court, Sridhar asked Senior Parasaran as to what the judgement would be in his opinion. The lawyer was confident while the bhakt in him sometimes got anxious. After some thought, he replied, 'No one will go empty-handed from my Ram.' The Supreme Court of India had turned into a fortress that day, with security personnel everywhere. The Chief Justice of India's court was jam-packed.

The judgement, inter alia, gave the following answers with a unanimous verdict:

1. In Para 771 the court delineated the challenge it faced. 'In the absence of historical records with respect to ownership or title, the court has to determine the nature and use of the disputed premises as a whole by either of the parties. In determining the nature of use, the court has to factor in the length and extent of use.

2. The evidence of both the Hindu and Muslim witnesses was analysed and it was held that *'the following facets can be gleaned' in Para 531.* Some of these points also find mention in Para 788.

   i. *Hindus consider Ayodhya as the birthplace of Lord Ram. Hindu Shastras and religious scriptures refer to it being a place of religious significance;*

   ii. *The faith and belief of Hindus is that Lord Ram was born inside the inner sanctum or Garbh Grih right below the central dome of the three-domed structure;*

   iii. *What Muslims call the Babri Mosque, Hindus consider as the Ram Janmabhumi or the birthplace of Lord Ram;*

   iv. *The faith and belief of Hindus that Lord Ram was born in Ayodhya is undisputed. Muslim witnesses also stated that Hindus have faith and belief in the existence of the Janmasthan;*

v. *Both Hindu and Sunni witness testimonies indicate that the disputed site was being used for offering worship by devotees of both faiths;*

vi. *Both Hindu and Sunni witnesses have described the physical layout of the disputed structure in the following manner:*

(a) *There were two entrances to the disputed premises—one from the East through Hanumat Dwar and the other from the North through Singh Dwar. There were on both sides of Hanumat Dwar black touchstone (Kasauti stone) pillars with engravings of flowers, leaves and Hindu Gods and Goddesses. Hindus used to pray and offer worship to the engravings on the pillars. Two Hindu witnesses spoke about the 'Jai and Vijai' engravings;*

(b) *Outside the main gate was a fixed stone with the words 'Janam Bhumi Nitya Yatra' written on it. On entering through this gate, the Ramchabutra was on the left upon which the idols of Lord Ram had been placed. Kirtan was carried out near the Ramchabutra by devotees and saints;*

(c) *In one corner of the outer courtyard, idols of Ganesha, Nandi, Shivlingam, Parvati and others were placed below a fig and a neem tree;*

(d) *There existed a structure with a thatched roof, which had provisions for storing food and preparing meals;*

(e) *Outside the disputed premises, in the south-eastern corner, Sita Koop was located at a distance of 200–250 paces;*

(f) *The Northern entrance gate to the disputed site was Singh Dwar above which a pictorial representation of Garuda was engraved in the centre with two lions on either side. On entering through Singh Dwar, Sita Rasoi was accessed, which included a Chauka-Belan-Choolha, Charan Chinha and other signs of religious significance; and*

(g) *To the West of the Ramchabutra, there was a wall with iron bars. Inside the railing was the three-domed structure which Hindus believed to be the birthplace of Lord Ram. Hindus believed this as the 'Garbh Grih' which was considered a holy and revered place. There existed black Kasauti stone pillars in the three-domed structure. The witnesses stated that the pillars had engravings of flowers, leaves, Hindu Gods and Goddesses on them;*

(vii) *A pattern of worship and prayer emerges from the testimonies of the witnesses. Upon entering Hanumat Dwar, Hindus used to offer prayers and worship the idols of Lord Ram placed upon the Chabutra in the outer courtyard followed by the idols placed below the fig and neem tree. Prayers were offered at the Sita Rasoi and then pilgrims used to pay obeisance to the 'Garbh Grih' located inside the three-domed structure, while making their offerings standing at the iron railing that divided the inner and outer courtyard. Hindus performed a parikrama or performed circumambulation of the Ram Janmabhumi.*

(viii) *Both Hindu and Muslim witnesses stated that on religious occasions and festivals such as Ram Navami, Sawan Jhoola, Kartik Poornima, Parikrama Mela and Ram Vivah, many Hindu pilgrims from across the country visited the disputed premises for darshan. Worshippers used to take a dip in the Saryu River and have darshan at Ram Janmabhumi, Kanak Bhawan, and Hanumangarhi. Pilgrims would perform a customary circumambulation around the disputed premises; and*

(ix) *Both Hindu and Muslim witnesses have referred to*

Panchkosi and Chaudahkosi Parikramas that were performed once a year during the month of Kartik, which attracted lakhs of pilgrims to the city of Ayodhya.

3. The court in Para 781 analysed history and held that from *the documentary evidence, it emerges that:*
    1. *Prior to 1856-7, there was no exclusion of Hindus from worshipping within the precincts of the inner courtyard;*
    2. *The conflagration of 1856-7 led to the setting up of the railing to provide a bifurcation of the places of worship between the two communities;*
    3. *The immediate consequence of the setting up of the railing was the continued assertion of the right to worship by Hindus who set up the Chabutra in the immediate proximity of the railing;*
    4. *Despite the existence of the railing, the exclusion of Hindus from the inner courtyard was a matter of contestation and at the very least, was not absolute;*
    5. *As regards the outer courtyard, it became the focal point of Hindu worship both on the Ramchabutra as well as other religious structures within the outer courtyard including Sita Rasoi. Though, Hindus continued to worship at the Ramchabutra which was in the outer courtyard, by the consistent pattern of their worship including the making of offerings to the 'Garbh Grih' while standing at the railing, there can be no manner of doubt that this was in furtherance of their belief that the birthplace of Lord Ram was within the precincts of and under the central dome of the mosque; and*
    6. *The riots of 1934 and the events which led up to 22/23 December 1949 indicate that possession over the inner courtyard was a matter of serious contestation often leading to violence by both parties and the Muslims did not have exclusive possession over the inner courtyard. From the above documentary evidence, it cannot be said that the*

Muslims have been able to establish their possessory title to the disputed site as a composite whole.

4. The issue about the identity and nature of the disputed structure was resolved in Para 769 of the judgement. It was held that the *'disputed site has witnessed a medley of faiths and the co-existence of Hindu and Muslim practices, beliefs, and customs. A blend of Hindu and Muslim elements emerges from the religious and architectural tradition associated with the erstwhile structure.' The structure embodied features both of a temple and a mosque. While the distinctive architectural elements overlapped, they were yet easily recognizable. They were symbols of a syncretic culture. Specific sculptured finds such as the black Kasauti stone pillars along with the presence of the figurines of Varah, Garuda, Jai and Vijay suggest that they were primarily meant for decoration of a Hindu temple facade and served as deities to be worshipped. At the same time, the distinctive appearance of a mosque emerged from the three domes, the Vazoo, the stone inscription with 'Allah', the mimbar and the mehrab. These features indicate that the disputed premise was constructed as a mosque. Within the premises of the same complex there existed two religious faiths. Their coexistence was at times, especially before 1856, accepting and at others, antagonistic and a cause of bloodshed. Yet, the distinctive features of the site, embodying both Hindu and Islamic traditions led to the creation of a space with* <u>*an identity*</u> *of its own. The real significance attached to the composite structure is evidenced by the nature and the length of use by both of the parties.*
5. The judgement in Para 788 went into the fact whether the accounts of travellers were corroborated with other evidence or not. The court held:

   IV. Historical records of travellers (chiefly Tieffenthaler and the account of Montgomery Martin in the eighteenth century) indicate:

> (i) *The existence of the faith and belief of the Hindus that the disputed site was the birthplace of Lord Ram;*
>
> (ii) *Identifiable places of offering worship by the Hindus including Sita Rasoi, Swargdwar and the Bedi (cradle) symbolizing the birth of Lord Ram in and around the disputed site;(iii) Prevalence of the practice of worship by pilgrims at the disputed site including by parikrama (circumambulation) and the presence of large congregations of devotees on the occasion of religious festivals; and(iv) The historical presence of worshippers and the existence of worship at the disputed site even prior to the annexation of Oudh by the British and the construction of a brick-grill wall in 1857 were all considered. The court held that beyond the above observations, the accounts of the travellers must be read with circumspection. Their personal observations must carefully be sifted from hearsay—matters of legend and lore. Consulting their accounts on matters of public history is distinct from evidence on a matter of title. An adjudication of title has to be deduced on the basis of evidence sustainable in a court of law, which has withstood the searching scrutiny of cross-examination. Similarly, the contents of gazetteers can at best provide corroborative material to evidence which emerges from the record. The court must be circumspect in drawing negative inferences from what a traveller may not have seen or observed. Title cannot be established on the basis of faith and belief alone. Faith and belief are indicators towards patterns of worship at the site on the basis of which claims of possession are asserted […]*

In addition to the above analysis of evidence the court further concluded inter alia the following in Para 788 relying on witness testimonies with respect to use, length of use and presence of structure:

(xiii) After the construction of the grill-brick wall in 1857, there is evidence on record to show the exclusive and unimpeded possession of the Hindus and the offering of worship in the outer courtyard. Entry into the three-domed structure was possible only by seeking access through either of the two doors on the eastern and northern sides of the outer courtyard which were under the control of the Hindu devotees;

(xiv) On a preponderance of probabilities, there is no evidence to establish that Muslims abandoned the mosque or ceased to perform namaz in spite of the contestation over their possession of the inner courtyard after 1858. Oral evidence indicates the continuation of namaz;

(xv) The contestation over the possession of the inner courtyard became the centre of the communal conflict of 1934 during the course of which the domes of the mosque sustained damage as did the structure. The repair and renovation of the mosque following the riots of 1934 at the expense of the British administration through the agency of a Muslim contractor is indicative of the fact the despite the disputes between the two communities, the structure of the mosque continued to exist as did the assertion of Muslims of their right to pray. Namaz appears to have been offered within the mosque after 1934 though, by the time of incident of 22/23 December 1949, only Friday namaz was being offered. The reports of the Waqf Inspector of December 1949 indicate that the Sadhus and Bairagis who worshipped and resided in the outer courtyard obstructed Muslims from passing through the courtyard, which was under their control, for namaz within the mosque. Hence the Waqf Inspector noted that worship within the mosque was possible on Fridays with the assistance of the police.

(xviii) The net result, as it emerges from the evidentiary record is thus:

1. *The disputed site is one composite whole. The railing set up in 1856-7 did not either bring about a sub-division of the land or any determination of title;*

2. *The Sunni Central Waqf Board has not established its case of a dedication by user;*

3. *The alternate plea of adverse possession has not been established by the Sunni Central Waqf Board as it failed to meet the requirements of adverse possession;*

4. *Hindus have been in exclusive and unimpeded possession of the outer courtyard where they have continued worship;*

5. *The inner courtyard has been a contested site with conflicting claims of Hindus and Muslims;*

6. *The existence of the structure of the mosque until 6 December 1992 does not admit any contestation. The submission that the mosque did not accord with Islamic tenets stands rejected. The evidence indicates that there was no abandonment of the mosque by Muslims. Namaz was observed on Fridays towards December 1949, the last namaz being on 16 December 1949;*

7. *The damage to the mosque in 1934, its desecration in 1949 leading to the ouster of Muslims and the eventual destruction on 6 December 1992 constituted a serious violation of the rule of law; and*

8. *(viii) Consistent with the principles of justice, equity and good conscience, both Suits 4 and 5 will have to be decreed and the relief moulded in a manner which preserves the constitutional values of justice, fraternity, human dignity and the equality of religious belief.*

(xviii) The Hindus have established a clear case of a possessory title to the outside courtyard by virtue of long,

continued and unimpeded worship at the Ramchabutra and other objects of religious significance. Hindus and Muslims have contested claims to the offering worship within the three-domed structure in the inner courtyard. The assertion by Hindus of their entitlement to offer worship inside has been contested by Muslims.

7. The issue of the parties substantiating their use of the disputed premises or the parties proving long user of the disputed premises was resolved in Para 771 of the judgement. The court came to the following conclusion:

   The oral witness accounts of Hindus show their faith and belief that the "Garbh-grih" was the birthplace of Lord Ram and the existence of long continued worship by Hindus at the disputed site. As regards namaz within the disputed site, the evidence on record of the Muslim witnesses, indicates that post 1934, namaz was being offered until 16 December 1949. However, the extent of namaz would appear to have been confined to Friday namaz particularly in the period preceding the events of December 1949. Both Hindu and Muslim witnesses state that active measures were being taken by the Sadhus and Bairagis to prevent Muslims from approaching the disputed premises and from offering prayers. This primarily shows that the disputed site witnessed use by worshippers of both the faiths. Obstructing Muslims from accessing the mosque did not mean that they had had no claim to or had abandoned the disputed site. However, it needs to be remembered that the present case relates to title or ownership of this composite place of worship.

8. With respect to three-way division of the land, the court held in Para 799 that dividing the land may not be a solution of lasting peace.

   We have already concluded that the three-way bifurcation by the High Court was legally unsustainable. Even as a matter of maintaining public peace and tranquillity, the solution which commended itself to the High Court is not feasible. The disputed site admeasures all of 1500 square yards. Dividing the land will not subserve the interest of either of the parties or secure a lasting sense of peace and tranquillity.

9. Five acres of land was awarded to the Muslim community for a mosque in Para 801.

The area of the composite site admeasures about 1500 sq. yd. While determining the area of land to be allotted, it is necessary to provide restitution to the Muslim community for the unlawful destruction of their place of worship. Having weighed the nature of the relief which should be granted to Muslims, we direct that land admeasuring 5 acres be allotted to the Sunni Central Waqf Board either by the Central Government out of the acquired land or by the Government of Uttar Pradesh within the city of Ayodhya. This exercise, and the consequent handing over of the land to the Sunni Central Waqf Board, shall be conducted simultaneously with the handing over of the disputed site comprising the inner and outer courtyards as a consequence of the decree in Suit 5. Suit 4 shall stand decreed in the above terms.

10. Finally, the court concluded with an acknowledgement of the assistance rendered by the counsels with a special mention:

In crafting this judgment, the forensic contest before this Court has provided a valuable insight in navigating through the layers of complexity of the case. The erudition of the counsels, their industry, vision and above all, dispassionate objectivity in discharging their role as officers of the court must be commended. We acknowledge the assistance rendered by Mr. K. Parasaran and Dr Rajeev Dhavan, learned Senior Counsels who led the arguments. Their fairness to the cause

> *which they espouse and to their opponents as, indeed, to the court during the course of the hearings has facilitated the completion of the hearings in the spirit that all sides have ultimately been engaged in the search of truth and justice.*

It was to the credit of Mr Parasaran and Dr Dhawan that they would guide their teams as the lead parties in the suit to complete a case peacefully—which otherwise had seen too many contests. We are grateful to destiny that we could be part of a historic legal discourse where advocacy and lawyering were taken to their highest level.

As people congratulated Senior Parasaran on the day of the judgement, bringing a closure to the centuries-old dispute, he had a very distinct perspective. According to him, the credit goes to all those who struggled over centuries when the country was ruled by those who were hostile, and later under colonial rulers who sought to divide the society. Post-Independence, it became a socio-religious movement for reclaiming the civilizational identity of Indians.

The efforts of the Advocates who conducted the trial, researchers who collected documentary evidence, and members of the community who patiently waited for the final verdict were to be acknowledged. For him, the efforts in the Supreme Court involved a few months of preparation and 40 days of hearings, which pale in comparison with the efforts put in by several generations of Indians who persisted with their faith against all odds. He wondered if he would be able to see the temple in his lifetime. The responsibility for the temple's construction lay in other hands, and the task would prove arduous in its own right.

Afterword/Client's Corner

Ayodhya, 06 July 2025

Jai Shri Ram.
Venerable Advocate Keshav Parasaran Ji
As I Saw him

....

1. Just about when 2010 was to begin, preparations were on for the final arguments before the Lucknow Bench of the Allahabad High Court on the civil suit concerning Shri Ram Janmabhoomi (Sri Ram's Temple of Nativity). As Shri Ravi Shankar Prasad Ji was busy formulating and drawing his arguments in Delhi, a group of lawyers, namely Shri Bhupender Yadav (currently a Cabinet Minister in the Government of India), Shri Vikram Banerjee (currently an Additional Solicitor General in the Supreme Court), Shri Saurabh Shamseri (currently a Judge of the Allahabad High Court), and the youngest lawyer of the lot Shri Bhakti Vardhan Singh were assisting him. Every day they used to sit together for five to six hours, brainstorming the minutiae. After thorough preparations, Shri Ravi Shankar Prasad Ji and many others, including me, had gone together to the residence of Shri Keshav Parasaran Ji to seek his blessings. This was my first opportunity to meet Shri Parasaran Ji, who received us with extreme warmth.
2. In September 2010, the three-judge bench of the Lucknow Bench of the Allahabad High Court delivered its verdict in the Shri Ram Janmabhoomi case. While substantially the verdict was in favour of Sri Ram Lalla, the decision to divide the entire land of nativity into three parts was not accepted

by any party. As a result, a decision was made to approach the Supreme Court.

3. There was prolonged discussion on whether to appeal in the Supreme Court or file a review petition before the Allahabad High Court; the merits and demerits of both the approaches were discussed threadbare. Finally, it was decided to file an appeal in the Supreme Court. Top senior advocates like Shri Ranjit Kumar and Shri P.S. Narasimha had played their part in preparing the appeal, the draft of which was thoroughly vetted and finalized by venerable Parasaran Ji, after which he wrote a letter to Shri Bhupender Yadav Ji that the appeal was ready to be filed in the Supreme Court. The appeal finalized by Ven. Parasaran Ji was moved before the Supreme Court.
4. From 1992 till the verdict in 2010, Ayodhya resident advocate Shri Madan Mohan Pandey Ji had handled the Ram Janmabhoomi case before the Lucknow Bench of the Allahabad High Court with complete dedication. The case moved with him like his own shadow. Shri Madan Mohan Pandey Ji and another dedicated Karyakarta, the late Shri Triloki Nath Pandey Ji, often used to go to Delhi to meet Ven. Shri Parasaran Ji for discussions on the case. Upon being introduced to Shri M.M. Pandey Ji for the first time, Ven. Parasaran Ji had stood up from his chair out of respect for Shri Mishra's work and expressed his appreciation, even though Shri Madan Ji was much younger not only in age but also in legal profession. Ven. Parasaran stated affirmatively that Shri Madan Ji had laid a very solid foundation for the case. Mr Parasaran's gesture was rare as in our society, the professional world in particular, it is rare to come across instances of seniors being so courteous and respectful towards one much junior.
5. The frequency of meetings with Ven. Parasaran ji gradually increased. In Delhi, based on the advice from Advocate Shri Bhupender Yadav and others, a team of Advocates-on-

Record was formed. Advocate Yogeshwaran Ji (from Tamil Nadu), Advocate Bhakti Vardhan Singh Ji (from Lucknow), and, whenever required, Advocate Madan Mohan Pandey Ji and late Karyakarta Triloki Nath Pandey Ji kept visiting Ven. Parasaran Ji for preparing the appeal. The team of AoRs used to visit Ven. Parasaran Ji at both Delhi and Chennai. Many a time, I also accompanied them.

6. With us, he was never formal. He always made us feel as if we were his own family members; not once did we feel that the usual lawyer-client equation was at play; this was greatness personified.
7. While discussing the case, he would suddenly remember something, call his clerk, tell him the year and the name of the book; many a time the book he asked for was very old. When the book was brought before him, he would browse, and in an instant, place his hand on the exact page! I used to be totally enamoured at this regular occurrence. Such a great memory at an advanced age could only be attributed to God's grace. I never even saw him in a state of anger or fury. In Bharatiya philosophy and Hindu ethics, akrodha (being free from anger) is considered to be an integral characteristic of dharma; Ven. Parasaran ji is a natural dharmic.
8. During the arguments, his regular presence in the coat for as long as five hours straight, neither tired nor jaded, surprised many. This would be due to God's grace alone. His punctuality was exemplary. We never had to wait once we reached his place.
9. Shri Yogeshwaran Ji and Shri Bhakti Vardhan Ji used to go to Ven. Parasaran Ji's residence in Delhi no less than five evenings a week. In these times, giving so much time is indeed rare. Perhaps the Ram Janmabhoomi case had become a part of his life. I guess, even in solitude he would be only thinking about this case.
10. In the Supreme Court, finally a Bench of five judges had been

constituted to hear the Ram Janmabhoomi case. At our end, to ensure that our court work was completed in a systematic and timely manner, a taskforce of about 60 young lawyers was formed. These lawyers themselves apportioned different tasks among themselves. Shri Sridhar Pottaraju Ji and Shri Anirudh Sharma Ji—the young lawyers assisting Ven. Shri Parasaran ji in the Ram Janmabhoomi case—along with their other colleagues used to meticulously write down the arguments presented by the advocates of both the sides.

11. From 6 August 2019 to 16 October 2019, the Bench heard the arguments for 40 days: about 170 hours of hearing had taken place. I assumed that the senior lawyers, after presenting their arguments, would either proceed to their next task, or head home. But despite being the oldest, at 92, Ven. Shri Parasaran ji would listen to the arguments of all the lawyers attentively, i.e., he sat for the entire 170 hours. This was so heart-warming. Once he stood up to present his arguments, he would stand and speak for two hours at a stretch; all in all, he presented his arguments for about 16 hours standing.
12. Considering the advanced age of Ven. Shri Parasaran Ji, the Bench had conveyed to him that he could present his case while sitting. I very well remember his reply: 'In the past, I have presented cases of many people while standing, how can I speak while sitting today; this case is of my Aradhya, after all!' This touched me!
13. He has often shared how since his days of youth itself he had been a regular reader of the Valmiki Ramayana. No surprise, then, that alongside the arguments on the nuanced points of law, he used to effortlessly bring in the words of Maharishi Valmiki to garnish his arguments. He had also said that not only was it his solemn wish for this case to be decided in his lifetime, the case of Shri Ram was also to be the very last accepted case of his life.
14. Within three weeks of the verdict being announced by

the Supreme Court (on 9 November 2019), he had come to visit Ayodhya with his fellow young advocates. He had ungrudgingly accepted the very humble arrangements made by us. Everyone was accommodated in Vedanti Mandir, the abode of Ven. Rajkumar Das Ji Maharaj. His simplicity and gentleness are indeed worth emulating. It was his pious wish to have a holy bath in the Saryu river, where he reached very early in the morning. He took a bath sitting on a chair. He then worshipped Saryu Maharani and offered tarpan. He sat on the banks of the Saryu for a long time. All the other young lawyers were watching this with sheer amazement.

15. Even afterwards, he came to Ayodhya several times, even with his family. In Ayodhya, he had also stayed at the Amawa temple in Mohalla Ramkot, but wherever he stayed, he invariably bore all the expenses himself.
16. It must be kept in mind that Ven. Keshav Parasaran Ji not once expressed any desire for even a token sum for preparing the case of Bhagwan Shri Ram, or for coming to Ayodhya. I, Champat Rai, affirmatively state in my personal capacity that even on day of the hearing it was Ven. Parasaranji who bought me the afternoon tea. These little gestures were endearing.
17. I can never forget one particular moment. It was probably in the year 2023, when, on a visit to Ayodhya, he saw the ongoing construction work of the temple and was preparing to leave after getting darshan and puja of Shri Ram Lalla. All security officials were present, and he had boarded, when he suddenly opened the door of the car, came out, called me with a gesture, and embraced me. He had tears in his eyes. Such spontaneous outpouring of affection from my father figure brought tears to my eyes. I also got overwhelmed with emotions.
18. Advocate Shri Anirudh Sharma, who is an associate of Ven. Shri Parasaran Ji, thought that the 40-day-long proceedings

of the Supreme Court totally deserve to be recorded and published. He already had everything in writing with him. Advocate Shri Sridhar Potaraju uploaded the entire range of proceedings and documents. They have put together a remarkable book that indicates all the actual SC proceedings of this historic case on the covered aspects.

19. This book will show the way to tide over grave challenges, like the subject of Shri Ram Janmabhoomi, through process of law. This book will help all those readers who have an interest in such subjects and will be a valuable addition in libraries.
20. I pray at the feet of the divine for Ven. Keshav Parasaran Ji's good health and long life.

With gratitude and my respects at Ven. Keshav Parasaran Ji's feet.

(Champat Rai)
Secretary General
Shri Ram Janmbhoomi Teerth Kshetra

Ayodhya Dham, Devshayani Ekadashi

Annexures

A. Palkhivala
SENIOR ADVOCATE
HIGH COURT

Commonwealth
151 Backbay Reclamation
Bombay-400 020

April 27, 1988

My dear Parasaran

I came back here last night and would like to take this opportunity — the earliest possible — to express to you my deep gratitude for your great courtesy and goodwill in permitting me to have some time yesterday to give my final reply. It is noble acts like these which make life at the Bar so gracious in the living.

You are the undisputed leader of the Bar not only as the Attorney General but in the ethical values which you adhere to so conspicuously. I always like to have you as the opponent because you will state the case as high as it can possibly be put but, at the same time, never try to take an unfair or unjust advantage of the other side. ~~I wish~~ other ~~Government~~ Counsel would follow your laudable example.

With affectionate regards, and every good wish for many more years of your continuance in the office which you have done so much to adorn,

Sincerely ever
Nani A. Palkhivala

Nani A. Palkhivala

The Hon'ble Shri K. Parasaran,
Attorney General of India,
New Delhi.

V. R. Krishna Iyer
(FORMER JUDGE, SUPREME COURT)

Phone: 363088
"SATGAMAYA"
M. G. ROAD, ERNAKULAM
COCHIN - 682 011

3rd October 1987

My dear Parasaran,

Time and tide wait for no man and so, the compulsion of the calendar declares your age as 61. Be the biological age what it may, your energy rates you much younger. Your passionate plea for judicial justice and your proud heritage of ancient wisdom make your personality an asset and your advocacy admirable. What has fascinated me in you is your commitment to Truth, come victory, come defeat. It would have been soulful to be present on the occasion of the celebration, but wandering as I do all over the Indian earth, I am not the master of my own time. I hope to be in Madras on 9th and if you are still in the city I may call on you. Meeting with men of your calibre is a spiritual experience. I wish you long years of service to God and Man. In the last analysis, compassion for all living creation is the realisation of the highest in the human and the divine.

Each day, as it dawns, is a fresh birthday, and as it sets heralds the next. So, life is a dedication every morning and a stock-taking every night. Let me wish you many days, several hundred months and long years to fulfill your tryst with Truth that is God!

With warmest wishes,

Yours sincerely,
V. R. Krishna Iyer
(V.R. KRISHNA IYER)

Sri K. Parasaran,
Attorney General of India,
MADRAS

List of Lawyers who Participated in the Case on behalf of Lord Ram Lalla

1. Mr K. Parasaran, Sr Adv.
2. Mr C.S. Vaidyanathan, Sr Adv.
3. Mr Ranjit Kumar, Sr Adv.
4. Mr P. S. Narasimha, Sr Adv.
5. Mr Bhupender Yadav, Adv.
6. Mr Madan Mohan Pandey, Adv.
7. Mr D. Bharat Kumar, Adv.
8. Mr P. V. Yogeswaran, Adv
9. Mr Bhakti Vardhan Singh, Adv
10. Mr Sridhar Potaraju, Adv.
11. Mr Anirudh Sharma, Adv
12. Ms Aditi Dani, Adv.
13. Mr Ashwin Kumar D.S., Adv.
14. Mr Nachiketa Joshi, Adv
15. Mr Santosh Kumar, Adv.
16. Ms Ruchi Kohli, Adv.
17. Mr Mukul Singh, Adv
18. Mr Praneet Pranav, Adv.
19. Mr Amit Sharma, Adv.
20. Ms Archana Pathak Dave, Adv.
21. Mrs Swarupama Chaturvedi, AOR
22. Mr Avdhesh Kumar Singh, Adv.
23. Mr V.V.V.M.B.N. Pattabhiram, Adv.
24. Mr Ayush Anand, Adv.
25. Ms Shiwani Tushir, Adv.
26. Mr Sindoora VNL, Adv.
27. Ms Ankita Sharma, Adv.

28. Ms Gavaraju Ushasri, Adv.
29. Ms Aditi Tripathi, Adv.
30. Mr Vikash Chandra Shukla, Adv.
31. Mr Rahul G. Tanwani, Adv.
32. Mr Yash Mishra, Adv.
33. Mr Ankit Raj, Adv.
34. Ms Indira Bhakhar, Adv.
35. Mr Rajesh Singh, Adv.
36. Mr Vineet Pandey, Adv.
37. Ms Nidhi Jaiswal, Adv.
38. Mr T. Bhaskar Gowtham, Adv.
39. Ms Srishti Mishra, Adv.
40. Mr Vikas Singh Jangra, Adv.
41. Mr Sarthak Nayak, Adv.
42. Mr Prakash Gautam, Adv.
43. Mr Rishi Raj Sharma, Adv.
44. Mr Sayooj Mohandas, Adv.
45. Mr Sandeep Singh, Adv.
46. Mr Pranav Kumar, Adv.
47. Ms Ankita Chaudhary, Adv
48. Mrs Babita Yadav, Adv.
49. Ms Baby Devi Bonia, Adv.
50. Mr Gobind Kumar, Adv
51. Mr Aniket Seth, Adv.
52. Ms Kanti, Adv.
53. Mr Ashish Kumar Upadhyay, Adv.
54. Mr Babu Lal, Adv.
55. Mr Abinesh Karthik, Adv.
56. Mr Jitendra Tripathi, Adv.
57. Mr Udayaditya Banerjee, Adv.
58. Mr Shubhendu Anand, Adv.
59. Mr Akshay Nagarajan, Adv.
60. Mr Vineet Pandey, Adv.

LIST OF PARALEGAL STAFF

1. Mr Mahender Singh
2. Mr R Muthusamy
3. Mr M. Ramachandran
4. Mr Devender Singh Bisht
5. Mr Ravi Tiwari
6. Mr Raj Kumar Tiwari
7. Mr Ritesh Kumar
8. Mr Shripal Singh Rawat
9. Mr Sunil Kumar Tiwari
10. Ms Ritu kohli
11. Mr Dharmender Kumar
12. Mr Gyanendra Yadav
13. Mr Shyam Lal Arya
14. Mr Manohar

Acknowledgements

The present book is a tribute to the Indian judiciary, which has navigated voluminous records running into thousands of pages of evidence and deliberated on issues involving several branches of law and jurisprudence. The legal teams contesting their respective cases put in great hard work with diligence and professionalism both before the Hon'ble Allahabad High Court and the Hon'ble Supreme Court of India. The hearings before the Hon'ble Supreme Court were extensively reported. This book seeks to present the untold story of preparation and presentation for the 'Case for Ram'.

The authors are fortunate to be part of the team led by Shri K. Parasaran representing 'Shri Ram Lalla Virajman' before the Hon'ble Supreme Court of India. The present book seeks to share their experience and the happenings in the court as they have perceived them.

One of us, who conceived the idea of the present book, discussed the plausibility of the same with Late Prakash Narayan Singh, Patna, who encouraged him to undertake the work of documenting the journey of preparation and presentation of the case before the Hon'ble Supreme Court.

Smt. Geeta Sharma, mother of Anirudh Sharma, took pains to read the initial draft and gave invaluable inputs and feedback. We would like to express our deep gratitude to Ms Lipika Bhushan and Mr Gautam Vig who helped with their inputs, which proved to be very valuable in structuring the book, and we thank them for being available to discuss issues concerning the book.

Since the book involved sharing a lot of personal details of what transpired in the chambers of Shri K. Parasaran, his consent and approval were taken. The role played by Shri Mohan

Parasaran and the encouragement given to undertake this exercise needs to be specially mentioned, as he supported the work in several ways including by persuading his father to agree to a book of this nature to be written. In the course of writing of this book, Shri Satish Parasaran and Vishnu Mohan spared time from their busy schedule to go through the drafts.

We are grateful to Shri Parasaran and his family for wholeheartedly supporting our endeavour to document the making of history. Sri C.S. Vaidyanathan and Sri Ranjit Kumar have been kind enough to give their consent to document the story of the preparation and presentation of the case, which stands out in human history as the only instance where a bitterly contested inter-faith dispute which originated in AD 1528 was resolved by a peaceful legal adjudication on 9 November 2019.

Sri K.K. Venugopal, former Attorney General of India, a true leader of the Bar, agreed to give his foreword to this book. We could not think of anyone else more accomplished than him for writing the foreword, to which he agreed immediately.

We would like to express our deep gratitude to Shri Champat Rai ji, who has dedicated his life to the cause of Shri Ram Janmabhoomi Temple. He has been very supportive and encouraged the idea of publishing a book. He has been kind enough to share his message for the book recalling from his memory his interactions with Shri K. Parasaran over the past decade, commencing from the days of preparation of appeals against the judgement of Hon'ble Allahabad High Court till date.

We would also like to thank Shri D. Bharat Kumar and his team of lawyers from Supreme Court Adhivakta Parishad, who all were part of the case and contributed.

We would like to acknowledge the support and wholehearted dedication of our colleagues Ms Niharika Singh, Ms Shivani Tushir, Mr Prateek Prakash, Mr Rajiv Dalal, Mr

Sanjeev Kumar Sharma, Mr Apoorv Tayal, Ms Kritika Arora, Mr Varun Kesarwani, Mr Mihir Jha, Mr Abhaid Parikh, Mr Shourya Mehra and Ms Chamundeswari Pemmasani, who assisted in finalizing the book with not only their time but also their valuable inputs. We would like to thank Dhriti Krishna and Vedang Krishna. We also extend our gratitude to Ms Ritu Kohli, Mr Sunil Kumar Tiwari and Mr Dharmender Kumar, who patiently and efficiently managed several versions of the drafts and all other related work.

This book would not have been possible without referring to various newspaper reports, digital media reports of the day-to-day hearings before the Hon'ble Supreme Court.

A special mention needs to be made of Mr P.V. Dinesh, Co-Founder *LiveLaw*, an old friend from the Supreme Court Bar, and Ms Mala Dixit, journalist reporting from the Supreme Court.

We would like to thank *LiveLaw*, *The Hindu*, Legal Observer Trust (*Supreme Court Observer*), *LatestLaws* (portal), *The Indian Express*, *India Today* and Vartha Bharathi, who were kind enough to grant us copyright permissions for reproducing their reports.

Digital and print media have reported the proceedings of the court extensively. We would like to acknowledge their reporters for the diligent reporting of the day-to-day hearings.

As the book took shape, we discussed the idea behind writing the book and the manner of presentation with several persons whom we would like to acknowledge with gratitude and apologize for not being able to name each one of them individually.

The designers at Rupa have come out with a very apt cover design, which was enriched by Ms Pranati Potaraju, our design consultant.

The support received from family and friends has given us the strength to sustain our efforts over the past five years for completing this book.

This acknowledgement would be incomplete without

expressing our gratitude to our parents and gurus who shaped our lives and outlook towards the world within and outside.

मातृ देवो भव! पितृ देवो भव! आचार्य देवो भव!
maatr devo bhav ! pitr devo bhav! aachaary devo bhav !.

Glossary

Adverse possession	Right of ownership of a squatter emanating from continued hostile possession of a piece of land.
Advocate-on-record	An advocate who is entitled under Supreme Court Rules to act as well as to plead for a party in the Court.
Amicus	Lawyer who is not a party to a lawsuit is requested by the court to assist the Court.
Appeal	To challenge a lower court's decisions before a higher court both on facts and law.
Balance of probability/ Preponderance of evidence/ Preponderance of probability	The greater weight of evidence, not necessarily established by the greater number of witnesses testifying to a fact but by evidence that has the most convincing force; superior evidentiary weight that, though not sufficient to free the mind wholly from all reasonable doubt, is still sufficient to incline a fair and impartial mind to one side of the issue rather than the other.
Bar	In a courtroom the railing that separates the front area, where court business is conducted, from the back area, which provides seats for lawyers as well as observers; by extension, a similar railing in a legislative assembly.
Bench	The raised area occupied by the judge in a courtroom.

Case brief/Case file	A short statement/note summarizing a case, especially the relevant facts, the issues, the holdings, and the court's reasoning.
Cause lawyering	Lawyers who take up and promote causes they believe in, irrespective of what others think about that cause.
Caveator	A party who is successful before a lower court and lodges a request with the appellate court not to pass any adverse interim order without hearing him in an appeal likely to be filed by the other side.
Chabutra	An elevated platform rectangular or square in shape.
Civil suit	A petition filed asserting violation of civil rights and seeking relief against a named opponent or against unknown opponents before a court duly constituted under the Civil Procedure Code, 1908.
Constitutional bench	The minimum number of judges who are to sit for the purpose of deciding any case involving a substantial question of law as to the interpretation of the Constitution of India under Article 145(3).
Court commissioner	An officer possessing certain minor judicial or quasi-judicial powers; he is a subordinate officer of the court of which he is commissioner.
Court of first instance (trial court)	A court of original jurisdiction where the evidence is first received and considered.
Court master	Court officer who assists the judge in the conduct of proceedings.

Deposition	A statement on oath made by a witness in legal proceedings reduced in writing. It also includes cross-examination.
Easementary	An easement is a right which a person who is not the owner of the land possesses, as such, for the beneficial enjoyment of that land, to do and continue to do something, or to prevent and continue to prevent something being done.
Evidence	Something that tends to prove or disprove the existence of a fact. It can be oral or a document.
First appeal	The appeal against an order passed by the court of first instance which adjudicated the dispute after recording evidence both oral and documentary.
Hearsay evidence	Something which the witness speaks about without having personal knowledge, based on what they have heard from others.
Injunction	A court order commanding or preventing an action.
In personam	[Latin: against a person] Involving or determining the personal rights and obligation of the parties.
In rem	[Latin: against a thing] Involving or determining the status of a thing, and therefore the rights of persons generally with respect to that thing.
Judgement	Decision given by a court
Juristic/Juridical	Of relating to or involving a jurist.

Juristic person/ personality/ entity	Legal recognition conferred on non-humans as having rights with capacity to carry on activities akin to a human; e.g., banks, private companies.
Next friend	Someone who appears in a lawsuit to act for the benefit of an incompetent or minor plaintiff, but who is not a party to the lawsuit, and is not appointed as a guardian.
Order	A command, direction, or instruction given under authority of law.
Opposing/ Opposite party	An adverse party in a court case.
Pari materia	In connection with the same subject/similar.
Res extra commercium	A thing which, by law, is excluded from the sphere of private transactions.
Res judicata	An issue that has been settled by judicial decision.
Res nullius	[Latin: thing of no one] Thing that belongs to no one; an ownerless chattel.
Ruling	The outcome of a court's decision either on some point of law or on the case as a whole.
Shebait/Sevait	The manager and superintendent of an endowed Hindu temple.
Shebaiti	Shebaitship means trusteeship and pujariship; it has in itself all the incidents of property and is thus inheritable.
Submission	A statement made before a court in support of the party.
Suo moto	One's own motion, usually when court takes notice on its own.

Testimony	Evidence that a competent witness under oath or affirmation gives at trial or in an affidavit or deposition.
Witness	Someone who sees, knows, or vouches for something.

Index

Agarwal, Sudhir, 33, 165, 169, 205, 376, 378, 382, 384
Ain-i-Akbari, 240, 241, 242
Ali, Mir Rajjab, 234, 381, 384
Allahabad High Court judgement, 3, 7, 25, 41, 100, 113, 378, 396
An Encyclopedia of Indian Archaeology from the Earth, 272
Archaeological Survey of India, 115, 121, 128, 132, 139, 143, 198, 258, 262, 265, 267, 268, 276
Archaeology from the Earth, 272, 282
Arora, Meenakshi, 161, 189, 258, 262, 264, 266, 269, 272, 276, 327, 329
Asghar, Mohd., 56, 234, 236, 252, 254, 339, 376, 381, 382, 383, 384, 385
Association of South-East Asian Nations (ASEAN), 321
Attorney General of India, 16, 17, 62, 284

Babri Masjid, 3, 49, 50, 103, 107, 121, 122, 123, 133, 134, 141, 144, 162, 163, 164, 168, 170, 176, 179, 196, 201, 202, 229, 230, 234, 235, 238, 240, 241, 242, 246, 252, 254, 276, 326, 336, 357, 374, 379, 380, 385, 387, 391, 392, 393, 407, 413, 418, 420, 422
Bahoranpur, 162, 382, 405
Baqi, Mir, 242, 376, 379, 384
Bar & Bench, xii
Bennett, W.C., 199
Bharati, Keshavananda, 293
Bharatiya Janata Party (BJP), 20, 340
British Museum, 119, 317, 319

Carnegy, P., 119, 149, 156, 199
Chandrachud, D.Y., 8, 90, 121, 188
Chidambaram, P., 110
Chidambaram Temple, 217, 298, 302, 303, 304, 308, 343, 348
Chidambara rahasyam, 300, 302, 303
Chief Justice of India (CJI), 8, 9, 91, 89, 92, 97, 104, 122, 179, 226, 230, 270, 278, 287, 288, 326, 327, 332, 336, 342, 421, 422, 424, 425

Das, Mahant Raghubar, 230, 237, 238, 242, 247, 249, 251, 252, 254, 255, 388, 408
Das, Mahant Suresh, 8, 35, 56, 125, 357, 375, 406, 407

Description Historique et Géographique de l'Inde, 50, 116, 196
Dhavan, Rajeev, 7, 69, 94, 103, 123, 134, 135, 158, 161, 165, 166, 167, 168, 171, 174, 178, 179, 186, 187, 196, 201, 202, 210, 211, 214, 216, 222, 223, 225, 227, 228, 229, 284, 308, 323, 324, 327, 333, 336, 344, 346, 347, 349, 359, 364, 367, 370, 376, 387, 388, 397, 399, 400, 401, 402, 408, 419, 421, 422, 434

Faizabad, 36, 42, 44, 119, 121, 156, 167, 174, 175, 193, 231, 235, 236, 239, 241, 242, 246, 247, 249, 260, 339, 341, 363, 381, 383, 386, 388, 393, 395, 408
Fakir, Nihang Singh, 54, 390
Father Joseph Tieffenthaler, 50, 196, 206, 338

Gandhi, Mahatma, x, 36
Gogoi, Ranjan, 8, 9, 91, 92, 93, 103, 122, 187, 226, 270, 326, 332, 336, 407, 421, 424

Hindu Mahasabha, 65, 341
Historical Sketch of Tahsil Fyzabad, Zillah Fyzabad, 199

International Court of Justice, 6, 217, 310, 320, 321, 322

Jain, Sushil Kumar, x, 77, 90, 91
Janam Asthan, 50, 54, 55, 58, 59, 63, 66, 67, 68, 80, 87, 100, 104, 105, 106, 115, 140, 141, 144, 181, 192, 226
Jawaharlal Nehru University, 205, 271
Jethmalani, Ram, 69
Jilani, Zafaryab, 161, 207, 237, 241, 246

Kamaraju Venkata Krishna Rao v. Sub Collector, 295, 305
Karnataka High Court, 286
Khan, S.U., 3
Koran, 158
Kumar, D.V. Shylendra, 286

Live Law, x, 112, 168, 210, 269, 287, 291, 292, 309, 322, 323, 324, 333, 342, 344, 345, 397, 406, 407, 420, 421, 422

Mehta, Tushar, 5, 6, 7, 284
Mutthuswamy, Rama (Mutthu), 24, 26

Nanak, Guru, 45, 338, 340, 355, 356
Nariman, Fali S., 69, 287
Nataraja, 214, 310, 316, 317, 318, 319

Oudh, 50, 119, 121, 162, 199, 224, 338, 339, 390, 401, 405, 430

Pandey, Madan Mohan, 20, 340, 437, 438, 444

Pasha, Nizam, 161
Potaraju, Sridhar, 26, 57, 82, 292, 441, 444

Ram Chabootra, 184, 185, 197, 198, 199, 200, 206, 221, 226, 228, 230, 232, 245, 247, 298, 364, 388, 390, 416
Ram Chabutra, 43, 44, 54, 56, 65, 183, 184, 185, 188, 193, 197, 211, 225, 226, 241, 242, 244, 246, 250, 262, 381, 387, 397, 414, 416, 420
Ram Janam Asthan, 54, 58, 68, 80, 87, 100, 104, 105, 115, 140, 141, 192, 226
Ram Lalla Virajman, ix, 17, 38, 60, 62, 77, 80, 86, 87, 88, 93, 94, 103, 104, 105, 147, 150, 153, 155, 157, 165, 189, 191, 192, 208, 255, 370, 371, 374, 375, 405, 416
Ram Setu, 20, 21, 76, 92
Royal Treasury, 162, 372, 374, 378, 405

Salve, Harish, 62, 69
Sharma, Anirudh, 26, 439, 440, 444
Shiva, 129, 132, 215, 235, 272, 302, 315, 316, 319, 320, 326, 329, 330, 331
Shivalinga, 326, 329, 330
Sholapur, 162, 382, 405
Singh, Bhakti Vardhan, 20, 23, 436, 438, 444
Singh, Rajender, x
Sinha, Lal Narayan, 15, 28, 61, 210
Sita Rasoi, 43, 44, 65, 183, 185, 187, 360, 388, 414, 427, 428, 430
Skanda Purana, 21, 195, 196, 201, 202, 216, 243, 324, 355
Solicitor General of India, 6, 7, 11, 16, 20, 26, 76, 110, 111, 281, 284
Sree Kadampuzha Bhagavathy Temple, 304
Supreme Court Observer, x, 6, 7, 104, 105, 106, 133, 137, 140, 148, 149, 156, 165, 167, 185, 200, 225, 237, 241, 244, 253, 264, 273, 275, 327, 380, 391

Thayarammal v. Kanakammal, 305, 306, 349
The Gazetteer of the Province of Oudh, 199
Tulsidas, Goswami, 124, 195, 196, 355

Uttar Pradesh (UP), 6

Valmiki, vii
Valmiki Ramayana, 49, 96, 124, 196, 243, 311, 312, 355, 439
Verma, T.P., 197
Vikramaditya, 49, 175, 198
Visharad, Gopal Singh, x, 32, 65, 172, 357, 372, 413
Vishnu, xii, 37, 116, 132, 140, 143, 197, 198, 283, 299, 329, 330, 350, 355, 359, 424, 425